Front Cover Photographs: Charles Gates Dawes in Paris, November 1918, from the Evanston
History Center archives, Evanston, Illinois.
American Troops in Paris, July 4, 1918, from the William B. Croka Collection (COLL/3218),
Marine Corps Archives & Special Collections.
Page from Charles Dawes' original war diary, from the Charles G. Dawes Archive,
Charles Deering McCormick Library of Special Collections, Northwestern University Libraries,
Northwestern University, Evanston, Illinois.
Back Cover Photograph:
Guard at Eiffel Tower -- Wireless Station, c. 1914-1915
Bain News Service, Library of Congress (LC-B2- 3251-14)
Charles Gates Dawes' *A Journal of the Great War* (1921) is a work in the public domain.

The legacy of Charles Gates Dawes reminds us all to reach beyond our capabilities through service to our fellow women and men with selfless faith and to develop strength of character for future generations.

Marian McNair, 2016

Written in honor of her great grandparents, Charles and Caro Dawes, her grandmother, Carolyn Dawes Ericson, and the many other Dawes family members who played their roles on the home front and on the battlefront during the momentous days of World War I.

Charles Gates Dawes in Paris, November 1918,
Evanston History Center Archives.

A Journal of the Great War

1917-1919

Charles G. Dawes

Brigadier-General Engineers

With Illustrations

Originally Published 1921

Edited by Jenny Thompson

CONTENTS

APPENDICES

Editor's Note and Acknowledgements

The Evanston History Center's publication of this critical edition of Charles Gates Dawes' *A Journal of the Great War* is part of a larger effort to examine the history of World War I during the war's centennial years. The new edition re-introduces an important war narrative, first published in 1921, into the contemporary public forum. It also provides a wider historical context for that narrative. Based on the vast resources of two of the most significant archival collections related to Charles Gates Dawes, two new essays accompany this new edition. The first essay, " 'An American in Paris:' Charles Gates Dawes in World War I," provides an introduction to the journal and examines the larger context surrounding Dawes' service overseas, including his personal motivations for going to war. The second essay, "Homecoming: Charles Gates Dawes and the Shadow of World War I," examines the war's impact on Dawes' postwar career and also provides a larger picture of his family's wartime experiences. Each essay seeks to provide an analytical and biographical context to Dawes' story and to provide readers with a broader understanding of Dawes' war experience and its impact on him both personally and professionally.

In researching Dawes' war experience, I have drawn from a wide variety of primary and secondary sources. I drew most heavily from two major archival collections related to Dawes: the collections of the Evanston History Center Archives, housed in the former home of Charles Gates Dawes, and the Charles G. Dawes Archive at the Charles Deering McCormick Library of Special Collections, Northwestern University Libraries, Northwestern University, both in Evanston, Illinois. These collections include a wealth of Dawes' correspondence, documents, photographs, scrapbooks, and ephemera, and, at the Charles Deering McCormick Library of Special Collections, his original handwritten manuscript of *A Journal of the Great War*. I also drew from a variety of newspapers, numerous U.S. government publications, including the various reports and hearings surrounding the A.E.F. during World War I, and a variety of biographical information contained in the annuals and yearbooks of organizations and institutions. I also relied on the resources of Ancestry.com in order to provide biographical information.

This new edition includes the original and complete text of *A Journal of the Great War*. The text has been annotated in order to provide a historical context to the journal. Dawes' own original notes to the text are also included and are marked with his initials "CGD;" otherwise, all other notes are those of the editor. Also included in this edition are the materials that accompanied the original edition, such as Dawes' letters to his mother and other correspondence. Much of the material that appears in the appendices was published in the original version as lengthy footnotes. The citations directing readers to that material are placed in the exact locations Dawes used in his original text.

A Journal of the Great War was originally published in two volumes: the first volume included only the text of the journal proper and Dawes' "Report of the American Member of the Military Board of Allied Supply to the Commander-in-Chief, American Expeditionary Forces, March 27, 1919." The second volume included three appendices: Dawes' "Report of the General Purchasing Agent and Chairman of General Purchasing Board American Expeditionary Forces to Commanding General, Service of Supply, American Expeditionary Forces, February 28, 1919," a collection of his Daily Reports, and his Boat Drill suggestions, titled, "Report of Lieutenant-Colonel Charles G. Dawes on Boat Drill on Army Transports Information and Suggestions for Officers in Command of Troops." With the exception of the daily reports and the "Report of the General Purchasing Agent and Chairman of General Purchasing Board American Expeditionary Forces to Commanding General, Service of Supply, American Expeditionary Forces, February 28, 1919," the original appendices have been restored to this new edition. The other material was not included owing to space limitations.

Most of the photographs that first appeared in the original edition are included here, reproduced with their original captions. A "Gallery of Portraits" at this end of this volume includes many of the portraits of Dawes' colleagues that he included in the original two volume edition. Additional photographs have been added, the majority of which are drawn from the archives of the Evanston History Center.

I am grateful to the many people who have helped with and supported this project. First, I would like to thank Eden Juron Pearlman, Executive Director of the Evanston History Center, for her tremendous support and for her friendship. I am grateful to the staff at the Charles Deering McCormick Library of Special Collections, Northwestern University Libraries, Northwestern University, for their assistance. In particular, I would like to thank Scott Krafft, curator, and Sigrid Pohl Perry, library assistant. Sigrid has managed the Charles G. Dawes Archive for many years and her vast knowledge related to the archive has been invaluable to me. I am grateful to her for her help with this project and for reading through drafts of the essays and providing insightful suggestions.

I am greatly indebted to Matthew Marchione for his careful and thoughtful copy editing of the manuscript and the essays. His work has been crucial to this project. Marian McNair deserves special thanks for her wonderful enthusiasm and assistance, and also for writing such a lovely dedication. I owe many thanks to Lee May for his insightful reading of the manuscript. I am grateful to Linda Showalter, Special Collections Associate at the Marietta College Legacy Library, for her help, and for allowing use of the image of Dawes' father, General Rufus R. Dawes, which was taken in front of the Dawes family home in Marietta, Ohio. Many thanks to Nicole Milano of the Archives of the American Field Service and AFS Intercultural Programs for her assistance and for granting permission to publish the photograph of William Mills Dawes that appears in this volume. I also wish to thank Lisa Marine, Image Reproduction and Licensing Manager at the Wisconsin Historical Society, for her assistance in securing the image from the Rufus R. Dawes diary.

I also wish to thank my colleagues at the Evanston History Center, Eston Gross, president of the Evanston History Center Board of Trustees, and the board members of the Evanston History Center for their support. Finally, I thank my family for their help and encouragement.

Jenny Thompson
Director of Education, Evanston History Center

Preface to the New Edition

It can be difficult to appreciate the extent of the Great War's impact. The war was truly a world-wide war, pitting the Central Powers, Germany, Austria-Hungary, Turkey, and Bulgaria, against the Allied Nations, Great Britain, France, Russia, Belgium, and the United States.[1] After the war broke out in August 1914, many people believed it would end by Christmas, when the Germans would be driven from the lands they occupied after invading Belgium and France. As most wars do, this one would not go as planned. Quickly becoming a war of attrition, the conflict saw the armies on the Western Front dig in, and there they would stay — for years. Meanwhile, fighting would break out in other territories and countries around the globe.

Soldiers were sent into combat facing new forms of mass killing: machine guns, high explosives, and chemical warfare. Troops lived in trenches; whole units were killed in a single day; often soldiers who hailed from the same town were killed together. Battle casualities would reach staggering figures; roughly 58,000 British soldiers, for example, were killed in just a single day during the 1916 Battle of the Somme. Airplanes flew overhead and tanks made their debut on the charred earth, torn up from the massive artillery shells that decimated the lands. Only the poppy was said to grow on the ghostly landscape of the Western Front.

The role of the Americans in the war was vast and unprecedented. In total, roughly 4,500,000 Americans were mobilized for service, with more than two million soldiers reaching France at a critical juncture in the war. In the summer of 1917, when General John J. Pershing led the first American troops down the streets of Paris to claim "*Lafayette, nous sommes ici*" ("Lafayette, we are here"), victory against Germany looked anything but certain. The Allied powers had expended vast resources and tens of thousands of men in the war. By March 1918, Russia would withdraw from the war as the country faced revolution from within, and German troops launched one of their largest and most successful offenses of the war. At this pivotal moment, Pershing would begin to deploy increasing numbers of American soldiers, using strategies and tactics that were innovative at the time. While he fought the pressure from the Allies to offer American troops for use as replacements in the Allied armies, Pershing struggled to overcome immense political obstacles. Although the Americans had been deployed in combat beginning in 1917, it was the Meuse-Argonne Offensive, a series of battles involving over one million American soldiers and fought along the Western Front in the fall of 1918, that finally brought the German government to sue for peace.

When the war came to an end with the declaration of an armistice on

November 11, 1918, the more than four years of fighting had taken a staggering human toll: an estimated forty million soldiers and civilians had been killed or wounded. Ultimately, a total of roughly 320,710 casualties were counted among the Americans, with 116,516 killed in combat.[2] In the war's final year, 1918, an international influenza pandemic broke out, brought on by the global movement of people at war. Ultimately, it would claim an estimated 30-50 million lives worldwide, with an estimated 675,000 people dying of the illness in the U.S. alone.[3]

For the Americans, who declared war on April 6, 1917, participation in the war would last just 18 months; but those months were seismic. American industries and financial institutions were given over to the war effort. There was a massive shift within the population as people moved to take up war industry jobs. Americans were asked to ration food and other supplies. The nation imposed the first ever federal system of "selective service"— the draft — with a total of 2,810,296 men drafted into the armed forces.[4] The country witnessed an unprecedented movement to recruit, draft, train, and deploy an army to fight overseas, and ultimately, more than 4 million American men would join the military during the war. The size and power of the U.S. government would grow exponentially, as the country opened its first official propaganda bureau, imposed censorship of the press, and jailed dissenters and "slackers."

In the preface to *A Journal of the Great War*, Charles Gates Dawes observed that "an elemental convulsion of humanity has occurred, so profound in its effects upon life on the earth that it will be studied and described for thousands of years." The four years of war had overturned empires, ended and upended countless lives, re-drawn national boundaries, caused fundamental shifts in societies, and re-ordered world power. The "old order" had vanished.

Ultimately, the war did not resolve the conflicts that had given rise to it in the first place, and in many cases, new conflicts emerged as the Paris Peace Conference concluded in 1919. Today, looking back at the Great War and reading Charles Gates Dawes' war journal provide contemporary readers with insight into our shared past; while the war proved not to "end all war," it did shape the 20th century and its impact can still be seen around the world today.

Notes

1   Other Allied nations (and colonies of the main allies) were Australia, Canada, Italy, India, New Zealand, Newfoundland, South Africa, Greece, Japan, Romania, Serbia, Greece, Portugal, and Montenegro. Both the Allied nationas and the Central Powers also included other territories and colonies.

2   Anne Leland, "American War and Military Operations," in *Casualties: Lists and Statistics*. Washington, D.C.: Congressional Research Service, 2010, 2. Statistics for World War 1 casualties and deaths vary depending upon the source. See also Lance Janda, "Casualties, Combatant and Noncombatant," in *The European Powers in the First World War: An Encyclopedia*. Spencer C. Tucker, editor. New York: Routledge, 2013, 273.

3   For more about the influenza pandemic see: Sandra Opdycke, *The Flu Epidemic of 1918: America's Experience in the Global Health Crisis*. New York: Routledge, 2014.

4   Gary Mead, *The Doughboys: America and the First World War*, Woodstock, NY: The Overlook Press, 2000, 71.

Charles Gates Dawes, c. 1917. Evanston History Center Archives.

Introduction

"An American in Paris:"
Charles Gates Dawes in World War I

There is no use trying to write you of my experiences.
I will have to wait and tell you about them after the war.[1]

Charles Gates Dawes, November 4, 1918

War Diary

In his room at the Hôtel Ritz at 15 Place Vendôme in Paris, Charles Gates Dawes wrote entries in his journal.[2] He wrote in longhand, using pages from a ledger or the letterhead from his office with the American Expeditionary Forces (A.E.F.). Occasionally, he used the stationery from the Hôtel Ritz. He diligently dated each entry, usually noting the time of writing. His entries were mostly made at night, around 9 or 10 p.m.

Paris was living beneath the ominous shadow of the war that had raged since August 1914. The German army's invasion of France had been thwarted soon after the war broke out, with French soldiers and citizens stopping advancing troops just outside the city limits. The opposing armies had then dug in, entrenched for years now along the Western Front. German pilots flew bombing raids over Paris, and "Big Bertha's" gun fire could be heard booming in the distance, with an occasional shell hitting the city. And Charles Dawes, an American officer with the A.E.F., was, as he wrote, living in the "midst of events."[3] From August 1917 to July 1919, Dawes lived in Paris, mostly working out of an office at the Élysée Palace Hotel and living in a room on the fourth floor of the Hôtel Ritz. Despite his swanky digs, this was not a time of fun or frivolity.

While living in Paris, Dawes served as the General Purchasing Agent for the A.E.F. in Europe. He had been appointed to that position by his longtime friend, General John J. Pershing, commander of the A.E.F.[4] After the U.S. declaration of war against Germany, Dawes had enlisted in the 17th Engineers, received a commission as a major, and soon sailed for Europe.[5] He had been in France for less than two weeks when Pershing asked him to undertake the role of General Purchasing Agent for the A.E.F.[6] His job would be to coordinate the acquisition of all the supplies—coal, horses, et al—for the A.E.F. For Pershing, having his close friend nearby would be both a personal and professional asset during his trying days in France. He needed a confidant, and moreover, he saw in Dawes a man who could play the business counterpart to his own role as military commander. Pershing knew that his friend "Charley" had a "decided talent for business."[7]

After Dawes accepted this new appointment, he would spend the next two years working out of Paris. He worked long days in his office with his faithful staff. He traveled frequently, visiting the front lines many times, and often going by automobile to Chaumont, roughly 170 miles from Paris, where the A.E.F. and General Pershing were headquartered. Later, he would represent the Americans on the Military Board of Allied Supply (MBAS), which he helped to establish. In that role, Dawes often traveled to Coubert, about 30 miles from Paris, where the MBAS was headquartered. But he spent most of his time in Paris, in meeting rooms, conducting seemingly endless "conferences," as he called them, with allied officials. He would be away from his home and family for more than two years, remaining in France long after the declaration of the November 1918 armistice that ended the war. In February 1919, he reluctantly agreed to serve on the U.S. War Department's newly created Liquidation Commission, which oversaw the sale of surplus supplies and equipment to the French government. While he was away, he celebrated his 52nd and 53rd birthdays, and his first grandchild, Charles Ericson, was born. By August 1919, just a month after the signing of the Treaty of Versailles that officially ended the war, Dawes, now holding the rank of Brigadier General, had returned home to the United States.

The length of his overseas service stood in stark contrast to the relatively brief time that unfolded between Dawes' jettisoning of civilian life and disembarking in Europe dressed in khaki. In May 1917, just a month after the U.S. declared war against Germany on April 6, 1917, Dawes traveled to Washington, D.C., where he went about "applying for my commission."[8] His friend Samuel M. Felton[9] was recruiting "railroad men" for service in France, and Dawes decided to join the newly formed 17th Engineers.[10] He had little real experience as an engineer, and so, as he later said, he "faked [his] way into the engineers."[11] While in Washington, Dawes had lunch with Pershing, who was preparing to sail for France where he would take up command of the A.E.F. Pershing spent the day helping his good friend navigate the various steps involved in applying for a commission, including visiting the War Department for a physical examination. Further assisted by Felton, who worked through a bit of red tape for him, Dawes received his commission in the 17th Engineers.[12]

On May 27, 1917, Dawes left his home in Evanston and traveled to Atlanta, Georgia, where he would live for two months, recruiting for and training with his unit.[13] In June 1917, he was promoted to lieutenant colonel.[14] On July 28, 1917, roughly three months after he had enlisted,

Dawes set sail on the British liner, the *Carmania*. He was one of roughly 2,000 American men from the 17th and 12th Engineer Regiments on the ship bound for Europe.

Dawes' enlistment made headlines. He was a "banker soldier," one of "the wealthiest men in the country," who had given up his comfortable position to serve his country.[15] At the time, Dawes was indeed a wealthy man; his 1917 income alone was an estimated $477,791.92.[16] He was president of the Central Trust Company of Illinois, a bank he founded in 1902. Along with his brothers, Henry, Beman, and Rufus Dawes,[17] he had made a fortune in industries and finance. He had friends in high places, and had made a foray into national politics when he served from 1898 to 1901 as U.S. Comptroller of the Currency in the administration of his close friend and mentor, President William McKinley, for whom he had campaigned in Illinois.[18]

Dawes' involvement in the war started in 1915 when he signed on as the only Chicago banker to the "biggest foreign loan in Wall Street history," a $500 million Anglo-French loan initially created and underwritten by J.P. Morgan and Company.[19] This loan, and the others that preceded and followed it, would ultimately amount to a total of $1.5 billion in loans which American financial institutions made to Great Britain and France to finance the cost of the war.[20] Dawes regarded the 1915 loan as "the greatest single achievement in the history of American finance,"[21] and looked upon the financing of the war as a great and courageous act.[22] J.P. Morgan and Company would prove to be "a most friendly and appreciative business ally" that would "make much difference in my financial life," he noted.[23]

That American financial institutions made profits from the war and from postwar reparations has long been known, and there is no question that Dawes benefited from these financial dealings.[24] With his role as a financier secure, he could well have remained comfortably stateside, supporting the Allied war effort from the home front. But he chose not to.[25]

"When Dawes recently offered his services to the government, he did so without heralding the fact," *Leslie's Weekly* reported. "And when he received his commission, he shut himself up in his home in Evanston with his personal secretary [and] wound up his affairs. Then, so quietly the newspaper boys missed him, he slipped away to Atlanta and donned a uniform."[26] While in Atlanta, Dawes notified his bank that his salary should cease while he was in service, and soon after, he sailed for Europe.[27] In doing so, he left behind his family, bank, various companies, complicated investments, and three low income hotels which he had opened in recent years. In Chicago, his brother, Henry M. Dawes, looked after his business affairs while he was away. His wife, Caro Blymyer Dawes, maintained their Evanston household, located in a 28 room mansion near the shores of Lake Michigan. His married daughter, Carolyn Dawes Ericson, and two young children, Dana and Virginia Dawes,[28] would write to him often while he was away.

On August 11, 1917, the *Carmania* docked in Liverpool. The 17th Engineers then traveled to the port of St. Nazaire, on the west coast of France, where the unit would be stationed. There, on August 21, 1917, Dawes wrote the first entry in his wartime journal, stating that he was keenly aware that the details of his wartime experience were "liable to pass from memory unless recorded."[29] He would try to write in it at least "once a week," he stated. But later, he admitted to his dilatory writing habits and the obligations of his high-pressure job that kept him from his diary. "[O]ne cannot live a life of action over here and do much writing,"[30] Dawes remarked in a letter to his mother, Mary Beman Gates Dawes.[31] To his brother Henry, he admitted that he was indeed a "poor correspondent." "When after the war you see how much I have to write and understand how carefully it has to be prepared," he explained, "you will realize why I am so poor at letter writing."[32] To his brother Rufus he simply stated: "I am too busy to write."[33]

With all that he had to do, and with all that he confronted during the war, Dawes still returned to what at times must have been a chore: writing in his war diary. In a letter to his wife, Caro, written just a few months after his arrival in Paris, Dawes recounted the bitter cold of the oncoming winter, his first overseas, when he held his hands over a lamp to keep them warm so that he could continue to write.[34]

Despite the challenges of keeping a journal, Dawes knew that it was a critical task. "It is so important," he wrote to his brother Rufus, "to preserve the lessons of this war that I endeavor once in a while to write something worthy of preservation."[35] And so he dutifully, if exhaustedly at times, recorded his diary entries.

Nearly every entry begins with Dawes' own comment on the writing of the journal itself— "Now that I have a little breathing spell this afternoon I will struggle at this diary," he wrote on September 2, 1917, and, "I regret that the disinclination to write has prevented me from commenting on the many interesting and historical characters whom I constantly meet," he recorded on April 11, 1919. "Have about concluded to cease these notes," Dawes wrote on March 27, 1918, "as writing them in the evening consumes more or less energy which should be conserved for the momentous work of the days." Even though days or as much as a few weeks could pass before he returned to his journal, he always came back to it.

Despite his claim of being a poor correspondent, the one thing he seemed to do most in France (aside from attending those endless conferences) was write. He wrote official daily summaries of his work. He wrote reports and confidential messages. He wrote cablegrams, telegrams, and letters to military officials, officers of the A.E.F., his colleagues at his bank, his brothers, his sisters, his mother, his wife, his children, and other relatives.[36] He wrote lengthy business and investment instructions to his brothers stateside. He wrote letters of introduction and inquiries to military officials on behalf of friends and relatives.

For all of this writing Dawes enjoyed the assistance of a stenographer (Lieutenant Dalton Mulloney often took dictation). But the journal was his alone. He did not entrust it to anyone, and he even went so far as to safeguard it, keeping it "under seal" at the offices of the bank, Morgan, Harjes and Company, located at 31 Boulevard Haussman in Paris.[37] This he did, as he wrote, so that "I can write freely and contemporaneously in it and yet not run any risk of losing it and thus doing injury."[38]

On July 3, 1918, Dawes notified his brother Henry by telegram that he was sending "extremely important papers" to his bank's office in New York City. He instructed Henry: "Go personally to New York and take papers to Chicago placing them in safe deposit box."[39] "They are tremendously interesting," Henry wrote to Dawes after he had retrieved the pages in New York.[40] Henry informed him that Caro had also had a chance to read them, safeguarding them in her own safe while they were in her temporary possession.

It is likely that the papers Henry picked up in New York were the pages (up to that point) of his brother's journal. Dawes would continue to write for more than one year after that until he returned home. He made his final entry aboard the SS *Leviathan* as he sailed across the Atlantic Ocean for home, docking in Hoboken, New Jersey, on August 6, 1919.

Dawes' original handwritten journal entries—loose sheets of paper arranged in chronological order within roughly 16 files—are today preserved in their entirety at the Charles G. Dawes Archive at the Charles Deering McCormick Library of Special Collections at Northwestern University in Evanston, Illinois.[41] To see the pages is to confront that very record of a man in the "midst of events." Dawes' handwriting spreads over pages that vary in color and size; his script appears widened or condensed, owing, perhaps, to his energy at the time of making an entry; occasional numerical notations or squiggles appear in the margins or on the backs of the sheets of paper; some pages bear the long-dried stains of water drops or ink smudges, and one page displays an apparent thumb print made in ink.

Despite the original journal's appearance as a manuscript written "in the midst of events," Dawes clearly sought to keep it in good order. Along with dating each entry, he numbered the pages, and he collected other items, such as copies of the letters he wrote to his mother, that he would

A page from Dawes' original war journal, written in Paris, on stationery from the Hôtel Ritz. Dawes wrote this entry at 6:15 pm on the day the armistice went into effect, November 11, 1918. He wrote: "The greatest struggle of humanity ended today with the signing of the armistice by the Germans. Col. Robert Bacon called me by telephone at 8 in the morning saying it was signed at 5 A.M. After breakfast on my way to my headquarters at the Élysée Palace Hotel was met by my faithful aide Lieut. Kilkenny who said Genl Pershing. . . ." Courtesy of the Charles G. Dawes Archive at the Charles Deering McCormick Library of Special Collections, Northwestern University Libraries, Northwestern University.

eventually include in the published version of the journal.[42] Lines drawn diagonally across the written text in some sections of the original journal indicate material that Dawes deleted from the published version; still, and perhaps surprisingly, nearly the entire published text is a verbatim version of the entries Dawes made during his time overseas.

Indeed, it is important to note that the published version of Dawes' journal is a near replica of what he wrote in France. His journal constitutes a record of days (a literal diary). Accordingly, Dawes occasionally quotes a famous London diarist, Samuel Pepys,[43] in his own, underscoring the fact that his journal was being composed as things happened, when events were fresh in his memory. The meetings, journeys, plans, personalities, emotions, and events that constituted Dawes' experience in France are laid out within the pages. To this end, Dawes' journal is a valuable war record.

Dawes himself noted that the "contemporaneous notes here published were made under pressure," but they were made "always with a sense of responsibility and a desire for accuracy."[44] In preparing it for publication, Dawes altered the original version in only two ways: he added elements (photographs, correspondence, official war records, etc.) to enhance the larger picture, and he deleted only a word or a line here or there—as much as roughly four or five pages total from the original journal; the rest was published intact.[45]

In the summer of 1921, two years after he returned from France, Dawes published his war diary in two volumes under the title, *A Journal of the Great War*.[46] By that time, Dawes was riding a wave of popularity that had begun during his service overseas. His association with Pershing, the universal praise for his work, and his numerous awards had all attracted widespread attention by the national press.[47] But his prominence was heightened by the fiery testimony he gave in February 1921 in front of a U.S. Congressional committee investigating expenditures during the war. His statement became a "best seller" as many Americans thrilled at his words. (It was also peppered with so many expletives that Dawes became known as a "champion cusser."[48]) He had stood up for the "little guy" as he railed against what he perceived to be the investigative committee's political agenda to undermine the achievements of the American war effort. "This was not a Republican nor was it a Democratic war," he fumed when accused of things such as making "absurd" purchases. "It was an American war."[49]

Following his testimony and its attendant interest, and just months before his journal was published, "Charles Dawes" had become a household name. In the wake of Dawes' testimony, President Harding appointed him to serve as the first director of the U.S. Bureau of the Budget (a job he seemed perfectly suited for based on his war experience of overseeing spending and cutting out waste). And, as the reviews of *A Journal of the Great War* came forth, universally praising both it and Dawes himself, Dawes had become famous. His prominence on the American political landscape would only increase; by 1925, he would take office as Vice President of the United States in the administration of President Calvin Coolidge.

Dawes' fame had been achieved in a country that had changed significantly since its prewar days. By the 1920s, the current generation of Americans had "lived amidst such a succession of great events that it has ceased to be greatly impressed by them," he noted at the time. "Among our people the war is largely forgotten."[50]

Indeed, in the years following the war, many Americans (along with citizens all over the world) did suffer from "war weariness." And many likely did wish to put the past, rife with war and death, behind them; now, many wanted the country to turn toward the future and bury the war in the past. In this postwar period, gone was the old order and the old life. And Dawes appeared to be the man of the hour; he had emerged on the world stage as a new man for a new, modern age. (See the essay "Homecoming" at the end of this volume for the full story of Dawes' testimony and his postwar career.)

But despite any wish to move forward, the reality of the war, and its impact, remained. Its memory cast a shadow upon the new and the now of the postwar period. For Dawes, there remained those pages from a Paris hotel room, written late at night, through many cold winter days when a longing for home made him sorrowful, and during long summer nights when hopeful moments would emerge as victory seemed near. Those pages would tell a story that Dawes hoped readers would want to hear.

Enter the Americans

History is replete with the failures of coalitions.[51]
General John J. Pershing

Nearly a century after it was written, Dawes' journal tells a story to a new generation. Interpreting it requires an investigation into its background and meanings, for it is a wartime record that can be read on various levels. Most simplistically, it is an account of Dawes' time overseas.

In his account, Dawes relates his experiences as they unfolded. He seems intent upon simply making the record itself, and as such, he includes accounts of the details of his days, stories of various encounters, and his reactions to his experiences. These various threads are woven intricately throughout the journal. Given his acknowledgement that his work was part of a larger, important American story, he believed that his record would not always be for himself alone.[52]

But after the war, he did not polish his journal, re-working it so that its meanings would shift or intensify. Instead, he published it in the form he initially created; a "first draft" of history rendered in a series of entries; a stream of personal reportage. Although Dawes clearly supported the war and believed in its overall purpose, he did not elevate it by espousing hyperbole concerning its ideals. The wartime fashion of using flowery prose to describe the war's aims—the proclamation of making the world safe for democracy, for instance—is absent in his volume; instead, his tone is decidedly modern—crisp and to the point. Accordingly, he downplays the very importance of what he has written in light of the war's larger reality: "I really don't know whether anything I have written is worth while," he noted at one point. "Everything is on such an immense scale these days that one feels very small and humble."[53]

Where Dawes does present a heightened sense of idealism is in his praise for General John Pershing, whom he calls "a very great man — and a very dear friend."[54] One of his stated intentions in publishing his journal was to provide "a true picture of the great American Commander-in-Chief in action" and "give to the thoughtful people of our nation the true measure of his greatness."[55] To this end, Dawes offers the American public a simple fact: the Allied victory was not a lucky accident. In Dawes' opinion, the role the United States played in contributing to it was indisputable, and that achievement was largely attributable to Pershing. Dawes sees in Pershing a man of talented leadership, deft skill in waging innovative tactical combat, and ingenuity in managing his part in an allied war. Pershing's abilities to resist political pressures, maintain the integrity of the American forces, and help bring into fruition an allied command structure in the war's final year were, according to Dawes, the reasons the Allies won the war.[56] Dawes saw his journal as a means by which he could portray these facts, especially in light of what he knew would be the inevitable criticism that would emerge in the post war era.[57] "Now that the war is about over," Dawes wrote ten days before the Armistice, "I am resigning myself to the inevitable future in which the critic and the politician take center stage. If there is any way in which General Pershing *can* be attacked, they may be trusted to find it."[58] His account would be important to maintaining (or even elevating) his friend's well-earned reputation. After all, it "is not the applause that greets one on entrance," Dawes remarked, paraphrasing one of his favorite philosophers, "but on exit, which is important."[59]

The key to Pershing's vision was his belief in establishing alliances in both the waging of the war and in the coordination of supply. In this,

Pershing and Dawes were perfectly in sync. Both men agreed that a lack of coordination was the primary reason the Allies had failed to win the war before the Americans entered it. "The absence of an entire united effort between the Allied armies on the Western Front during the earlier years of the war was probably due merely to lack of understanding between commanders, but its continuance would have undoubtedly lead to their defeat," wrote Pershing after the war.[60] In Dawes' words, the lack of coordination resulted in "the stupendous and unnecessary loss of life and waste of wealth, man power, and material due to the selfish resistance among the Allies to an earlier central control of military and supply operation."[61] Dawes' own brilliant execution of the plan to create a system of coordinated supply was the mirror image of Pershing's work to help bring about the coordination of the Allied armies. And the chief ingredient in victory, they concurred, was the creation of these coalitions.

There is no question that within the grand narrative of the A.E.F., Dawes played no small role. He was "a key figure in Pershing's inner circle," as historian Gary Mead noted.[62] In dealing with the stresses of their work, Dawes had Pershing to turn to, and vice versa. They were, Dawes wrote, "occasionally given in our close friendship to shutting the door and indulging in strong comments upon a hostile world — after which it is always easier to deal meekly with it."[63] As Pershing's right hand man, Dawes was in continuous contact (almost daily) with him throughout the war, either in person or "telephonically," as he put it. "Pershing came to rely heavily not only on [Dawes'] social company," Mead notes, "but also on his advice concerning military strategy."[64]

Dawes was Pershing's "procurement genius,"[65] operating behind-the-scenes, part businessman, part negotiator. "Everybody in the United States thought I bought everything for the Army," Dawes later remarked, "and I never bought a lead pencil."[66] Indeed, Dawes' role was that of a manager, not purchaser. He saw the war from the viewpoint of an administrator, whose ledgers kept track of ship tonnage, coal, and locomotives, who negotiated deals with military officials and politicians, recruited laborers from around the world, and acquired items to keep the Allied armies fighting.

While Dawes seeks to maintain a level of humility in recounting his experiences, he also presents a portrait of himself at work. His first aim in his role as General Purchasing Agent was to impose a new system of coordinated supply for the A.E.F. Indeed, Pershing believed that transatlantic ships should be devoted to transporting what would amount to over two million American troops to France. Thus, supplies had to be found in Europe, not in the United States. This was the idea behind Pershing's creation of the General Purchasing Board. Not only would such a board be more efficient and help eliminate waste, but it would also cut out the potential for corruption or graft. And ultimately, so both Pershing and Dawes believed, it would speed the Allies toward victory. In carrying out this plan, Dawes focused on coordinating the American supply system by "superimposing a business organization over the Regular Army."[67] This was, in fact, revolutionary. At the time, no such coordination existed among the various branches of service.

Next, Dawes sought to impose the same kind of coordinated supply system for all the Allied armies, an idea that came to him after Pershing successfully helped to bring about the unification of the military front under a supreme command in March 1918. Pershing agreed to Dawes' idea of creating an allied board of supply, but it proved to be far more difficult to establish since the "notion of centralizing and coordinating the supply process," as Gary Mead observed, "was completely novel for the British and French."[68]

While eventually the plan was realized, Dawes first had to get the leaders of the Allied nations (France, Great Britain, Belgium, and Italy) to agree.[69] Who would be in charge of such coordination? Who would have final say in decisions? Because so many Allied leaders were vying for authority, none wanted to relinquish their own power in favor of a truly allied effort. Dawes met with resistance and occasional downright obstructionism as he tried to forge agreement to this novel system. "[W]e did not realize the enormous obstacles in the way of it having their root in individual selfishness and ambition," he noted.[70]

Thus, most of his work in France—at those endless conferences—was largely focused on convincing, manipulating, persuading, and sometimes berating others into agreeing to work toward a common goal: the unification of supply. Trying to coordinate the various personalities among the Allies was, in a sense, Dawes' most important job. As his close friend, the French General Charles Payot said of the endless squabbles, disagreements, and power struggles within the Allied power structure: "I am working sixteen hours a day, four hours fighting the Germans and twelve hours fighting my own people."[71]

Just how to manage the Allied military and political commanders, and to a certain degree, manipulate them into working together— (men, it should be underscored, who were fighting the war on the same side) — were the challenges Dawes faced. His journal, therefore, can be seen as a blueprint for achieving the feat of teamwork— managing supply itself is a mere footnote to the more elusive aspect of orchestrating the massive egos of those who wanted nothing if they did not have power. Dawes may not have been fighting in the trenches, but he fought a symbolic battle that took place around the conference tables of military councils, in fancy and ornate drawing rooms within aging palaces in the French countryside, where spittoons were laid at the polished boots of the men who determined the fates of millions of soldiers and scores of nations.

While going about his work, Dawes rubbed shoulders with some of the most powerful men in the world. Some he admired, and others he could have done without. In giving an account of the many personalities he confronted, Dawes offers a brilliant study of an aspect of war that exists beyond the battlefield: the more elusive and psychological struggle over power; and his journal is an unintended chronicle of relationships among men, their dealings and their friendships.

World War I would be a test case for the United States, the first true chance for the country to take a powerful role on the international stage, going head to head with the Old World European empires that had so long dominated the world. As he went about his job, Dawes found himself faced with the difficult task of introducing ways of doing business that, in earlier eras, his European peers would likely never have considered. But even though this was the Old World where Dawes was operating, he still knew this kind of world quite well—the world of men and power, of handshakes and formal dinners, of meetings and reports, of power plays, and of carefully veiled insults and threats. As a businessman with experience in politics, Dawes was at home in this kind of arena. But he also introduced something new to it.

In some ways, Dawes symbolized the very entrance of the "American character" into the mix. And his stroke of genius lay in the way he managed that entrance as he brought a new element into the war — "American-ness." There can be no doubt that for some Europeans, the Americans — viewed as naïve, friendly, eager, innocent — may have appeared too simplistic or informal, or operating without a dignified level of pomp and circumstance. In some respects, they were regarded with vague suspicion by the imperial rulers and military officers who wore their decorations on their uniforms like works of art on the walls of Europe's most famous museums. Indeed, many of the portraits of Americans overseas emphasize the stark contrast between their no-frills, "businesslike" attitudes and the ornate formality of the Old World imperial culture. And Dawes was certainly no exception. His very office at the Élysée Palace Hotel in Paris revealed such a contrast. The hotel had been "the favorite stamping ground . . . of the beauty, chivalry and royalty of Europe before the war," reporter Isaac Frederick Marcosson wrote after visiting Dawes' office. But the hotel's grace and charm had been requisitioned by American war operations: "General Dawes' office is in the stately and paneled salon of what was, in happier days, the Grande Suite,"

Marcosson wrote. "But it is shorn of its trappings and save for the noble ceiling and ornate mantel is just like the work-room of the President of a great corporation. In the centre is the long table where the occasional meetings of the General Purchasing Board—the Directors of this vast Purchasing Corporation—are held. Facing the door and at a simple flat-top desk sits General Dawes."[72]

The very simplicity of Dawes' office, and the ways in which he worked, underscore his mastery at performing his public role; he was a humble American focused on getting his job done without frills or formality, without pomp or circumstance. "Knock 'em down if they refuse to buy," Dawes reportedly said when asked how to respond to anyone who failed to purchase Liberty bonds in support of the war.[73] This was the kind of "no nonsense" talk for which Dawes would soon be well known. His folksy, American-y talk was stripped of any appearance of formality. (Dawes was known for giving a "pip snorter" of a speech, to stir up crowds and rally support.)[74] It was just this kind of attitude that very likely played into Pershing's choice of Dawes.

Dawes was (to use a modern term) a "connector," able to navigate the complex map of human relationships, putting people in touch with each other, cultivating alliances and friendships, and always remaining profoundly loyal to each and every one of his friends. "It is said that everyone who worked under him," one reporter said of Dawes, "would have fought for him at the drop of a hat."[75]

In all of his complicated dealings, Dawes ultimately believed that being "natural," as he called it, was essential. "How majestic is naturalness!" he observed of Americans' simple attitudes. "I have never met a man whom I really considered a great man who was not always natural and simple. Affectation is inevitably the mark of one not sure of himself. It is above everything the real hallmark of inferiority. We are liked for ourselves over here [in France], if we will only be ourselves and not try to imitate anybody."[76]

Throughout the journal, Dawes injects into his narrative the sense of that "American-ness"— both as a characteristic of the United States and as part of his own self-portrait, which can read quite comically at times.[77] Here was Dawes: always a bit unkempt (as far as military appearance), overcoat buttons undone and reportedly wearing his puttees over his garters for a time, causing him a great amount of discomfort;[78] sometimes sick with a cold or struggling on crutches owing to a foot injury; smoking a cigar (which was a no-no during military reviews or when approached by men of a higher rank); observing and recording the speeds and travel times of his various cars, from a Panhard to a Cadillac;[79] addressing the Belgian Minister of Finance not as "your excellency" as protocol dictated, but as "boss;" kicking high-ranking officers out of his hotel room when any of the enlisted men from his unit came calling; and politely arguing with a waiter at the Hôtel Ritz after declining to order the requisite soup course and thereby subverting the French belief in the "sacredness of fixed procedure at dinner."[80]

Dawes was the quintessential "aw shucks" American. And he was, by his own admission, notoriously undisciplined when it came to following military protocol. Pershing often chastised him for various un-military behaviors and violations of protocol. " 'Charley,' " Pershing said on one such occasion, " 'while I'm in front of the men don't come up with your cigar in your mouth and say, 'Good Morning, Jack.' I don't give a damn what you call me when we're alone, but after all, I'm the official head of the A.E.F. and you're one of my officers.' "[81] At another time, Dawes remained seated, cigar in his mouth, when Pershing entered the room. The other officers present were reportedly stunned by Dawes' nonchalance. Pershing ribbed him: Charley, he addressed his good friend, "when the commanding general walks into the room it is customary to move your cigar from one side of your mouth to the other."[82]

Pershing may have been able to chide Dawes for his behavior,[83] but others were less willing to do the same. In a letter to his brother Henry, Dawes recounted an incident that "appealed greatly to my amusements and somewhat to my satisfaction. Charles Schwab[84] remarked to General Fox Connor that he noticed that 'you don't have Dawes very well disciplined.' 'That is correct,' Connor answered, 'and at the beginning of this war a number of regular army officers got ready to hand him something but when they looked him over once they decided not to do it.'" "He was referring," Dawes explained, "to a period of my military existence when I never appeared before the General Staff without breathing fire and brimstone."[85] That period, and Dawes' penchant for losing his temper, were noted by a wide range of his colleagues. General James Harbord, Pershing's chief of staff, described Dawes as "outspoken and apparently impulsive."[86] (But he also called him "the most outstanding civilian in the American uniform.")[87]

Dawes was nothing if not shrewd. "When Dawes blows up," one reporter observed, "it is according to schedule and plan. It is seldom, if ever, spontaneous; never emotional."[88] He knew how to use his temper only in service to a desired aim. And he also knew when to remain silent, survey a tense situation, and cleverly defuse conflict. (His inability to understand French, he noted, was an asset in his work. He was never ruffled or distracted by comments made by his French colleagues. He just simply did not understand them.)[89] He described some of the other tactics he deployed during inter-Allied conferences when faced with "bitter difference" among the parties: "By smoking cigars, by great emphasis, by occasional profanity no matter how dignified the gathering or impressive the surroundings," he wrote, "I generally got everybody earnestly in discussion of the very crux of the question in the first half-hour. My disregard of the conventions was studied and with a purpose."[90]

His own observation that "One does not, of course, play politics and do it naively, at least not for any length of time" is a keen insight into Dawes. He was well aware that his role was not of mere paper pusher; he knew he wielded tremendous power. "With the latitude John [Pershing] gives me," he wrote, "I feel as if I were exercising the powers of one of the old monarchs. To negotiate single-handed with governments comes to but few men."[91] But in exercising his authority, he did not throw his weight around. "My experience in working for coordination teaches me that the coordinator must himself coordinate his mental activities with others," he noted. "To seek to display authority is to embarrass progress. Reason must be king. A good reason carries one farther than a General's stars . . . It is all just a matter of common sense."[92]

Ultimately, Dawes was, in fact, able to effect what he called "great changes" in the way the war was run.[93] On June 28, 1918, the first meeting of the newly-formed Military Board of Allied Supply took place at his Paris office. The MBAS, chaired by Dawes' good friend, General Payot, would thereafter pool supplies, transportation, and storage, coordinating the services of the rear in much the same way that Pershing worked to help coordinate the front. The Allied leaders had finally agreed to form the board only after Dawes suggested that no single member would be given ultimate authority over the others. This was Dawes' genius, and it was a masterful stroke of political maneuvering; it was the League of Nations writ small; American democracy on the Western Front.[94]

The idea that Dawes brought some simple American "common sense" to the business side of the war is central to understanding both his journal and his work overseas. He was able to realize his goal of unification after much negotiation, a little bit of psychological maneuvering, and the outright soothing of egos. "The glimpses we get in these pages of clashing personalities among the allied civil and military leaders," the New York Times noted in a 1921 review of A Journal of the Great War, "taken with other disclosures of what happened behind the scenes during the war, rouse fresh our wonder how, even after four years' fighting, a victory by united forces was possible."[95] Dawes' "particular kind of genius," the Times continued, "is co-ordination, or — to give it a simpler, everyday name — teamwork."[96]

The self-portrait Dawes reveals in his journal is no less literary, in a sense, for being written in a hurry, in the "midst of events." His journal is a record of a man who, in many ways, appears as a near stereotype of the "self-made" American. In writing his account, Dawes can be seen to walk along the literary path forged by Benjamin Franklin in his posthumously published autobiography.[97] Like Franklin, Dawes appears as an "average" man doing his bit; through hard work, discipline, and sacrifice, he succeeds in completing a day's work. He is a man who is full of humility, scorns formality, and if he can be criticized, it is for being somewhat undisciplined.

This, in essence, is the picture Dawes paints of himself through his journal. And in doing so, he sketches a portrait of America itself with much the same humble characteristics as he grants to himself. To this end, Dawes provides a story of how a job was done, how and why the workers on the job succeeded, and what was intrinsic in the American character that helped bring about victory for the Allies in World War I. Dawes offers his journal to readers as a primer of sorts, a manual for students of history and for future generations. "In the pages of this journal," he states, "may be traced the evolution, under great difficulties, of certain military principles whose recognition hereafter is necessary if allied armies are to be effectively fought as one army."[98]

Along with this grand story, however, there is another tale of "evolution" within Dawes' journal. Indeed, the journal can be read as a kind of rough memoir, an account that measures Dawes' own transition, from a life of business to a life whose primary focus was public service. Through a careful reading of the journal and an excavation of Dawes' biography, that story of transition, of "becoming," emerges, deepening the journal's meanings, and casting light upon Dawes himself.

Memorandum in Pencil

In the course of the "day's work" I have become a military man.[99]
Charles Gates Dawes, 1917

Some might wonder why, at the age of 51, Dawes would choose to go overseas to serve in World War I. But in 1917, doing your "bit" for the war effort was not unusual. In fact, the press delighted in finding "business and professional men" who gave "up positions of executive responsibility and large salaries" to serve their country.[100] "This is a big game, this game over here," observed A.E.F. General Peyton March. "The men of Dawes' type are the very best men we are getting; men of affairs and ability, and used to handling big things."[101]

Those men who did "big things" in the war were, by and large, Dawes' peers. Many of the men with whom Dawes served in France were his close friends or business associates. They were men who operated in powerful financial and political circles, some of whom Dawes personally recruited to serve on his staff of the General Purchasing Board. Indeed, Dawes would be surrounded by his peers during his service overseas: wealthy business-men, lawyers, politicians, and, especially, bankers. Too old to join the enlisted ranks for service at the front, they took up the vast number of volunteer or administrative positions so necessary to support the A.E.F.[102] These men were nearly all of the same generation. Almost to a man, they were born in the two- or three-year window surrounding the end of the American Civil War. *This* was the generation that ran World War I, —the men who served as the nuts and bolts of the administrative side of the A.E.F. These were the men who financed the war, made profits, and played no small part in shaping the American postwar era.

When Dawes enlisted, however, he did not elect to join his colleagues in one of those support roles. "I did not enter the army as a pastime," as he observed.[103] His choice was to enlist in the 17th Engineers — a unit that would undertake hard, physical labor near the war's battlefields. It was quite unusual for a civilian of Dawes' age to enlist in a unit that would be down and dirty in the hard work of war. In fact, Dawes himself was careful to instruct all interested recruits that the overseas work of the 17th Engineers would be "no picnic."[104] In a letter to his brother Beman, Dawes noted that he had "yielded" to the "temptation" to go to war, but he instructed Beman not to do the same.[105]

So why did he go? One possible reason that Dawes yielded to "tempta-tion" lies in his family history. His father, General Rufus Robinson Dawes (1838-1899) served as a soldier in the American Civil War.[106] He was a military hero, commander of the famous "Iron Brigade," and tales of his bravery followed him throughout his life. Charles Gates Dawes was his first son, born just four months after the war's end, his father having been mustered out of service in August 1864, after three harrowing years with the Union Army.

When war was declared in 1861, Rufus Robinson Dawes was a 22 year old recent graduate of Marietta College, living in Mauston, Wisconsin. In April 1861, he organized a volunteer unit "to defend our country and sustain our government."[107] He was "elected" as an officer of the unit that later became the Sixth Wisconsin Volunteer Infantry. Like so many others, he believed the "Rebellion" would be crushed in sixty days.[108] Little did he know what lay waiting for him as a soldier in the Union Army: three years of war and involvement in major military campaigns from Antietam and Chancellorsville to Gettysburg and Spotsylvania.

After the war, he was brevetted as a general for "meritorious service," and entered politics, serving in the U.S. Congress as a representative from Ohio from 1881-1883. His first born son, Charles Gates Dawes, was twenty-five years old when his father published his own wartime memoir, *Service with the Sixth Wisconsin Volunteers* in 1890.[109] In it, young Charles would read accounts of his father's (and other relatives') war experiences, their fates, idealism, enthusiasm, bravery, fear, suffering, and, in some cases, death.[110]

"A box of old letters and papers, collected during the war and carefully arranged and preserved by my wife," General Rufus Dawes noted, served as the "chief source" for the memoir he wrote twenty-five years after the war.[111] But he had also kept a diary during the war, recording his experiences in two (extant) volumes of handwritten entries, now in the possession of the Wisconsin Historical Society in Madison, Wisconsin. The two diaries cover the period from 1860 to 1863, tracing the enthusiasm with which he enlisted, his visits home to Marietta, (and references to Mary Gates, his future wife), and his life in the army: the marches, bivouacs, and battles. His account is devastating to read. His loss of spirit and increasing sense of anxiety and horror at what he witnessed unfold on his diaries' pages. "Soldiering is tiresome, miserable life, entirely in the power of the Caprice of Superiors," he wrote on May 6, 1862. "Rain again," he wrote a few days later. "War is horrible."[112] Interspersed within the entries are lists he made of the men in his unit, with notations of who had been killed or wounded, and also included is one particularly harrowing entry, titled "memorandum in pencil," written on the field during the Battle of Gettysburg in July 1863.

As the son of a veteran, Charles Gates Dawes knew from personal experience that war constituted a unique and important reason to keep a diary. But more importantly, he knew how being "subject to the extreme perils of war" could affect a person's well-being.[113] His father was said to have lived a "storm tossed" life following the war.[114] He died at the relatively young age of 61, having suffered in the wake of his "awful battle experiences" that left him "prematurely old."[115]

Still, Dawes "wanted to go to war."[116] His initial plan was to "get into the line" and serve in the artillery, as he later said, but "they would not take me."[117] But he was intent on serving. As an eldest son, descended from a line of soldiers, Dawes was likely influenced by his family legacy.[118] "There is not a drop of fighting blood in me," his mother wrote to him after he arrived in France, "but I am thankful that my boys inherited from their father his patriotism, his love of justice and willingness to sacrifice for the right." She was, she told her son, "glad and proud to be the mither o' ye."[119]

In serving in his "own" war, Dawes follows in his father's footsteps. One can imagine that the memory of his father's "storm tossed" life was keen in Dawes' mind as he embarked on his own war experience. While in training in Atlanta, he took a few side trips, including one in June 1917 to his hometown of Marietta, Ohio, for a "farewell family reunion."[120] At the Dawes family home at 508 Fourth Street, he bade good-bye to everyone, including his mother.[121] During that visit, did he pause on the pathway in front of his childhood home and think back on his life? Did he picture his father, General Dawes, dressed in uniform, posing on that very same path with Dawes' young children, Carolyn and Rufus, on either side of him? "Truly, we can not tell what is in store for us," his father had observed during the war.[122]

Despite the uncertainty of what lay before him, Dawes knew what lay behind him. And he chose to go. His service would allow him to join the ranks of those who have "seen war as it is."[123] Situating himself within a larger historical narrative, he traces his own legacy: The son of a famous Civil War general is now a part of a new generation, involved in a modern war. Occasionally in the pages of his journal, he refers to his father's influence, expressing his own intensified connection to him and his other relatives, born of his time in France. To "have been in eighteen battles of the Civil War," he wrote in October 1918, "means something more to me now about my father."[124] While he admitted that his own experiences "are nothing as compared" to his father's, he acknowledged that they are "enough to give me knowledge of what a long continuance of such an experience entails in physical and nervous strain."[125]

Precisely what he knew from his father about war's effects Dawes does not reveal in depth. But there is no question that Dawes was no stranger to the "nervous strain" wrought by war. In his journal, he refers to his own "nerves" and the tremendous pressure under which he worked. In his many tours around the Western Front, one can assume that he encountered something of war's horror. At one point, he refers to "the atmosphere of tragedy unspeakable" in which he lived. "The hand of death seems laid on this city," he observed of Paris when he arrived. "Can hardly realize it is the same Paris I visited twenty years ago."[126] While he saw the war from a closer viewpoint than the vast majority of Americans, he chose to refrain from describing its nightmarish scenes. "I shall not write of [war's] horrors as I run across them. Others will do that," he stated simply.[127]

As Dawes extended the legacy of war into another generation, he pays tribute to his father's memory. But there is another Rufus to whom he also pays tribute. For Dawes reveals himself not only to be a son who has lost his father, but also a father who has lost a son. And his desire to go to war might also lie in a tragedy that had befallen him just five years before he arrived in France.

Don't Give Up the Ship

I, his father owe him one last and solemn duty, to project the high lesson of his life, as far as lies within my power.[128]

Charles Gates Dawes, 1912

On September 5, 1912, Charles and Caro Dawes' eldest son, twenty-one year old Rufus Fearing Dawes, drowned while swimming in Lake Geneva, Wisconsin, the likely result of a weakened heart he suffered after having contracted typhoid in the summer of 1909.[129] Dawes and his family were shattered. Rufus had been their first born, a promising young man about to enter his senior year at Princeton University. His loss produced a palpable and seemingly immovable pall within the family. According to Dawes' first biographer, Paul R. Leach, Charles and Caro were so grief-stricken that they "virtually retired from public life" following their son's death.[130] Dawes himself later stated that "the tragic loss of our boy Rufus well-nigh overcame us."[131]

By the time Dawes reached France in 1917, nearly five years had passed since Rufus died. Those five years had seen Charles and Caro attempt to grapple with their loss: they adopted two young children (Dana and Virginia), and they found solace in providing assistance to others. In Dawes' tribute to his son, read by Reverend W. T. McElveen at Rufus' funeral, Dawes enumerated the many ideals by which he had lived; his humility, kindness, generosity, and spirit of charity towards others.[132] As much as Dawes may have been a man keen on capitalism and making money, he was also a man of an earlier age who took Andrew Carnegie's lessons to heart.[133] He believed in giving back, and he did so, making generous gifts to individuals and charities, often anonymously, and supporting his family members, including his mother and youngest sister. ("We live a very happy and peaceful life thanks to you," Dawes' sister wrote to him in 1917.[134])

After Rufus' death, Dawes would renew his commitment to living according to the ideals his son represented. "The five years since Rufus' death have been ones of my business progress," Dawes wrote in a section he later expunged from the published version of his journal, "making me a wealthy man and enabling me, Thank Heaven, to help many others less fortunate. The most blessed prerogative of wealth is the ability to aid others."[135] In those sorrowful years, Dawes seemed to have thrown himself into his work. "The bank, my gas and electric and other enterprises have all prospered beyond expectations," he noted.[136] With his wealth secure, Dawes saw fit to do something of meaning that would help him move beyond his grief. Shortly after Rufus died, Dawes launched a project to open

Charles Dawes before leaving for training, 1917.
Evanston History Center Archives.

hotels for unemployed men (and later, for working class women) with the philosophy that everyone deserves a decent, comfortable residence where they are respected and assisted. The first of the three such hotels which Dawes would open explicitly paid tribute to his son. On New Year's Day, 1914, the Rufus F. Dawes Hotel on South Peoria Street in Chicago opened its doors.[137] There, men were not only fed and housed (5 cents bought a "bed and bath"), but they also found a place that was designed to "help and inspire men to get work." Downstairs in the hotel lobby, a portrait of Rufus was hung, and also a flag that read: "Don't Give Up the Ship."[138]

Dawes himself seemed to be in sore need of following the same advice. As readers of the journal will find, the loss of Rufus is like a specter haunting his time overseas (especially, one imagines, given the intensity of mourning and loss in France with so many young men killed). He also reveals that he shares with General Pershing far more than friendship and a love of each other's company. "Hardship, self-denial, tragedy have all been his lot," Dawes notes of his good friend.[139] Tragedy, indeed. Dawes and Pershing were drawn even closer since they had "both passed through the greatest grief which can come to man."[140] On August 27, 1915, General Pershing's wife, Helen, and three young daughters died in a fire at their home in the Presidio in San Francisco. Only Pershing's six-year old son, Warren, survived. Dawes understood something of the black depths of Pershing's grief, and it was this connection that deepened their relationship. Dawes recalls one moment when they were driving together in France: "there occurred an instance of telepathy which was too much for either of us. Neither of us was saying anything, but I was thinking of my lost boy and of John's loss and looking out of the window, and he was doing the same thing on the other side of the automobile. We both turned at the same time and each was in tears. All John said was, 'Even this war can't keep it out of my mind.' "[141]

From the very first line of his journal and throughout the pages that follow, Dawes alludes to the impact his son's death had on him, especially as he witnessed the march of so many young men on their way to war—men who were contemporaries of Rufus. "I do not seem to get over the loss of my dear, dear boy," Dawes wrote.[142]

In many ways, enlisting can be seen as Dawes' effort to move beyond the private realm of his own personal sorrow. Born in the shadow of his father's war, Dawes might have been part of a generation that would miss its "own" war. War service was a duty that would fall to his father and to his son, for Rufus would have been of prime age for enlistment in World War I. And indeed, many of Rufus' college friends and young relatives would go to war. But Rufus was not to go. And, in some ways, Dawes goes in his stead.

It is only once he is overseas and within a "new environment" that

Dawes finds that he has "a new interest in life" and "a new career, however humble, to make."[143] "My hours of work, my time of rising and of going to bed, my food, my habits, my exercise are changed in a revolutionary way from my former life," he notes.[144] He is purposeful now, going about his work. "The old banking hours of labor with me are a thing of the past," he wrote to Caro.[145]

While overseas, he also takes up a fatherly role as he assists young friends and relatives as they navigate their own war experiences. Three of Dawes' nephews, contemporaries of his son Rufus, would serve in the war, and all were in constant touch with their uncle both in person and via correspondence while they were in France. (See the essay "Homecoming" at the end of this volume for more about Dawes' nephews and others.)

Dawes had given up his habit of keeping a diary after Rufus died. And it was not until he arrived in France that he would begin again. The very first line of his wartime journal reads: "I gave up a journal in 1912 after the tragic death of my dearly beloved son Rufus Fearing," he tells readers.[146] The very act, then, of creating his journal, can be seen as a method by which Dawes coped with his loss. It is his own "memorandum in pencil," written on the battlefield of grief. Dawes' service overseas was thus an act of "becoming," of hope. It is only after embarking on a transatlantic journey and into the First World War, that Dawes again takes up his pen, and plunges into the task of keeping a diary. When he begins again to keep a journal, he was following the advice on that hotel flag. He is not giving up the ship.

Dawes' journal is far more than a simple record of his time overseas. It was the means by which he sought to measure his own evolution. As he tells his war story, he portrays an image of himself, the man he was upon setting off to war, and the man he became while overseas. In the great tradition of American autobiography, Dawes' tale recounts both a personal and national evolution; it is an account of a man and country undergoing a test of faith and character. By the end of the experience, Dawes has become a better man, and America a stronger country.

"Life is an adventure," Dawes was quoted (most likely apocryphally) saying, "and this will be my part in it."[147] Here, Dawes begins his journal; here, he begins his tale. As in any grand literary adventure, Dawes sets off on his wartime journey, in the process of becoming something different, and something better than he was before.[148]

Jenny Thompson

A tight-knit family: Mary Beman Gates Dawes, back row center, with her children (clockwise) Charles Gates Dawes, Mary Frances Dawes (Beach), Henry Dawes, Beman Dawes, Betsey Dawes (Hoyt), and Rufus Dawes. Evanston History Center Archives.

Some of those left behind: clockwise, Caro Blymyer Dawes,
Dana Dawes, and Virginia Dawes. Evanston History Center Archives.

The 17th Engineers (above), Atlanta, Georgia, summer 1917. Evanston
History Center Archives. Dawes' friend "Jack," (below) also known as
General John. J. Pershing. Library of Congress.

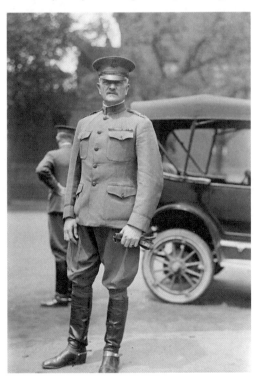

Paris, c. 1917. Dawes' spent most of his time in Paris working out of an office in the Élysée Palace Hotel (above, left). The hotel was located at 102 Avenue Champs-Élysée. Evanston History Center Archives.

Allied leaders, France, c. 1918. Dawes, seated 5th from the left, holds his signature cigar in his hand. Evanston History Center Archives.

Another "endless conference:" A meeting of Allied leaders, France, c. 1918.
Dawes is seated at the head of the table. "This picture was not posed," Dawes
wrote on the back of this photograph. Evanston History Center Archives.

Rufus Robsinson Dawes in his Union Army uniform,
c. 1861-1864.
Evanston History Center Archives.

"Memorandum in pencil," a page from the diary of Rufus
R. Dawes, recorded at 2 p.m. on the first day of the Battle
of Gettysburg, July 1, 1863. It reads, in part:
"Bloody desperate fight. Major Stone of the 2nd Miss.
Infantry surrendered his sword and <u>regiment</u> to me - 230
men. If I am killed today let it be known that Corporal
James Kelley of Company 'B' shot through the heart and
mortally wounded, asked to tell his folks he died a soldier."
Courtesy of the Wisconsin Historical Society.

General Rufus R. Dawes (center) in front of his home at 508 Fourth
Street, Marietta, Ohio, c. 1897-1899. Five Marietta High School Cadets are
pictured behind him, having performed, according to a note on the back of
the original photograph, a dress parade in his honor. Pictured are (left to right):
Knowlton Ames (in suit), Carolyn Dawes, General Rufus R. Dawes, Rufus
Fearing Dawes, and John Shedd.
Courtesy of the Harry Philip Fischer Collection,
Marietta College Special Collections.

Rufus Fearing Dawes, 1890-1912. Evanston History Center Archives.

"Don't Give Up the Ship," Rufus F. Dawes Hotel, Chicago, IL.
Evanston History Center Archives.

Notes to "An American in Paris:"
Charles Gates Dawes in World War I

1   Letter from Charles G. Dawes to Rufus Dawes, November 4, 1918. Box 71, Charles G. Dawes Archive, Charles Deering McCormick Library of Special Collections, Northwestern University Libraries, Northwestern University, Evanston, Illinois. Hereafter referred to as Dawes Archive, Northwestern.

2   Dawes' Paris office was first located at the Hotel Méditerranée at 98 quai de la Rapée, and later, in May 1918, at the Élysée Palace Hotel at 103 avenue des Champs-Élysée. For a brief time, Dawes also had an office at 3 rue de Berri. Mark D. Ells, *America and World War I: A Traveler's Guide*. Northampton, MA: Interlink Books, 2015.

3   Charles G. Dawes, *A Journal of the Great War*, August 21, 1917.

4   By 1917, Dawes and Pershing had been friends for three decades. Both men were in their twenties when they met while living in Lincoln, Nebraska. Pershing, who hailed from Missouri, but whose parents moved to Lincoln when he was young, taught military science and tactics at the University of Nebraska from 1891 to 1895. (He also earned a law degree from the same school in 1893.) Dawes moved to Lincoln in 1887 after graduating from law school. He left in 1895 and moved with his wife and two young children to Evanston, Illinois.

5   The 17th Engineers was one of many units composed of engineers, "raised for the emergency" of war. It was designated for the construction of railways in France. The men in the unit were largely recruited from the Chicago area, with recruitment headed up by Dawes' colleague, Samuel M. Felton (see note below). The unit was authorized on May 5, 1917 and arrived in Liverpool, England, on August 11, 1917. It traveled to St. Nazaire, France, where it would remain, operating under the Services of Supply, for the war's duration. The unit returned to the United States on March 25, 1919. It was demobilized on April 12, 1919. "Report of the Chief of Engineers, September 30, 1919," in *Annual Reports, War Department, Fiscal Year Ended June 30, 1919*. Washington, D.C.: Government Printing Office, 1919, 3.

6   In a meeting in Paris on August 30, 1917, Pershing asked Dawes to take on the new position. He would also serve as "head of a board of ten officers representing all the purchasing departments of our army, including also the Red Cross and Army Y.M.C.A." (*A Journal of the Great War*, September 2, 1917). "The responsibilities of my position are hard for myself to comprehend at times," Dawes wrote to his brother Rufus just after assuming his new roles. "I am sort of an Ambassador—Plenipotentiary for the American Expeditionary Force with the other Governments as well as our own." (Letter from Charles G. Dawes to Rufus Dawes, December 28, 1917. Dawes Archive, Northwestern, Box 71.) "[Pershing] gives me practically unlimited discretion and authority to go ahead and devise a

system of coordination of purchases," Dawes wrote in describing his position, "to organize the board; to arrange the liaison connections between the French and English army boards and our own; to use any method which may seem wise to me to secure supplies for the army in Europe which to that extent will relieve our American transports in their enormous burden." *A Journal of the Great War*, September 2, 1917.

7   John J. Pershing, *My Experiences in the World War*. Volume 1. New York: Frederick A. Stokes Company, 1931, 24.

8   *A Journal of the Great War*, August 21, 1917.

9   Samuel Morse Felton, Jr. (1853-1930). During the war, Felton served as Director General of Military Railways, overseeing the supply of railway material and the organization of railway operations and construction troops. An engineer with extensive experience in railroads, Felton served as manager and president of numerous railroads. He also served on the Board of Directors of Dawes' bank, the Central Trust Company of Illinois.

10   At the time, newspapers erroneously reported that Dawes was to "have charge of expenditures" on a commission for manning and reconstructing railroads in France. "Dawes To Hold Purse of Rail Army in France," *Chicago Daily Tribune*, May 25, 1917.

11   Dawes later explained that he "faked" his way in "on the theory that when I was about thirty years old I was the chief engineer of a railroad, and one of the directors of my bank was in a position to put me in, and I had him by the hair, and he put me in." U.S. House, *Select Committee on Expenditures in the War Department, Hearings Before Subcommittee No. 3 (Foreign Expenditures)*, Testimony of Hon. Charles G. Dawes, February 3, 1921. Washington, D.C.: Government Printing Office, 1921, 4508. According to one source, by the time he had graduated from Marietta College in 1884, Dawes "had already done considerable work as a railroad civil engineer and after graduating in law became chief engineer of a small line which is now part of the Toledo & Ohio Central Railroad." Josiah Seymour Currey, *Chicago: Its History and Its Builders*. Vol. IV. Chicago: The S.J. Publishing Co., 1918, 16.

12   See the essay "Homecoming" at the end of this volume for more details concerning Dawes' war experience.

13   Dawes left Evanston, traveling in a private railway car that he had hired for himself; he would live for two months on the car, while he trained with his unit in Atlanta in preparation for overseas service. ("Millionaire Dawes Here in Private Car to Join regiment," *Atlanta Georgian*, May 21, 1917. Scrapbook, Dawes Archive, Northwestern, Box 84.) The unit opened a recruiting office at 601 West Madison Street. The city of Atlanta was thrilled at the presence of Dawes and reported on the unit's training leading up to a farewell parade on Peachtree Street. ("Seventeenth Engineers Are Given Godspeed by Atlanta on Eve of Departure for France," *Atlanta Journal*, July 24, 1917.)

14   When Dawes arrived in Atlanta, it was not yet known publicly what his position was, since, as the *Atlanta Constitution* reported, Dawes "as yet holds no rank in U.S. Service." Dawes had been spotted by newspaper men, but "refused" to give a statement to the press. ("Mystery Surrounds Arrival in Atlanta of Charles Dawes," *Atlanta Constitution,* June 2, 1917.) At least two rumors surrounding his role in the war were bandied about in the press. It was reported that Dawes might remain stateside and serve under Herbert Hoover on the National Food Commission, and later, a rumor surfaced that he might join the Shipping Board. ("Colonel Dawes May Not Go to Europe," *Marietta Journal,* July 31, 1917; "May Join Shipping Board," *Philadelphia Telegram,* July 31, 1917.) In fact, Dawes' name was indeed being considered for an appointment to Hoover's food commission. Dawes himself had met with Hoover, who wanted him very much. Dawes' business savvy, well known among the higher echelons, was in demand. But Dawes refused. The reasons for Dawes' initial silence concerning his military role lay in the fact that his commission had been held up with a bit of red tape. On May 28, 1917, S.M. Felton cabled Dawes: "Washington advises your commission will be major promotion later." (Telegram from S.M. Felton to Charles G. Dawes, May 28, 1917, Dawes Archive, Northwestern, Box 69). Dawes received his first commission as a major on June 11, 1917. On July 15, 1917, just days before embarking on the trans-Atlantic journey, he received a promotion to Lieutenant Colonel. On January 16, 1918, he was promoted to Colonel, and on October 15, 1918, he was promoted to Brigadier General.

15   "Millionaire Dawes Here in Private Car to Join Regiment," *Atlanta Georgian,* May 29, 1917, Scrapbook, Dawes Archive, Northwestern, Box 84.

16   Letter from Henry Dawes to Charles G. Dawes, January 9, 1918, Dawes Archive, Northwestern, Box 71.

17   Henry May Dawes (1877-1952) and his wife Helen Dawes (1881-1974) lived in Evanston, Illinois. Henry was a lawyer who would later serve as U.S. Comptroller of the Currency, a position his older brother Charles held from 1898-1901. He was appointed to that position by President Harding and served from May 1923 to December 1924. He left that position to become president of the Pure Oil Company, a company he and his brothers founded as the Ohio Cities Gas Company in 1914, expanding it during World War I. In 1920, the name was changed to the Pure Oil Company. Henry served as the company president from 1924 to 1952. Beman Gates Dawes, Sr. (1870–1953) and his wife Bertie Burr Dawes (1872-1958) lived in Ohio. Beman served as a representative from Ohio's 15th District from 1905 to 1909. He also served as president of the Pure Oil Company and as chairman of its board of directors. Rufus Cutler Dawes (1867–1940) and his wife Helen Palmer Dawes (1868-1941) lived up the road from Charles and Caro Dawes in Evanston. After the war, he served on the commission, headed by his brother, Charles, to manage Germany's postwar reparations. All the Dawes

brothers graduated from Marietta College, in Marietta, Ohio, and were members of Delta Upsilon fraternity. They worked together in various businesses throughout their careers. Charles Dawes also had two sisters, Mary Frances Dawes Beach (1872-1956) and Betsey Gates Dawes Hoyt (1880-1972).

18   Dawes called his friendship with William McKinley "one of the most precious memories of my life." According to Dawes, the president treated him "as a father would a son. He made of me a constant companion and a trusted confidant." Charles G. Dawes, *Notes as Vice President, 1928-1929*. Boston: Little, Brown, and Company, 1935, 49.

19   According to historian Ron Chernow, the "loan ultimately had sixty-one underwriters and 1,570 financial institutions marketed the bonds." (Chernow, *The House of Morgan: An American Banking Dynasty and the Rise of Modern Finance*. New York, Grove Press, 1990, 200.) J. P. Morgan and Company and its many subsidiary and partner banks (known collectively as the "House of Morgan") served as the primary purchasing and financing agent of both Great Britain and France. The interest in the House of Morgan's financing the war was clear, and throughout Dawes' journal, he refers to his own meetings with numerous bankers and financiers who were playing no small role in the financing the war.

20   Jerry W. Markham, *A Financial History of the United States: From J.P. Morgan to the Institutional Investor, 1900-1970*. Volume 2. Armonk, NY: M.E. Sharpe, 2002, 73.

21   Charles G. Dawes, handwritten original manuscript of "A Journal of the Great War," Dawes Archive, Northwestern, Box 86, np.

22   Telegram from Charles G. Dawes to T[homas].W. Lamont, October 1, 1915, Dawes Archive, Northwestern, Box 85. Other Chicago bankers declined to participate in the loan. The *Wall Street Journal* chastised them as being "American at heart, but had to be German in pocketbook." ("He Was Not Affrighted," *Wall Street Journal,* December 8, 1915). Dawes' willingness to sign on to the loan caused some controversy. He received some negative publicity and even a death threat, but his bank's board of directors "ratified my action in subscribing for five hundred thousand," he noted, with only one dissenting vote. "I congratulate you most heartily," J.P. Morgan's Tom Lamont cabled to Dawes upon his joining the loan. "Your action is patriotic, high minded, courageous and wise. You will have no trouble with your depositors but if you do we will back you to the limit." (Cablegram from T.W. Lamont to Charles G. Dawes, September 30, 1915, Dawes Archive, Northwestern, Box 85.) The story of American banking and its intimate connection with the financing of World War I is central to Dawes' story. Numerous influential American bankers, who were part of the American war effort, make appearances in Dawes' journal, including Morgan bankers E.C. Grenfell, Tom Lamont, and Henry Herman Harjes. The war would mark the entrance of the United States onto the world stage as an international creditor, with U.S. banks,

(primarily J.P. Morgan), ultimately financing the war for the Allies through loans made to the French and British governments.

23   Charles G. Dawes, handwritten original manuscript of "A Journal of the Great War," Dawes Archive, Northwestern, Box 86, np.

24   This issue deserves more attention than the essays in this volume provide. A broader look at the complicated nature of U.S. financial and political institutions and the financing of the war can be found in Nomi Prins, *All the Presidents' Bankers: The Hidden Alliances That Drive American Power.* New York: Nation Books, 2014.

25   Aside from Dawes' involvement in the financing of the war, Charles and Caro Dawes also purchased U.S. war bonds, called "Liberty Bonds." In June 1917, Dawes sent a telegram to his brother Henry instructing him to "subscribe in my name for twenty five thousand dollars of Liberty Bonds." (Telegram from Charles G. Dawes to Henry Dawes, June 6, 1917. Dawes Archive, Northwestern, Box 71). In October 1917, he purchased another twenty-five thousand dollars' worth of Liberty Bonds. (Cablegram from Charles G. Dawes to Henry Dawes, October 23, 1917, Dawes Archive, Northwestern, Box 71.) His wife Caro, who had her own trust, also purchased bonds, buying, for example, $10,000 in Liberty Bonds in October 1918. (Letter from Henry Dawes to Caro Dawes, October 17, 1918, Dawes Archive, Northwestern, Box 71). These would not be the last of the Dawes' substantial purchases of bonds during the war and the couple also funded other war-related causes. By his own estimate, Dawes donated a total of $22, 028.64 in 1918 alone, which included a $10,000 donation to "the French orphans," while out of her own trust, Caro donated $1500 per month in supplying yarn for the Red Cross. (Letter from Charles G. Dawes to Henry Dawes, January 15, 1919. Dawes Archive, Northwestern, Box 71). See the essay "Homecoming" at the end of this volume for more about Caro Dawes' wartime work.

26   Emory Marshall Young, "Builders of America," *Leslie's Weekly,* February 9, 1918.

27   Telegram from Charles G. Dawes to Henry Dawes, June 6, 1917. Dawes Archive, Northwestern, Box 71. While overseas, Dawes continued doing some private business, particularly selling stock on a venture with his brothers, the Ohio Cities Gas Company (later known as Pure Oil). He also made investments for numerous people including the King of Belgium. (Letter from Charles G. Dawes to Caro Dawes, December 22, 1917. Dawes Archive, Northwestern, Box 71). He also helped his own household staff with their investments, writing at one point, for example, to his brother Henry to tell his servants to sell a given stock and "reinvest in Liberty Bonds thus realizing their profits." (Letter from Charles G. Dawes to Henry Dawes, May 5, 1919, Dawes Archive, Northwestern, Box 71.) While training in Atlanta, he cabled his bank for more check books, presumably to open accounts for the men in his unit.

28   Dana McCutcheon Dawes (February 12, 1912-1998) and Virginia Dawes

Cragg (February 20, 1914-1993). When Dawes left Evanston for Atlanta in 1917, Dana was five years old and Virginia was three years old.

29   Letter from Charles G. Dawes to Mrs. Mary B. Dawes [Mary Beman Gates Dawes], November 14, 1918, Evanston History Center Archives.

30   Ibid.

31   Mary Beman Gates Dawes (1842-1921) lived in Marietta, Ohio.

32   Letter from Charles G. Dawes to Henry Dawes, May 21, 1918, Dawes Archive, Northwestern, Box 71.

33   Letter from Charles G. Dawes to Rufus Dawes, March 31, 1918. Dawes Archive, Northwestern, Box 71.

34   Letter from Charles G. Dawes to Caro Dawes, November 2, 1917, Dawes Archive, Northwestern, Box 71.

35   Letter from Charles G. Dawes to Rufus Dawes, March 9, 1918. Dawes Archive, Northwestern, Box 71.

36   During the war, the letters written to and from various Dawes family members were usually shared, with correspondents asking that letters be passed along after recipients had read them.

37   The Paris branch of the American bank, J. P. Morgan and Company, with which Dawes did quite a lot of business before, during, and after the war. The bank was founded in 1868 as Drexel, Harjes & Co. In 1895, J. P. Morgan took control of the bank and renamed it.

38   *A Journal of the Great War,* August 29, 1917.

39   Telegram from Charles G. Dawes to Henry M. Dawes, July 3, 1918. Dawes Archive, Northwestern, Box 71.

40   Letter from Henry M. Dawes to Charles G. Dawes, September 14, 1918, Dawes Archive, Northwestern, Box 71.

41   The archive contains the collection of Dawes' papers that were stored in his bank until his death in 1951.

42   Along with a vast amount of documents and correspondence contained within the Charles G. Dawes Archive at the Charles Deering McCormick Library of Special Collections, Northwestern University Libraries, at Northwestern University, is a host of ephemera Dawes saved related to his war experience, including tickets to events, dinner programs, banquet menus, and much more. Along with these items, he saved copies of his correspondence, telegrams, and cablegrams. A clipping service kept track of the press coverage related to his work and his family. Articles from newspapers and journals from all over the country were dated and pasted into scrapbooks which are also housed within the archive.

43   Samuel Pepys' (1633-1703) diary, comprised of his accounts of life in London spanning nearly a decade, was published in 1825.

44   Preface, *A Journal of the Great War.*

45   In putting together the published version of his journal, Dawes had

relatively little work to do to the manuscript proper. At some point, he deleted some words and lines by crossing them out (usually no more than a single line) in just a few instances. The most extensive cut was the deletion of the journal's first two pages after the first line. One other section, roughly a paragraph, was cut out (literally with scissors) from the page and another page had the bottom cut from it. Otherwise, the deletions were usually brief references to some kind of disagreement or emotion. Dawes wrote mildly negative things about a handful of people and either crossed out their names or deleted the section entirely. He also changed the term "Boche," which he used once, to "Germans." Boche is a derogatory term for German people which was widely used by the Allies at the time.

46   Volume I of *A Journal of the Great War* included the war diary, along with added material, such as letters and telegrams (reproduced in this new edition). Volume 2 included appendices comprised mostly of Dawes' various reports and photographs.

47   Dawes received nearly every possible award and honor for his wartime service, including the Distinguished Service Medal and the *Croix de Guerre*.

48   "Dawes a Modest 'Cusser,'" *New York Times,* April 23, 1921.

49   U.S. House, Testimony of Hon. Charles G. Dawes, February 3, 1921, 4492.

50   Preface, *A Journal of the Great War.*

51   Pershing, *My Experiences in the World War.* Volume 1, 34.

52   Dawes would later publish more of his journals including: *The First Year of The Budget of The United States.* New York: Harper & Brothers, 1923; *Notes as Vice President,* 1928–1929. Boston: Little, Brown and Company, 1935; *A Journal of Reparations.* London: Macmillan and Co., 1939; *Journal as Ambassador to Great Britain,* New York, Macmillan Co., 1939; and *A Journal of the McKinley Years.* Chicago: The Lakeside Press, 1950.

53   *A Journal of the Great War,* March 27, 1918.

54   Ibid, August 25, 1918.

55   Preface, *A Journal of the Great War.*

56   Pershing was pressured by the Allied commanders in various ways throughout the war. He was chastised for what was perceived to be the slow deployment of U.S. troops in France, even though Pershing argued that they had to be trained properly. He was also pressured to allow the Allies to deploy U.S. forces within their own armies—essentially using them as replacement troops for France and Great Britain. Pershing resisted fiercely and faced various consequences, including the attempt by some French officers (namely Foch) to have him removed from his command. While he had some American critics, Pershing had the support and backing of President Woodrow Wilson and the Secretary of War, Newton Baker, throughout the war.

57   Pershing did not publish his own account of the war until 1931. The two

volume *My Experiences in the World War* (1931) would be awarded a 1932 Pulitzer prize.

58   *A Journal of the Great War,* November 1, 1918.

59   Baltasar Gracián's original quote reads: "Felicity consists not in having the applause of the people at one's entrance; for that is an advantage which all that enter have. The difficulty is to have the applause at one's exit. Baltasar Gracián, *The Art of Prudence: Or, A Companion for a Man of Sense.* Trans. Mr. Savage. London: D. Browne, 1714, 62.

60   Pershing, *My Experiences in the World War.* Volume 1. 34.

61   Preface, *A Journal of the Great War.*

62   Gary Mead, *The Doughboys: America and the First World War,* Woodstock, NY: The Overlook Press, 2000, 121.

63   *A Journal of the Great War,* February 28, 1919.

64   Mead, 121.

65   Byron Farwell, *Over There: The United States in the Great War, 1917-1918.* New York: W.W. Norton and Company, 1999, 288.

66   U.S. House, Testimony of Hon. Charles G. Dawes, February 2, 1921, 4459.

67   Ibid, 4449.

68   Mead, 151.

69   Russia, also an Ally, was not involved in the coordination of supply owing to the fact that most of its troops were stationed on the Eastern Front.

70   *A Journal of the Great War,* June 13, 1918.

71   Ibid, August 28, 1918.

72   Isaac Frederick Marcosson, *S.O.S. America's Miracle in France.* New York: John Lane Company, 1919, 313. Prior to the publication his book, Marcosson (1876-1961) published a shorter magazine piece on "The Business of Managing War" which included sections about Dawes' operations. Marcosson dedicated his 1919 book, *Peace and Business* (New York: John Lane Company) to Dawes "who revealed in war, as in peace, the high spirit and indomitable courage of American business."

73   "Use Fist to Sell Liberty Bonds, Dawes' Advice," *Chicago Daily Tribune,* May 20, 1917.

74   Emory Marshall Young, "Builders of America," *Leslie's Weekly,* February 9, 1918.

75   Ibid.

76   *A Journal of the Great War,* August 21, 1917.

77   Dawes recounted one humorous instance when he was caught in the "old world" style of manners: At a dinner held in honor of Herbert Hoover in Paris, the French Minister of Commerce "inexpressibly horrified me by kissing me on both cheeks before a large audience of which the American part must have been tremendously amused . . . As we sat at the table together I told [Hoover] our old friends in Cedar Rapids, Iowa, and Marietta, Ohio, who knew us better, would

never have made the mistake either of making us so prominent or of kissing us."
A Journal of the Great War, February 16 1919.

78   Carolyn Wilson, "Col. Dawes and His Overcoat," *Chicago Daily Tribune,*
October 4, 1918.

79   Dawes travelled frequently by automobile in France. One of his favor
ite hobbies was tracking the speed of his various cars. His first car in France was
a French Panhard, but by July 1918, he had acquired "a good automobile — a
Cadillac — which takes the French roads easily and continuously from thirty-five
to fifty miles per hour without shaking us up much." Dawes also paid attention to
the automobiles his friends drove. Van de Vyvere, for instance, had a "fine Rolls-
Royce machine." Letter from Charles G. Dawes to Mary [Beman Gates] Dawes,
October 23, 1917, reprinted in *A Journal of the Great War.*

80   *A Journal of the Great War,* October 12, 1917.

81   Quoted in Edward A Goedeken, "The Dawes-Pershing Relationship
During World War I," *Nebraska History* 65 (1984): 114.

82   Quoted in John Perry, *Pershing: Commander of the Great War.* Nashville:
Thomas Nelson, 2011, 136.

83   Dawes and Pershing apparently derived quite a bit of amusement over
the various stories about Dawes' lack of discipline. After the war, Pershing told an
audience one of his favorite stories about Dawes appearing at an official function
with his cigar in his mouth and only one button of his overcoat buttoned. After
Pershing finished the story and the two men were departing, Dawes quipped: "'He's
taking me away so I can't tell the story I know about him.' " "Pershing tells on
Dawes," *New York Times,* April 15, 1925. "Some soldiers told me that in England
there was a Kodak taken of John with one breast-pocket unbuttoned," Dawes
notes in his journal. "For this picture I am going to search that country — to use
it for justifiable defensive personal purposes." *A Journal of the Great War,* April 21,
1918.

84   As head of Bethlehem Steel Company, Charles M. Schwab (1862-1939)
had a virtual monopoly on contracts with the Allies to manufacture certain types
of munitions. In April 1918, he was appointed Director General of the Emergency
Fleet Corporation which oversaw all shipbuilding in the United States. After the
war, Schwab (among others) refuted serious charges of war profiteering. See Robert
Hessen, *Steel Titan: The Life of Charles M. Schwab.* Pittsburgh, PA: University of
Pittsburgh Press, 1975. See the essay "Homecoming" at the end of this volume
for more about postwar investigations into war expenditures.

85   Letter from Charles G. Dawes to Henry Dawes, January 15, 1919, Dawes
Archive, Northwestern, Box 71. "It amuses me," Dawes wrote, "to think of what
must have been the first impressions of me of these splendid officers and dear
friends — so used to conventional military methods of statement and address —
when, breathing fire and brimstone, I made my incursions into the system after

results, my mind fixed upon the red hot poker of dire necessity pressed against the lower part of my back and oblivious to nicety of expression or conventional forms of military salutation," *A Journal of the Great War,* January 11, 1919.

86   James J. Cooke, *Pershing and His Generals: Command and Staff in the AEF.* Westport, CT: Praeger Publishers, 1997, 11.

87   Farwell, 104.

88   James B. Morrow, "Our Field Marshal of Figures," *The Nation's Business,* November 1922, 28.

89   "That defect," Dawes later admitted about his inability to understand the French language, "stood me in good stead whenever I had to carry out a difficult project in which French officers were concerned. I would submit my proposition and steadily stick to my text, being wholly unembarrassed by the criticisms, objections and discussions in the intervals. It is a great advantage at times to be ignorant of a foreign tongue." "Dawes is Pride of Chicago Financial District," *Commercial West,* August 23, 1919, Scrapbook, Dawes Archive, Northwestern, Box 84. "Here and elsewhere," he added, " I was singularly fortunate in having the backing of General Pershing. The general stood by me throughout."

90   *A Journal of the Great War,* March 9, 1919.

91   Ibid, November 9, 1917.

92   Ibid, June 8, 1918.

93   Ibid, March 31, 1918.

94   Dawes supported the League of Nations, and did in fact, as he told Lloyd George, see the MBAS as "practically a 'League of Nations' operating just behind the Allied line of battle." *A Journal of the Great War,* May 9, 1919.

95   Austin Hay, "Behind the Scenes with Foch, Pershing and Haig," *New York Times,* August 21, 1921.

96   Ibid.

97   Franklin's autobiography, first published in Paris in 1791, remains a classic American text, with a voice and style that heavily influenced subsequent autobiographies. Franklin's self portrait also reflected the nascent characteristics of the literary "American character."

98   Preface, *A Journal of the Great War.*

99   *A Journal of the Great War,* August 21, 1917.

100   "Recruited from 'Big Business' to Serve Nation," *Chicago Daily Tribune,* July 8, 1917.

101   Letter from P[eyton] C. March to Major General Wm. H. Carter, December 22, 1917, Scrapbook, Dawes Archive, Northwestern, Box 84. Peyton C. March (1864-1955) was a commanding general in the U.S First Army. Later he would serve as the U.S. Army Chief of Staff.

102   Dawes' fellow Chicagoans included Julius Rosenwald president of Sears, Roebuck and Co., who served on the munitions board, and Stanley Field,

nephew of Marshall Field. Many also served on the home front and were known as "Dollar a Year Men," men of means who were paid an annual salary of just one dollar for their service (owing to legal restrictions regarding volunteer service in the government).

103   *A Journal of the Great War,* November 26, 1918.

104   Telegram from Charles G. Dawes to J[oseph].E. Otis, June 1, 1917, Dawes Archive, Northwestern, Box 69.

105   Letter from Charles G. Dawes to Beman Dawes, October 18, 1917. Dawes Archive, Northwestern, Box 71.

106   Rufus R. Dawes was commissioned a major in 1862, a lieutenant colonel in 1863, and a colonel in 1864. On May 22, 1866, he was brevetted as brigadier general by order of President Andrew Johnson.

107   Rufus R. Dawes Diary, Vol. 2. "Dawes, Col. Rufus R. (1838-1899)," Wisconsin Historical Society, http://www.wisconsinhistory.org/. Accessed April 2016. The unit was known initially as the Lemonwier Minute Men, and was later designated at the Sixth Wisconsin Volunteer Infantry. It was mustered into service at Camp Randall, Madison, Wisconsin, on July 16, 1861. The unit members signed up for three years of service.

108   Rufus R. Dawes, *Service with the Sixth Wisconsin Volunteers.* Marietta, OH: E.R. Alderman and Sons, 1890, 5-6.

109   *Service with the Sixth Wisconsin Volunteers,* 5-6. As is the case with many war memoirs, a generation would pass before Rufus Dawes would record his experiences in his account of the war.

110   Rufus Dawes' brother, Major Ephraim C. Dawes (1840-1895), also served in the American Civil War. On May 28, 1864, in Dallas, Georgia, Ephraim was shot in the face. He survived, enduring unimaginable pain and suffering that included a facial operation performed without the benefit of chloroform; the operation took 90 minutes. Rufus Dawes was by his side throughout the entire operation, holding his brother's hands. The operation was performed in September 1864, months after the initial injury was sustained. (*Service with the Sixth Wisconsin Volunteers,* 312.)

Another of Charles Gates Dawes' uncles, Charles Beman Gates (1844-1864) died in the war. He was the younger brother of Dawes' mother, Mary. The two had been "inseparable companions." (Dawes, *Service with the Sixth Wisconsin Volunteers,* 284.) Mary had only been married a few months — (Rufus and Mary wed on January 18, 1864) — when news came that her brother "Charley," a soldier in the 148th Ohio volunteers, died on May 31, 1864. He had only just enlisted. He had been a student at Marietta College when the war broke out and had finally persuaded his parents to let him enlist. He had been "firm in his conviction that it was his duty to go." On May 23 1864, the train carrying his unit, which had just been mustered into service, had just departed Marietta when it derailed. Two men were killed and Charley and three others suffered injuries. It was said that Charley was unwilling to return home, and went on with his unit to Harper's Ferry. There, the unit camped in the open and withstood numerous rainstorms, and soon, the already weakened and injured Charley contracted pneumonia and died. He was 23 years old. D.E. Beach, "Lieutenant Charles Beman Gates," *History of Washington County, Ohio: With Illustrations and Biographical Sketches.* Cleveland: H.Z. Williams and Bro, 1881, 252. See also Whitelaw Reid, *Ohio in the War: Her Statesmen, Her Generals and Soldiers.* Volume 2. Ohio: Moore, Wilstach, and Baldwin, 1868, 678.

111   Preface, *Service with the Sixth Wisconsin Volunteers.*

112   Entry, May 14, 1862, Rufus R. Dawes Diary, Vol. 2.

113   Dedication, *Service with the Sixth Wisconsin Volunteers.*

114   Address by "One of His Sons," [Ed. Possibly Charles G. Dawes] Given at the Funeral of Rufus R. Dawes, August 3, 1899, in William E. Roe, *A Memoir: Rufus R. Dawes.* New York: De Vinne Press, 1900, 37.

115   Ibid.

116   U.S. House, Testimony of Hon. Charles G. Dawes, February 2, 1921, 4448.

117   Ibid.

118   One of Charles G. Dawes' ancestors was William Dawes (1745-1799), one of several people who rode with Paul Revere and warned of the approaching British forces on the night of April 18, 1775.

119   Letter from Mary G. Dawes [Mary Beman Gates Dawes] to Charles G. Dawes, November 13, 1917, Dawes Archive, Northwestern, Box 71.

120   "Colonel Dawes to Visit this City," *Marietta Journal,* June 23, 1917. Dawes Archive, Northwestern, Box 84.

121   Also on that visit to Marietta in June 1917, Dawes worked to recruit men for his unit (just as his father had done for his own unit in 1861).

122   Dawes, *Service with the Sixth Wisconsin Volunteers,* 284.

123   *A Journal of the Great War,* October 26, 1918.

124   Ibid.

125   Ibid.

126   In 1897, Dawes and his wife Caro had made a tour of the continent, including a stay in the city of lights. They had sailed on the *Majestic* from New York, New York, to Liverpool, arriving on July 7, 1897. They spent a month taking in the majesty of the "continent" and getting a bit of culture, before sailing on the *Teutonic* and returning home to "our own blessed native land" in August 1897. Charles G. Dawes, *A Journal of the McKinley Years.* Chicago: The Lakeside Press, 1950, 125.

127   *A Journal of the Great War,* September 12, 1917. Dawes frequently got close to the war with his visits to the Western Front. He traveled to the front lines numerous times, often staying with Pershing or other officers at their headquarters. He was at St. Mihiel in October 1918, and other hot spots through the periods of heaviest combat for the A.E.F.

128 "Tribute to Rufus Fearing Dawes," in Charles G. Dawes, *Essays and Speeches*. Boston: Houghton Mifflin, 1915, 1.

129 Rufus had taken ill while working as a surveyor with an engineering corps in South Dakota during a summer vacation. He had arrived home in Evanston very sick and would not recover for weeks.

130 Paul R. Leach, *That Man Dawes*. Chicago: The Reilly and Lee Co, 1930, 145.

131 Later, Dawes stated that "kindly time enables us now to speak of [Rufus] and the happiness he gave us." Charles G. Dawes, *Notes as Vice President, 1928-1929*, 254.

132 Rufus' funeral was held at the Dawes' home in Evanston.

133 In 1889, Andrew Carnegie first published his now famous treatise, "The Gospel of Wealth," in which he instructed the wealthy classes in the best ways to administer their fortunes. "In bestowing charity," Carnegie wrote, "the main consideration should be to help those who will help themselves; to provide part of the means by which those who desire to improve may do so; to give those who desire to use the aids by which they may rise; to assist, but rarely or never to do all." Andrew Carnegie, "The Gospel of Wealth," in *The Gospel of Wealth, and Other Timely Essays*. New York: The Century Company, 1901, 17.

134 Unsigned, letter to Charles G. Dawes from his sister [most likely his younger sister, Betsey Dawes (Hoyt)] June 5, 1917, Dawes Archive, Northwestern, Box 71. Dawes was generally fairly frugal. When he gave out financial advice to friends it involved keeping one's head when one is prosperous and always paying one's debts.

135 Charles G. Dawes, handwritten original manuscript of "A Journal of the Great War," Dawes Archive, Northwestern, Box 86, np.

136 Ibid.

137 At the hotel, 100 private rooms were let for 10 cents a night, and 400 bunks were available for 5 cents each. In its first few months, the hotel provided lodging to 74,161 men and 29,431 men were fed. A free employment agency was established in the hotel to assist guests in their search for jobs. In its first four months of operation, 1,063 guests found work. Chicago at the time had an estimated 100,000 men out of work. Mitchell Mannering, "The Dawes Hotel by the Side of the Road," *National Magazine,* August 1914, 787-788. "Opens Memorial Hotel," *New York Times,* January 2, 1914. Dawes would open another hotel for men in Boston in 1916, and, in February 1917, he opened one for women, the Mary Gates Dawes Hotel (named after his mother) at 327 Throop Street in Chicago. "Hotel Home for Women," *Chicago Commerce,* February 1917, 31. "Girls Find Home as Mary Dawes Hotel is Opened," *Chicago Daily Tribune.* February 18, 1917. Of the hotel, Dawes' mother, Mary, said, "it is a happy thing to know that through the kindness of my son many self-respecting girls may be given a clean and comfortable home under

my name." "Mary G. Dawes Women's Hotel to Open Today," *Chicago Daily Tribune,* February 17, 1917.

138 The famous line (or battle cry) was the dying command of American naval officer, James Lawrence (1781–1813), commander of the U.S.S. Chesapeake during the War of 1812.

139 *A Journal of the Great War,* December 22, 1917.

140 Ibid, September 2, 1917.

141 Ibid.

142 Ibid, February 5, 1918.

143 Ibid, August 21, 1917.

144 Ibid.

145 Letter from Charles G. Dawes to Caro Dawes, November 2, 1917, Dawes Archive, Northwestern, Box 71.

146 Dawes had kept a diary off and on for many years before, namely while serving in the McKinley administration. It was not until 1950 that he would publish it. Charles G. Dawes, *A Journal of the McKinley Years.* Chicago: The Lakeside Press, 1950.

147 *Davenport Democrat,* May 29, 1917. Scrapbook, Dawes Archive, Northwestern, Box 84.

148 Dawes' views on war as improving one's character were well-rooted in his era. At the time, war was popularly characterized as a great adventure, an experience through which young men grow stronger and cultivate virtues. The great rhetoric and propaganda that accompanied the U.S. involvement in the war was fuelled by this kind of imagery. The sobering realities of modern war would not be fully understood until after the war's end. For more on the "myth" of the war experience, see George M. Mosse, *Fallen Soldiers: Reshaping the Memory of the World Wars,* Oxford, UK: Oxford University Press, 1991, and Paul Fussell, *The Great War and Modern Memory.* Oxford, UK: Oxford University Press, 1975.

Military Board of Allied Supply
Coubert, France, 1918

General Enrico Merrone, Italian Army in France; Brigadier-General Charles G. Dawes, American Expeditionary Forces; Brigadier-General Charles Jean Marie Payot, French Army; Major-General Reginald Ford, British Expeditionary Forces; Major Cumont, Belgian Army

A Journal of the Great War
1917-1919

Charles G. Dawes

Brigadier-General Engineers

With Illustrations

Preface to the Original Edition

We, of this generation, are too near the Great War to write its history. Time alone can give perspective and then only to the historian and his readers. It alone can assign to past events their relative importance. This generation in the United States is living and has lived amidst such a succession of great events that it has ceased to be greatly impressed by them. Among our people the war is largely forgotten, or remembered because of some personal consequence or some prospective personal consequence. Yet an elemental convulsion of humanity has occurred, so profound in its effects upon life on the earth that it will be studied and described for thousands of years.

Of all ages and epochs this is the greatest, and the one to which all those of the future will hark back — this, in which, though we played our great part, we yet live heedlessly and with little thought of the future.

The war itself was conducted on so vast a scale, involved so many nations and armies, covered such an extent of territory, and included such a number of campaigns, that only the trained mind of the future military student will follow it in its details. But out of the study of the war in its larger aspects, already commencing in Europe, there is arising the first of many great generalizations, to wit: the stupendous and unnecessary loss of life and waste of wealth, man power, and material due to the selfish resistance among the Allies to an earlier central control of military and supply operation. When in March 1918, Foch,[1] who in my judgment will be regarded in history as the greatest of all soldiers, was finally conceded the central control of Allied army movement, it was as a result of a crushing defeat of the British which wiped out their already exhausted Fifth Army.[2] To the support of this army no Allied reserve could be called because bitter opposition to even such a partial measure of central control had thwarted a plan of the Supreme War Council,[3] suggested by Foch and Sir Henry Wilson.[4]

If the English had not then yielded a central control the British Empire, together with the Allied cause, would, in all probability, have fallen. To such extremities does the pride of nations bring them! The attitude of opposition toward any release of national power by one ally to another, either over operations or supplies, was essentially the same on the part of all. While emergency as a rule effected the only exceptions — and these exceptions are but few — yet this journal records the action of one great commander who offered to surrender power for the common good before an emergency became acute — John J. Pershing[5]— and whatever condemnation history may visit upon others in this regard, his fame will only shine the brighter. As the Chief of Supply Procurement for the A.E.F., under a plan devised by General Pershing, which superimposed a centralizing and coordinating authority over the decentralized services of our own army, the uncoordinated condition of the rear of the Allied armies in France naturally forced itself upon my attention.

About two weeks after the agreement for the Foch command on March 27, 1918,[6] I proposed a plan to General Pershing for coupling up the rear of the three Allied armies in France as they were coupled up at their front, which was, in effect, to be an extension over the Allies of his plan in our own army supply procurement which I was carrying out as an officer. He adopted the plan in principle, and appointed me as his representative to endeavor to secure its adoption by the Allies, authorizing me to offer his own control over the rear of the American army to French command provided the English would do likewise. The importance of such a plan, if adopted, cannot be overstated. With the theoretical power to command the movement of the three armies, Foch had no power over any lines of communication except those of his own army. With the central command he could fight the three armies as one army only so far as the rigid supply organization of the English and American armies, of which he had no control or essential knowledge, would allow of their movement. That he acutely felt this handicap is evidenced by the fact that in August, 1918, he asked that the supreme control over the Allied rear be given to General Payot,[7] of his staff, the Chairman of our Military Board — which was, in effect, exactly the same proposition that I had made the Allies in our inter-Allied conferences in April.

Apart from the unification of supply activity in the immediate rear of the armies, the release of men from the Service of Supply for the front which coordination would effect, and the creation of supply reserves as bearing upon future operations such as the motor reserves for surprise attack or pursuit of the enemy, this central control of the immediate rear would have extended its economizing influences, all tending toward increased military effectiveness, over the more distant rear of supply production — England, the United States, and the south of France. The continued piling-up behind each army of unnecessary supplies, many of them carried in ships otherwise available for the transport of combat soldiers, which resulted from the lack of any bird's-eye view of the supply situation of the three armies considered as one, would have been checked. Incalculable wasted effort and wealth would have been rendered effective in securing earlier victory and saving precious lives. But we succeeded, through international agreement, only in placing the control over the Allied rear in the hands of a Military Board which could issue orders to the Allied armies by unanimous agreement.

As a matter of fact, although our Board was called the "Military Board of Allied Supply," apart from its order pooling French and American ammunition, it concerned itself largely with matters other than supply. My journal and my official statements, printed with it, sufficiently cover what we did accomplish. My purpose in referring to this matter in this Preface is again to call attention to the results which we might have achieved, in addition to what we did achieve, if our Military Board, which, for over four months preceding the armistice, conducted many activities in the rear of the Allied armies, had come into existence at the beginning instead of the end of the war.

So important did I consider this demonstration to military students that, through this Board, of which I was the American member, I secured the issuance of orders to the Allied armies for coordinated reports of the status of the armies on October 31, 1918, and the history of their supply organization from the beginning of the war. This great compilation has taken two years of work by the staffs of the different armies, but is almost ready for publication, its form having been finally approved by representatives of all the Allied armies in Paris on October 19, 1920. From these records the military student of the future will continue the study where we ended it, just as any allies in war hereafter must start the work at the point where we ended it, if they are to wage war with their full effectiveness.

In the pages of this journal, therefore, may be traced the evolution, under great difficulties, of certain military principles whose recognition hereafter is necessary if allied armies are to be effectively fought as one army. In proposing and establishing them, notwithstanding the innumerable obstructions interposed by the authorities of the independent armies and governments, — doubly formidable because national pride can always be invoked against the establishment of a superior coordinating power, — results were effected important enough, from a military standpoint, to make these principles certain of acceptance in the next war fought by allied armies.

At the time I prepared the monograph on the "Principles of Army Supply and Purchase," which appears in these pages,[8] I was much burdened and pressed for time, but I knew then that in the future this exposition of principles must always be considered authoritative for the reason that under an organization based on them, there had been gathered, from countries in Europe supposed to be stripped of supplies, over ten million tons of material for the American army as compared with about seven million tons which were shipped to it from the United States. I have been amply repaid for its preparation in its recognition by the War Staff College of the United States in its course of instruction.

The contemporaneous notes here published were made under pressure, but always with a sense of responsibility and a desire for accuracy. From them can be obtained a true picture of the great American Commander-in-Chief in action. Here again time, and time alone, will give to the thoughtful people of our nation the true measure of his greatness.

Charles G. Dawes

1   French military leader Marshal Ferdinand Foch (1851-1929) commanded troops in the field and served on the Supreme War Council during World War I. In March 1918, he was appointed Supreme Allied Commander, overseeing all of the Allied forces. General Foch's experiences in the war ranged from commanding French troops in the face of the 1914 German invasion to waging a costly war of attrition. Overall, he was judged to have succeeded in holding the Allied armies together, an essential component in the Allied victory.

2   The British 5th Army was overrun by the Germans during the Spring Offensive, launched by the Germans in March 1918. The Offensive was to prove a turning point in the war. Reinforced by the troops that were moved from the Eastern Front to the Western Front (after Russia got out of the war), Germany attempted an all-out attack along the Western Front before the U.S. forces were fully deployed. German forces gained more territory at that time than they had since the war began in 1914.

3   The Supreme War Council, comprised of representatives of the Allied nations, was formed in November 1917 and met once a month in Versailles. The council was formed in reaction to three years of failing to coordinate operations, something that Dawes and Pershing both considered to be the primary problem in waging the war.

4   Sir Henry Hughes Wilson (1864-1922) was a military advisor to British Prime Minister Lloyd George and served as a representative on the Supreme War Council. In 1918 he served as Chief of the Imperial General Staff.

5   John Joseph Pershing (September 13, 1860 – July 15, 1948) was born in Laclede, Missouri. He graduated from the United States Military Academy (West Point) in 1886. He served in the Frontier campaigns against the Sioux and Apache from 1886-90. From 1891 to 1895, he taught Military Science and Tactics at the University of Nebraska. He went on to serve in the Spanish American War and in the Philippine–American War. He commanded U.S. troops near the Mexican Border, and in 1916, led the U.S incursion into Mexico, known at the time as the "Punitive Expedition" and now known as the Mexican Expedition. In May 1917, he was appointed commander-in-chief of the American Expeditionary Forces in France. After the war, he served as Army Chief of Staff from 1921-1924.

6   The March 1918 agreement established a unified command for the Allied armies, with Foch at the head. General Pershing had advocated a unification of the forces for some time, arguing that by maintaining separate commands, the Allied armies operated ineffectively.

7   Colonel (later Brigadier General) Jean Marie Charles Payot (1868-1931) of the French Army, one of Dawes' closest friends in France.

8   See Appendix A for Principles of Army Purchase and Supply as suggested by Experience of American Expeditionary Force in France.

A JOURNAL OF THE GREAT WAR

August 21, 1917 ~ August 2, 1919

Section 1

August 21, 1917 ~ September 24, 1917

CHARLES G. DAWES
Brigadier-General Engineers

St. Nazaire, France
August 21, 1917

I gave up a journal in 1912 after the tragic death of my dearly beloved son Rufus Fearing.[1] In the course of the "day's work" I have become a military man, and am living in the midst of events so important that a record of them will be interesting to others and to myself later. Through the friendship of S. M. Felton,[2] Director-General of Railways, a member of the Board of Directors of the Central Trust Company of Illinois, and with the cooperation of John Pershing, my old friend, I received a commission as Major in the Engineers (17th Regiment, National Army[3]). I reported at Atlanta, Georgia, leaving Chicago May 27, 1917, with Colonel Sewell (then Major) who commanded the regiment.[4] I cannot overemphasize my debt to Colonel Sewell. My selection was approved by him. In all circumstances, some of which must have been extremely annoying to him, he was the courteous, kindly, loyal friend. He is a man of great executive ability, of wide engineering experience, of broad culture and high education. A graduate of West Point with twenty years' experience in the army and ten in an active business in civil life, he is the ideal commander of a regiment of engineers.

I took a private car with me to Atlanta and Colonel Sewell and I lived on it while we were there. Mrs. Sewell and Caro and Carolyn[5] joined us for several weeks. During the two months I was with the regiment in America, Colonel Sewell and I, together with Captain Coe[6] (of Co. A, the engineer of the Florida East Coast "Sea-Going" Railway during its construction) and our families, went to Marietta and New York. At Marietta, my old home, we recruited forty men for our regiment under the direction of D. B. Torpy and H. E. Smith. I bade "good-bye" to my mother and to the rest of the Marietta branch of the family. My mother is a great and good woman. She is also a dear mother.

Assisted somewhat in recruiting the regiment (17th Engineers, Railway) through my railroad friends in the North. At length we had about three hundred and fifty men from the North and seven hundred and fifty from the South — a splendid group. Our time at Atlanta was spent in hard work, drilling and organizing. The tactics came a little hard for me; but I was soon drilling a battalion and feeling thoroughly at home in it. Colonel Sewell was more than kind in giving me every opportunity to develop along military lines. I found I did not mind long marches or horseback riding, and became acclimated soon.

Our battalion drilling-grounds were on South Gordon Street, Atlanta, probably named after the famous and splendid old Confederate

Major-General, John B. Gordon, whose name is reverenced throughout the South and especially in this section.[7] I rode out to see his old home "Southerland," a fine example of the best Southern architecture.[8] Talked with many who knew him. One told me of a remark of his to a young man who wanted to get his uniform quickly so that he could drill his men. "Young man," said Gordon, "if you are not a Captain in your shirt-sleeves, I can't make you one with a uniform."

We left Atlanta for France on July 26. I had in the meantime received my commission as Lieutenant-Colonel[9] and Colonel Sewell his commission as Colonel. I forgot to say that when I was in Washington applying for my commission I met my old friend John J. Pershing, who had been put in command of the United States Expeditionary Force in France. I took lunch with him and Charlie Magoon at the Metropolitan Club and spent the balance of the day with him and his staff at his headquarters at the War Department. He sent one of his aides, Captain Margotte, to the Army Surgeon with me for my physical examination, and made himself a lot of trouble in helping me get my commission. At lunch Charlie Magoon[10] remarked that he (Pershing) would become the great hero of the war, etc. John answered: "Tell me one man who started in this war in supreme command who lasted. What I am going to do is simply the best I can, and there is nothing in what you say worth thinking about."

I also took lunch with Hoover[11] (the food control man) and Fred Delano, of the Federal Reserve Board.[12] Hoover wanted me to become the head of the organization he proposed to make to control the prices of grain in the United States. He talked with me an hour or so, and was very emphatic in his invitation. He said, "I can find a hundred men who will make better Lieutenant-Colonels of Engineers and I want you right here." He is an extremely able man. He will succeed if any one can in such a difficult task as confronts him.

After reaching Atlanta and receiving my commission, Hoover gave me a great scare by wiring, "Would you bear me implacable resentment if I asked the President to assign you to me?" I answered: "Under no circumstances do such a thing. It would be unfair and cruel, and I know you would not consider it." Heard no further from the matter to my great relief.

We reached New York on July 28 and were embarked on the ship *Carmania*, together with the 12th Regiment of Engineers. In all there were about 2500 soldiers on board. The ship was commanded by Captain Charles, the senior Captain of the Cunard Line, formerly Captain of the *Lusitania*, though not on her when she was torpedoed. The Chief Officer was J. Close and the First Officer E. W. Bamber.

Colonel Sewell placed me in command of the regimental "boat drill," to

OFFICERS OF THE 17TH ENGINEERS (RAILWAY) AT ATLANTA, JUNE, 1917

Left to right, first row: Colonel Sewell, Lieutenant-Colonel Dawes, Major Atwood. *Second row:* Captains Causey, Coe, Cooper, Ryan, Lieutenant Bullard. *Third row:* Lieutenant Roop, Captain Maddox, Captain Perkins, Lieutenant Howard, Lieutenant Rhodes. *Fourth row:* Lieutenants Dickinson, Halleck, Yarcho, Farrington, Welch. *Top row:* Lieutenants Heinz, James, McCarty.

COLONEL JOHN STEPHEN SEWELL AND LIEUTENANT-COLONEL CHARLES G. DAWES
17TH REGIMENT ENGINEERS (RAILWAY) AT ATLANTA

devise the method of getting the men on deck most expeditiously opposite their assigned boats and rafts in case of submarine attack. It was a very important and responsible assignment, and I worked hard at it, gradually getting it into good shape.

We went from New York to Halifax Harbor, where we spent two days and where we met the balance of our fleet, the *Adriatic*, the *Ordena*, and the *Bermudian* — the latter loaded with colored troops from Bermuda. As we steamed out of the harbor in the evening of a wet and foggy day, the crew of an English battleship in line on the decks gave three cheers while their band played the "Star-Spangled Banner," to which our men responded.

From the commencement of my assignment in command of boat drill I slept with my clothes on in the "after wheel house"[13] where the "officers of the night" could reach me at a moment's notice, and from where I could reach the top of the "after island" which was to be my post in case of attack. During the long nights I made friends of the gunners who served the six-inch gun on the stern and of the after crew of the boat. They were very considerate. If they thought I was sleeping they all walked on "tip-toe." They were interesting companions all the way over. From them I gained much information about the submarine warfare, as I did from the ship's officers, who had most of them been on torpedoed vessels. A torpedo travels about thirty-five knots per hour. The submarine itself has to be aimed to discharge it at its mark. Hence the zigzagging of the ships expecting an attack. Our fleet zigzagged all the way across. Ships are continually attacked, and the situation is much more dangerous than would seem to one on shore. From the beginning of the voyage I endeavored to gather information, and after having made a good record in the time consumed in getting the regiment on deck from the hold, I compiled a report which was commended to General Pershing by Colonel Sewell and recommended for distribution by Captain Charles. This report and my instructions to our Captains in case of attack I shall sometime attach hereto, as it will give a better idea of what a ship and its officers constantly confront than anything I could write here.[14]

During one night when we were in the danger zone the sea was rough, and while it would have been difficult for a submarine to hit us I realized that if it did our loss of life would have been very large. It was very dark and cold, and it would have been almost impossible for the men to reach the rafts as we threw them off. To hear a discussion of a raft detail on a cold, dark, and foggy deck as to whether it would not be better in case of a sinking ship to take to the water without life preservers, in order to have things over quicker, only indicates how hopeless the outlook sometimes seems when one is on the sea and up against it, as compared with a discussion as to a course of action held on land before sailing.

THE GREAT ADVENTURE

While I do not know what use General Pershing may make of my report, I feel that something of the kind should be sent to landsmen officers in command of troops on army transports. During the whole voyage I worked so hard at "boat drill" and making up my report that I had little time for anything else. After a long time one foggy evening a little light appeared away to the front. It was the signal light on one of the six British destroyers sent out to convoy us in. Captain Charles told me afterward how relieved he was when he saw it. His rendezvous with the convoy had been changed on the way over and our course was very erratic — made so to avoid submarines. We went apparently far north and then south again. We were about eleven days at sea from Halifax to Liverpool, and two weeks traveling from New York to Liverpool. The *New York*, which sailed from New York after us, reached Liverpool before us, and was attacked on the way over. The *Belgic* was attacked just before we arrived, and two of our destroyers left us to chase the submarine. And here I may say that there are a large number of hostile submarines off this coast now hovering around this American base (St. Nazaire).[15] Yesterday (or the day before) five torpedoes[16] were discharged at *The Finland*. I suppose the most dangerous part of our passage was the trip from Southampton to Havre. At some time some of our transports will likely be struck, and with the crowded-in soldiers the casualties will be large, in all probability.

We arrived at Liverpool on the 11th of August and found trains at the dock ready to carry us to Oxney Camp near Borden. The English liaison officer assigned to us was Lieutenant F. C. Covell, with whom I became "good friends." I was put in command of the train carrying the first battalion of our regiment, Colonel Sewell following on the second train. It was a long but interesting trip across England. Everywhere the people were waving flags and cheering along the route. It took us until eleven o'clock at night to reach Borden. The men had had only a sandwich at noon. It was a cold, dark, rainy night. A British officer on our arrival asked me to form the battalion on the road near the station, which I did. And then occurred a demonstration of the reviving effect of music, for there appeared to lead us to camp a splendid British band. As it played the American marches and airs as we marched in the dark, it meant to us all that we were welcome, that after all we amounted to something, that somebody was glad to see us. I do not think that in the great London demonstration, when we marched for hours through cheering crowds, — the first American troops ever to pass through the British capital, — our men were so uplifted as when we marched along that lonely road that night, after a weary day, to camp. When we got there we found a fine supper waiting for us. I managed to get four lines of men passing the soup cans at once instead of the one line our

British friends had arranged, and in this way saved an hour of time at least.

In cordiality and the anxiety to show us kindness and make us welcome, the English officers could not have been surpassed. We slept under tentage and were comfortable. From that day to this our life as officers has alternated between luxury and the extreme opposite — from the routine work of a new and drilling regiment in camp to the most interesting and unusual experiences. For myself I find everything new and interesting — the few hardships and all. As summary court officer for the regiment, which I have been from the beginning, as a drillmaster and pupil, as a principal and a subordinate, as a ship officer and a military commander, I have found among these new friends and associates and in this new environment a new interest in life, a new career, however humble, to make, and in thinking back the only experience in my life with which I can compare it in its excitement are the early days of college life with its new friends and duties and competitions.

One's civil accomplishments help some, but not much. Young and bright men are around you engaged in similar tasks. Comparison is always present. Competition sits at your side. All the artificial barriers which civil success and wealth have built around one fall away, and leave you but a man among men to make or unmake yourself as in the time of young manhood. And then as before, work and character and personality — tact and initiative and common sense — will commence to count. Humbleness and naturalness are the great protection against ignorance. I feel that I learned much in military life from the beginning by letting those "who knew" know that I did not know, but that I wanted to learn. This was especially the case in my association with English officers. To "put on a front" because of my rank would have condemned me to perpetual ignorance, and so I sat at the feet of my inferiors in rank constantly, and will continue to do so in order to acquire knowledge. And while in civil life I felt I knew something, at this time and in this life I find I know very little or nothing. But I am learning every day. My hours of work, my time of rising and of going to bed, my food, my habits, my exercise are changed in a revolutionary way from my former life. And as a result I am vigorous, can endure more, eat more, and do more than I deemed possible heretofore. The outdoor life — the camp fare — I enjoy everything. I eat beans and cabbage and beets and rice with zest which I never could stand before. Even onions and a small degree of garlic do not stagger me. As for being particular as to whether the service is clean, as I used to be, it never occurs to me to look for dirt, I am so anxious to get something to eat. I am writing this right here for the benefit of middle-aged business men. The joys of youth are still within our reach if we will only give over physical and mental indolence. When in army life you have some hardships — and you certainly do have them — there are a lot of good fellows going through the same thing at the same time, and the whole thing becomes laughable.

The day before the London parade I went to London taking my orderly, Francis Kilkenny[17] and Eddie Hart[18] with me. I called on the firm of Morgan, Grenfell and Company[19] and was cordially received. Mr. Grenfell and Mr. Whigham took us to lunch at the City Club and devoted their time to us when we were at their office. Lieutenant Covell joined me in the afternoon. We stayed at the Ritz and dined in the evening at the Carlton, going afterward to the theater.

The next day Covell and I went to the depot with an American flag for the regiment, which I borrowed from Captain Warburton, of the American Embassy, our own colors being still on the way.

In the parade there were four regiments of engineers, about 4500 men in all. To each regiment was assigned a fine English band, the best in the Empire. Our regiment was the fourth in the column. Walked with Colonel Sewell at the head of the regiment and with a British peer—Lord Erskine, I think —as the liaison officer. From the station to the end of the march, and in the afternoon on the return to the depot, the streets were jammed with lines of cheering people, and the American flag was everywhere. We were reviewed by the King and Queen[20] and by the American Ambassador.[21] Lunch was served to the officers and troops in a park near the palace. After lunch the officers were taken to the British officers' quarters near by, where every attention was given us. In the afternoon we marched back to the Waterloo Station through the poorer parts of the city.

As we did not expect to leave Borden until Friday, Colonel Sewell gave permission to the officers to remain in London. I gave a dinner, which Covell very efficiently arranged for at the Carlton, to the Colonel and regimental staff officers and Captains. While at this dinner, which was served at a large, decorated table in the main dining-room, there suddenly came the order to move the next morning, which was entirely unexpected. As a result the Colonel and the necessary officers took taxicabs for the fifty-mile ride to Borden — the balance of us taking an early morning train. We left with the regiment about noon, arriving at Southampton in about three hours, where we were put aboard a cattle ship. It was a very cold afternoon and night. The men were quartered in the stalls and the officers in one room — none too large — on the upper deck. All through the ship the men in the stalls imitated the "mooing" of cows and the bleating of sheep. In the night we sailed — every man wearing a life preserver all the time. We officers slept on the floor so crowded that if any one left his place in the night to go on deck the natural expansion that ensued made it impossible for him to get back and find space enough to lie down in. As a result he slept thereafter on deck. It was a contrast to the Ritz at London. We lived on travel rations, but had a ship's breakfast in the morning when we landed at Havre.[22]

At Havre we marched to camp headed by our band, for which organization, by the way, I am responsible, having presented the instruments to the regiment after we had failed to get them from the War Department. During the day I heard that the Belgian seat of government was in the city and determined to call on M. Van de Vyvere,[23] the Belgian Minister of Finance, whom I had met on his trip to Chicago and with whom I had become well acquainted. We found in America that we had a liking for each other, and he spent most of his day in Chicago in my company, going to the opera with me and deserting his suite most of his time. Instead of calling him "Your Excellency" as did most of the Americans and his retainers, I called him "Boss," which I explained to him was the American way of conveying an idea of companionability and good-fellowship as well as authority. So on going to the seat of the Belgian Government I sent in my card to him presenting my compliments to the "boss." Out he came, and thereafter during my stay I became the guest of the Belgian Government. He sent for his big automobile and went to camp with me for my things and set aside a suite of rooms for me at the Villarie, the hotel assigned to the Belgian Cabinet by the French Government. He insisted on my making up a dinner party for him to entertain in the evening, which I did by inviting Colonel Sewell, Major Atwood, and Major Cushing.[24] In the afternoon at the camp at regimental inspection I had the regiment "present arms" to him. We spent an interesting evening with him and the Minister of the Interior on a balcony overlooking the beautiful bay of the sea.

After the guests were gone, we two sat up until nearly midnight, and he talked over the affairs of his unhappy country — now only about twenty miles long and ten miles wide, so narrow that great shells from the German army sometimes pass over it. He is a friend of King Albert and he invited me to visit the King (who is at the front) with him and go over the Belgian line, which I hope to do later. There are 160,000 Belgians still in the army. As he talked in his quiet, earnest way of his plans for his countrymen — of their probable plight after the war — of the difficulties and perplexities with which he was contending, my heart went out to him and he seemed more the "boss" than ever. How majestic is naturalness! I have never met a man whom I really considered a great man who was not always natural and simple. Affectation is inevitably the mark of one not sure of himself. It is above everything the real hallmark of inferiority. We are liked for ourselves over here, if we will only be ourselves and not try to imitate anybody. I stayed all night at the Villarie, and after breakfast and another visit with my friend and the Minister of the Interior I went back to camp in M. Van de Vyvere's automobile which he insisted on my keeping during the day.

In the afternoon we took the train for St. Nazaire. We were rather crowded in the officers' car and I don't think I ever passed a more uncomfortable night, being half-frozen from the waist down. We arrived at St. Nazaire in the evening, were met by the American officer in charge of the base, and were conducted to the camp in which we are at present quartered. This was on August 19 (Sunday). The camp is situated about two miles from the docks on high ground. The officers' quarters are floored; the men's quarters are similar to the officers' except they are not floored. The camp has been erected by the French and by German prisoners of whom there are said to be about three thousand in the city. These prisoners work around the camp under a French guard. They are given plenty to eat and receive good treatment. A more contented set of men I have seldom seen. Talking with them is prohibited for military reasons.

Our regiment was almost immediately set to work in connection with improvement of the camp, as it is yet unfinished. We are leveling it and putting in drainage. We have furnished several hundred men for changing the location of about 1200 tons of coal in the hold of a transport. This is extremely hard work for the men, but they stand up under it finely. A splendid spirit exists throughout the whole organization.

The 147th French Regiment is quartered here in St. Nazaire, being back from the front for a rest which they sorely needed. During our stay here there have occurred several engagements with German submarines, which attack our ships as they approach the harbor. It is said two submarines have been destroyed, but this is not authentic. There is much exaggeration.

Colonel Rockenbach,[25] the American commander of the base, took Colonel Sewell and myself to dinner at La Baule, a watering-place situated about ten miles away. He talked over the situation he confronts and the next morning took Sewell, Atwood, and myself over the entire dock and transportation system of the base. Rockenbach strikes me as an exceptionally competent and able officer. He has decision and energy, and common sense. He is sadly overburdened with work. Five transports arrived the day after we did, and I had an opportunity of judging how the embarkation of men and troops compared with the Liverpool experience of our own. Notwithstanding shorter preparation and more inadequate facilities, the way the men and freight were handled here seemed fully up to the Liverpool standard save what was due to lack of facilities. Too much freight is now warehoused here which should be immediately forwarded and thus saved extra handling. But this will be bettered in time.

The camp life here is not especially exciting. We were all greatly disappointed not to be sent to the front as we had expected, but we hope that will come later. While here we received our first mail from home. All our letters sent from the regiment have to be censored. This task falls to the company officers and it is a heavy one. After a while, when the men come to understand that one cannot write home about anything much except the state of their emotions, the work will be less.

From this point on I shall endeavor to keep a diary by days.

St. Nazaire, France
August 24, 1917

After mess went with Captain Ryan, Regimental Supply Officer, to St. Nazaire. Called at American base office. Brought back regimental mail in a truck. Studied Court Martial Manual preparing for Special Court Martial of which I am President, the first session being held to-morrow.[26] At camp in the evening.

St. Nazaire, France
August 25, 1917

Spent the morning at regular Saturday inspection of the men of the regiment and their quarters. Presided at Special Court Martial in the afternoon. The trial of one of the Master Engineers for attempt to commit manslaughter occupied nearly five hours. The Court was composed of Major Cushing, Captain Burkhalter, Lieutenant White, and myself. Lieutenant Kraft was Judge Advocate and Captain Estes counsel for the defense.

At camp in the evening. Colonel Sewell is having a report made relative to possible improvements in present methods of handling freight at this base. When this report is completed it will point out important improvements which should be made. Major Atwood, Major Cushing, and Captain Causey, all experienced railroad men, are studying the situation. It seems desirable that the regiment be kept together as a construction unit, but it is authoritatively intimated that some of our officers may be taken on details on outside work. We hear that the 13th Regiment Engineers is at the point where we had hoped to be, wearing gas-masks and steel helmets and building narrow-gauge roads behind the lines. If we are not ordered to the front am going to make an effort with Pershing to be sent there myself.

St. Nazaire, France
Sunday, August 26, 1917

The officers of the American base here, and some of the officers of the different military units in the camp and five hundred men are to be the guests to-day of the city of La Baule, the French watering-place which I have already mentioned. As we shall not start for a time I will indulge in a few generalities.

At the time the United States entered the war I judge the Allies were much more discouraged than we had supposed. The French, having stood up under the worst of it, were, and perhaps are, a little more that way than the English. But it was not the discouragement which for a moment suggested anything but a fight to a finish. The spirit and determination of the French and English under discouragement are wonderful. One has to be here, to see the long daily hospital trains from the front — not here as yet, but to the French and English bases — to see the columns of fine men crossing the Channel and others going north from this port to France to be fed into the awful furnace of modern war, to understand what these people have stood up under for three years. The women are in black everywhere. The faces of the men from the trenches bear a look which often haunts one.

The French have been fought until they feel the war in every phase of life, but one realizes that this cannot be so in France and England and not be so in even greater degree in Germany. There being in Germany a military aristocracy against which the inevitable psychological reaction against continued war can find an outlet in attacking, I feel that the war will be ended by the internal revolt of the people of Germany. If that does not come, the end of the war now seems several years off. Yet who knows what will happen in this tremendous and unprecedented upheaval of the whole world!

St. Nazaire, France
Sunday evening

Colonel Sewell, Major Atwood, and I are back in camp after an interesting afternoon. The Mayor and city officials of La Baule gave the American officers a fine banquet at the Royal Hotel. They made addresses welcoming the American troops, of which we were the first to visit their town in a body.

The streets were crowded with people and lined with French and American flags. Colonel Sewell made a very happy response to the speech of the Mayor — much the best of the occasion. Spent some time discussing the facilities of this base and what ought to be done in preparation for the immense number of troops and large amount of freight to be unloaded here. Major Atwood, Major Cushing, and Captain Causey, in addition to Colonel Sewell, are studying the situation.

American freight is not packed so as to be economically and quickly handled in the small cars on the French railroads. The average loading of French freight per car averages at this port only thirteen tons, while the average loading of American freight, owing to the way it is packed, averages only a little over eight tons a car. Much of the handling of freight cars in the yard is done by manpower. It would seem, in view of the tremendous burden soon to be placed on the facilities of this port, that the railroad from this base to the front should have American equipment with its larger units, and more machinery and less men should be used in unloading and handling freight from the ships. It is extremely important to have the naval bases operating at full efficiency. Through these funnels must be passed the military resources of our great nation. Congestion here may mean defeat further north.

The purpose of our discussion was to equip me with the technical points from a railway standpoint to be urged upon Pershing when I see him next week in Paris. Additional dock facilities are needed. Think I have the situation fairly in mind. The investigation is being conducted with the cooperation and sanction of Colonel Rockenbach, the present commander of this base. What I want to do in Paris, if possible, is to have proper weight attached to the expert railway advice on railway and dock matters. Major Cushing, for instance, in connection with the Southern Pacific ships and railway system, has gained an experience directly applicable to this situation. If I can be of assistance over here in carrying out the admirable policy of President Wilson as indicated by his conduct of military affairs in America, and help get large tasks in competent hands, I shall be glad.

St. Nazaire, France
August 27, 1917, Monday. (My 52d birthday)

The figures look large — but they will never grow smaller. A very heavy wind and rain. In the morning put on my raincoat and struggled down to headquarters at St. Nazaire. On my return found the wind had blown the roof off the barracks over my little room, and that my baggage, clothes, etc., had received a baptism. Last night there was considerable trouble between our men and the adjoining Marines. A Marine policeman in St. Nazaire, very much intoxicated, was found beating a negro. One of our Southern privates interfered to stop it, and the drunken policeman drew his revolver and attempted to shoot the private. Thereupon the private, who — accidentally, according to him — happened to have a bottle of champagne in his hand, delivered the same with telling effect across the head of the policeman, knocking him out. He then divested him of his revolver and immediately came to camp and surrendered himself (in a rather dilapidated state) and the

Marine's revolver to me. Turned him and the revolver over to the officer of the day with instructions to make an immediate and thorough investigation. Some of the Marines, hearing of this encounter in which their man had been worsted, proceeded to arrest and beat privates of the 17th as they came back to camp and took eighteen of them to the guardhouse in the town. Investigation of the affair by Marine officers resulted in an apology being sent Colonel Sewell by the Marine officer (Major Weston). The offenders will be punished. All of which illustrates what will happen around camps where liquor is sold.[27] At Atlanta where there was strict prohibition there was little trouble with the men. The transition from a drought to a flood region of drink has proved too much for the equilibrium of many of our men. The action of the Southern man who intervened to protect a poor colored man from a severe and undeserved beating, and went into a fight for him, recalls what someone has said, "The North may be a friend to the negro, but the South is a friend to a negro."[28]

Major Cushing told an incident which occurred yesterday. There are a number of American negroes from the South who were brought here as workmen. Their lot — wages and work — has not been satisfactory to them, to say the least. One of them approached the Major and said, "I done think sumfin' is wrong inside my head." Upon the Major inquiring the cause of his belief he said, "'Cause I'se over here, Majah, an' I didn't have to come. Jes 'cause I'se over heah. Did anybody fetch you over heah, Majah, or did you jes come?"[29]

In the evening at the Hotel de Bretagne the regimental staff and the Captains gave me a birthday dinner. Their kindness and their evident regret that I am to leave them for detached duty affected me very much. Colonel Sewell tells me they have commissioned him to buy me a loving-cup; but I asked him just to get a small cup which I could carry with me all the time in remembrance of them. I hope I may see them often. I can understand now after three months with them why army associations are so binding. The life makes intimate all acquaintance among officers. There were about fifteen at the dinner.

At camp all night very windy and wet.

Paris, August 28, 1917

Took train for Paris.[30] Had sent Francis Kilkenny on the night before. On train all day, arriving at Paris about 8 P.M. Chauncey McCormick[31] and Francis met me at the train and took me to the Ritz Hotel[32] where I had engaged rooms. Chauncey took dinner with me. He has done splendid work at the front caring for French children.

Paris, August 29, 1917

Called on General Pershing in the morning. Spent an hour with him. He tells me he wants me to organize and head a board which will coordinate all purchasing for the United States Army in France, including the Red Cross; that he expects to publish for the use of the army my report on "boat drill" and method. Went over the method of handling freight on line of communications and gave him what ideas I had gathered, chiefly from the experts of our regiment — Colonel Sewell, Majors Atwood and Cushing, and Captain Causey. He had already anticipated to a large degree the situation. He is fully alive to the dangers of congestion. Agreed entirely as to necessity for wooden docks; for one supervision of entire process of unloading from ship to trains; for authority to rest in a railway expert. Thinks Wilgus is equal to it. Agrees that American equipment must be used to large extent and gave me the number of engines and cars he has already ordered. He is selecting men for results and holding all to a rigid accountability to produce results. He issued an order attaching Francis to me as an orderly.

Pershing is the man for this great emergency. He has an immense faculty for disposing of things. He is not only a great soldier, but he has great common sense and tremendous energy.

Went to Morgan-Harjes office.[33] They were very kind. Mr. Carter called in his purchasing experts and I asked them some questions as to their methods. Wish I had time to discuss the appearance of Paris, etc., but cannot get my mind upon details to-day.

Since I apparently am to be closely associated with headquarters as a member of Pershing's staff I am going to have this book deposited under seal at Morgan, Harjes and Company so that I can write freely and contemporaneously in it, and yet not run any risk of losing it and thus doing injury. I will probably be able to write in it once a week anyway.

Paris, Sunday, September 2, 1917

Now that I have a little breathing spell this afternoon I will struggle at this diary. On reaching Paris I reported to General Pershing. He has made me head of a board of ten officers representing all the purchasing departments of our army, including also the Red Cross and Army Y.M.C.A. In addition he has made me General Purchasing Agent in Europe for the American Expeditionary Force in France. He gives me practically unlimited discretion and authority to go ahead and devise a system of coordination of purchases; to organize the board; to arrange the liaison connections between the French and English army boards and our own; to use any method which may seem wise to me to secure supplies for the army in Europe which to that extent will relieve our American transports in their enormous burden. He gives me authority to select my assistants from within or without the army. He will ask for commissions as Captains of such civilians as I may desire to impress into the service. He gives me such authority as I may deem wise to execute in regard to all methods of purchase and general supervision of them. In other words, he makes me an important element in this war.

As I proceed to build up the organization, the communications which pass between me and the Commander-in-Chief will contain the best record of what I shall or shall not accomplish and these will be available after the war. I called the first meeting of the board yesterday (Saturday). The following reported to me for duty:

Lieutenant-Colonel Wilkins, Quartermaster Corps.
Lieutenant-Colonel Charles E. Stanton, Quartermaster Corps (General Disbursing Officer).
Major D. P. Card, Medical Corps.
Colonel Thomas A. Jackson, Corps of Engineers.
Major Edgar S. Gorrell, Aviation Service, Signal Corps.
Captain James B. Taylor, Signal Corps.
1st Lieutenant Olney Bonar, Ordnance Department, U.S.R.
1st Lieutenant J. H. Matter, Signal Corps, U.S.R.
Carl Taylor, Purchasing and Disbursing Officer, Red Cross.
F. B. Shipp, Purchasing and Disbursing Officer, Y.M.C.A.

— representing all purchasing departments of the army in France. Announced to board its functions and my purposes in connection therewith. Appointed James E. Dunning, Captain Quartermaster Corps, Purchasing Agent for England. General Pershing later in day issued him orders to report to me. Ordered Red Cross to make all its English purchases through him. Instructed Corps of Engineers and Red Cross to take joint action in lumber purchases to avoid competition.

However, it will be impossible for me to make any comprehensive record of my military activities. They will relate to many outside matters, as, for instance, I found and brought to Pershing's attention that probably three ships instead of one could be used in transporting supplies from England to our army in France. He will immediately ask for such additional ships as I find can be effectively used — a matter I am now engaged on. Each boat working from England to France will do the work of three from America to France if we can fill them. We must have from the 1st of September (to

1st of June), for instance, 30,000 tons of coal per month. We hope to get all this from England and in my judgment shall if we can furnish the transports.

General Pershing expects me to study and make decisions for reference to him of questions relating to what shall or shall not be requisitioned from America in the matter of supplies. It is a man's work, but I am thankful beyond words that, now that I have come here instead of remaining in America, it is work which will count for my country in its time of greatest trial.

In the occupation of work I find little else to write of. Colonel Harbord,[34] Pershing's Chief of Staff, took dinner with me at the Ritz and spent the evening Thursday. I have been with General Pershing each day, taking lunch on Friday at the house (or rather palace) at which he is staying.[35] Dear fellow, and loyal friend. I hope I do not fail him. We have both passed through the greatest grief which can come to man.[36] As we rode up together there occurred an instance of telepathy which was too much for either of us. Neither of us was saying anything, but I was thinking of my lost boy and of John's loss and looking out of the window, and he was doing the same thing on the other side of the automobile. We both turned at the same time and each was in tears. All John said was, "Even this war can't keep it out of my mind."[37]

We lunched in a house owned by Ogden Mills, which was formerly the palace of Marshal Lannes.[38] Colonel Harbord and the Adjutant-General — Colonel Alvord — and Captain Collins[39] were with us. As I looked around me I said, "John, when I contrast these barren surroundings with the luxuriousness of our early life in Lincoln, Nebraska, it does seem that a good man has no real chance in the world." To which John meditatively replied, "Don't it beat hell!"

Colonel Sewell arrived Saturday morning. Took him to see General Pershing. Am getting even with him by degrees for all his kindness and forbearance with me. Got him to agree to let me have James, Ryan, and Grafton from the regiment. Am going to send Ryan to Spain and Grafton to either Switzerland or Italy as representing me. Pershing is issuing the orders for them to report for duty.

In the evening my ankle broke down and I endured the torments of the damned until I got a physician who reset the little devil of a bone which every year or so will persist in slipping out of place for a few hours. Why it does not do this during a ten-mile march, but only when I am quiet, is an anatomical mystery.

My nephew, Beman Gates Dawes,[40] dined with me on two days. Called at an American Field Service[41] office for him and my nephew William, but the latter was at the front somewhere at work.[42] John Pershing moved his headquarters yesterday to the front. My headquarters will be in Paris. We shall have quick telephonic communication, Harbord says. The hand of death seems laid on this city. Can hardly realize it is the same Paris I visited twenty years ago this year.[43] Pershing has ordered my "boat drill" report printed for the benefit of the American army.

Paris, Monday evening, September 3, 1917

I only hope that I will persevere in keeping this record contemporaneously with my connection with events here. There is such a field for my useful activity that the evenings find me tired.

Discovered this morning that the arrangement that requisitions for our army upon the French Government on purchases had to pass through our Chief of Staff, which resulted in two to three days' delay, which would be increased now that the Chief of Staff has moved to Chaumont.[44] Discussed this over the telephone with Harbord (C[hief]. of S[taff].), and then personally with General Pershing, which resulted in orders being issued passing all these requisitions for approval through my office instead of that of the Chief of Staff. This will save much delay, as my headquarters will remain in Paris. To consummate this arrangement General Pershing took me with him this afternoon to call upon the French Minister of War, M. Painlevé,[45] and acquainted him with the arrangement. General Pershing told him that I was to centralize all our army purchases in Europe, taking control of them, and would organize a system in Europe for locating and transporting supplies to our army. The Minister expressed his satisfaction at this arrangement and said that the French Government would cooperate, notifying me of their prospective purchases and appointing a French liaison officer to attend my headquarters in furtherance of our understanding of unity of purpose and action; that in some cases he would wish me to represent the French Government in purchases outside of France. He and General Pershing arranged for a review of the American troops by the President of France. He also urged the importance of getting our engineers at work as soon as possible in cutting the French forests, stating that the need of lumber for the winter could not be overestimated.

Through Pershing and his War Department route wired W. T. Abbott, C. H. Sabin, and Clarence Dillon[46] in America with the purpose of getting Abbott, Dean Jay,[47] and Dillon to accept Captains' commissions and join my staff. These telegrams will appear in the records of my office which I am keeping. Took lunch with Colonel Sewell. My foot was so much better that I commenced to walk in the morning without crutches. Met William Allen White[48] at breakfast. Spent so much of the day with General Pershing

GENERAL JOHN J. PERSHING

MAJOR-GENERAL J. G. HARBORD
Commanding Second Division

THE HIGH COMMAND AT GENERAL HEADQUARTERS: THE COMMANDER-IN-CHIEF, THE CHIEF
OF STAFF AND THE ASSISTANT CHIEFS OF STAFF, AND THE ADJUTANT-GENERAL

Front row, left to right: Brig.-Gen. H. B. Fiske, G-5 (Training Section); Maj.-Gen. J. W. McAndrew,
C. of S.; Gen. John J. Pershing, C. in C.; Brig.-Gen. Fox Connor, G-3 (Operations Section); Brig.-
Gen. G. V. H. Moseley, G-4 (Coördination of Supply Services). *Rear row, left to right:* Brig.-Gen.
A. D. Andrews, G-1 (Administrative Section); Brig.-Gen. LeRoy Eltinge, Deputy Chief of Staff;
Brig.-Gen. D. E. Nolan, G-2 (Information Section); Brig.-Gen. R. C. Davis, A. G.

CHAUMONT
General Headquarters of American Expeditionary Forces

that he had time to fully discuss the situation as it was when he came and as he sees it at present. What I write he has said to no one else, but it will be safe in Morgan-Harjes's vaults until after the war. He said that when America entered the war the wonderful French spirit was enduring its greatest strain; that it almost seemed to him, after he had met the French and English authorities, that they realized that through exhaustion the end was near; that matters were better now since the recent offensive. He said that one trouble which he saw was the difficulty the French, English, and Italians experienced in securing between themselves the best methods of cooperation; that this condition was improving, but that the recent offensives of the French and English, though arranged to be simultaneous practically throughout, failed to be so, and as a result after one offensive was through the Germans could move and did move their troops over to combat the other. He stated that the Russian situation[49] was bad, and that it might result in the releasing of more German troops for the Western Front. He stated that Spain[50] was under great internal strain; that if strikes or revolutions tied up their transportation the Allies would run out of lead within a short time; that German influence was strong in Spain. While he called attention to these difficulties, however, he said the encouragement to our allies from America's entrance in the war was tremendous. He emphasized the necessity and importance of my work to increase the volume of European purchases for our army so as to save as much ship space as possible, and thus get his army and American supplies over as soon as possible; that he could hope to have twenty divisions over by spring, but had told Haig[51] and Pétain[52] that he could not do anything effective before that time. He felt, however, that now there was no question, whatever happened in Russia or Spain, that the Allies would hold out and that the aid of America would inevitably bring a victory. He predicted this would come by Christmas, 1918. He thinks we may have to bring 2,000,000 Americans over, and believes that the United States is equal to the task of in some way providing the. He especially praised Cadorna[53] whom he said he had met. He said he had told him and Haig and Pétain that the United States was in this war to the finish with all its resources of men and material, but that America, like England had been, was unprepared when it entered the war, and it would take time for its full strength to be felt. He believes that everything he said in connection with the exhaustion of strength of France and England applied in as great if not greater degree to Germany; that in estimating his difficulties he never forgot that; that victory for the Allies is certain.

Paris, Saturday night, September 8, 1917

The operations of my office are so vast, the matters of vital importance with which it is concerned are so varied, the demands it makes upon my time so pressing that of necessity this record can only be of things of a very general nature. The record of what I am accomplishing, however, will all be kept in the shape of my official correspondence with the Commander-in-Chief and his replies thereto in the orders carrying out my requests and suggestions. I am keeping copies of what I consider especially involves personal decision and initiative in a file which after the war I will have bound to accompany this journal.

Being in a position with power to control, supervise, and direct purchases of the army in Europe—the head of each purchasing department reporting to me for duty — I am not only coordinating purchases between the different branches of our own army and between our army and the English and French Governments, but I am engaged in the organization of effort both within and without the purchasing departments of the army to locate supplies and the transportation therefor in Europe in order to lessen the burden upon the American transport system across the sea. I am therefore fighting German submarines. In exactly the proportion that I secure supplies here which otherwise would have to be transported across the Atlantic, I offset the result of hostile submarine activity.

The General Purchasing Board of the Army, which I head, owes its existence to the resourceful mind of the Commander-in-Chief, who overrode an adverse report upon the advisability of its creation. To my suggestion that it, and my powers as General Purchasing Agent, be used in the effort to broaden and extend, as well as to centralize, European purchases, he immediately acceded. In every possible way he is using his vast power to strengthen and uphold my hands. Now that he has gone to Chaumont he telephones me on important matters, and I am in daily telephonic communication with the Chief of Staff and Major McCoy[54] of his staff. He has sent word to me through Major McCoy that no written request for the issuance of orders from me will ever be denied; that if they disclose any tendencies which he believes need discussion from his standpoint it will be verbal. He has asked me to come to Chaumont every week, but until I have my organization better built up to handle the volume of important matters passing through it, I have asked him to communicate with me by telephone and through his staff.

Underneath me I feel his strong support as does every other officer who is doing his work as it should be done. General Pershing demands results. Unless one can show them, he must step aside. When one does show them, the General does not stint his appreciation either in word or act. He has told me how much he relies upon me and how gratified he is at what I am doing and at what his officers say of it. He will never know how much these words mean to one in the quiet of the night, when, weary with the work and battle of the day, he takes mental account of himself and his task. Great is a commander who inspires in his followers a love and devotion toward him only second to that which they feel for the cause of their common effort.

Paris, Sunday, September 9, 1917

General Pershing called me by telephone at my headquarters this morning and we discussed the coal situation for the army. I told him we needed 60,000 tons of freight space in ships from England to France now— 50,000 for coal and 10,000 for general supplies; that by the 1st of February when our railroads here would commence to consume coal, we should need space for 150,000 tons of coal monthly in addition. England notifies us she can furnish coal at government regulated prices, but can give us no transportation. Discussed form of request to make of War Department for dispatch of colliers[55] or barges to England immediately to get this coal started. Pershing sent me copy of notification he has wired War Department of my appointment as head of the General Purchasing Board. Logan of staff at Chaumont called. Pershing at first wanted me to go to England at once, but finally decided my presence here just now is more important. Logan says they are working over form in which my "boat drill" method will be published for the American army. Discussed with Pershing idea of borrowing Great Lakes shipping during time lake navigation is closed, to work between England and France. Suppose American Shipping Board has already looked into that, but Pershing says he will suggest it and be sure in this way it has consideration.

Spent a time with my nephew Beman and we went for a short time to the Louvre, my first "sight-seeing" in Paris.

Busy at consultations and plans most of day. Am thinking now of sending Captain Ryan, of the 17th Engineers, to England, keeping Captain Grafton and Lieutenant James, both of the 17th Engineers, at my headquarters.

Received letter from William C. Dawes,[56] head of the English family of Dawes, urging me to come to England; but anything but work is out of the question now for me until the war is over. Decided man for Switzerland[57] and also for Spain.

Paris, September 12, 1917

The more one learns of the actual conditions the less certain he feels as to the outcome of things. I came to France believing an Allied victory was only a matter of time. Now I can only feel that it is probable. The loss in tonnage (ships) for two weeks has been submitted to me. It is about 240,000 tons, or at the rate of nearly 500,000 tons per month. French officials are apprehensive as to the effect of the coming winter on the morale of the army and the people of Paris. Unless they can be kept warm, revolution is feared, or rather disorganization. General Pershing has placed upon my shoulders largely the responsibility of securing from England the coal supply for our army the coming winter in addition to my other work. He has ordered our officers there to wire me direct from England to save it passing through the General Staff office with ensuing delay. Am in contact with the French Government on the situation. We must and shall get the coal, but we have to get the transportation facilities for it as well. There is a great shortage of lumber. Pershing telephones me every day. He wants simplicity in operations of the army as far as possible, and immediately puts into effect any of my recommendations along these lines. He telephoned me about the organization of a general supply and shipping commission between the three allies, concerning which he had asked for a general recommendation from me, which I had given. Says decision should be reserved until Mayo gets here on account of England's reluctance to release any degree of control of her shipping, and that then he wants me to discuss matter with Mayo. Lassiter has already recommended such a commission to the War College. I agree as to its great desirability.

The submarine figures emphasize the great importance of my work. The official records of correspondence with the Commander-in-Chief will show what I am doing in the formation of my organization. It is no use for a tired man to try and epitomize it in the evening. There is too much of it. Spent the evening at the hotel with Captain Grafton, Junior Ames,[58] and Francis Kilkenny. My foot has given me great trouble and pain the last two days, and I am temporarily on crutches. General Pershing has ordered me a limousine for my use in getting around on official business. Want to get to see the front anyway, where I had hoped to go, but am tied like a dog to a stake when it comes to anything not connected with my duty.

Hope the Russians will make a stand.[59] Everybody—Germany included—except America seems "fed up," as the English put it, with the war. No wonder, for they have been in it for three years. I shall not write of its horrors as I run across them. Others will do that.

Paris, Sunday, September 16, 1917

Over and above all is the problem of coal and transportation for it for our army. This Pershing has put up to me alone at this time. Winter is coming. France fears a revolution unless her people and army are kept warm, and can give us no coal and little wood. England can give us coal without transportation for it. I have caught up the threads of information from the different branches of the army. I am rapidly getting the elements of the problem of handling the coal when we get it from England to France. I know now what we need, where we can get it, how we can get it from the ports in France to the points of consumption, and it only remains to get the transportation from England to France. That "only" seems an inappropriate word. Some one has said that authority like the nettle must be firmly grasped if one is not to be stung by it. It may not seem modest (if anything I write does I am surprised), but I must, in justice to the facts, state that if I fail in my military career it will not be because I have failed to firmly grasp all the authority within reaching distance of me.

General Pershing having asked me to handle the coal situation and suggest the cable to go to the War Department requisitioning the ships, there was so much information to get to do this intelligently that I had to go to headquarters everywhere. Finding that Admiral Sims[60] was in the city I called on him and endeavored to get the navy to help us out. The minute I said "coal" he started on a strong complaint that the situation needed some one to handle it who knew it, that it was being handled piecemeal, that "this and that" was the way to do it. What I came for was to borrow a ship, not to get a statement of what I knew to be the fact up to the time I took hold of the coal matter about a week ago. I got (apparently only) angry and proceeded to give him a good imitation of a man who knew what he was talking about, descending, I regret to say, to extreme statement. Immediately the gold lace dropped away and a clear-headed, helpful man emerged — one who could not give us a ship, for he did not have one to give, but one who gave helpful suggestions and kindly encouragement. I realized then that Sims was a big man, and what he had said at first was to find out whether I was, or not, in the shortest possible time.

After failing with Sims, to our mutual regret, I met with Major-General Blatchford [61](a constructive, natural leader of men), General Langfitt, Colonel Stanley, and Captain Moore (a ship expert).[62] They met to discuss my requisition on them for Moore whom they want to use at Bordeaux and I want to use here. Blatchford said that absolutely nothing was more important than to help in this coal crisis and gave me Moore. Have used him all day and shall try to get through with him soon in order to release him for his own most important work.

I saw Beckingham of England and put him in contact with Moore. My official papers will explain who Beckingham is, and my relations with him, therefore.

By to-morrow morning I shall have for Pershing the form of a cable for the War Department, and a statement of the whole coal situation as I have found it, with recommendations for appropriate action.

Dined with Greyson [sic] Murphy,[63] Perkins, and Swan Saturday evening and agreed upon the relation of Red Cross to army activities here and in England.

Am writing this between 6 and 7 P.M. and start into conferences again on coal matters after dinner to-night.

Paris, September 19, 1917

Having rounded up the coal situation for the army, and General Pershing having requested me to write the necessary cablegrams to the War Department for him to send making the requisite suggestions and requisition for ships, I took automobile for Chaumont Monday afternoon after having had the first meeting of my French Auxiliary Committee with the Purchasing Board in the morning. Took Chauncey McCormick (who speaks French) and my army chauffeur with me. We made good time and covered the 156 miles by about 9:30 P.M. The General and his staff were at his quarters where I spent the night. John and I sat up in conference and visiting until nearly one o'clock. He approves my selection of Moore to take charge of coal and supply transport from England. Major-General Blatchford (C.G., L. of C.)[64] has agreed to loan me Moore for thirty days; but am inclined to think the Commander-in-Chief will be insistent on his remaining on this detail permanently owing to its vital importance.

The next morning I worked incessantly until about 1 p.m. preparing my cablegrams and report on coal. Then presented the matter to Pershing with Rogers (Chief Quartermaster),[65] Harbord (Chief of Staff), and Alvord (Adjutant-General)[66] present. Programme and cables all were approved. They cover suggestion of requisitioning lake vessels during winter, methods of adapting them for salt-water service, methods of loading to utilize all space, and a requisition for ships (steamers) to carry 41,000 tons dead weight. In addition they provided for Moore to take charge of transporting from England and eventual control of this work by the Commanding General, Lines of Communication.

After lunch with the General and his staff spent a time with Major Robert Bacon, who took me to see the old tower and wall. Bacon is commander of the Post at Chaumont. He was formerly Ambassador to France and Secretary of State, U.S.A.[67] Chauncey and I then started for Paris. Everything went well until about 10.30 P.M., when we got our automobile, a big Panhard,[68] in an impossible tire difficulty. We turned off at Grisy[69] (I think that is the name), a little village twenty miles from Paris and off the main road. It was dark as pitch, and there were no lights anywhere. Everybody was in bed and everything barred and bolted. We gave up looking for an inn and were about to compose ourselves for the night in the machine, when Chauncey spied a light through a crack in a street window on a side street. He knocked on the shutters and they were opened on a French wedding party of about twenty people seated around a table. They all rose and crowded around the window. They passed us out wine to drink the bride's health. The groom was a young French soldier on a week's leave, the bride a beautiful girl of the village. She took some of the white wax flowers from her bridal wreath and handed them through the window to Chauncey and me. The groom's father left the party and walked with us a long distance and helped us rout out a sleepy innkeeper. I told Chauncey to ask him if he would take a wedding present back to the bride and he answered that a Colonel's wish was to him a command. So I gave them a start for housekeeping when the war is over; that is, if the poor fellow comes back. It was not a gay wedding party, but one from the class of people who make France glorious before the world.

We stayed all night at the clean little inn, and this morning, our automobile having been repaired by our chauffeur, reached Paris. The French of our chauffeur is confined to two words — "Oui" and "Tray Bone" — and he greatly feared he would be left alone to get back to Paris.

Had a conference with General Blatchford and Moore in the morning. (Moore is going to be made a Major for the good work he has done for us.)[70] Worked hard all day and here is where I go to bed.

Paris, Monday, September 24, 1917

Last Thursday General Pershing took me to lunch with Admiral Mayo[71] of the navy, Commander Sayles,[72] Atterbury (Director of Railways),[73] and two or three other officers. There we discussed the cooperation of the navy with the army in France. At the request of Lindeboom (French navy) and Chairman of the French Naval Purchasing Board for America, who brought me a letter from the highest French naval authority, I arranged with General Pershing for the transmission of a cable from him to Washington requesting authority for the transfer to the French Government of about twenty vessels (aggregating about 31,000 tons) from the American Shipping Board, which after the purchase by the French had denied permission for the ships to leave. The French naval authorities impressed upon me the desperate need of coal for their navy which these ships would transport from England. Some of their warships had only two or three days' supply ahead. Since a part of these steamers would patrol and help make safer the French ports where we are landing American soldiers and supplies, and since this war involves France and America in a common effort, it seems to me extremely important that these ships go to the French. This war from our (the Allies') standpoint resolves itself into a question of holding out until America can really come into the struggle. Am bending all my efforts to carry out the policy of Pershing to make the influence of the United States strongly felt in creating a better coordination of effort between the three armies which he feels is needed.

It is a joint struggle for a joint cause. What helps one helps all. We must not lose sight of the common need in search for relief for our own needs. This I am especially mindful of in my operations involving European purchases. Shall allow nothing to be done to weaken out allies for our own benefit. Distrust of each others' intentions is fatal to quick action in time of emergency. The French seem greatly to appreciate my attitude.

In trying to think back over the past five days I find this record will be less interesting if I try to catalogue all important things—my official correspondence and papers must do that—and will be more valuable if I speak at greater length of a few things than to merely mention many. The important things above everything else is coal, and I rejoice that in the last two days great progress has been made. General Pershing telephoned me from Chaumont this afternoon that the War Department had answered his cable which I had drawn up at Chaumont; that our suggestions as to the requisitioning of Great Lakes boats while navigation is closed on the lakes in the winter, for use in bringing us coal from England, was being acted upon; that the result of Admiral Sims's refusal to me of a collier, which he (Pershing) had reported to the War Department, had been a cable to him (Sims) to turn over to us one or two colliers, and instructions to help us in every way possible; that coal was starting to us from America. Pershing seemed much relieved, especially since we heard from Lassiter yesterday that coal shipments would start from England this week. We seized the *Berwind*[14] at Dartmouth, having been too late at Havre to catch her. Wired Lassiter hoped he could provide tonnage capable of landing us 30,000 tons monthly. Ordered first two cargoes to Bordeaux. I now hope, with the better cooperation of the navy, that we can do better than this from tonnage secured on this side, having the 41,000 tons dead weight carrying capacity which we asked for from America in addition.

(The night-flying aeroplanes guarding Paris has an irresistible attraction for me, and I have stopped three times while writing this to watch one from my window. They carry lights. They are so high up at times that the sound of their propellers resembles the buzzing of a mosquito.)

To-day I lunched with the officer second in command of the French navy and Mr. Lindebloom, and Marshal Joffre's[75] secretary (whom I asked Lindebloom to bring, as he helped me out of an embarrassment at the Joffre meeting at the Stockyards[76] arising out of the jealousy of Viviani of Joffre's popularity).[77]

To-day sent Pershing the outline of the order establishing the organization for handling the transports from England to France. Blatchford and Rogers approved of same, and Pershing will issue order immediately. Have put the power and its twin sister, responsibility, in the hands of Captain Moore (who because of his great help to us is soon to be a Major).

Pershing telephoned me asking if I could use in my work Major Harjes,[78] of Morgan, Harjes and Company, Paris, and I gladly requisitioned him. Verily, war gives me an authority to which peace is a stranger. The weather has been beautiful, though I have not had time to enjoy it. Lindeboom is going to America and will take with him the beautiful birthday gift of the 19th Regiment to me. It is inscribed, "A token of the respect, admiration, and affection of the personnel of the 17th Regiment Engineers." I greatly value it and the more because of my own attachment to those who gave it; but I remember Balthasar Gracián's[79] caution that it is not the applause that greets one on entrance, but on exit, which is important.

1   Rufus Fearing Dawes (1890-1912) was the son of Charles and Caro Dawes. In 1912, in the summer before his senior year at Princeton, Rufus drowned in Lake Geneva in Wisconsin. See the introduction for more about the impact of Rufus' death on Charles and Caro Dawes.

2   President of the Chicago and Great Western Railroad, Samuel M. Felton served as adviser to the chief of army engineers in relation to railroad affairs. He oversaw the work to send American "railroad men" to France. He was awarded the Distinguished Service Medal. "Samuel M. Felton Heads Engineers to France," *The Cornell Daily Sun*, Volume XXXVII, Number 166, May 23, 1917.

3   Formed after the U.S. declared war against Germany in 1917, the National Army was comprised of volunteers and those who were drafted into service. It was distinct from the Regular Army and the National Guard. The National Army comprised the vast majority of the U.S. military during the war, although units of the Regular Army and National Guard were first to engage in combat in France. In 1920, the National Army was disbanded and all personnel remaining in service were reverted to Regular Army status.

4   A graduate of the United States Military Academy, class of 1891, John Stephen Sewell (1869-1940) served in the military for several years before the U.S. went to war in 1917. In 1908, as a major in the Army Corps of Engineers, Sewell retired. He was serving as Vice President of the Alabama Marble Company when he reactivated in January 1917 and joined the Engineer Officers' Reserve Corps. In May 1917 he went on active duty and was appointed to command what would become the 17th Engineers. He later served as commander of the Base Port at St. Nazaire. Cullum, George Washington, *Biographical Register of the Officers and Graduates of the U. S. Military Academy at West Point*. Volume 6. Part 1. Saginaw, MI.: Seemann & Peters, Printers, 1901:1891. Sewell served with great distinction and was later awarded the Distinguished Service Medal.

5   CGD: My wife and daughter.

6   Clarence Coe (1865-1939) was an engineer who joined the 17th Engineers and served in France, stationed at St. Nazaire. He was promoted to colonel in March 1919. Later, he was awarded the Cross of the Legion of Honor for his service. "Foreign Railways," *Railway Review*, November 1, 1919, 673.

7   John Brown Gordon (1832-1904) served in the U. S. Senate after the American Civil War and later served as governor of Georgia. His 1903 memoir, *Reminiscences of the Civil War*, was hugely successful at the time. His reputation, however, has dramatically changed in more recent decades. He was, according to a recent biographer, the "titular head of the Georgia Ku Klux Klan." Ralph Lowell Eckert, *John Brown Gordon: Soldier, Southerner, American*. Louisiana State University Press, 1989, 149.

8   Also known as "Sutherland," the home was demolished in 1942. Franklin M. Garrett, *Atlanta and Environs: A Chronicle of Its People and Events, 1880s-1930s*.

Volume 2. Athens, GA: University of George Press, 1969, 470.

9   Charles Dawes received his first commission as a Major on June 11, 1917. On July 15, 1917, just days before embarking on the trans-Atlantic journey to France, he received a commission as Lieutenant Colonel. On January 16, 1918, he was promoted to Colonel, and on October 15, 1918, he was promoted to Brigadier General.

10   CGD: Charles E. Magoon, now deceased, was an old Lincoln, Nebraska, friend of General Pershing and myself. He was at one time Governor General of Cuba.

11   In April 1917, President Wilson appointed Herbert Hoover as head of the U.S. Food Administration. His efforts to control food consumption in the U.S. during the war (in order to encourage conservation of resources and preserve food for the overseas military) came to be known as "Hooverizing." After the war Hoover served as Secretary of Commerce and was elected U.S. President in 1928.

12   Former railroad executive and uncle to Franklin Delano Roosevelt, Frederic Adrian Delano (1863-1953) would soon leave the board and join the Army Corps of Engineers, serving as a major. Delano had played a key role in the creation of Daniel Hudson Burnham's 1909 Plan of Chicago, a project in which Charles Dawes had also been involved.

13   A rounded steel structure which contained a second steering wheel.

14   See Appendix B, Report of Lieutenant-Colonel Charles G. Dawes on Boat Drill on Army Transports.

15   Saint-Nazaire, an established port and fishing center on the west coast of France, was the location of the first of seven American "base sections" for the A.E.F., dedicated to receiving troops and supplies. The base section at Saint-Nazaire was established officially by the U.S. military in June 1917. Throughout the war U.S. personnel made various improvements to the port.

16   CGD: (Later.) This report is recently denied. [Ed: *The Finland* was torpedoed on October 28, 1917 on her return voyage. Nine people onboard were killed. *The Chicago Daily News Almanac and Yearbook for 1918*, Ed. John Langland, Chicago: Chicago Daily News Company, 1917, 542.]

17   Francis J. Kilkenny (1876-1933). See the essay "Homecoming" at the end of this volume for more about Kilkenny.

18   Lieutenant Edward "Eddie" J. Hart (1887-1956) had been a star football player at Princeton University. He was in the class one year ahead of Charles Dawes' son, Rufus.

19   The U.K. branch of J.P Morgan, headed at the time by partner E.C. "Teddy" Grenfell. During the war, the London-based bank would serve as "the financial and purchasing agent in the USA for Great Britain (as well as for France, Russia, Serbia, Belgium, Italy, Greece and Romania)." *Handbook on the History of European Banks*. Manfred Pohl and Sabine Freitag, eds. Great Britain: Edward

Elgar Publishing, 1994.

20   King George V and Queen Mary.

21   Walter Hines Page (1855-1918) was a journalist, editor, publisher, and diplomat. He was partner and vice president of Doubleday, Page and Company from 1900-1913. He also served as a literary adviser to Houghton, Mifflin and Company and editor of *The Atlantic Monthly*. He served as United States Ambassador to Great Britain from 1913-1918. The same post would later be held by Charles Gates Dawes. In 1926, Dawes donated the money he received for his 1925 Nobel Peace Prize to the endowment for the Walter Hines Page School of International Relations at Johns Hopkins University, which had been established in 1924.

22   The French city of Le Havre.

23   Aloys Van de Vyvere (1871-1961) later served briefly as Prime Minister of Belgium.

24   Edward Benjamin Cushing (1863-1924) worked for the Southern Pacific Railroad before being commissioned as an officer and going overseas to serve with the 17th Engineers. He then joined Pershing's staff. He was awarded the *Croix de Guerre* after the war and returned home to work as a federal bank examiner. He served on the board of directors of Texas A&M University (his alma mater) and also as board president. On November 23, 1927, the Texas A&M library was named the Cushing Memorial Library in his honor. Hugo Ellis, "Cushing, Edward Benjamin," *Handbook of Texas Online*, Texas State Historical Association, accessed April 10, 2015, http://www.tshaonline.org/handbook/online/articles/fcu33.

25   Samuel D. Rockenbach arrived in France in June 1917. He served as quartermaster of Base Section 1 at St. Nazaire until December 1917. Afterwards, he became Chief of the Tank Corps, and was later awarded the Distinguished Service Medal. Joseph Cummings Chase, *Soldiers All: Portraits and Sketches of the Men of the A. E. F.* New York: George H. Doran Company, 1920, 297.

26   A Special Court-Martial is the intermediate level of three kinds of military trials (the others are Summary and General Courts-Martial). During the American Civil War, Dawes' father, Rufus R. Dawes, also served on Special Court-Martials. Dawes, Rufus Robinson. *Service with the Sixth Wisconsin Volunteers*. Marietta, OH: E.R. Alderman and Sons, 1890: 190, 216.

27   The incident recounted here underscores the overt racism that ran rampant throughout American society during this time. According to historian Chad L. Williams, African-American troops in the A.E.F. faced often brutal treatment and violence. "The ports of St. Nazaire, Brest and Bordeaux," Williams states, were "virtual racial battlegrounds." Chad L. Williams, *Torchbearers of Democracy: African American Soldiers in the World War I Era*. Chapel Hill: University of North Carolina Press, 2010, 112. In his book, Williams includes Dawes' own account of the above incident.

28   The U.S. military was strictly segregated during World War I. Roughly 368,000 African-American men enlisted or were drafted into the military during the war. Most were relegated to working manual labor jobs, such as serving as stevedores, and all faced discrimination and often substandard supplies and equipment. About 40,000 men served in combat units, most notably in the 92nd (Buffalo) Division, a black division commanded by white officers, and in units of the (incomplete) 93rd Division, whose regiments were integrated into French Army units. These soldiers, which included units famous for their bravery, such as "Harlem's Hellfighters," were among the highest decorated Americans in the war. David Woodward, *The American Army and the First World War*. Cambridge University Press, 2014.

29   Unfortunately, Dawes' use of this kind of racially-loaded language, intended as humor, would not have been unusual on the part of white Americans at the time. In fact, this kind of racist joke has roots far back in American culture.

30   The 17th Engineers would remain stationed in St. Nazaire for twenty months where the members built a railway yard. The unit returned to the United States in March 1919.

31   Chauncey McCormick (1884-1954) hailed from a famous Chicago family. His relatives were founders of McCormick Harvester, which merged in 1902 with the Deering Harvester Company, founded by William Deering and others, to form the International Harvester Corporation. In 1914, McCormick married into the Deering family when he wed Marion Deering (1886-1965) in Paris in 1914. McCormick enlisted in the A.E.F. and was commissioned as a captain. During the war, his work primarily focused on getting food and medical supplies to refugees in Europe. He was awarded the *Croix de Guerre*.

32   By the time Dawes registered at the Hôtel Ritz at 15 Place Vendôme in Paris, the hotel's reputation for luxury was already well-established. Cesar Ritz opened the hotel in 1898, and by 1917, it was being run by his wife, Marie-Louise Ritz. Other wartime guests included Marcel Proust, Winston Churchill, and Edith Wharton. Aside from undergoing air raids throughout the war, the hotel also served as a hospital, with one of its floors given over to that function. Elaine Denby, *Grand Hotels: Reality and Illusion*. London: Reaktion Books, 1998, 276, 278.

33   A Paris-based investment bank that later partnered with American banker, J. Pierpont Morgan. During World War I, the bank secured loans for the Allied nations to purchase American manufactured supplies.

34   James Guthrie Harbord (1866-1947) played significant dual roles in the war, both as an advisor to Pershing and as a military leader. He was a longtime friend of Pershing's, the two men having met in 1898 when they were lieutenants. Harbord enlisted in the army in 1889, received his commission

in 1891, and served under Pershing during the Mexican Expedition of 1916. In May 1917, Pershing appointed Harbord as his Chief of Staff, a position he held until June 1918 when he took command of the 4th Brigade of the 2nd Division during the Battle of Château-Thierry and the Battle of Belleau Wood. In August 1918, Harbord was appointed to command the Services of Supply for the A.E.F. Harbord was awarded the Distinguished Service Medal. In November 1918, he was promoted to Brigadier-General and reappointed as Chief of Staff. In September 1919, he was promoted to Major-General and, in 1920, took command of 2nd Division in the U.S. In 1921, Pershing was appointed Army Chief of Staff, with Harbord as Deputy Chief of Staff. He retired from the military in 1922, and later served as president and chair of RCA. In 1942, he was promoted to Lieutenant General, retired. Charles A. Endress, "James Guthrie Harbord," in *The United States in the First World War: An Encyclopedia.* Anne Cipriano Venzon, ed. New York: Garland Publishing Inc., 1995, 270-274.

35   General Pershing's Paris headquarters was located within GHQ headquarters, a five-story town house at 49 rue Pierre Charron in the 8th Arrondisement of Paris, near the Champs-Élysées. The townhouse was built in 1890 by the Comte de Paris, heir to the French throne. In 1919, it became the headquarters of the newly-formed American Legion. Today, the building is known as Hôtel Pershing Hall, a 26 room hotel.

36   In 1915, General Pershing's wife and three daughters died in a fire at their home in the Presidio in San Francisco. Pershing was away at the time. Only Pershing's six-year old son, Warren Pershing (1909-1980) survived.

37   CGD: The death by fire of the General's wife and three children at the Presidio and the death by drowning of my son.

38   Marshal of the Empire, Jean Lannes (1769-1809) was one of Napoleon's most famous generals. The luxurious Paris home of Ogden Mills was located at 73 rue de Varenne; Mills later allowed Pershing to use the home as his private residence during the war. Mills also maintained a home in New York City. A lawyer and businessman, Mills later enlisted in the army during World War I, and after the war, he served as Secretary of State under Herbert Hoover.

39   James Lawton Collins (1882-1963) was a graduate of the United States Military Academy. He served in the Philippines before being appointed aide-de-camp to General Pershing. He served as Pershing's aide in the Mexican Expedition and went with him to France in that same role. Later, he became Secretary of the General Staff at General Headquarters, A.E.F.. In the final months of the war, he took command of a battalion of the 7th Field Artillery of the First Infantry Division. He eventually achieved the rank of Major General.

40   Beman Gates Dawes, Jr. (1895-1968), known as "Gates," was the son of Bertie Burr Dawes (1872-1958) and Charles Dawes' brother, Beman Gates Dawes, Sr. (1870-1953). On May 26, 1917, Gates enlisted in the American Field

Service (AFS). He went overseas and served with the AFS for three months before transferring to the 17th Engineers. He was part of the "Marietta College" AFS unit, organized and financed by his father, Beman Dawes, Sr. "Dawes, An Organizing Genius," *Petroleum Age*. November 1920, 66. See the essay "Homecoming" at the end of this volume for more about Gates Dawes and Dawes' two other nephews, Charles and William, who also served in France during World War I.

41   The American Field Service (AFS) was comprised of American volunteers who drove ambulances and other vehicles during the war before the United States declared war against Germany. Organized in December 1914 by Abram Piatt Andrew Jr., the AFS was funded by donations from Americans. It operated in the front lines in all areas where the French Army fought. After the U.S. went to war in 1917, the AFS ceased to operate as a volunteer organization. Ultimately 2,500 people served in the AFS. See James William Davenport Seymour, ed., *History of the American Field Service in France*. Boston: Houghton Mifflin Company, 1920.

42   William Mills Dawes (1895-1984) lived just up the road from Charles Dawes in Evanston, Illinois. He was the son of Dawes' brother Rufus Cutler Dawes (1867-1940) and Helen Palmer Dawes (1868-1941) who lived at 1800 Sheridan Road. William attended Northwestern University, class of 1919. On May 26, 1917, he joined the AFS and went to France where he served 6 months with the AFS before enlisting in the U.S. Motor Transport Corps. See the essay "Homecoming" at the end of this volume for more about William Mills Dawes.

43   Charles and Caro Dawes sailed on *the Majestic* from New York to Liverpool, arriving on July 7, 1897. They spent about a month touring Europe. Charles G. Dawes, *A Journal of the McKinley Years*. Chicago: The Lakeside Press, 1950, 125.

44   In order to be closer to the American training areas, the General Headquarters of the American Expeditionary Forces was moved from Paris to Chaumont on September 1, 1917 by order of General Pershing. The staff was housed in the regimental barracks at Caserne de Damrémont in Chaumont. John Votaw, *The American Expeditionary Forces in World War I*. Oxford, UK: Osprey Publishing, 2005, 27.

45   In March 1917, Paul Painlevé (1863-1933) was appointed War Minister for France. Just days after Dawes made the above entry, Painlevé became Prime Minister of France, serving only until November 1917. He was succeeded by Georges Clemenceau.

46   W.T. Abbott was a Chicago-based lawyer, active in the railroad industry; Charles Hamilton Sabin was president of the Guaranty Trust Company of New York; and Clarence Dillon (1882-1979) was co-founder of Dillon, Read Company, an investment bank. During the war, Dillon served on the War Industries Board.

47   Nelson Dean Jay (1883-1972) was an old friend of Dawes. The former vice president of Guaranty Trust Bank in New York, Jay was recruited by Dawes

to serve on the Purchasing Board staff in France. The close ties among the banks of J.P. Morgan and its loans to the Allies would be underscored in 1919 when Jay was hired by Paris-based Morgan-Harjes, becoming a partner in 1920. Martin Horn, "A Private Bank at War: J.P Morgan & Co. and France, 1914-1918," *Business History Review* (Spring 2000).

48   William Allen White (1868-1944) was a Pulitzer-prize winning journalist from Kansas.

49   In March 1917, the Russian government collapsed in the midst of a revolution. This led to the withdrawal of Russia from the war. Pershing's concern was quite real: German troops were thus being withdrawn from the Eastern front and moved to the Western front, making victory for the Allies look improbable.

50   Spain remained neutral throughout World War I, but it confronted significant economic and social turmoil during the war.

51   Field Marshal Douglas Haig (1861-1928) commanded the British Expeditionary Force (B.E.F.) from 1915-1918. Roughly two million soldiers died under his command, earning him the nickname, "the butcher," (a nickname attached to many World War I generals). His reputation post-World War I suffered greatly once more was revealed concerning the extent of the casualties suffered during infamous battles such as the Somme (1916) and Passchendaele (1917). During the nearly five-month Battle of the Somme, for example, one million soldiers were killed or wounded. In just a single day of the battle, 60,000 British soldiers were killed.

52   Philippe Pétain (1856–1951) served as a general before serving briefly as Army Chief of Staff and later Commander-in-Chief of the French Army. During World War II, Pétain was Chief of State of Vichy, France. After the war, he was accused of collaborating with the Nazis. He was convicted of treason and sentenced to death, a sentence the court asked not to be carried out because of Pétain's age. President Charles de Gaulle commuted his sentence to life imprisonment and Pétain was stripped of all military ranks and honors, except for the distinction of Marshal of France.

53   Luigi Cadorna (1850-1928) was an Italian Field Marshal who served as Chief of Staff of the Italian Army. In October 1917, he would lead disastrous campaigns (particularly at Caparetto) resulting in the near collapse of the army and the surrender of 275,000 soldiers. The Allies urged the removal of Cadorna. He was also accused of using excessive disciplinary measures, including summary execution, toward officers and troops under his command. After he was removed as Chief of Staff, he was appointed to the Allied Supreme War Council.

54   Frank Ross McCoy (1874-1954) was one of the many experienced officers that Pershing and Harbord recruited to serve on the GHQ of the A.E.F. A graduate of the United States Military Academy, McCoy had years of experience in the field and would command two units during World War I, the

169th Infantry Regiment (the famed "Fighting 69th") of the 42nd Division and the 63rd Infantry Regiment of the 32nd Division. John J. Pershing *My Life Before the World War, 1860-1917: A Memoir.* Lexington, KY: University Press of Kentucky, 2013, 551.

55   A cargo ship that carries coal.

56   William Charles Dawes (1865-1920) lived on the Mount Ephraim estate in Faversham, Kent, England.

57   CGD: My selection for Switzerland was Harold F. McCormick, now President of the International Harvester Company, who as the representative of our army there secured thousands of tons of material and supplies at a most critical period. His service was distinguished and invaluable. [Ed. Harold McCormick (1872-1941) was from Chicago, and, at the time, married to Edith Rockefeller, the daughter of John D. Rockefeller. The couple divorced in 1921.]

58   Junior Ames was Knowlton Lyman Ames, Jr. He was the son of Charles Dawes' second cousin, Knowlton Ames, Sr., (nicknamed "Snake" because of his star maneuvers on the football field when playing at Princeton University). "Among the Alumni," *The Princeton Alumni Weekly,* May 22, 1931, 805. Dawes was very fond of Junior and in October 1917, Dawes recommended Junior for a commission. Dawes wrote to his brother Henry that Junior "has real initiative and is very useful." Charles G. Dawes letter to Henry Dawes, October 12, 1917, Box 71, Charles G. Dawes Archive, Charles Deering McCormick Library of Special Collections, Northwestern University Libraries, Northwestern University, Evanston, Illinois. Hereafter referred to as Dawes Archive, Northwestern. Junior, a 1917 Princeton graduate, also played football. Junior eventually did receive a commission and served as 2nd Lieutenant in the 122nd Field Artillery of the 33rd Division and later went on to own and manage the *Chicago Evening Post. Illinois in the World War: An Illustrated History of the 33rd Division.* Chicago: States Publications Society, 1920, 568.

59   Most likely referring to what would be the final battle of the Russian army against the German Army at Riga.

60   Admiral William Sowden Sims (1858-1936) commanded the U.S. naval forces operating in European waters during World War I. He was instrumental in formulating strategies to combat U-boat attacks on Allied ships. After the war, he was publicly critical of the U.S. Navy, resulting in a Congressional investigation. He refused to accept his Distinguished Service Cross. For his 1920 account of the war effort, *The Victory at Sea,* he was awarded a Pulitzer Prize. John C. Fredriksen, *American Military Leaders.* Volume 2. Santa Barbara, CA, 1999, ABC-CLIO, 731-732.

61   Richard Blatchford (1859-1934) was a longtime friend of Pershing's; he had served under Pershing during the Mexican Expedition. While Pershing had great faith in appointing him to a monumental task of overseeing various

aspects of the transport and supply of troops in France, Pershing soon decided that Blatchford was not up to the job and replaced him with Francis Kernan. Jim Lacey, *Pershing, A Biography*. New York: Palgrave Macmillion, 2008, 118.

62   Possibly Calvin Moore, a naval officer with many years experience in sailing. He had sailed on commercial ships prior to enlisting in the U.S. Navy in 1917 where he commanded army transports from Europe to the U.S. John Smith Kendall, *History of New Orleans*, Volume 3. New York and Chicago: The Lewis Publishing Company, 911.

63   Grayson Murphy was the High Commissioner of the American Red Cross in Europe.

64   Commanding General, Line of Communications. A line of communication refers to the route between a unit and the unit's supply base. The A.E.F. operated a complex system of supply and transportation. For more, see U.S. War Department, *Organization of the Services of Supply*, Washington, D.C.: Government Printing Office, 1921.

65   Major General Harry Lovejoy Rogers (1867-1925) enlisted in the U.S. Army in 1898 and was later appointed by Pershing to serve as Chief Quartermaster for the A.E.F., a position that required him to supply the entire American Army overseas. He was both innovative and successful in his duty. He continued to serve in the Quartermaster Corps until he retired in 1922. "Major General Harry L. Rogers," Arlington National Cemetery, Accessed March 11, 2015. http://www.arlingtoncemetery.net/hlrogers.htm.

66   Brigadier General Benjamin Alvord, Jr. (1860-1927) was a graduate of the United States Military Academy, and served in the Philippines and on the Mexican border. He returned to the United States from France in 1918 after falling ill. He was later awarded the Distinguished Service Medal.

67   Robert Bacon (1860–1919) was Assistant U.S. Secretary of State from 1905-March 1909, U.S. Secretary of State from January to March 1909, and U.S. Ambassador to France from 1909 until 1912. In 1914 he went to France with the American Field Service. In May 1917, he was commissioned as a major in the U.S. Army and joined Pershing's staff. In 1918, he was promoted to lieutenant colonel and served as Chief of the American Military Mission at British General Headquarters. He returned to the United States in April 1919 and passed away after complications from surgery. Benedict Crowell and Robert Forrest Wilson, *The Road to France, Vol. II, The Transportation of Troops and Military Supplies*. New Haven, CT: Yale University Press, 1922, 394.

68   Panhard (originally *Panhard et Levassor*, est. 1887) automobiles were favored by military officials during the war. Until 1920, Panhard supplied all the official presidential vehicles to the French government.

69   Grisy-Suisnes.

70   CGD: The first promotion for efficiency made in the A.E.F. (H. B. Moore).

71   Henry Thomas Mayo (1856-1937).

72   William R. Sayles was Naval Attache at the American Embassy in Paris. "Army and Navy Register," April 27, 1918, 532.

73   W.W. Atterbury, former head of the Pennsylvania Railroad. In 1917, he was appointed Director General of Transportation for the A.E.F.. "W.W. Atterbury Appointed Director General of Transportation," *Railway Age Gazette,* September 21, 1917, 513.

74   The *Berwind* was an American ship that was secretly used to supply the German forces under cover of falsified shipping permits.

75   Joseph Jacques Césaire Joffre (1852-1931) was commander-in-chief of the French forces from 1914 through December 1916. He was largely reviled by 1917, and his role in the war was by then ceremonial. At the outbreak of war in 1914, Joffre played a leading role, and although he was judged to have successfully thwarted the German Army at the Marne, his later campaigns resulted in astronomical casualty rates. In 1915 alone, France lost an estimated 1.5 million men. In 1916, under Joffre's command, the French would lose another 800,000 men at the battles of the Somme and Verdun. Gary P. Cox, "Joseph Jacques Césaire Joffre," in *The United States in the First World War: An Encyclopedia,* 312-314. Joffre was succeeded by Robert Nivelle (1856-1924) who had a similarly disastrous command. Nivelle was succeeded by Philippe Pétain in May 1917.

76   In May 1917, Rene Viviani, the French Minister of Justice, and General Joseph Joffre, Marshal of France, traveled aboard a "secret" train (for their protection, according to officials) to Chicago from Washington, D.C. They were part of a tour designed to rally support for the American entry into the war. Chicago Mayor, William Hale Thompson, was less than enthusiastic about their visit, referring to Chicago as the "sixth German city in the world." Illinois governor, Frank O. Lowden, along with the city council, countered Thompson's rhetoric with a formal welcome, and public crowds turned out in their honor. Dawes presided over their appearance at the Dexter Pavilion, near the stockyards. James Langland, ed. *The Chicago Daily News Almanac and Year-Book for 1918.* Chicago: The Chicago Daily News Company, 1918, 571.

77   CGD: In the early part of the year I had presided over the meeting at the Chicago Stockyards, Chicago, Illinois, held in honor of Joffre and Viviani.

78   Henry Herman Harjes (1875-1926) was an American banker who lived in Paris. In 1909, he inherited management of his father's Paris-based bank, the Morgan, Harjes & Co. The bank made major loans to the Allies during the war, which were later subject to criticism concerning war profiteering. In 1915, prior to the U.S. entry into the war, Harjes founded, with Richard and Eliot Norton, the Norton-Harjes American Volunteer Ambulance Service, whose most famous volunteers included poet e.e. cummings and writer Ernest Hemmingway. Chris Dickon, *Americans at War in Foreign Forces: A History, 1914-1945.* Jefferson, North

Carolina: MacFarland and Co, 2014, 17. Harjes also served as High Commissioner of the American Red Cross Society of France and Belgium.

79   Balthasar Gracián (1601-1658), born in Spain, was a Catholic priest and philosopher.

Section 2

September 29, 1917 ~ April 15, 1918

GENERAL PURCHASING BOARD, A.E.F., NOVEMBER, 1918

Seated, left to right: Brigadier-General Charles G. Dawes, Engineers, General Purchasing Agent A.E.F., and Chairman of Board; Colonel C. E. Stanton, Q.M.C.; Colonel W. R. Grove, Q.M.C.; Colonel F. C. Boggs, Engineers; Colonel E. D. Bricker, Ordnance; Colonel D. P. Card, M.C.; Lieutenant-Colonel L. F. Gerow, Signal Corps. *Standing, left to right:* Lieutenant-Colonel N. D. Jay, Q.M.C., Assistant General Purchasing Agent, A.E.F.; Major Ralph Ward, Chemical Warfare Service; Captain H. H. Tolman, Motor Transport Corps.

Paris, Saturday, September 29, 1917

For the last five days have devoted most of my time to the matter of coal supply for our army, endeavoring to complete the organization which I have already at work. At my suggestion a group of officers was appointed by General Pershing to formally meet the French authorities in charge of the fuel situation in France, to close definitely with them the question of the joint action necessary to handle properly the fuel question — both wood and coal. He appointed Brigadier General Taylor (Engineers),[1] Chief Quartermaster (Colonel) Rogers, Director of Transportation Atterbury, Lieutenant Colonel Wilkins (Assistant Chief Quartermaster),[2] and myself (General Purchasing Agent). This morning we held a preliminary meeting at my office and outlined our position to present to the French. Captain Hill (a very able man) reduced it to writing. I was selected to verbally present our position to the French whom we met at 5 P.M. at the office of the French Minister of Supplies. All the French officers having authority to definitely close the matter were present. Our interview was satisfactory and the French will outline in writing the principles agreed upon, leaving the method of carrying them out for further consultation. My official papers will show the action in full.

Yesterday (Friday) General Ragueneau,[3] the head of the French Mission at Pershing's headquarters, called with a letter of introduction from General Pershing, and we discussed the relation of our purchases for our army to the French situation. He pointed out how France was practically stripped of supplies, and asked the closest cooperation of our army in the matter of purchases. I told him I was determined that we should do nothing without the approval of the French Government; that I was holding up independent purchasing; that as Pershing had put me in control of the matter he (General Ragueneau) and his associates must if possible place a liaison board of the French at my headquarters empowered to act with the same authority as to the French attitude on any question as I had in regard to that of the American army — this to simplify and expedite as much as possible our work. He agreed as to this. I earnestly hope and shall steadfastly endeavor to keep in closest coordination of purpose and action with the French Government.

In the afternoon (Friday) Lieutenant-Commander Lindeboom of the French navy (General Staff) called for me and took me to call on Marshal Joffre. Took Major Cushing and Captain Coe of our regiment (who happened to be in the city) with me. At Joffre's office met Colonel Fabry and Lieutenant De Tessant, and a French naval commander who with Lindeboom had all been to America with Joffre and Viviani. Had an extremely pleasant visit with them. The Marshal was delighted with his American reception, as were all the others. He was very cordial. They all spoke of how they were impressed at the Stockyards meeting with the singing of the "Battle Hymn of the Republic" — "Glory, Glory, Hallelujah, for God goes marching on." They repeated these words.

While very busy on the fuel situation during the week have progressed in my organization for securing supplies in England, Spain, and Switzerland. Christie, the man I have appointed to take charge in Spain, will leave for there the coming week. Upon him much will depend. Shall have him report on the matter of the possibility of importing Spanish labor to help build our railroads.

Am cooperating with the officers of the 17th Regiment Engineers in presenting their plan for building piers at St. Nazaire capable of handling 50,000 tons of freight a day.[4] Colonel Sewell and his staff have discovered that this can be done at this harbor, despite French engineering advice to the contrary. Their discovery has come in time, I think, to check the other plans, which are much less desirable. Took Captain Coe to Major-General Blatchford and other officers of the Lines of Communication who will decide the matter.

General Pershing telephoned his appreciation of my coal work. I have had a busy but a satisfactory week. If the plan of the 17th Regiment is adopted, it will be a wonderful contribution to the effectiveness of our army and to the reputation of the regiment.

Paris, Sunday, September 30, 1917

At our conference with the French yesterday an interesting incident occurred. Some time ago, hearing that the French coal mines were not being operated to full capacity, I started a plan to have a report made as to this with the idea of suggesting the sending of miners from the United States if this proved the case. The French Government heard that I was about to send an expert to make the examination and requested that I defer doing so. Yesterday, in answer to my question as to whether this would be agreeable to them, they said that the labor situation and trades-unionism in France were such that the importation of miners would involve them in great domestic embarrassment. We therefore had to give up a plan which I am sure would have greatly relieved the coal situation both for them and us.

Having finished the organization for supplying coal and moving it, which has consumed much thought and a large part of my time, I spent some time to-day preparing orders for submission to the Commander-in-Chief which when issued will relieve me from attention to the details of coal operation. Coal will start landing in a few days, and the machinery being in motion will continue throughout the war. Its foundations are so broad that it will expand as the burdens upon it increase.

At the Saturday afternoon conference the French Government also suggested that we turn over to them the ship tonnage we had, and were gathering, to transport coal from England, and in return they would give us our entire supply of coal from France. I had had an intimation that they would make this proposal and called General Pershing by telephone and discussed it. He instructed me to decline the proposition if made. In doing so at the conference I referred to the cooperation of the General in the matter of endeavoring to secure transfer to the French Government of certain seagoing barges and tugs — as well as the 31,000 tons of shipping to which I have before referred in these notes. It would not do for us to lose control of our transport system from England to France in any degree. The reasons for this are too obvious to discuss. I hear much criticism from the French themselves of their complex organization and the delays it entails — and this from those highest in authority. As for my own contact with it, I can say it has worked so far very well in its relations to us, offering the minimum of reasonable objections to our movements.

Paris, October 4, 1917

This war involves the United States in a supreme test as to its ability to coordinate — not only the various lines of effort relating to its own military preparation, but its collected and consolidated results of preparation with those of its allies. As one laboring constantly to effect this coordination, its importance is daily the more impressed upon me. When the source of main military supply is so far distant from the point of use, as is the case with the United States and its army in France, the importance of coordination increases in proportion to its difficulty. What, as officers on the field of consumption of military supplies, we are seeking, is to locate the control of the movement of supplies from America as a base, at the point of use. The President and the War Department indicate, by their every action and their endeavor to speedily comply with Pershing's suggestions, that they recognize the importance of this principle; but to put it into effective operation will require time and thought.

Priority in shipments, route of shipment (ports of disembarkation), and relative necessity of material should be, barring exceptional emergency, determined here and not in America. Ships now come loaded with material for St. Nazaire and Bordeaux. Since a steamer cannot land at both ports, land transfer and double handling of freight result. If loading and routing of ships were determined here and not in America, freight for two ports would not be mixed — freight needed most three months from now would not displace freight whose lack holds our engineers idle, and delays work on our lines of communication, keeps our foresters out of the forests of France from lack of sawmills and axes when Paris fears revolution this winter from lack of fuel, and the armies in the field face a fuel shortage.

Coordination of our own activities is our first problem. We are rapidly — but none too rapidly — solving it. And then must come effective co-ordination of supplies, and military effort with our Allies. The war would best be fought if one commander-in-chief controlled the movement of the ships, supplies, and men of the three nations. Since that is impossible, liaison boards, representing the three governments, with final power, are desirable. It is conceivable at times that the most effective military results would be obtained if our United States ship tonnage was devoted largely to supplying England's fighting army; at another time that England's ton-nage would be devoted to carrying supplies for the army of France and the United States. If we fail (that is, the Allies) in this war it will be because we do not coordinate quickly enough. Pershing and all of us see this. We are working for it night and day. I am glad that my particular service is largely along these lines. The enormous destruction of shipping by German sub-marines makes coordination the salvation of the Allies — the lack of it, their defeat. We must not deceive ourselves.

General Pershing over the telephone indicated that in addition to my other heavy duties he wishes me to take up the question of labor. We need 50,000 men for the building of our railroads, and to do other construc-tion work. Where to get them, to what extent we can use our troops, to determine the Spanish and Italian situation in this connection — all this is involved. I do not quite know to what extent he wishes me to take hold of the matter. If I cannot do it thoroughly I must not attempt it. He wanted me to supervise the selling of Liberty Bonds to the soldiers for its stimu-lating effect on American subscriptions, but I asked him, in view of my present heavy burdens, to assign this work to others.

Received letter from Van de Vyvere relative to going to the Belgian lines with the Belgian Cabinet who meet the King there every Monday; but how in the world I am going to get the time to do it I do not know.

Paris, Saturday, October 6, 1917

Spent most of the morning at my office with Major-General Bartlett, who is to succeed General Lassiter as Military Attaché of the American Embassy at London. Went over the character of problems he would have to meet based on those we have encountered the past thirty days. Informed him as to the relations of the General Purchasing Agent and Board to his organization as we understood them. Had him meet Captain (Major) Moore and Lieutenant-Colonel Wilkins, who are now handling the coal transports and shipments and the coal exchange at ports with the French for coal at the points of our use. We reached a good understanding. I explained to him that the serious questions in my judgment which confronted him were those which would arise out of the request of England for use of our tonnage from America to England in return for the coal and other supplies she is furnishing us in England for use in France. The request for the use of the 41,000 tons' capacity of steamers we have just requisitioned, to carry on the first trip steel billets to England, is in point. My feeling is that we must go to every extreme in our efforts to cooperate with England and France. If we do not the war may be lost before we are ready to enter it.

On Friday called with my aide, Major Harjes, on Mr. Sharp, the American Ambassador.[5] Was cordially received and assured of his hearty cooperation in my work. At his request and that of the French Minister of Blockade, who was present, am delaying sending army purchasing officers to Switzerland until diplomatic negotiations are nearer completion looking toward an adjustment of the embargo situation between the United States and Switzerland.[6] Hope that our country will make some concessions to Switzerland which will result in Switzerland's lifting the embargo on certain supplies which we can get there for our army. In the afternoon met the French Minister in charge of medical and surgeons' hospitals, etc. (*Service de Santé*)[7] and his staff in formal session, and arranged the details of coordination in this work and securing medical supplies between the French and our own army. The interpreter at this session was James H. Hyde,[8] formerly of the Equitable Life Assurance Society, New York.

Was greatly pleased (to-day — Saturday) to receive the word of our large coal loadings in England. Moore has just returned from a hurried trip there.

The war has resolved itself in a large degree into a freight tonnage situation for the present. Great Britain is making a splendid offensive while the mighty work of American preparation goes on.

Paris, Tuesday, October 9, 1917

Yesterday Colonel Stanton[9] and I, having received orders from General Pershing, met the representatives of the French Treasury and considered the matter of the material furnished by the French Government to our army up to September 30, the payment therefor, and the method of payment hereafter after the system of checking material and accounts is more fully worked out. After going over the statements presented we wrote the Commander-in-Chief recommending that $50,000,000 be placed to the credit of the French Government in the Federal Reserve Bank of New York as against material already delivered. We also recommended that Major H. H. Harjes be appointed to represent the United States in determining amounts, and carrying out a system in the future for settlement of balances. The French officials estimated they would furnish us from $60,000,000 to $100,000,000 per month of supplies including ordnance and aviation material. Agreed upon the desirability of fortnightly settlements, as France needs the credits for use in America. This matter took us the entire day.

To-day am considering the question of our relation to Swiss and Spanish markets, having received a letter from the American Ambassador Sharp and the French Minister of Blockade in this connection. The matter is one of more or less delicacy owing to the necessity for complete cooperation between us and the French and English.

Our army system here seems more centralized than that of either the English or French, of which I am glad. I believe in extreme centralization in army matters. Through it comes a quicker perception of the necessities of a situation, and a more rapid correction of a difficulty. Heaven knows we need quick action these days!

Am delighted that Congress has made John a General[10] — settling once and for all questions of relative rank among not only our own Generals, but among those of our allies.

Paris, Friday, October 12, 1917

Busy days. Thursday at a long conference with General Carter,[11] the Director of Supplies, British Expeditionary Force, laid the foundation for what I hope will be the eventual coordination of all Continental purchasing and handling of supplies among the Allies. Carter and I prepared a cable which General Pershing has sent to Lord Derby[12] opening the way for a London conference, and we also reached an agreement between us which we shall now take up with the French for joint action in Spain. My official correspondence will show the details. General Pershing telephoned me Wednesday that he would come in and spend Thursday evening with me. He did so and we took dinner and spent the evening in war discussion. He is naturally pleased at his promotion to the great position of Lieutenant-General, but is properly impressed with the great responsibilities of his position. Read me a letter from Baker[13], Secretary of War, commending his course thus far; said (that is, Pershing said) Wilson told him he had chosen him to be the Commander-in-Chief in France because of the way he had conducted himself in Mexico.[14] He has suggested to the French that we use some of the Russians now in France as laborers. It has been kept a profound secret, but two divisions of Russian troops — about 40,000 men — on the French line revolted after killing many of their officers. The French have them in barbed-wire enclosures, and are rather at a loss to know what to do with them.[15]

I told him that it would be impossible for me to properly attend to the labor situation in addition to my other duties as he suggested. He was greatly pleased with the way I am cooperating in the Switzerland and Spanish supply situation with the American Ambassadors to France, Spain, and Switzerland. Pending the diplomatic negotiations on embargo between the United States and the latter two countries my constant cooperation, as controlling the activities of our supply departments with our diplomatic representatives, is essential. My official correspondence, prepared with much care, shows the questions at stake and our method of procedure.

John is master of his great place. It has not affected his perspective or changed him in any way. He has the proper mixture of caution along with his tremendous initiative and executive capacity. He thinks a thing out, and then acts without indecision. He is very wise. When he starts our offensive it will be kept up. His mind is on essential things, and yet he does not overlook the importance of details in their relation to greater things. I have never worked in greater accord with any one than with Pershing. Reason, and never prejudice, rules with him. He is in the midst of great events — and still greater ones await him, and those of us associated with him in our humbler posts.

The French believe in the sacredness of fixed procedure at dinner. When I told our head waiter at the Ritz that General Pershing was to dine with me, and was ordering dinner in advance, he was much distressed because I ordered no soup. His protests were polite, but extremely insistent. Soup should be served. The General would expect soup. Was I sure he did not want it? He would prepare it anyway — and if the General did not want it, it would not be put on the bill. Was I very sure that the General could get along without soup? "Well," I replied finally, "when the General and I patronized Don Cameron's 15-cent lunch counter at Lincoln, Nebraska, he was able to get along without soup and nearly everything else I have ordered that costs over ten cents." This remark, designed to impress his sense of humor, was unnoticed in his profound depression over my obstinacy — and so I let him make his soup and pass the question directly to the great chieftain himself for decision. When the General, dining at my expense, decided for soup, the waiter's joy was so evident that sacrilege had not been committed when threatened, that I was glad I had raised the question for his sake.

Letter to my mother
Paris, October 23, 1917

My Dear Mother:

I realize that my letters to you have been brief and unsatisfactory, which arises not out of any lack of affection or consideration for you, to whom I owe in every way so much, but from the fact that during my whole life my training in correspondence has been to eliminate what has from a business standpoint seemed to be non-essential. In that way I have lost the art of narrative letter writing. When I start to write such a letter I am constantly sitting in judgment upon the question as to whether the facts are important enough to record, forgetting that to those we love and who love us most no fact is trivial if it concerns ourselves. And so to-night, despairing of any effort to write you, I have brought my stenographer to my room to undertake to dictate an account of the trip to the Belgian front from which I have just returned. As a matter of fact none of the personal incidents which I shall mention are really important as compared to the incidents of the work which General Pershing has given me to do, but the latter would prove uninteresting as compared with what follows.

I have told you of my friend Mr. Van de Vyvere (pronounced Van de Fever), the Belgian Minister of Finance, of whom I have come to think so much. His Bureau is concerned with all matters of Belgian finance and I had some questions to discuss with him relative to the coordination of the work of securing supplies for the Belgian and the American armies. I met him at Abbeville, to which point I went by motor from Paris, starting Saturday morning. I took with me on the trip Major H. H. Harjes, one of my aides, a member of the firm of Morgan, Harjes and Company, Paris, and my friend Cornelius N. Bliss, Jr.,[16] of the Executive Council of the Red Cross, who happened to be here. I had arranged to take Colonel Sewell of the 17th Regiment Engineers, but at the last minute he had written me of his inability to come. After lunch with Mr. Van de Vyvere at Abbeville I got into his motor, a fine Rolls-Royce machine, and at a speed which I think must have averaged forty-five miles per hour, reached the old French town of St. Omer, where we waited an hour before my own machine with Harjes and Bliss joined us. Mr. Van de Vyvere took me to visit the old cathedral, to which no one could have a more interesting guide. In culture, education, knowledge, and ability, he is a most unusual man. Fortunately for their own present stock of interesting reminiscences, Harjes and Bliss got into Mr. Van de Vyvere's automobile with us for the balance of the journey to La

Panne, the point of our first destination.

Dunkirk is the town in which, sometimes at noon and sometimes at seven o'clock in the evening, practically each day, there is received a German shell fired from a gun about thirty-three miles distant. Signals are given from the flash at the gun from points far ahead and the inhabitants have about one minute from the time of receiving the signal to seek shelter in the cellars. The town is, of course, considerably damaged. We passed through this town a little after seven o'clock in the evening. As the entire section is under more or less bombardment, especially from airplanes, we ran with no lights at a comparatively slow pace. Just after we had passed the town a siren sounded and Mr. Van de Vyvere announced that an airplane raid was in progress. This first raid had but a comparatively mild interest for us, since the bombs struck at a very considerable distance. We could hear the antiaircraft guns and saw the searchlights seeking the hostile airplane. We had not proceeded, however, more than half an hour when we suddenly found ourselves surrounded by great shafts of white light directed toward a spot above us in the sky, which, of course, we could not see through the top of our limousine. We were proceeding slowly in the dark very near a factory used for making shells, to destroy which was the evident purpose of the hostile airplanes. Around us on all sides the anti-aircraft guns were firing at the airplanes. It seemed to us even then that we had a center seat for an interesting performance. Suddenly to the right of the road occurred about four great crashes, each one of them sounding like a ten-story sky-scraper falling down, and then, a few seconds later, three more tremendous crashes occurred on the other side of the road. If the Germans had been aiming for our automobile instead of the munition factory, they would have been considered extremely good marksmen, for two days later when we came past this spot on our return we paced the distance from the nearest crater to the point on the road where our automobile stood, with an estimated allowance for the small canal at the side of the road, and the distance was about one hundred and forty yards — only a little over four hundred feet. Into the crater formed by this bomb a small-sized house could be comfortably placed. Our safety consisted somewhat, no doubt, in the fact that the nearest bomb struck a soft, swampy field instead of rocks or hard earth. When the bomb struck I did not notice that it gave off any light, but only sparks such as would be caused by striking red-hot iron with a hammer in a blacksmith shop. There were not very many sparks at that.

We finally reached La Panne, where Mr. Van de Vyvere took us to the apartment rented by him and the Minister of the Interior for use when they go to La Panne at the time of their cabinet meetings with the King of Belgium.[17] Mr. Van de Vyvere lives at Havre, France, which is the present

Belgian seat of government. The apartment was plain and simple, but very comfortable. We arrived at about nine o'clock at night and after dinner had a most enjoyable evening. Sunday morning, October 21, two Belgian Commandants called at eight o'clock to take us to the Belgian front. I went in the automobile with Commandant Le Due and Mr. Van de Vyvere, and Mr. Harjes and Mr. Bliss followed with Commandant Scheldt. On the way Mr. Van de Vyvere stopped at the office of his colleague, General De Ceuninck,[18] the Minister of War, a man of very pleasant but aggressive character, to whom he presented me. He was living in a handsome house which in some lucky way had escaped bombardment.

And now a word about Belgium. Belgium is now only about twenty miles long and six to eight miles wide. Upon this narrow strip of territory the King of Belgium and his army, consisting of about 160,000 men, have made their stand against the Germans. The whole country is subject to constant bombardment, and the larger guns of the Germans constantly fire clear across it into French territory. Its little villages are many of them practically demolished, but a considerable proportion of their original inhabitants dwell in some of them. The Belgian front extends for a long way through what is called the "flooded district" in Flanders. At the cost of immense labor the Belgian army has built into the flooded regions roads and erected trenches which consist of ramparts of sandbags for the most part. The roads leading to the Belgian front are protected by camouflage strung on wire screens and consisting apparently in large part of straw and reeds. Practically all the distance which we traveled from the office of the Minister of War to the front was thus protected.

About halfway we stopped and left the automobiles and proceeded on foot along the road which at that time was not bombarded, but which at night, when supplies are brought forward over it, is subjected to constant bombardment and machine-gun fire. We spent a time in the second trenches and then went forward to the first trenches, walking about forty feet apart so as not to attract special attention. We reached the front-line trenches and spent quite a time talking with the Major commanding the battalion there. At that time the artillery firing from the Germans and the Belgians was quite light and we decided to go still further to the most advanced posts from which we could get a better view of all the proceedings. We reached these points by going behind a rampart part of the way and then through a narrow lane of sandbags arched over at intervals with iron where an enfilading fire from the Germans could otherwise be directed along the trench. On the way I was taken to an observation post which was hidden halfway up a ruin of a farmhouse. I climbed the ladder to the observation station and with the glasses of the soldier who was there looked at the German line which was about four to five hundred yards further on.

About this time the firing became more general between the Belgian and German lines. The shells would pass over our heads. Some of them sounded almost like a railroad train; some of them whined,[19] and others made a sound similar to the firing of a sky-rocket. The airplanes were very active. Whenever the French or Belgian airplanes would come near the line, the German guns would open upon them and we could see the shells bursting around them. The Germans would also fire at them with machine guns. A machine gun sounds a good deal like a pneumatic hammer on a skyscraper which is being built, but since in Marietta you have probably not heard one I will bring you to a realization of it by stating that when in our childhood we boys used to run along the pavement in front of the house holding a stick hard against the pickets of the old fence the resultant noise sounded like an infant machine gun. Finally a German airplane almost directly above my head was engaged by four Allied machines. I counted eight or ten shells bursting at one time around the Allied machines. Machine guns also were firing from the German lines, from the airplanes themselves, and from a little Belgian who was in the trench where we were. The engagement ended by the German airplane flying back to its lines with apparently no casualties on either side. All this time, while an intermittent firing was going on around us, there was a dull and continuous roar to the east. It was an inspiring sound, like the roar of distant thunder — or rather it was the roar of the splendid British lion, grievously wounded, but fighting the greatest winning fight of his life.

From my observation post I could see the town of Dixmude [*sic*][20] in the distance, which is in the hands of the Germans, and just beyond this town the English guns were at work. The blood of my ancestors stirred in pride within me when I realized the tremendous scope of this magnificent artillery effort. We stayed in the trenches all the morning. No shell burst near us with the exception of one after Mr. Van de Vyvere and I had gotten into the automobile quite a distance back of the second line. The name of the point which we visited I have written down and in peace-times I should like to revisit it. I shall never be able to remember the name. Here it is — Stuyvekenskerke. At one o'clock we went to the headquarters of the Belgian army. The attentions which were paid to us you must not attribute to my own military standing, but to the high regard in which my friend the Minister of Finance is held by everybody in Belgium. We found the American flag flying from the headquarters and we were greeted by Lieutenant-General Ruquoy of the Belgian Army,[21] First Chief of Staff, General Detail, Second Chief of Staff, Colonel Maglinse, and the General in Command of Artillery, General Arnould.[22] Here we were entertained at lunch. It was a most interesting occasion, and while the General and his staff could not talk English, Mr. Van de Vyvere and Mr. Harjes and Commandant Le Duc interpreted for all. The Commanding General lost his only son, a boy of twenty-two years, the year before in action, and himself was badly wounded. He is a simple, unaffected, energetic, kindly man. As we left he asked me to step out on the porch and there had the official photographer take a picture of the party, which, when I receive it, I shall forward.

I cannot speak too highly of the work of the Belgian army. What it was in the early history of the war the world knows, but in the interest inspired by the larger armies within the last two years it has been almost forgotten. But there it stands, fighting in the midst of swamps, mud, and conditions of indescribable discomfort with the same steadfastness and unflinching courage which drew from Julius Caesar his praise of two thousand years ago. Later in the afternoon we visited one of the ruined villages of little Belgium and a base hospital. We then returned to La Panne, where with Mr. Van de Vyvere at his apartment we passed the evening and night. The Belgians insisted the next morning upon carrying us by automobile from La Panne to Amiens, about one hundred and fifty miles on our way home, since their fine machines outclassed my own.

On the way we passed the reserves of the magnificent British army, some of them just starting for the front to go into action. It is difficult to state in terms which will convey a proper impression, the strength, fitness, and splendid bearing of these men. In equipment of all kinds, in thoroughness of preparation, in esprit de corps, and, above all, in morale, they have no superiors, but in time we know they will find an equal in the troops of the United States, with which so many of their blood will march. As we passed along the road a regiment of Gordon Highlanders[23] in their kilts passed us, headed by a splendid band including its squad of bagpipers. The effect of the music upon the men and upon us who saw them reminded me of what the men of the 17th Engineers felt the night they marched through the rain and in the dark from the railroad station at Borden to their camp at Oxney, led by an English band. I had commanded the train which carried the first battalion of our regiment from Liverpool to Borden. The boys had had only a small ration at noon and we did not arrive until late at night. They came out of the cars tired and hungry and formed in the darkness and rain along the road. When this band came down from the English camp and marched back at the head of our line, playing American airs, it seemed to say to the discouraged and tired men, "You amount to something after all." "You are welcome." "You are one of us." I do not think that the march afterwards through the crowded streets of London produced the effects upon the minds of the regiment as did this march in the night along the

IN THE BELGIAN TRENCHES, OCTOBER, 1917
Major Harjes and Lieutenant-Colonel Dawes

Left to right: BRIGADIER-GENERAL FRANK McCOY, MAJOR-GENERAL J. G. HARBORD, BRIGADIER-GENERAL GEORGE VAN HORN MOSELEY

124

LIEUTENANT FRANCIS J. KILKENNY

LIEUTENANT DALTON H. MULLONEY

quiet lanes which led to Oxney.

This letter is long, but the burden will fall chiefly upon my stenographer. I cannot take time to write often in this way.

My work is exacting, but inspiring, for it is related to the general preparation of the army which before long will march by the side of the Allies in the final effort. I am glad to be here, and am glad that William and Gates are here. Between the three of us we will try and leave the family mark on the record. If Rufus were alive he would be with us too. I hope you keep well. I wrote you on our mutual birthday and the length of this letter is in part an apology for having written only once since.

With much love,
Your affectionate son

Paris, Thursday, October 25, 1917

I reached Paris from my trip to the Belgian front Monday evening. In a letter to mother I have recorded the incidents of the trip and will file a copy of the letter in these notes.

Before leaving I wrote to the American Ambassador to France suggesting a method of solving the grave exchange situation between France and Spain and France and Switzerland by having the Governments of Spain and Switzerland establish a debit balance on the books of the Treasury of the United States which would be created by their purchase of cotton for their factories direct. The United States would pay the cotton producers of the United States direct and charge Spain and Switzerland on its books for the amount. The debit balance our purchasing agents would extinguish by the payment of the amount due for importations for our army of supplies — simply giving Spain and Switzerland memorandums of the amount due which would be credited against the debit balance in the United States. The Ambassador cabled my letter to the State Department strongly urging the plan, and Ribot[24] for the French Government stated that he would cable the French Ambassador to the United States to urge the adoption of the same. The United States is considering the lifting of the embargo on cotton to Spain and Switzerland in return for embargo concessions from them.

Spent much of Wednesday afternoon with General Pershing discussing important problems, the chief being the relations of our purchases to those of France in connection with the effort I have inaugurated to centralize all Continental purchases of the Allies. The General has placed the Claims Settlement Bureau, to adjust the claims for supplies currently furnished us by the French Government, under my board (G.P.B.).[25]

My organization is now well in successful operation, and the General is inclined to constantly extend our responsibilities. This is gratifying in one way, but as our army operations grow, our energies are going to be heavily taxed. The executive ability of Pershing impresses me more and more as time passes. He is the man for the place. He has just returned from the French offensive[26] which was so successful. Nothing counts with him but results. The law of the survival of the fittest among his officers and the army is at work. It is cruel, but inexorable. In war no excuses count. Performance alone answers. Conducted as this war is, no reputations will be made by accident. But whether it is the military method or not, I am trying, where I find men unfitted to carry out certain lines of work assigned them, to change them, without breaking their hearts and spirit, to work better adapted to their abilities. In proportion as power has come to me in life, I seek to avoid its ruthless use. Its exercise is no less effective — indeed, I have found it much more effective — when with it is exhibited patience, reason, and moderation. The law of compensation is ever at work. Unhappy will be the man in power who for one minute forgets it. God keep us all humble in mind.

Paris, Saturday evening November 3, 1917

How to save shipping space from America — that is the greatest problem which engrosses me and my office. I am trying to effect this, first, by locating supplies in Europe which otherwise would have to come from America; second, by ordering prime materials like sheet tin which can be manufactured here with resultant saving in space; third, by endeavoring to substitute in army use articles of less bulk for greater serving the same purpose. I requisitioned ten thousand and fifty tons of sheet tin the other day for manufacture into milk cans and other bulky articles which will save from sixty to ninety thousand tons cubic capacity shipping space. In our work there can be no cessation of effort. Every ship sunk increases its importance. In the meantime I am securing a steadily increasing coordination in the work of securing and purchasing supplies. My efforts to make this coordination inter-Ally are progressing. My official correspondence indicates the steps taken. General Pershing has now ordered the entire volume of European purchasing through my office. I have prepared for him a statement of the conditions which surround us which General Harbord tells me he is going to place in the official war diary. It is for the purpose of having a contemporaneous statement preserved of the reasons for important decisions in supply matters.

General Pershing took a trip to St. Nazaire and other ports last week and part of this. He was here two or three days, leaving for Chaumont Saturday morning. Was in daily consultation with him. Thursday night we had planned to spend alone in going to dinner and the theater, but a party of fourteen Congressmen arrived,[27] and the General gave them a dinner at the Ritz which I attended. We then all went to the circus.

Friday night General Harbord dined with Major Atwood and me. Friday afternoon the delegation of Congressmen called on me at my office. In the early part of the week Colonel Sewell and Coe were also here. Had Pershing invite Sewell to his dinner. John is in good spirits. He is gratified at the way things are progressing. Says Haig is nervous all the time over the politicians at home, but that President Wilson, the censorship,[28] and the distance home all unite to save him such worry.

The Italian reverse is sobering.[29] Eighty-five thousand French and English troops have been rushed there. But it seems to me that this war will be won or lost on the Western Front. No reverse elsewhere will shake the morale of the great English troops soon to be joined by Americans. And the splendid French are advancing. Next year Germany should be conquered in the west. In my judgment she will not have time to organize for great military assistance her conquered territory. It seems to me that in unconquerable spirit will come the final test of victory. Who will break first in spirit under the tremendous punishment both sides must bear? Not the Allies in the west with America just entering the war. In the meantime into the maelstrom is pouring a large part of the best life of the earth.

Paris, Friday evening, November 9, 1917

The last two days have been ones of progress. I met M. Metin,[30] the French Minister of Blockade, at the office of the American Ambassador, and arranged to start our purchases in Switzerland. We also discussed the plan for the coordination of all Allied purchases in Spain and Switzerland, and arranged for a meeting at 6 P.M. Saturday at which the representative of the French army and the representatives of the French War Office and Treasury will be present. There we expect to complete the plans for inter-Allied cooperation in the securing of supplies. We shall start with an agreement between France and the A.E.F. to which we shall ask the acquiescence and cooperation of England and Italy later. Am in constant contact with the American Ambassador, who is helping in every way possible in my efforts to secure an opening for supplies for our army in Spain and Switzerland. Much depends upon the action of our State Department in connection with embargo negotiations.

During the week spent a time with the Commander-in-Chief, who asked me to lunch. We took a long walk. When we rode my nephew Gates, a private soldier, was our chauffeur.[31] Italy seems breaking down, but the English and French troops are rushing to her assistance. This afternoon read the final proof of my "Boat Drill" soon to be standard for the American army. The torpedoing of two transports adds to its importance. My official correspondence indicates how continuous is the procession through my office of important decisions. To help the Commander-in-Chief — my dear friend — to carry his burden, to help my country in this time of need, to push onward and look upward, to be patient, to get things done, to count for something in every way — all this is my weary but happy lot. But it is not difficult to be happy when one feels the sense of progress.

I miss my dear ones on the other side of the ocean sorely. I have little sense of the passage of time. The weeks pass like days. The disinclination to write grows with the sense of the impossibility of delineating the magnitude both of our task and our accomplishments. With the latitude John gives me I feel as if I were exercising the powers of one of the old monarchs. To negotiate single-handed with governments comes to but few men.

Paris, Friday, November 30, 1917

Am fighting a disinclination to write due to weariness at night which, unless conquered, will be a great source of regret to me after the war when I look back on things. So much happens — I talk and negotiate with so many people of importance on things of importance — that the temptation is to make of these brief notes a catalogue of names and conferences. Tonight I shall try and picture the situation as the thinking heads of our army look at it, just stating matters of apprehension and then matters of encouragement.

1st. We fear invasion of France by the Germans through Switzerland. Eighty per cent of the Swiss army is said to be pro-German. If Germany starts through, it is doubtful if Switzerland will fight them. She may fight for Germany. The situation there seems bad.

2d. If the Germans come through Switzerland the frontier defense calls for troops which it will be difficult to furnish.

3d. France is "fed up" with war. Only the entrance of the United States into war prevented her from going to pieces before this. In the case of invasion through Switzerland the effect on the morale of France may be disastrous.

4th. In getting troops and supplies from America we are not as yet handling the shipping problem right. We are not loading ships to fifty per cent of their carrying capacity — lacking coordination on the other side between the source of supply and the docks, and proper handling of the docks. We are not unloading ships expeditiously on this side. In America the control of ships is still considering commerce with South America, for example — when we are in a death struggle.

5th. Military coordination between the Allies is sadly needed.

6th. Revolution is feared in Spain which will much lessen France's current supplies if it occurs.

7th. Our line of communications is delayed by lack of equipment (engineering, etc.) from the United States. In this our danger lies in our being blocked with freight when its real movement commences, say three months from now.

8th. The release of the German divisions from the Russian line, the capture of over 2,000 Italian guns, means increased pressure on our French lines eventually.

9th. Peace seems in the atmosphere.

The matters of encouragement are these:

1st. France will probably hold for another season. If she does, especially on the western part of the Western Front, a general retirement of the Germans can be forced. This should greatly impair German morale and perhaps cause internal and political collapse in Germany.

2d. English morale is in no danger. The United States is new in the struggle, and if she gets in in time will greatly improve the general morale.

3d. Germany probably cannot organize any considerable system in her conquered territory which will prove of immediate military importance to her. She is wearing down in manpower. The Allies are still increasing.

4th. We probably underestimate the extent to which the German army and morale has been affected, and also the strength of the internal desire for peace which, with a proper basis such as an important military reverse, should crystallize into revolution.

5th. We have the best of the food and supply situation.

6th. Coordination is improving, though far from what it should be along all lines.

7th. Only about 40 of say 160 German divisions released from the Russian lines will probably be effective military forces.

8th. Italy is holding.

9th. The status quo is against Germany.

The commission headed by Colonel House[32] is here. The members have been in constant consultation with me as the authorized spokesman for the supply needs of the army. So far as advice as to how to coordinate our army business, they seem to realize, being able businessmen, that we have it accomplished. I am impressed with their ability. Mr. Vance McCormick[33] is a clear-headed, practical businessman. The commission should carry home information as to our needs which should enable the work of coordination there to be expedited. Mr. McCormick having the embargo treaties in hand is getting a grasp of the situation which should enable him to force supplies to us from Spain and Switzerland if they do not collapse as governments. McCormick was broad and wise enough, however, to recognize that our steps to coordinate Spanish and Swiss purchases with the Allies were well taken, and instead of objecting to them at the conference with the Ministry of Blockade, when the French Government officials read my note and their answer of November 13 making full provision for the matter, adopted them. The French have promised to name their members of the Franco-American board this week (to-morrow). Mr. McCormick's visit expedited this action I am sure. His commission cannot, however, help us in handling purchases, but in making Spain and Switzerland agree to let us buy and ship from there.

Have furnished Perkins[34] and his statistician my collected estimates, just being completed, of the needs of the army for the next three months. When I met formally the members, many of them at McCormick's room at the Hotel Crillon[35] at first, I took occasion to express the appreciation of the A.E.F. of Ambassador Sharp's cooperation with army activities. Have not met House yet, but expect to meet him at Harjes's at dinner to-morrow night with Pershing and Sharp.

Yesterday was Thanksgiving, and I took about my first half-holiday since coming to Paris. General Harbord, — also a little in need of rest, — of whom I have become very fond, came to the office in the morning. Took him, Major Cushing, Wade Dyar,[36] and Dean Jay to lunch at Frederic's. Then Harbord and I dug into second-hand books at Brentano's[37] for an hour; then we went to my hotel room after a walk to read them; then at 5 P.M. we went to a reception of United States Army officers at Ambassador Sharp's; then to the hotel; then to John's (Paris) house; then to dinner with Colonel and Mrs. Boyd;[38] then with the Boyds to the circus. When it was over made up my mind I had not rested much. Everybody has a bad cold including myself. Have moved a piano into my bedroom at the Ritz, and will get my mind off work a little with it in the evenings. Also got a fox terrier for company which the servants at the hotel take care of for me.

Paris, Monday night, December 3, 1917

I feel weary and ill from this cold which for weeks seems sapping my strength, but so far I am able to keep the pace. The last two days really deserve attention for their accomplishments. But first merely interesting things!

On Saturday night I went to dinner at Harjes's, which he gave for Pershing and House — only the latter did not come, sending word at the last minute. Those present were the General, Colonel and Mrs. Boyd, Mrs. House, Frazier of the Embassy, Carter (Harjes's partner), his wife, her cousin (a naval Lieutenant), and myself. During a lull in the dignified conversation at a wonderful table in a wonderful house, I said in an earnest way so that all could hear, "General, I know Mrs. Harjes will be interested if you tell her about the old Spanish nobleman, Don Cameron, who used to entertain us in this same way in the old days." (Don Cameron kept a ten-cent lunch counter at Lincoln, Nebraska, where John and I used to eat in our days of poverty.) John never relaxed his dignity, but entered upon a forcible statement of the impossibility of properly militarizing an old friend. He then told her in detail.

Sunday I worked hard — explained in detail the army system to Perkins of the War Industries Board for his use in the United States and also arranged with Van de Vyvere, who is here representing Belgium at the Inter-Allied Conference, an effort to get Belgium to turn over to the A.E.F. 600 locomotives which are now rusting on the tracks idle, and which Belgium declines to give to England or France, having already given them 1100 and wishing to retain these so as to be sure to have them to start business with in that poor country when the war closes. He took me to a dinner given by the Belgian Minister to France Sunday evening. Here, let me add, that England and France (that is, their War Offices) are very angry with Belgium for not turning over these last 600 or 700 engines. At this dinner was the Belgian Minister of Transportation (Paul Segers). (Also General Ruquoy, the Belgian Minister to The Hague, and other leading Belgians.) Both he and my great and good friend Van de Vyvere agreed to my representation that here was the opportunity for Belgium to show her appreciation of what the United States has done for her in her distress, and, to make a long story short, agreed to give us the engines on the same terms as the other ones had gone to our Allies.

Realizing that we must turn them over at first to France (and perhaps a part to England), since we are not yet in charge of any operating railways, I secured their agreement that we could so turn them over if we desired; in other words, the A.E.F. by this initiative settled something desired by all the Allies. Monday (to-day) Segers called on me and we closed the matter. I took him to Pershing who formally thanked him; also to General Patrick who did the same. Took lunch at Harjes's with Van de Vyvere (dear man), Tom Lamont,[39] of New York, and young Whitney. Am sick and tired to-night — but "got there" as the official records will show.

Just a little more: Harjes saw Joffre — I think it was on Friday. Joffre is very apprehensive about the military situation. Is feeling aggrieved because he is not given "unique command"; that is, over all the Allied armies.[40] Says Lloyd George[41] prevents — also blames Clemenceau for not demanding it. Says Military Committee of Allies is not sufficient. Says Lloyd George is influenced by political considerations, which, however, Joffre does not underestimate. Says Painlevé had no right to agree with Lloyd George in Italy on committee programme when he (Painlevé) knew he was about to go out of power.[42]

The labor problem is still a matter of discussion between the Commander-in-Chief and myself. I dread, and yet want, to take hold of it.[43]

Paris, Sunday, December 9, 1917

The reason why valuable contemporaneous comments on war are scarce is because so many important things happen in such a short space of time that any one in important relation to them loses the sense of their importance. One becomes so accustomed to the unusual that it seems the usual, especially when one becomes fatigued. The Belgian locomotive matter — the series of interesting things about it — I should like to write about, but I shall let my official files tell the story.[44] What I do must be forgotten or some one else must tell about it — that is, must tell about the details.

I am finding so much material in Europe for our army that we really run the gauntlet of criticism from the different departments that we are finding them too much too quickly. They say now we have found too many machine tools. Of course we do not have to take them if this is the case. Notwithstanding 400,000 ties (railroad) are at present under requisition from the United States and 2,400,000 are needed in all, the Engineer Department seemed dazed when I got them an offer of 145,000 in Portugal, 50,000 in Spain, and some from France which they had not located, just as a starter. But it is a gratification unspeakable to feel that if you make criticism, it is by doing work well instead of poorly.

The regular army is a magnificent organization. I work with it incessantly and without friction. One of our officers has been criticizing Belgium, saying it is not playing its part. "Belgium not playing its part!" Belgium — twenty miles long by six miles wide — all under bombardment — holding the line as Russia did not! Belgium, ground to atoms under the heel of Germany because it did "play its part" and fought like a tiger against overwhelming odds until a battle of the Marne could be fought, and a world saved!

My cold is better. But I stay in my room in the evenings, and outside of my business endeavor in every way to save my nerves. They have got to last through the war — and then, if we win, I guess they will remain in my possession.

Have finally asked Pershing not to give me labor. I have ten men's work now, it seems to me; and yet, evidently at the suggestion of headquarters, I find a question relating to 9,000 Italian laborers on my desk for action. Have suggested Woods,[45] Police Commissioner of New York, to head labor under an organization to be attached to the Lines of Communication. Tom Lamont called my attention to Woods.

Paris, Saturday, December 22, 1917

Nothing seems important any more except the tremendous task on which I am engaged — the saving of shipping space for our army by securing its needs on this side of the ocean. Any incidents connected with that stand out clearly in my mind. It is, however, unnecessary to write of them here, for official records and history must preserve them for those who are interested in the great economic side of the greatest struggle of the ages. Each day brings its new problems — each day, thank God, sees something done toward meeting them.

I think I wrote last about two weeks ago. To-night I shall note a few personal things. Last Sunday I went to Chaumont to place before General Pershing the Spanish and Swiss situations relative to army supplies. He had telephoned me to come, and that he would return to Paris with me to insist on action along my suggestions on the part of the French and English. I reached Chaumont and took lunch with John and Harbord and others. With them I discussed matters at length. I had intended to return on the afternoon train, but John wanted me to stay and meet General Pétain, Commander-in-Chief of the French army, who was coming to dinner. In the afternoon late John and I took a long walk. Pétain is a very alert man. After dinner he arranged with John for the latter to visit him at French headquarters to go over the plans for the winter for the French army which I understand John is doing to-day.

The following will be of interest to those who do not know our Commander-in-Chief. When I got up next morning it was very cold and snowing. General Harbord came to my door and asked me to come and dress in his room as he had a wood fire. Notwithstanding the fire it was freezing cold, and I was quite proud of myself for forcing myself through my morning gymnastic exercises. While I was so engaged I looked out of the window, and there was "Black Jack"[46] clad only in pajamas, bathrobe, and slippers, his bare ankles showing, running up and down in the snow outdoors. I never saw a man more physically fit at his age.

I spent the day hard at work with the Staff — Harbord, Logan, Rogers, and McCoy. In the evening went with John in his private car to Paris. General Ragueneau,[47] Chairman of the French Mission at General Pershing's headquarters, and his aide, Colonel de Chambrun (a descendant of Lafayette), went with us. The General and I took Ragueneau into a compartment and secured his acquiescence in the changes we desired in the methods of handling requisitions on the French Government by the A.E.F., all of which centralize in the hands of Ragueneau and myself. Then John and I had a long visit together alone going over the old times and the old struggles and the old friends. He said the first speech he ever made was at the dinner I gave for him in Chicago in 1903. I am so proud of him, and of his mastery of his great opportunity. Hardship, self-denial, tragedy have all been his lot, but work — always work — has brought him to the heights.

I am in splendid health again. The Chief of Cabinet of the King of Belgium, Comte Jehay,[48] called on me and took lunch with me Thursday. He invited me to visit the King, whom I should like to meet, of course — but I cannot leave my work.

We are all expecting a great attack from the German forces. Germany must make its supreme effort before the American army becomes effective. Work — work, always work — that is the meaning and the only meaning of time to those preparing the American army for action.

To-night the sirens sounded for an expected air raid on Paris. The lights in the hotel were extinguished, but nothing happened. The Parisians seem very confident that the Germans will never make an air raid on Paris — why, I do not know. I have been told, however, that the French will not allow the English to raid Alsace-Lorraine nor do they do so themselves. Perhaps there is reciprocity here.

Paris, January 6, 1918

I do not remember when I wrote last — whether after the first of my two recent trips to see General Pershing at field headquarters at Chaumont or not. The second trip was to discuss the cable from the State Department at Washington asking him to permit me to represent the Government of the United States in negotiating the commercial treaty covering imports and exports with Spain. Important as this task was, it was so much less important than my work here, which I would have to leave, that the General was compelled to decline the request, much to my relief, for it would have been impossible for me to leave even for a week without endangering most important tonnage-saving negotiations. Was at Chaumont on this matter New Year's Day, and stayed as usual at the General's house. I had my nephew William visit me at the house, and he came fresh from his hard work as a private soldier up to General Pershing's bedroom, where before a wood fire he talked with the General and myself. I also took him to General Harbord's room. After a long conference with him gave my approval of his desire to go into the artillery, and Harbord ordered him to the artillery officers' training school. William has made a splendid record and wants only to be useful. He is a fine and brave boy.

My Auxiliary Advisory Committee joined in a "roundrobin" attack[49] upon our department of army service this last week, for "purposes of record" among other things. They accomplished it all right; but I am doubtful if they will be pleased with the "record." I dissolved the committee in consequence. General Pershing has recommended me for promotion to rank of Colonel, cabling really more than I deserve. William spent the evening with me. Worked at office most of day. Wired the General about my advisory (civilian) committee revolt. In preparing my answer to their letter I kept in mind that that defense is best which is concurrently planned with aggressive attack.

Paris, Friday, January 11, 1918

The following may sometime be interesting. John Pershing called me over to his house yesterday and after a conference we went to the Ritz for lunch. He was passing through the city. After disposing of business relating to my department of the Staff he told me that he had ordered the American troops into the line on January 15 — that is, a large part of them. Told me the British and French wanted them divided between them, and discussed this, deciding — at least it was my inference that he decided — to keep them together as an American unit. America has a pride which should not be ignored unless extremely strong military considerations demanded it. These do not seem to exist. Our country would be disappointed at any loss of what might be termed the "individuality" of our troops. I strongly urged him, for its moral effect and for its expediency, to immediately announce this movement to the world. It should have a strong effect if Germany is wavering. He was inclined to agree, but said he must have due regard for the War Department in the method of announcement. I pointed out that peace seemed in the air; that I diagnosed Wilson's address to Congress as an able modification of his former positions to place him and our country in proper relation to an early armistice request from Germany and a peace to result from it on the general lines of the Lloyd George proposals. Wilson omitted former references to the impossibility of negotiating with present German authorities. His present address will always be considered properly as one of the causes of what seems to me to be a rapidly approaching peace; but in making it I think the President had in mind, nevertheless, the wisdom of the ancients who understood so well the working of the public mind when they coined the phrase, "Post hoc, ergo propter hoc."[50] I told John he could well think of the same thing in deciding to move quickly. And yet, who knows how long the war will last!

In my dealings with the higher French authorities I notice an accession of spirits, an increase in activity, and promptness in business cooperation, which have been especially marked the past two weeks. Somehow I think, like myself, they feel victory in the air — in other words, internal collapse in Germany. With all the world war-weary except the United States, our entrance into war has tipped the balance.

Sent Colonel Sewell and Major Atwood to the Belgian front in Harjes's automobile and by arrangement with my friends Van de Vyvere and General Ruquoy — the latter wiring that he was sending two officers to meet them at the Belgian frontier.

Called my officers of the General Purchasing Board together in the morning to consider proposal of methods of expediting the filling of requisitions submitted to me by the French.

Am in good health. Am very proud of the magnificent work done by my wife in furnishing sweaters to our troops. By this time she must have equipped over two full regiments — one of them the 17th Engineers. Our men would have suffered much without them. My nephew William has gone into the artillery.[51] Gates is hard at work. They are both fine soldiers. My nephew Charles[52] has also enlisted in America.

Paris, January 16, 1918

Returning his hospitality to me at the Belgian front, on Sunday took my friend Van de Vyvere and Major Harjes to Chaumont. We went out with General Pershing in his private car. On the way out we discussed the Belgian locomotive and freight-car situation with the General. It is possible that by furnishing the iron parts we can get a large number of freight cars manufactured by Belgian workmen out of lumber they furnish from French forests.

At the General's house, where we stopped, Major-General Bell[53] was visiting. At General Pershing's request I had not bought any eagles to mark my promotion, as he said as a matter of sentiment he wanted to give them to me. And so just before we went to lunch John appeared and pinned the eagles on my shoulders. We spent the night at John's house, and then in the morning Van de Vyvere and I went to Neufchateau, the headquarters of Major-General Edwards, commanding the 26th Division — an old acquaintance and friend of my Washington days. He devoted all his time to us, entertaining us at lunch and then taking us to the practice trenches where we saw a battalion drilled in the new warfare. Edwards is a splendid soldier. If the Germans hit his front they will get action even before his men are fully trained. When he gets them ready he will lead them anywhere. Was much impressed with his qualities of leadership and personality. Returned and had a little time with John before leaving for Paris on the late afternoon train. John said that Pétain objected to the announcement as to the entry into the line of American troops, as it might provoke a German attack on his front. The troops will get into line by the 22d at least. Bullard's division will be the first, I understand.[54] Am suffering from a severe cold again — and with my daily burden of work find it very annoying. Junior Ames on his way to the artillery school spent the afternoon at my office and took dinner with me at my room at the hotel. He is a very promising young man with high purpose and fine ambition. He will succeed.

Paris, Monday, January 28, 1918

We live in the midst of events. Colonel Boyd is making contemporaneous notes of the conferences of General Pershing on the important question of the hour — the manner in which the A.E.F. shall continue to enter the line; but it may be interesting to note the impressions which in his confidential talks the General gives me. The English, notwithstanding their steadfast refusal to mix small units of their own troops with others — even their colonial troops with their own — and the French, are endeavoring to persuade the United States to scatter their troops in small units throughout the French and British line. General Bliss[55] has acceded to the idea. General Pershing is obdurate in his position against it.[56] Bliss has not yet gone to the extent, as I understand, of making to Wilson a recommendation contrary to Pershing. John is therefore in one of those crises at the beginning of military movements alike so annoying and yet so valuable as establishing his unquestioned leadership. To me, his firmness and his great strength of statement — his breadth of view and his utter indifference to the personal importance of any one opposing him — are a source of pride and satisfaction as well as relief. The President of France, the British authorities, Lloyd George, General Bliss — all arrayed against John — mean nothing to him except as they present reason. This sense of the relative importance in great matters of fact and reason and of the relative lack of importance of personality is one of the essential attributes of greatness. No man who unduly reverences name, reputation, title, who is awed by pomp or circumstances, who unduly cares for the semblance as distinguished from the substance of things, is fit to be entrusted as a military commander and negotiator with the lives and fortunes of his fellowmen. John Pershing, like Abraham Lincoln, "recognizes no superior on the face of the earth." He is the man for this great emergency — and I know Wilson will stand by him in his position, for he is right.

John wants his troops to go into the line in divisions, thus preserving their esprit de corps, the pride of their country, the support of the American public, the honor of our nation. He has no objection to their going into the British or French lines, provided they go by divisions. Despite Bliss's disagreement on policy John regards him as a good and loyal friend.

General Pershing spent yesterday and Saturday in the city. Was with him in his room Sunday afternoon. In the evening had him, Colonel and Mrs. Boyd, General Harbord, and Colonel Bacon to dinner at my hotel, and we then went to see "Thaïs" at the Opera House.[57] As usual the General and I talked only war and army organization. He has decided to put labor under me — and this time I have accepted. It is my duty — for an emergency exists — but I am heavily laden already. Still, "between us girls," I am glad of the opportunity. If I only keep well! I can't understand why I should want to risk my reputation for success in this additional and great undertaking, for, like the jumping horses at the horse show, if one fails to clear the seventh bar the audience forgets that he negotiated the sixth. And unlike the horse-show bars, the bar I have to jump is nailed to the posts. If I don't clear it I shall break my legs. But I shall clear it — with space to spare.

Paris, February 5, 1918

General Pershing has placed upon me the responsibility of procuring labor in Europe for the work of the A.E.F., which will require in the aggregate 100,000 men, 50,000 of whom are needed now. I am forming a labor bureau in my office and have appointed Major Jackson, formerly Labor Commissioner of Pennsylvania, as chief.[58] This afternoon I took up, at a formal meeting with the Chairman of the French Mission in charge of French relations with A.E.F. (Maurice Ganne),[59] the subject of the French relation to our efforts. I stated our immediate needs at 50,000 men. Requested permission to import Spanish labor. Ganne is to take the matter up with the Council of Ministers. I asked for an allotment of the military labor about to be brought by France from Italy, on the ground that it would result in the release of a proportionate number of our troops now engaged in labor for combative contact with the enemy in the line.

I have also established, under authority given by the Commander-in-Chief, a Board of Contracts and Adjustment and appointed F. W. M.

Cutcheon[60] chairman of the same. By means of this board we will try and settle difficult business questions and contracts with the French and British Governments as we go along — not leaving a mass of unfinished and complicated negotiations to consume the time of international commissions after the war. I consider this board a very important body.

Have also recommended an organization for the supervision of the technical service of the A.E.F. to function under me.

General Pershing took dinner with me last night. Have been much with him lately, as he has been in the city in connection with the meetings of the Supreme War Council. At his request I called this afternoon on the new Chief of Staff, General March,[61] who is about to leave for America, and gave him a general picture of the work of the A.E.F. in France to date, as General Pershing asked me to do. Had the pleasure of telling him our European purchases now amounted to 2,690,000 tons, and that in my judgment 300,000 tons would cover our replacement agreements, making the tonnage from America saved net 2,400,000 tons. To try to keep a record of what my organization is accomplishing is comparatively useless. Have made up my mind that everything is so important these days that our work will always be comparatively obscure. But so far we have done "our bit" all right. It is relative and not abstract importance nowadays that determines what should be a matter of public consideration. I liked General March very much. He is a friend of my good friend General William H. Carter.[62]

Major Belmont got back from Spain after a very effective trip representing the State Department in the Spanish commercial treaty matter. Sent him to the United States to make a verbal report to State Department and War Trade Board.

Am in splendid health again. Colonel Sewell is in the city. Wayne Stacey, one of Rufus Fearing's classmates and friends, called on me to-day. He is a Major. I do not seem to get over the loss of my dear, dear boy.

Paris, February 24, 1918

This is a war to win. Any officer in the United States Army who puts system above success, who does not exercise his initiative and his ingenuity to adopt any and all means to secure results, had better leave France upon his own request before he is sent back. This is the spirit of General Pershing. In the ultimate struggle of a war like this, system, precedent, habit must give way to emergency. The system of military procedure is devised to win battles, and to win them because its methods bring out the ultimate possible effectiveness of troops and their machinery of the rear at the time it is needed in battle. If peace-time army methods and customs fail to do this at the test, they must be, temporarily at least, altered to meet the test.

In connection with the transfer of my section of staff work in certain particulars to the jurisdiction of the C.G.S.O.R. [63] (so that the C. in C.[64] can take his place in the field) along with all the other sections of the administrative and technical staff, I discussed certain principles before the committee of the General Staff and Staff of the C.G.S.O.R. at the request of the C. in C. These principles will be found applied practically in my section of work set out in my orders, directions, and correspondence, which, because of the magnitude and importance of the transactions and their relation to the military and business activities of the army, must hereafter be the subject of study and discussion by students of military science. But realizing that in the mass of documents underlying principles may long be buried, or misunderstood when extracted by the student, I took advantage of a few hours' leisure this afternoon to dictate to a stenographer some of my conclusions, based upon a unique experience, as to the proper principles which should govern modern army purchase and supply. This I hope to do again and from time to time, for I have learned from experience that mental work is best done by me when I am under pressure and theoretically have no time for it. Then again I am writing more than mental conclusions; I am only recording the principles which necessity has compelled me to adopt as right. Let those who attack them — and there will be many who will maintain that I am wrong about them — remember that for six months I have been (put there by General Pershing) in a position relative to our army supply and purchase operations in France to which there is nothing similar in the armies of England and France.

I am in control of purchase and supply matters relating to all services of the army — not only one or a few of them. The board of which I am chairman has purchased in six months in Europe over 2,900,000 tons of material and is still at it. In addition, I am in control of labor accumulation. I feel the pressure from all points of demand, and am in touch with all sources of supply. I get the viewpoint from the mountain peak of hard and burdensome experience. It is not a theory which has confronted me. My conclusions are compelled by fact; and the commentator upon them, before he condemns them because some of them seem inconsistent with principles of business axiomatic in peace, must consider and keep in mind the vast experience from which they are drawn. And then it must be remembered that I am primarily a business man and business organization man, and entered my great work a firm believer in the infallibility of certain business principles in their application to any collective effort of man, including war. I have been convinced in spite of myself by experience. And thus convinced I have succeeded in my task.

These remarks occur to me in connection with what I dictated this afternoon, which after revising I shall attach to these notes.[65] I keep no track of the passage of time, and do not recall when I last wrote at these notes.

Major-General Kernan,[66] C.G.S.O.R., called me to Tours this last week and we talked over the relations of my work to his new position. He gave me a large portion of the day, taking me to lunch at his house with General Patrick and his aides.

Reached a very satisfactory understanding with Kernan and feel that our relations will be extremely cordial. He has a difficult place — none more so — and he shall receive my undivided loyalty and help. He is giving me the same wide discretion as the Commander-in-Chief and the General Staff. The latter (through Colonel Logan) wires, however, to-day that the Commander-in-Chief is issuing special instructions that in all my work involving negotiations and relations with other governments I must remain in first-hand relation to the C. in C. This is because, although still a member of the Staff of the C. in C., I told him, when he called me up over the telephone, that unless the General Staff and G.H.Q. ceased to deal with me direct that he would embarrass me in my relations to Kernan; that if I am to work at my best there must be no sense on Kernan's part or mine of a divided responsibility on my part. I had before made this a matter of record by wire, as I do not want any system to spring up at the beginning of Kernan's and my association which later may lead to embarrassments.

John has to be at the front. The service of the rear must no longer divert him from his greater task. The change in staff organization is imperative to free him for more military and combative activity. But his success depends on the proper functioning of the S.O.R.,[67] and I wanted to see it start in a way that will enable me to do as good work in the future for Kernan as I have done for him in the past.

Am busy at the labor organization. My papers at the office tell the story. Try to walk outdoors an hour each day. Have to take lunch on my desk, but stay quietly in my room at night and am keeping in the best of health.

Paris, March 27, 1918

Have about concluded to cease these notes, as writing them in the evening consumes more or less energy which should be conserved for the momentous work of the days. I do not remember when I wrote last. The Chief of Staff, C.G.S.O.S.,[68] has asked me officially to send each day a report of activities and I have been doing it since March 9. These brief reports of the general nature of my work will preserve the record which I want to keep.

The great and long-expected German offensive[69] is on as I write. Two days ago matters looked dark, but they are improving. Officials of the French Government sent for me and asked me to get ready to receive at any moment militarized French laborers (miners) employed in coal mines behind the English lines from which (four mines) they said nearly one half of the coal produced by France was being taken. They are under bombardment. If these mines have to be abandoned it will be an irreparable loss. But at my conference with the Minister of Mines and his staff this afternoon, when I announced to him that the American army had completed its preparations to receive the laborers and discussed the methods, it was hoped that the emergency would not arise. My labor organization is well under way in its work. We have already secured about 6,000 men monthly from the French. I am now certain of success in it. From the C. in C., the C.G.S.O.S., and General Patrick I have received words of commendation and appreciation, all of which are most welcome and stimulating. I try and pass them on to my faithful associates, so much of whose efforts and abilities are going to enhance my own prestige when it should wholly go to their own. But thus it is always in life — that credit crowns especially the head rather than the members of the body of organization.

I have a splendid group of men with me. Many interesting things happen which will never be recorded. Let me register one hope — that this war will end the custom of our country of appointing men of wealth only in our diplomatic service.

Sharp has done well. ----- [70] is a failure. Poor -----[71] is pathetic, from a military standpoint at least. My official papers in the latter case will indicate my reasons for this opinion. To pass an ultimatum through ----- [72] is like trying to pass live steam from a locomotive boiler to the cylinders through a rubber hose. The State Department at home is virile; but their agents, such of them as we inherited from peace-times, have not well represented them with the exception of Sharp.[73] They have recognized this and are using others to help us. George McFadden, who was sent by Vance McCormick, the able head of the War Trade Board, is a success and is really helping us.

In war every man who succeeds must work on his toes. God save us from leaders of society as agents to wield in time of war, for the assistance of an army, the mighty powers of the civil branches of our Government.

Secretary McAdoo[74] cabled through the War Department to Pershing that he had recommended me for appointment as one of the directors of the proposed government finance corporation, but the C. in C. answered that my field of highest usefulness was here. I do not think I could survive being taken away from this great work of mine here, to which I am giving and shall give all that is in me. As compared with it, nothing that I have done heretofore in life seems important.

We have had a bombardment here in Paris this week, and one morning a shell fell every fifteen or twenty minutes; also some air raids from time to time. But when we think of what is going on on the Western Front this is not worth notice.

I really don't know whether anything I have written is worthwhile. Everything is on such an immense scale these days that one feels very small and humble.

Paris, March 31, 1918 (Easter Sunday) (Evening)

Some things disquiet me; for instance, an offer wired this morning to me from the British Government, through my representative there, offering us 500,000 camp outfits, as the troops for which they were intended "will not be available." Cutcheon arrived in the afternoon and telephoned me. Cutcheon made his point, and if the events of war do not upset our transportation as it is doing now we will get this labor. Everything in war is liable to change overnight. Cutcheon says no word has been received from Washington as a result of the cable of Pershing and myself, but the fact that we told them in Italy that we sent it may have done a little stimulating. Cutcheon deserves a promotion for this service alone — to say nothing of his other splendid work.

"Big Bertha" (the long-range German gun) has been pretty active yesterday — and started again this afternoon. Went for a minute into the church where the shell killed and wounded 160 at one shot on last Friday.[75] As I came out of the door of the church another shell exploded in the neighborhood. The crowds were kept away from the church, but the officers passed me through. We are being bombarded and "air-raided" right along these days.

I was interrupted here by an officer who came to my room with reports from the front which he said he had received from the French. These reports may be inaccurate, but they must be similar to those we shall receive later. He says the 69th New York[76] is practically wiped out; that the Americans in the line have suffered terrible losses; that a division of the English in front of Amiens was almost destroyed (this must refer to the first two or three days); that the line is now being held. I doubt whether the 69th was in the battle. Cutcheon also telephones that Italy expects an attack on April 8 and that we must hurry our labor shipments. But the railroads are burdened to the limit with the English and French troops recalled from Italy to take part in repelling the offensive on the Western Front.

General Pershing made a wonderful statement when he offered our army to the French.[77] He made it in his own characteristic way. His sincerity will ring through the world.[78]

He called me by telephone yesterday to congratulate me on my labor work and I told him how the French officers had come to my office with tears in their eyes to express their appreciation of his statement to Foch. We do not know what a day will bring forth — except that men will die for duty. Thank God for our American soldiers! They will not have died in vain, whatever comes.

Sunday evening, March 31 (continued on arriving from Davison's)

Took dinner with Harry Davison[79] and his Red Cross staff at Perkins' apartments. He has done a great work and the Red Cross cooperation with the army has been wonderful. We are on the eve of great changes. My work is so entirely engrossing that I have not time even to ask any one about outside happenings during the daytime, and at night-time I seldom see any one. My news from the front is never very quick unless it concerns some need of action on my part, and then it is immediate. One cannot be an onlooker and observer and do his work right at the same time. Therefore, as a rule I have only written about the things I know of my own personal knowledge. Everything is on the verge of momentous change. All I know is that we have done and shall do the best we can.

Paris, April 13, 1918

From: The General Purchasing Agent, A.E.F.
To: The Commander-in-Chief, A.E.F.
Subject: Military control, allied service of supply.

My Dear General:

From the time that you landed in France you have exerted an influence for coordination of effort and centralization of authority on inter-Ally activity which has had the most far reaching results. You have exerted this influence among the Allies during the time that you were creating a coordinating and centralizing system in your command. To carry out the purpose of the centralization of purchase and supply in your own army, to become connected with which effort you called me from St. Nazaire, you have as a matter of fact devised the plan the extension of which to the entire Allied operations would seem now vitally essential to Allied success in the war. What I am to suggest to you arises from conclusions based upon knowledge and experience gained in the position in which you have placed me. Even with the conviction which I have of the vital importance of the matter, I should hesitate to call it to your attention, were it not for your constant demonstration of the desire to subordinate everything, including your own personal authority as an independent commander, to the common purpose of an Allied victory. To willingly sacrifice individual authority and individual prestige in time of emergency for the sake of a common cause is the highest test of greatness and one which, in all your actions over here, you have stood. The power and influence of the great people of the United States, and their assets in men and material with which to secure victory, are in the hands of the President and yourself, and you have rightly interpreted their spirit when you notified General Foch to do with you and your army as he might desire. In this offer you have already taken the step, the proper carrying out of which I am going to suggest in this letter. The peculiar position of the United States in this situation, including your own relation thereto, is such that upon the initiative of our Government alone is it possible to accomplish it.

The general proposition is this, that just as there is now a unified military command of the Allies at the front — in other words, a merging and consolidation of three distinct independent military authorities into one military authority (General Foch) — there must be a corresponding merging of all separate individual authority of the Allies, in reference to the service of supply, into one military authority responsible to the corresponding military authority at the front.

One is just as necessary as the other. In fact, for every argument for the necessity of the Foch command at the front, there exist two arguments for a similar authority for supply and transportation in the rear. I mean by this, supplies from America, supplies from England, supplies from France, and the land and sea transportation therefor, warehousing and handling thereof. The Foch command at the front necessitates similar control of the rear, and in this case the rear means France, England, the United States, and perhaps Italy. Before discussing the method of accomplishing this, let me illustrate, in a manner which has no doubt often occurred to you, its overwhelming importance. The United States is at this time using an immense amount of tonnage for the purpose of building enormous warehouses and dockage facilities. It is doing this notwithstanding the warehouses of France and England are being emptied and will continue to grow emptier. The French Government has used to a very large extent private warehouses for storing of supplies. Owing to the steadily lessening amount of supplies there is a large amount of French warehouse capacity now idle, and at the same time we are proceeding, at the heavy expense of current tonnage, on plans to immensely increase our warehouse facilities. Who is there, with authority to act, to determine from a bird's-eye view the relation of existing English and French warehouse capacity in France to the present warehousing and transportation projects of the A.E.F.? It cannot be done, except in a haphazard and inefficient way, unless by one man with military authority extending over all the Allies. This man, for the same reason that led to the selection of General Foch, must be a Frenchman, and England and the United States must accept him. He must be given exactly the same authority toward the ocean and land transportation, engineering and supply activities of the entire Allied forces, which you have given me in connection with purchase and supply and certain other activities of the A.E.F., his authority being created by the same method. The position of General Purchasing Agent, A.E.F., you built up by a system of compelling the partial cession of independent authority. The weight of your own great powers and personality was thrown into the effort of compelling the creation of this authority, and when any independent head showed signs of not recognizing the necessity for it or bending to it, you broke him on the cross. What has made the success of the organization of my office is its now unquestioned power and authority over independent agencies. I never have had a meeting of the General Purchasing Board except on minor matters such as the distributing of office space or matters relating to the collection of information — never on the determination of action. Our organization is military. The reason why our Allied boards fail is because action has to be by a board and not by an individual. The organization of the entire transportation and supply of the Allies must be military in its nature and not based upon the principles of either oligarchy or democracy. I do not have to argue this to a man like you. Sometime after this war is over get Herodotus and read the discussion of the seven Persian Generals when they were riding horseback on their way to Persia, discussing the best form of government for them to set up in the place of the monarchy of an assassinated king. If we do not have military management and military control, we may fail and a German army at the ports may save us the trouble of unloading some of our engineering material from ships, thus devoted, which should have been bringing men and food to have stopped our enemies where they are now. It may be that our present plans may not have to be abandoned or materially altered, but the point I make is that it is impossible, with this great multiplicity of civil boards, criss-cross authority between the Allies, and lack of coordination in supply effort, to properly determine the matter or properly act after its determination. Take the question of joint supplies. Impelled by the same emergency pressure that compelled unity of command at the front, the French and the English are calling upon me for information as to supplies of our army, with intimations of the necessity of pooling, etc. I am working the best I can in coordination with the French and English in all these matters, but I am in a position where I realize that these questions can only be settled, in time to be of avail, by military authority, which, gathering its information, acts, and does not discuss. Who knows today, considering the Allied forces as one army, whether or not the great supplies of steel, oil, barbed wire, rubber tires, chloroform, sugar, picks and shovels, forage, clothing, etc., existing in France, England, and the United States are being marshaled in Foch's rear by the quickest routes to proper points, to warehouses built or to be built, considering both present and future needs and the present military emergency? In this present great military emergency shall we again pursue the time-worn policy of appointing an Allied board to secure this information, and then, after long delay, subject the self-evident conclusions arising therefrom to the discussion of three separate authorities, influenced by personal or national considerations, personal ambitions, and counter-purposes?

In writing this way I almost feel as if I was insulting your intelligence, who have been the chief leader and have made the greatest personal sacrifice in the effort to apply remedies for this sort of business. If the suggestions herein you cannot force into adoption with the weight and prestige of your country and your own personal power, then we must go back at this time to a new effort to concentrate authority in a new board of the Allies, to do by common consent and town-meeting methods that which should come at once from central military authority extending over all. No one knows better than you what this means in delay, and what delay may mean in a time like this, in a war like this. Can you not force the Allies to agree to adopt immediately the principles involved in the relations of your own military purchasing board to the entire service of supply of your own army, through which this entire Allied supply and transportation situation shall be placed in the hands of a French military officer with the same kind of authority over the Generals in command of the different services of the rear of the Allies that your General Purchasing Agent has over the separate purchase and supply services of the American army? The authority for the French command of these services could be created by the same method through which you have placed authority in me for our purchase and supply situation in the A.E.F. The three Generals in command of the Allied rear should be coordinated and controlled by French military authority as are the members of the General Purchasing Board by the General Purchasing Agent. As in the case of the purchasing board of the A.E.F., this does not mean the radical interference with the conduct of current activities. It does not even mean the lessening of current activities. It means their proper coordination and intelligent direction, and above all it means that when once a necessity is determined, the authority is in existence to compel its immediate relief. The influence of such unified military command of the service of the rear of the Allies upon the question of tonnage, use of material, economy of construction, and general betterment of conditions, must be self-evident. To go with unified military action at the front must come unified military support at the rear. You are the only man that can bring this about. If it was anybody else than you, even under the tremendous pressure of the present emergency, I should hesitate to suggest it; for human nature is weak. Nothing but the weakness and ambition of human nature prevented the unification of military command which you have always advocated until the death of hundreds of thousands, and continued military failure brought individual and national ambition under the yoke of a common necessity involving existence itself.

General Harbord took dinner with me last night and spent the evening and I presented these views to him. He did not express himself, but I judge from his demeanor that he was not entirely unimpressed. I understand from Harbord that you may be here within the next few days. I had intended to come to Chaumont to present verbally what I am writing here. There is probably nothing in this letter which has not already been considered by you. However, now that unification of military command at the front has been secured, I am sure that the application of your General Purchasing Board idea to the service of the rear of the Allies is that which will go further just now in bringing a successful conclusion to this war than any other thing.

Charles G. Dawes
Colonel, Engineers, N.A.[80]

Paris, Monday, April 15, 1918 (11.10 P.M.)

I am tired, but I know that if I do not make some notes of this time of crisis I shall always regret it.

Colonel Boyd called me up and arranged for General Pershing to come to the hotel for dinner with him and me. We discussed my letter of April 13[81] relative to placing — or rather having the United States make an effort to place — all the Allied service of the rear under one (French) military command to correspond with the military unification of the front, already accomplished chiefly through General Pershing's insistence and self-effacement.

I feel that the General can now, with the prestige of our country and his own prestige, successfully initiate military control of the rear — and the rear means England, France, and the United States, and perhaps Italy. My contact is very close with the whole supply and transportation system of the Allies behind the front. Emergency is forcing us to joint action now reached incompletely through a common perception of necessity all along the line of command. The time has come for joint action compelled by one military authority. National and personal ambition must make way. A unified front necessitates a unified rear. Our backs are against the wall. England is fighting not only for Calais, but for Paris and a free New York. The time has come to abolish Supreme War Councils, Allied boards, town-meetings, and common consent discussions, and relegate discussions and diplomacy to their proper place — substituting military consideration and action. One man must control the rear, subject to one man who controls the front — a General, not a civilian, even though he be a prime minister.

I am sure that John agrees with me that for the Supreme War Council should be substituted a French General. I believe that John can and will bring it about and that he must bring it about if we are to win the war. He has devised in his own army, in my position, the plan which the Allies must now adopt for the control of their entire service of supply, including transportation. These matters are so important that I know what I write here must hereafter be discussed. I hope that my use of the personal pronoun may not create the impression that these ideas are more mine than John's. They are his ideas — for which ever since he has been here he has fought, for which he willingly sacrificed his independent command, for which to-day, if necessary, he would step aside. He is a great leader. I love and revere him. Whatever may be the outcome his country has had his best — unselfishly and unconditionally. Surely greatness requires no harder test than the willingness in an historical crisis to suggest supreme power for others at the expense of our own. But John never thinks of that — only the best way to accomplish it for victory's sake. He arrived from Chaumont last night. Sergeant Kilkenny delivered him my letter of the 13th on Sunday the 14th (yesterday noon). It contains a discussion of the steps which should be taken. To-morrow I am going with John and Boyd to the front, where John will address the officers of the First Division[82] before they go into battle.

During the week was at Tours arranging plans for the labor corps of the A.E.F. which I am collecting and will command. So far we have gathered 12,000 men, but we should add at least 2,000 per week to this number, perhaps many more. Ran down to St. Nazaire and visited for a day my old regiment. It was there that the thought occurred to me that only military unification of the rear could bring about a proper perception — and then take the action called for by it — of the relation of what we are doing and propose to do for our army as a unit to what we should do and propose to do for our army as merged with the other armies. I knew that as French warehouses were emptying we were building new ones, and that no one was in position to authoritatively coordinate the situation immediately as should be done. This idea must cover all supply effort — if we are to win.

1 Assistant Chief of Engineers Harry Taylor (1862-1930). After the war, he served as Chief of Engineers. During World War II, the USS *General Harry Taylor* was named in his honor.

2 Harry E. Wilkins (1861-1941) was also a graduate of the United States Military Academy, with many years of military experience. He was later promoted to Brigadier General.

3 Camille Ragueneau (1868-1956).

4 CGD: The beginnings of the Montoir project.

5 William Graves Sharp (1859-1922) was a lawyer and manufacturer. He served nearly three terms as a U.S. Congressman from Ohio. In 1914, he resigned from Congress before the end of his third term upon his appointment as U.S. Ambassador to France by President Wilson. He served until April 1919.

6 During World War I, Switzerland maintained an official position of "armed neutrality." The United States imposed a trade embargo on Switzerland in an effort to block the country, which borders Germany, from selling American imports to Germany.

7 Health Service.

8 James Hazen Hyde (1876-1959) was a multi-millionaire who had moved to Paris in 1905 after being forced out of his inherited position as majority shareholder in The Equitable Life Assurance Society in New York. A graduate of Harvard with a degree in French, Hyde volunteered for the American Field Service and opened his home for use by the Red Cross during World War I. He was commissioned as a Captain and appointed as an aide to Grayson Murphy, the High Commissioner of the American Red Cross in France. Hyde lived in Paris until the German occupation of the city in 1941. An avid art collector, Hyde amassed a vast collection, which, after his death, was distributed among several museums, including the Metropolitan Museum of Art. "Archives Directory for the History of Collecting in America," The Frick Collection, Accessed June 5, 2015. http://research.frick.org/directoryweb/browserecord.php?-action=browse&-recid=7478.

9 Charles E. Stanton (1859-1933). Upon the arrival of the first U.S. troops in France, Pershing and some of his staff participated in various public events in Paris. On July 4, 1917, they visited the tomb the Marquis de Lafayette, who had fought with George Washington in the American Revolution. At the wreath-laying ceremony, Colonel Stanton made the famous proclamation, "*Lafayette, nous sommes ici*" ("Lafayette, we are here").

10 In October 1917, Pershing was promoted to General (from Major General). In part, the promotion was the result of the concern that Pershing was otherwise outranked by European officers. Although Dawes refers to Pershing's promotion to "Lieutenant General," he was, in fact, promoted to the rank of full general. Cullom Holmes Farell, *Incidents in the Life of General John J. Pershing*. Chicago: Rand McNally and Company, 1918, 125. After the war, in 1919, Pershing

was appointed to the highest rank ever held in the U.S. military, General of the Armies. In 1976, the U.S. Congress posthumously awarded that same rank, of greater seniority, to George Washington.

11   Evan Eyare Carter (1866-1933).

12   Edward Stanley, 17th Earl of Derby, was British Secretary of State for War from December 1916 until April 1918 when he was appointed British Ambassador to France. He served a second term as British Secretary of State for War from 1922-1924.

13   Newton D. Baker, Jr. (1971-1937) served as U.S. Secretary of War from 1916-1921.

14   In March 1916, during the Mexican Revolution, Pershing led a U.S. military incursion into Mexico (the Mexican Expedition). The goal was to find Francisco "Pancho" Villa who had led an attack on the town of Columbus, New Mexico, on March 9, 1916, during which time buildings were burned and 18 residents were killed. Eventually, the effort to capture Villa involved 150,000 U.S. National Guard troops stationed along the U.S.-Mexico border. Villa was not captured, but Pershing was judged to have handled a potentially explosive situation—both militarily and politically—with great skill. John Perry, *Pershing: Commander of the Great War.* Nashville: Thomas Nelson, 2011, 109-113.

15   The fascinating story of the Russian soldiers in France is told at length in the book by Jamie H. Cockfield, *With Snow on Their Boots: The Tragic Odyssey of the Russian Expeditionary Force in France During World War I.* New York: St. Martin's Press, 1998.

16   Cornelius Newton Bliss, Jr. (1875-1949) served on President Wilson's Red Cross War Council as an advisor. The council oversaw relief work in the U.S. and overseas.

17   King Albert I (Albert Léopold Clément Marie Meinrad) (1875-1934), who reigned from 1909-1934, commanded the Belgian Army during the war, a time when ninety percent of his country was occupied by the German military. His wife, Queen Elisabeth, worked as a nurse at the front. Although the Belgian government had established itself in Le Havre, France, in October 1914 (just months after Germany invaded Belgium), the King remained in Belgium, in the town of Veurne, within the small area of unoccupied Belgian territory.

18   Armand De Ceuninck (1858-1935) served as the Belgian Minister of War from 1917-1918.

19   CGD: I came to know afterward that the "whining shells" were from the enemy and were nearing the end of their flight.

20   Diksmuide.

21   Louis Ruquoy (186-1937), Chief of Staff of the Belgian Army.

22   Henry Hector Maglinse, later appointed chief of staff and promoted to general, and General Henry Arnould would both be awarded the U.S. Distinguished

Service Medal. *Congressional Medal of Honor, the Distinguished Service Cross, and the Distinguished Service Medal Issued by the War Department, 1917-1919.* Washington, D.C.: Government Printing Office, 1920, 842, 938.

23   "One of the best known regiments" of the British Army, the Gordon Highlanders was formed in 1881, comprised of recruits mostly from northeast Scotland. Trevor Royle, *The Gordon Highlanders: A Concise History.* Edinburgh, Mainstream Publishing Company, 2007.

24   Alexandre Felix Joseph Ribot (1842-1923) served as French Minister of Finance from 1914-1917. In 1917 he was appointed Prime Minister (his final and fourth term in that office). Spencer C. Tucker. *The European Powers in the First World War: An Encyclopedia.* New York: Routledge, 2013, 594.

25   General Purchasing Board.

26   Part of the Second Battle of the Aisne, which began in April 1917, led by Joffre's replacement, Robert Nivelle. Nivelle had promised that the spring battles of 1917, known as the Nivelle Offensive, would bring about decisive victory for the Allies. Not only did they result in more horrendous casualties, but Nivelle's offensive was such a failure that it provoked widespread mutinies among the French troops (a fact censored by the Allied governments at the time). Nivelle was replaced by Pétain, and in October 1917, the French succeeded in taking control of the Chemin des Dames ridge. While this was, technically, a success, as Dawes notes, it came at the end of a disastrous year for the French Army. Public morale was at an all time low.

27   A delegation of U.S. Congressmen spent roughly two weeks in France, visiting the French and British front lines and American training areas. Along with dining with Pershing, they also attended a reception given by the U.S. Ambassador to France, William Graves Sharp. "Congressmen in Paris," *New York Times*, November 1, 1917.

28   Great Britain instituted complete censorship of the press following the outbreak of the war. Reporters on the front lines were arrested, and numerous other acts of censorship were performed, such as controlling the information soldiers' revealed in their letters home. Later, a system of accrediting the press was set up, which allowed for the official control of information. The U.S. Government also imposed wide ranging censorship both at home and abroad. The first official U.S. propaganda bureau, the Committee on Public Information (CPI), was established by executive order upon the U.S entry into the war in April 1917.

29   Dawes is referring here to the defeat of Italian forces by the German and Austro-Hungarian forces during the Battle of Caporetto (aka the Battle of Karfreit) which took place from October 21-November 19, 1917. Ten thousand Italian soldiers were killed, 30,000 taken prisoner, and 275,000 prisoners of war taken. British and French troops were sent to reinforce the positions. The defeat was not only demoralizing, but it was also to have great political impact. Cadorna,

whom Dawes mentions above, was forced to resign following the defeat at Caporetto.
30   Albert Métin (1871-1918) would soon head a mission to Australia, designed to form an economic alliance among the Allied nations. On his way to Australia, he died in his hotel in San Francisco on August 16, 1918 after suffering apoplexy. "Albert Metin Dies From War Strain," *New York Times,* August 16, 1918.
31   Gates Dawes, Charles Dawes' nephew, had recently enlisted in the 17th Engineers. See the essay "Homecoming" at the end of this volume for more about Gates (aka Beman Gates Dawes, Jr.)
32   Edward Mandell House (1858-1938), often referred to as "Colonel House," although he had no actual military rank or experience, was one of President Wilson's closest friends and top advisors throughout the war. House was involved in a variety of war-related projects. He served as a top advisor at the 1919 Paris Peace Conference (aka Paris Peace talks). Wilson and House had a falling out during the Paris Peace talks. Wilson reportedly felt House had made concessions that were unacceptable to Wilson's vision. See below for more about House.
33   Vance Criswell McCormick (1872-1946) was chairman of the War Trade Board. He would later serve as chair of the American Delegation to the Paris Peace talks in 1919. President Wilson created the War Trade Board by executive order on October 12, 1917. The board, comprised of representatives of the U.S. food administration, the chairman of the U.S. Shipping Board, and secretaries of state, treasury, agriculture, and commerce, had control over both imports and exports.
34   Thomas Nelson Perkins, most likely. Dawes mentions Perkins again below. Perkins was on the War Industries Board, a powerful federal agency created on July 28, 1917 to oversee industrial production, price fixing, and other matters during the war. Neil Alan Wynn, "The War Industries Board," in *The Home Front Encyclopedia: United States, Britain, and Canada in World Wars I and II.* Volume 1. James Ciment, Thaddeus Russell, eds. Santa Barbara, CA: ABC-CLIO, 2007, 493-494.
35   The Hôtel de Crillon, at 10 Place de la Concorde, opened in 1909 and was housed in a building constructed in 1758. Later, the hotel would be used by the members of the American delegation to the 1919 Paris Peace Conference.
36   William Wade Dyar (1860-1937) was a long-time friend of Dawes. The two men were both graduates of Marietta College, in Marietta, Ohio, and of the University of Cincinnati, School of Law. Dyar served as a major in the U.S. Quartermaster Corps.
37   Located on the Avenue de l'Opéra, Brentano's first opened in Paris in 1895. The first Brentano's was opened in New York City in 1853.
38   Colonel Carl Boyd (1879-1919) and his wife, Annie Peebles Boyd. Colonel Boyd served as General Pershing's aide-de-camp. A 1903 graduate of the United States Military Academy, Boyd had been an associate of and friend to Pershing for many years. He served on the Mexican border with him prior to World War I. A few years before the outbreak of World War I, Boyd was sent to Paris to serve as

a military observer. Upon the outbreak of World War I, he was appointed military attaché to the American Embassy in Paris. When Pershing and his staff arrived in France in 1917, Pershing immediately appointed Boyd to his staff. Through the war, Boyd served as Pershing's most trusted aid and interpreter. He was awarded the Distinguished Service Medal, the *Croix de Guerre,* and the Legion d'Honneur. See below for more on Boyd and his death from influenza in 1919.

39   Thomas William Lamont, Jr. (1870-1948) was a partner at J.P. Morgan and Company. He represented the U.S. Department of Treasury during the 1919 Paris Peace talks, and also took part in the 1924 formation of the Dawes Plan (which allowed the Morgan Guaranty Trust Company to lend capital to Germany in order for that country to pay its war debts). His influential role in the banking industry, politics, and the war is well documented in Ron Chernow's *The House of Morgan: An American Banking Dynasty and the Rise of Modern Finance.* New York: Grove Press, 1990.

40   Pershing strongly opposed allowing the Allied armies to absorb American troops into their ranks. His stance on this issue would win out, although initially the Americans, and Pershing in particular, faced quite a bit of pressure from the Allies. It should be noted that there were some American troops who did serve under another nation's colors: four units of the 93rd Division, comprised of African-American soldiers (the 369th, 370th, 371st and 372nd Infantry Regiments), were placed under French command and served in combat with the French Army. Wearing American uniforms, these soldiers were issued French equipment, including the distinctive French Adrian helmets. Later, the unit adopted a shoulder patch depicting the "blue hat."

41   Liberal Party member, David Lloyd George (1863-1945) was the Prime Minister of Great Britain. During the war, Lloyd George served as Chancellor of the Exchequer, Minister of Munitions, and Secretary of State for War. In December 1916, he became Prime Minister, and enjoyed popular support through the final years of the war and into the postwar period. (He won a second term as Prime Minister, 1918-1922.)

42   The year 1917 saw a re-ordering of power among the Allies. Not only was Lloyd George newly installed as British Prime Minister, but the Americans were also now on the scene. Georges Clemenceau (1841-1929), known as "*Le Tigre*" (the tiger), became Prime Minister of France on November 15, 1917, succeeding Paul Painlevé, and serving in that position until January 1920. Clemenceau had served a prior term as the French Prime Minister, from 1906-1909. He often visited the front lines, and was fairly well-liked by the French public and military. In the original journal, this paragraph's final sentence (which Dawes crossed out with his pencil) read: "All of this reminds me of something my father used to quote to me 'Little fleas have bigger fleas to bite" and "so on 'ad infinitum.' " Charles G. Dawes, handwritten original manuscript of "A Journal of the Great War," Dawes

Archive, Northwestern, Box 86, np.

43   Throughout Europe (and in the United States), the war had created a major labor shortage. Indeed, with so many people serving in the armed forces, the civilian labor pool had been drastically reduced. Laborers were needed in a wide variety of occupations from construction and factory work to clerical and domestic jobs, and to recruit tens of thousands of laborers that the A.E.F. needed was indeed a daunting task.

44   In November 1917, Dawes' staff managed to obtain damaged Belgian locomotives which American personnel then repaired, using tools from a newly-established machine tool section of the A.E.F. At that time, machine tools were not able to be shipped from the U.S., and thus Dawes' staff managed to secure "all machine tools available in allied and neutral countries." This feat of acquisition and repair provided the "absolutely essential locomotive power impossible at the time to be obtained elsewhere." Statement of Charles G. Dawes, November 4, 1919, *Hearings Before the Subcommittee on Military Affairs, U.S. Senate, Reorganization of the Army,* Washington, D.C.: Government Printing Office, 1919, 1730.

45   Colonel Arthur Hale Woods (1870-1942) served as New York Police Commissioner in 1914. He worked for the Committee on Public Information and later worked for the U.S. War Department.

46   A variation of a nickname given to Pershing by his students at the United States Military Academy. The original nickname uses a racial slur. The nickname's origin was Pershing's brief command of the 10th U.S. Cavalry regiment, a unit comprised of African-American soldiers. The unit was one of several in the segregated U.S. military. Along with members of the 9th U.S. Cavalry regiment, the soldiers were often referred to as "Buffalo Soldiers" because of their deployment in the American west during military operations waged against Native Americans. Pershing is still referred to as "Black Jack," although the original nickname was not intended as a compliment to him, but rather to deride him for having "lowered" himself to command black soldiers. Adam P. Wilson, *African American Army Officers of World War I: A Vanguard of Equality in War and Beyond.* Jefferson, NC: McFarland and Company, Inc., 2015, 194.

47   Camille Marie Ragueneau (1868-1956).

48   Fritz van den Steen de Jehay.

49   CGD: The committee really did not realize what they were doing, in my judgment. They were badly advised, and had been treated so well by me that they became a little unbalanced, and misconstruing my amiability as weakness, tried a little horseback riding. The great majority of them did not mean to do anything detrimental to the service.

50   "After this, therefore, because of this." A saying that posits the illogical nature of one thing causing another, simply because it occurred afterward.

51   In January 1918, William enrolled at the Field Artillery School in

Saumur, France. He received a commission as a lieutenant in March 1918, and joined America's first heavy tank battalion, the 301st.

52   Charles Cutler Dawes (1899-1970), son of Rufus C. Dawes and brother of William Mills Dawes, enlisted in the 21st Engineers with his childhood friend, Norman Johnson. By the time General Dawes wrote this entry, both were already on their way to France. "Young Dawes and Chum on Way to France," *Chicago Daily Tribune,* December 22, 1917. See the essay "Homecoming" at the end of this volume for more about Charles Cutler Dawes and William Mills Dawes.

53   James Franklin Bell (1856-1919), commander of the 77th Division, was sent to France in December 1918 to report on conditions. A West Point graduate, Bell served as Chief of Staff of the U.S. Army from 1906-1910. *History of the Seventy-Seventh Division, August 25th, 1917 to November 11th, 1918.* New York: The 77th Division Association, 1919, 163-164.

54   Robert Lee commanded the First Division from December 1917 through July 1918. Thereafter he was in command of the Second Army. As of the date of this entry in Dawes' journal, units from the First Division had already taken casualties, a result of their rotation in and out of the trenches—and combat—since October 1917. The 26th Division would enter into combat in April 1918, near the town of St. Mihiel. That encounter left the unit with 634 casualties.

55   General Tasker H. Bliss (1853-1930) was a graduate of the United States Military Academy, with many years of military experience, including service in the Spanish American War. He served as the Chief of Staff of the U.S. Army from September 1917 to May 1918. In November 1917, he was appointed to serve as the American Permanent Military Representative on the Supreme War Council. After the war he served as a member of the American delegation to the Paris Peace Conference. He was awarded the Distinguished Service Medal.

56   Pershing would continue to be obdurate.

57   French composer Jules Massenet's (1842–1912) opera, *Thaïs,* premiered in Paris in 1894.

58   John Price Jackson (1868-?) was professor and later dean in the School of Engineering at Penn State College. He was serving as Pennsylvania Commissioner of Labor and Industry when he was commissioned as a major in the Engineering Section of the Officers Reserve Corps of the U.S. Army. He arrived in France in November 1917. Throughout 1918, he would serve as chief of the Labor Board, and after the armistice, he assumed a number of different duties before returning to the U.S. in November 1919. *Penn State in the World War.* State College, PA: Alumni Association of the Pennsylvania State College, 1921, 37-38.

59   Maurice Ganne headed the *Office Central des Relations Franco-Américaines* until May 1918 when André Tardieu (1876-1945) took the helm. Statement of Charles G. Dawes, November 4, 1919, *Hearings Before the Subcommittee on Military Affairs, U.S. Senate, Reorganization of the Army,* 1919, 1740-1741. In both his journal

and in his Senate testimony of 1919, Dawes was full of praise for the work of the *Office Central des Relations Franco-Américaines,* but privately he did not care for Tardieu at times. He would later expunge comments concerning Tardieu from the published version of his journal. His original entries include an observation that Tardieu was trying to "usurp the work of the War Trade Board" and that he was hampered by "personal ambition." "This is no day for nonsense," Dawes wrote of Tardieu's antics. Tardieu went on to serve three separate terms of as the Prime Minister of France. (See below for more on Tardieu.) Dawes, Manuscript, np.

60   F[ranklin] W[arner] M. Cutcheon (1864-1936) was a New York lawyer with the firm Byrne, Cutcheon and Taylor. In 1917, he volunteered to work with the American Red Cross and was appointed acting head of the Department of Military Relief. *The Red Cross Bulletin,* August 20, 1917, 4. Later, in November 1917, he was appointed Secretary General of the American Red Cross. "Appoints F.W.M. Cutcheon," *New York Times,* November 4, 1917. On December 13, 1917, he received a commission as captain, was assigned to Pershing's general staff, and sailed for France. He worked on the staff of the Purchasing Board under Dawes, and later was appointed to use his legal expertise as chairman of the Board of Contracts and Adjustments, created on February 14, 1918. His work in this role took him to various countries, negotiating on behalf of the U.S. He was awarded the Distinguished Service Medal for his work during the war. After the war, he was appointed to the Reparation Commission, working under Charles Gates Dawes. "News from the Classes," *The Michigan Alumnus,* January 7, 1928, 292. For a detailed account of his career, including his work for Dawes, see James Byrne, *Memorial of Franklin Warner M. Cutcheon.* New York: Committee on Memorials of the Association of the Bar of the City of New York, 1937.

61   Peyton Conway March (1864-1955), a graduate of the United States Military Academy, had a long military career prior to World War I. During the war, he served as commander of the 1st Field Artillery Brigade, First Division, before being promoted to major general and commander of the artillery units of the U.S. First Army and all non-divisional artillery units. Dawes' mention of March's imminent departure for America might well have been owing to the sad fact that in February 1918, March's son, Peyton March, Jr. (1896-1918), a 2nd lieutenant in the Air Corps, died following a plane crash in Texas. In March 1918, March would assume the position of Army Chief of Staff, a position he would hold until 1921.

62   William Giles Harding Carter (1851-1925) served in the American Civil War and the Spanish American War. He was also active in the "Indian Wars" (against Native Americans) in the American Southwest. He was recipient of the Medal of Honor in 1881. He played a central role in the modernizing of the U.S. military, and was the author of several histories.

63   Commanding General, Services of the Rear.

64   Commander-in-Chief.

65   CGD: "Principles of Army Purchase and Supply as suggested by Experience of American Expeditionary Force in France." [Ed. See Appendix A.]

66   Francis Joseph Kernan (1859-1949) was a graduate of the United States Military Academy with a long military career. From May to August 1917, he served as Acting Assistant Chief of Staff, and then briefly served as a commander of Camp Wheeler and Camp Macon, in Georgia. In November 1917, he was appointed to oversee the U.S. Services of Supply in France, a post he held through July 1918. During the Paris Peace talks he was an advisor to the U.S. delegation.

67   Services of the Rear. See note directly below.

68   Commanding General, Services of Supply. The Services of Supply was officially organized on February 16, 1918. Prior to that date it had been known as the Services of the Rear. U.S. War Department, *Organization of the Services of Supply,* Washington, D.C.: Government Printing Office, 1921, 26.

69   On March 3, 1918, Russia signed a treaty with Germany, ending its participation in the war. Bolstered by fifty divisions of troops freed from combat with Russia, the German military launched what was known as the "Spring Offensive." On March 21, 1918, German troops began to attack along the Western Front, gaining more ground than it had since the war's start in 1914.

70   Dawes' original manuscript includes the names which were expunged from the published journal. The "failure" is noted in that original text as "Willard"— most likely Daniel Willard (1861-1942). President of the B&O Railroad, Willard was appointed by President Wilson in November 1917 to serve as chair of the War Industries Board. He left that post in January 1918. Dawes, Manuscript, np.

71   Thomas Nelson Page (1853-1922) was "pathetic," according to Dawes. Page was the U.S. Ambassador to Italy, serving in that post from 1913 to 1920. Dawes, Manuscript, np.

72   Again, Thomas Nelson Page. Dawes, Manuscript, np.

73   CGD: This only covers my personal opinion of those with whom I came in contact in army supply procurement matters.

74   William Gibbs McAdoo, Jr., (1863-1941) U. S. Secretary of the Treasury, 1913-1918.

75   On March 29, 1918, the St. Gervais et St. Protais Church at 13 Rue des Barres in Paris was shelled. The roof collapsed during a Good Friday service. Ninety-one people were killed and 68 were wounded.

76   The famous 69th Infantry Regiment, known since the American Civil War as the "Fighting Sixty-Ninth," arrived in France in November 1917 as part of the 42nd "Rainbow" Division. On February 26, 1918, in the woods known as Rouge Bouget, near the town of Baccarat, the unit came under fire for the first time. Along with other combat deaths, the unit suffered the deaths of 21 men when a dugout collapsed during bombardment. During the war, the unit suffered 644 killed in action and 2,587 wounded (200 of whom would later die of their

wounds) during the 164 days of combat the unit saw.

77   Pershing did not so much "offer" the American army to the French, as he did agree to the subordination of American forces under the leadership of a Supreme Allied Commander. As a response to the dire situation following the Germans' launch of the Spring Offensive, representatives of the Allies agreed to appoint Ferdinand Foch Supreme Allied Commander. The agreement, signed April 3, 1918, read: "Gen. Foch is charged by the British, French, and American Governments with the coordination of the action of the Allied Armies on the Western Front; to this end there is conferred on him all the powers necessary for its effective realization. To the same end, the British, French, and American Governments confide in Gen. Foch the strategic direction of military operations. The Commander-in-Chief of the British, French, and American Armies will exercise to the fullest extent the tactical direction of their armies. Each Commander-in-Chief will have the right to appeal to his Government, if in his opinion his Army is placed in danger by the instructions received from Gen. Foch." President Wilson approved the agreement on April 16, 1918. John J. Pershing, *Final Report of General John J. Pershing*. Washington, D.C.: Government Printing Office, 1919, 31.

78   CGD: *Au cours d'une reunion qui fut tenue le 28 mars 1918, sur le front et a laquelle assistaient le general Pétain, M. Clemenceau, et M. Loucheur, le general Pershing s'est presente au general Foch et lui a dit: "Je viens pour vous dire que le peuple Americain tiendrait a grand honneur que nos troupes fussent engagees dans la presente bataille. Je vous le demande en mon nom et au sien. Il n'y a pas en ce moment d'autre question que de combattre. L'infanterie, l'artillerie, l'aviation, tout ce que nous avons est a vous. Disposez-en comme il vous plaira. Il en viendra encore d'autres, aussi nombreux qu'il sera necessaire. Je suis venu tout expres pour vous dire que le peuple Americain serait fier d'etre engage dans la plus belle bataille de l'Histoire."* ("I have come to tell you that the American people will hold it a high honour that their troops should take part in the present battle. I ask you to permit this in my name and in theirs. At the present moment there is only one thing to do, to fight. Infantry, artillery, aeroplanes - all that I have I put at your disposal - do what you like with them. More will come - in fact, all that may be necessary. I have come expressly to tell you that the American people will be proud to take part in this, the greatest and most striking battle of history.")

79   Harry Pomery Davison, Sr. (1867-1922) was a banker and senior partner at J.P. Morgan and Company. During the war he served as chairman of the War Council of the American Red Cross. For his work he was awarded the Distinguished Service Medal.

80   National Army.

81   See Appendix C for Dawes' letter to Pershing, dated April 13, 1918, from the General Purchasing Agent, A.E.F. to the Commander-in-Chief, A.E.F. Subject: Military control, allied service of supply. (Dawes also includes this letter in the text of *A Journal of the Great War.*)

82   The First Division was organized in May 1917 and units from the division would arrive in France beginning in June 1917 through December 1917. On July 4, 1917, it was members of the First Division who marched with Pershing to Lafayette's tomb in Paris. In October 1917, the first American casualties were suffered by soldiers from the First Division. In April 1917, the First Division was deployed on the Western Front in support of a beleaguered French Army. The resulting battle of Cantigny ended with the first American victory on the Western Front.

Section 3

April 16, 1918 ~ August 16, 1918

GENERAL PERSHING ADDRESSING THE OFFICERS OF THE 1ST DIVISION AT CHAUMONT-EN-VEXIN
APRIL 16, 1918, JUST PRIOR TO THEIR ENTRY INTO BATTLE
General Robert Lee Bullard commanding the division stands at left of picture in fur coat

Paris, Tuesday night, April 16, 1918

General Pershing sent his automobile for me at 8.30 A.M., and at 9 A.M. we left for Chaumont-en-Vexin, the present headquarters of the First Division, Major-General Bullard commanding. Colonel Boyd and Captain de Marenches followed in a second automobile. Arrived at about 10.30. In the rear of General Bullard's headquarters were gathered the commissioned officers of the First Division — about 1,000, I should say.[1] The General (Pershing) addressed them, as they leave for battle (any time — probably to-morrow night) — our first division to be engaged in the great struggle which is now going on. It was a solemn occasion and an historical one. It marks the real entry of our nation into actual battle. General Pershing, in a few simple words, gave his message, and that of the President and the American people, of confidence in them and what they would do to uphold the traditions of their country. General Bullard afterwards said a few words. There was no effort on the part of either to be dramatic — the scene and occasion required no emphasis. They were a magnificent body of men. They are to give of their blood and young lives in the cause. They were as every American would expect them to be — calm, intensely earnest, and confident. I met many friends among the officers — Bertie McCormick[2] among the others, who asked me to do certain things if anything happened to him. Young Mayo of Evanston was there.[3] There we were joined by General Harbord and went to General Duncan's headquarters for lunch.

After a hurried lunch we left for General Foch's headquarters at Sarcus. He had asked Pershing to get there as soon as possible, as he had to leave at 3 P.M. to meet Haig at Abbeville. On arrival at the little town and small brick building where Foch was, the General took me in with him and introduced me to General Foch, who strikes me as very alert and very cool. I was not present at the conference, but John told me about it as we rode back to Paris together. It was in reference to our troops — what we should give and when. While we were there the guns of the French were sounding in the distance. Foch is confident.

On the way back General Pershing and I discussed military unification of the Allied rear much of the time. Harbord had written John of my views, but seems hesitant in his opinions of them. It must come, if we are to fight at our best. In this I believe the Commander-in-Chief fully and entirely concurs; but as the responsibility is upon him he must consider the matter in all its phases. No one in the A.E.F. is more in touch with the Allied supply situation than is my office, and I am feeling now a pressure of a great emergency. Let the Germans advance ten more miles and there will be no argument then. It will be done immediately. It will have to be done then. Then surely it ought to be done now. If it is the best step for relief after disaster, it is the best step now to avert it.

We arrived at John's house at about 6.30 P.M. Harbord, Boyd, and de Marenches went to dinner with me. The General went to work. He has every confidence in Foch. On most of our long ride we talked over war matters. He says he is ordering combatant troops rapidly to the front, trusting to me to fill their places by our rapidly recruiting labor corps. It was an important and solemn day. In a few days the splendid First Division will be in the fiercest and greatest battle of history. No one who knows them can doubt them. God be with them, and those of them so soon to die. I shall never forget them, whatever may become of them, as I saw them to-day.

Paris, Wednesday, April 17 (Night, 11 P.M.)

I think I should keep notes, for General Pershing's sake, of what he is considering and the environment under which he plans. Upon some of his decisions, soon to be made, depends the outcome of the present war, in all probability. Whatever may be the result of his decisions, this contemporaneous record of what confronts him should be made by some one. It cannot be made by him, for a man cannot be General and historian at the same time.

In the General's bedroom to-night (Rue de Varenne) — he is suffering from a cold contracted on our trip yesterday— he went over matters fully. Haig is calling him for a conference. What Haig wants is men — Americans — to be fed into his hard-pressed army. He maintains that unless he has a minimum soon of 150,000, and more later, his army may not be able to withstand the tremendous onslaught of the numerically superior enemy. He is being pressed in around the Channel ports. General Pershing must decide for himself Haig's real situation, and the full nature of the apparent emergency. The rate of destruction of men is so great that once in, the American 150,000 will be so reduced in numbers by counter-attacking that the foundation of the American military organization now forming will be largely destroyed. If the emergency is such that it seems necessary, the men will be fed in; if the emergency seems less acute than represented, more care can be had for the relation of present American losses to the future military effectiveness of the American section of the Allied forces. The General, and he alone, must decide in the next few days to what extent immediate amalgamation of American forces into the English army is necessary. With the natural intense desire of an American and an army commander for the preservation of national and personal independence, he yet will fearlessly make any decision inconsistent with their preservation which is necessary to ultimate victory or the escape from an immediate Allied defeat. If the emergency, in his judgment, does not involve immediate Allied disaster (after a personal inspection of the battle area), he must preserve from unnecessary destruction, as far as possible for the future of the war, the existing vital germ now here of the future vast army of the United States. This is what he tells me — and whatever his action, these are the principles which will control it. It is due to him to state them now *"in medias res."* His head is very cool. His judgment will be formed from conditions and facts uninfluenced by emotionalism, politics, ambition, or personal considerations of any kind. After three hours of a visit with him alone, all of which were devoted to a discussion of the situation, I came away knowing that he is the one American to be in his present place. He says again that Foch is very confident.

Am a little worried for fear of pneumonia attacking him, and made him promise to get a doctor to-morrow if he did not feel better. He wants to start for Haig's headquarters to-morrow. John expects to have fifteen divisions by June. Men are coming rapidly.[4] But of the men now going into the English and French battle lines it can be said that, though their numbers may be comparatively few, they may yet determine which way the balance of the nations shall swing.

Paris, Thursday night, April 18, 1918 (10.30 P.M.)

General Pershing sent word (telephone from Colonel Boyd) this evening to come again to his house. I had had another conference with him at his house this noon on the subject of military unification of the entire Allied service of supply along the lines of my April 13 letter. Pershing in the afternoon called on Clemenceau (also Milner).[5] He is to meet Haig to-morrow evening, but has not yet seen him in the matter of the new plan. General Pershing announced to me this evening that he had finally and definitely settled on a demand for the central military control of the Allied supply and transportation system; that he had proposed it to Clemenceau this afternoon; that the latter had immediately accepted it in principle, wondering (he said) why some one had not thought of it before; that Clemenceau had asked for a written statement of the idea for study which he (John) was preparing; that he (John) proposed to name me in his letter to the French to represent him in the formulation of the plan; that Clemenceau and he had agreed to pool for the French and Americans whether the English would come in or not (subject, of course, to approval of the President and War Department); that he (John) would see Haig to-morrow, but whether Haig approved or not would leave for England to urge it on the Government immediately after seeing Haig; that he (John) was preparing a cable[6] to the War Department which he would send to-morrow stating his intentions and reasons and asking approval of the extension of his General Purchasing Board principle (devised by himself) to the Allied service of supply and transportation and of his demand for it.

We discussed the matter further. The idea is to put a military control and military methods in the place of civil control and civil methods which have failed. The Supreme War Council has been a supreme failure. Our idea is that a General — one man — must take the place of the Supreme War Council. The latter never gets anywhere. Every reason in the world exists for the creation of an authority sought to be reached by the Supreme War Council. It has failed to exercise it effectively. Therefore its authority must be placed where it can be properly wielded. When this plan goes into effect, it means that military authority must practically control civil activities and civil bodies; that we shall control tonnage as a necessary result of the condition created; that order will come out of this chaos at the rear, and that we shall commence to win the war.

I do not want to criticize English obstinacy — thank God for it! It saved the Marne[7] — it is saving the Channel ports. It has justified and glorified itself in the blood of hundreds of thousands. But that obstinacy must now be broken. It must not lose us this war after having made victory possible. I pray God that the English may come in with the French and Americans without delay on this plan. If they do not, we must go ahead as best we can. But no other man can so forcibly present to the English their duty as General Pershing. In every great crisis where the great principles of human freedom have hung in the balance the great and fearless leader has appeared. In this one it is John.

Paris, April 21, 1918 (Sunday night)

The General sent me copies of his letter to Clemenceau and his cable to the War Department before he left for England. Am giving thought to the method of presenting plan to the French if summoned in accordance with the General's suggestion to Clemenceau.

My mind has been on so many important things that this evening it reverts to some of the amusing things of which one must train one's self to think in these times of horror. With all his grasp of the great things of military operation and organization, General Pershing by no means overlooks the important relations of some little things to a general scheme. His mind is certainly open to details, no matter how impressive the surroundings. My own somewhat pronounced indifference to certain military conventions, born as often of ignorance as of intention, — though not always, — is a matter at times of some embarrassment to him. After he had finished his conference with General Foch, he was standing across the road from me and some Frenchmen, with General Harbord, waiting for Foch to take his automobile for his trip to Abbeville to see Haig. This was last week. I saw him looking at me, notwithstanding the sound of the cannon, and the general surroundings, with the look of mingled friendliness, admonition, and concern which characterizes his expression during some of my interviews with his better-disciplined military associates. It led me to make a hasty self-appraisement of my attitude, in which, however, I could surmise no fault. He spoke to Harbord and the latter walked across the road to me. As Harbord carefully buttoned up my overcoat, which was opened, including the hooks at the top, he murmured in my ear, "This is a hell of a job for the Chief of Staff — but the General told me to do it."

Some soldiers told me that in England there was a Kodak taken of John with one breast-pocket unbuttoned. For this picture I am going to search that country — to use it for justifiable defensive personal purposes.[8]

Paris, Friday, April 26, 1918

I must keep note of these important things. General Pershing returned from England and I saw him to-day before and after Loucheur[9] called on him in reference to his letter to Clemenceau relative to joining the supply services of the Allies. It was agreed between Pershing and Loucheur that Clemenceau was to answer General Pershing's letter naming Loucheur to meet me to discuss methods. Before leaving for England, Pershing saw Haig and told him of the plan. Haig immediately began to raise objections. I do not like to criticize this great soldier. It may be unfair to assume that his reluctance to cede military authority either at the front or rear is in any way based upon the thought of its effect upon his personal prestige. I shall not do so — I really do not feel sure about it; but I feel a pride in the fact that no one can have such doubts about the personal unselfishness of our own leader. I feel as sure of the willingness of General Pershing to make a sacrifice of personal prestige for the sake of the common good as I should of Abraham Lincoln if he were in his place. And that is the most any one could say. General Pershing said that when he took up the matter with Lloyd George the latter agreed as to its advisability; but stated the difficulties with which he had contended in analogous efforts arising out of the perpetual strength of the English status quo in matters of authority and its location. Lloyd George spoke of General Nash, the English director of transportation, as one who would certainly favor it. Pershing said that he was going to write Lloyd George (this was just after his interview at his house with Loucheur this afternoon) stating that we — the Americans and French — were going ahead anyway.

From what he said it is General Pershing's present intention, after the plan is approved by him and Clemenceau, after being formulated by Loucheur and myself, to place upon me the responsibility of being his representative with the French which will automatically make my organization the instrument of coordination so far as the A.E.F. is concerned. He doubts whether the French will part with any large part of civil control of supply to their own military organization— that is, any considerably larger control than at present. If so, I must accept at first the present French machinery without much change as that with which to start cooperation along the new lines. But it is the General's hope and my own that once in continual contact with French authority, their views and my own as to the future steps best to be taken may not prove to be very divergent. Surely after we take some of the most important steps, the perception of their mutual benefit in the increase of our military effectiveness must make it difficult, and increasingly difficult as time goes on, for personal ambition and ulterior purpose to keep in existence machinery interfering with them. We have our backs to the wall. Each one must do his part. If he does not willingly do it, he must be made to do it. And there is no force in the world so potent in time of emergency and great crisis as a clear reason, fearlessly stated.

As a memorandum for the General's consideration I gave him my line of thought as to the way in which to proceed immediately — for if we leave this thing to the Supreme Council or to general discussion before decision, it will as usual require a few more defeats and thousands of lives to bring about its adoption.

Yesterday went over the graphics of the A.E.F. with Logan,[10] who is here. Logan has a great mind. But no one has at the same time not only the comprehensive grasp of the problem but the power of using his knowledge in correct decision and action that General Pershing has.

Paris, April 27, 1918

It is midnight and I ought to go to bed, but I shall regret it some time if I do not make contemporaneous notes of these things. Have just returned after five hours with General Pershing. At dinner the General and I put through "a course of sprouts"[11] in endeavoring to get a more virile cooperation from him in helping us to secure army necessities — in particular the Italian militarized labor. He agreed to another effort. In reply to a vigorous statement by General Pershing of the views he would like to present to ----- , who should be aggressive instead of pathetically mild in time of emergency. ----- said, "You might as well throw baseballs at a feather bed."[12]

The General and I, when we were alone again, discussed the military unification of the Allied rear. He is firm that it should be wholly military. Before Loucheur sees me the General (in his mind to-night) has decided to write notifying General Foch that he is ready to place our supply service at his disposal — thus tending to short-circuit what Loucheur is certain to propose, that American military machinery be coordinated with the semi-military and civil French machinery of supply. The idea is to establish by this letter a status quo with the French internally favorable to complete militarization in place of one now unfavorable to it. Listened to the verbal report to the General of Major Clark, liaison officer at French G.H.Q., in from the front. The General also read me his written report. The French are feeling bad about the loss of Mount [sic] Kemmel;[13] are criticizing the British against whom the whole German army is pressing; are confident, however, that the line will hold; feel (claim) that the British are holding 700,000 men under arms in Great Britain which should be in the fighting line (to which General Pershing remarked that that was absurd); feel that time for counter-attacking is almost at hand. General Pershing told Clark to state to French G.H.Q. that they were in error relative to the number of English armed troops in England, and that the six American divisions now coming to the English, which the French would like to have in their line, come in English tonnage under an arrangement made some months ago with Pétain's acquiescence.

I write all this as indicating the atmosphere in which we live. Pershing gave me estimate of losses thus far in the offensive as about 400,000 Germans, 250,000 for the English and 60,000 for the French. The use of tonnage for troop carrying purposes almost exclusively should enable the English and ourselves to bring over from the United States 200,000 to 250,000 troops per month for three months after the six divisions are landed. By fall, therefore, the United States should have 1,000,000 men here. Pershing told Clark to tell this to the French. He received detailed report from Clark as to location, movements, etc., of our American troops.

This morning met members of the U.S. Shipping Board — Stevens, Sherman, Rublee, and Morrow.[14] Called on them at Crillon Hotel. Afterwards they called on me at my headquarters. Received telegram from Smithers, [sic][15] H.Q., S.O.S., that War Department has authorized the organization of 200 administrative labor companies by me. For this they will give me 133 Captains, 133 First Lieutenants, 134 Second Lieutenants, 1,000 Sergeants, and 2,000 Corporals. With these officers I can handle 33,000 to 50,000

GENERAL PAYOT AND GENERAL DAWES AT ÉLYSÉE PALACE HOTEL HEADQUARTERS

MAJOR-GENERAL HARBORD, COMMANDING GENERAL SERVICE
OF SUPPLY, WITH THE GENERAL PURCHASING AGENT

labor troops easily. Have already secured about 15,000.

Paris, Sunday, April 28, 1918

Took lunch with General Pershing and spent most of the afternoon with him. At lunch were also General Crozier, Colonel Mott, and Colonel Boyd. Crozier, who had been to Italy, gave his opinions (which were favorable to action) on the matter of sending American troops to Italy, which General Pershing is again considering in connection with our conference with last night when we again urged that the United States use its advances to the Italians in assistance to us in getting labor. General Pershing, of course, cannot be determined in his decision by the comparatively unimportant matter of the labor; but since a favorable decision would probably settle the labor matter, if it is to be made, now is an opportune time. General Pershing discussed it at length in all its phases — from the standpoint of the immediate effect on Italian morale; from the standpoint of its ultimate effect on morale if undue expectations are aroused by the coming of a small number of troops at first and the fact that troops sufficient to be a military factor cannot be spared; from the point of view of the French and English (since we get more troops for the front by using labor from Italy to replace soldiers now at work, they will probably agree); from the standpoint of its possibly creating a false impression of the contemplated undue diffusion of American troops. After full discussion he was inclined to take the action after notifying Foch, feeling that the immediate effect on Italian morale is important enough to take some chances on the future — especially since the Italians are clamorous for the step.

When the General and I were by ourselves again we took up the procedure in the supply unification plan. He is sending Colonel Mott[16] out to see Foch, and get his ideas as to the extent to which he (Pershing) shall insist on French military authorities as the coordinators as distinguished from civil.

It was agreed that at my first interview with Loucheur I should handle the subject gingerly — as we are so anxious for complete supply coordination that we do not wish to make any ultimatums or propositions until every phase of the situation can be first carefully considered.

Paris, Friday, May 3, 1918 (night)

Harbord called by telephone from Chaumont yesterday morning saying that Clemenceau had asked me to meet Loucheur. Accordingly met him (Loucheur) at his office (Ministry Armament) at 4 P.M. yesterday. Took Lieutenant Chauncey McCormick as interpreter and Captain Barrington

Moore[17] to make notes of our agreements and discussion. Interview lasted about three quarters of an hour. I emphasized the military control feature. Loucheur very cordial in every way. Reached the agreement, which Moore has outlined, for submission to General Pershing and M. Clemenceau. Loucheur said he would not take the place — said Clemenceau desired an American. I strongly stated the reasons for the selection of a Frenchman, and it was agreed upon. Loucheur agreed to start between the French and Americans, inviting the British. Loucheur this morning sent his aide, Lieutenant de Neuflize, to change slightly the first draft of our report eliminating my reference to him as an acceptable choice. Took my copy to Pershing (who arrived late last night) at his house this morning. Spent most of the morning with him. He had taken up the matter with Clemenceau and Lloyd George at Abbeville on his trip and had arranged for a meeting at Clemenceau's office between him, General Travers Clarke, B.E.F. Quartermaster-General,[18] and myself for Monday afternoon, 3 P.M. The General told me he expected hereafter to be occupied largely at the front, leaving Allied coordination as affecting the rear under my direction. Discussed means for this. My suggestion was to form a new division of the General Staff — say Allied coordination division — making me Assistant Chief of Staff at the head of it, reporting to him. I could then order acts of coordination through directions, "by order General Pershing," without taking additional rank or being put in an unnecessarily conspicuous position, which I am very anxious to avoid, as I want to last through the war, and not sacrifice the permanent substance, for the temporary semblance, of power. I would then form my staff and coordinate our resources, construction, and transportation with our allies. The matter was left open until we shall have discussed it further with the Allies. Pershing says Clemenceau agrees to military control. Pershing, Clemenceau, and Lloyd George all seem to want to dodge the delays and discussion of the Allied Council and get started as soon as possible. I think nothing can stop it now — even if the Allied Council tried to expedite it.

Pershing told of his decision to send troops to Italy for the sake of influencing Italian morale — the French and English having approved. He notified Orlando at Abbeville. May start with a regiment and expects to build up to a division which was more than Orlando had hoped. He was somewhat impatient at the attitude of the French about our troops with the British as taken at the Abbeville meeting, and so expressed himself there. Expects 1,000,000 Americans in his army in France by the end of June.

If we get the Service of Supply of the Allies in a firm military control so as properly to use our resources, to match the military unification of control at the front, it will be the sure beginning of victory.

Varaigne[19] called on me at my room to tell me this evening that as a result of my visit with him, Jackson, and that good friend of our army, M. Ganne, on the President of the Council, Jeanneney,[20] the other day, the French had allotted us 5,000 additional laborers in addition to a liberal percentage of German prisoners.[21] This will give me a total of over 20,000 laborers in my organization. Am glad I succeeded in it, with Jackson's able assistance, before we amalgamate with the Allies. Labor, however, is one of the first things I hope to pool.

Gates took dinner with me. Got Cutcheon's well-deserved promotion to Lieutenant-Colonel at last.

Paris, May 9, 1918 (night)

I shall not make any extended notes of the inter-Ally conference of May 6 called to consider General Pershing's proposition to unify under military command the Allied rear, since Captain Moore's notes give a fair but very condensed summary of the meeting which consumed over three hours. I had assumed that only the B.E.F. Quartermaster-General, whom somebody had told me was General Travers Clarke, would represent England, but when we arrived England had Cowans[22] (Lt.-Gen., Q.M.G.),[23] General Crofton Atkins,[24] General Cannot, Sir Andrew Weir, and Sir J. W. Curry — a good battery well entrenched in conservatism. The Italian Q.M.G. for Italian troops in France was present. Colonel, of Foch's staff, Jeanneney, President of French Council of Ministers, and Ganne were there for the French. I appeared alone for the American army representing General Pershing. Had Captain Moore there to take notes and Chauncey McCormick as interpreter. By vigor and direct and forcible statement I soon dissipated the formal atmosphere which the weak always allow to retard their purposes.[25] Having the proposition to present gave me the direction of the argument for the most part.

Realizing that I must shake the English up thoroughly to start with, if we are to land anywhere, I tried to keep the minds of the conferees on the necessities of the immediate rear of the armies in coordination, and to prevent the English from focusing attention on the difficulties of a more widespread application of an unquestioned principle. I don't want to give an unfair picture of the attitude of these able leaders of England, but it was distinctly pessimistic as to the chances of success in securing agreement on the plan, to such an extent that one must assume on their part — or at least on the part of the members of the conference — an innate opposition. While agreeing on principles, they raised innumerable practical objections and difficulties. However, I did not become discouraged because little progress was made at this first meeting; but immediately went to work preparing an argument to the conference for the plan addressed to M. Jeanneney, the Chairman. This I sent out to General Pershing for suggestion and revision yesterday, and this evening received it back with his comments. I will to-morrow modify my references to the English as the General suggests and send it in for the consideration of the English and French Governments.

The General approves the argument. This afternoon at his request I met M. Loucheur, Minister of Armament, and discussed the situation. He agrees with me fully — and will send a representative to the next confer-ence to support me. In the meantime he and Clemenceau will consult and endeavor to expedite independent agreement between the French and American armies for S.O.S. coordination. The English at bottom are so splendid and fine that I do not fear for their full cooperation eventually. But they are careful, as they should be. My headquarters move from the old Hôtel Méditerranée to the Élysées Palace Hotel on the Champs Elysées to-morrow.

Letter to M. Jeanneney
Paris, May 8, 1918

To M. Jeanneney, President, Inter-Ally Conference of May 6, 1918 (called to consider General Pershing's proposition and plan for military unification of the Allied Services of Supply).

Relative to the three questions the conference proposed at its first meeting and in accordance with your suggestion that comments be filed thereon, I submit the following:

General Pershing's plan, in so far as it involves the coordination of military supply, transportation, and construction now located in the im-mediate Allied rear, is susceptible of adoption by the military commands as distinguished from the civil as a strictly military measure of coordination involving activities now wholly under military control, but as yet not coordi-nated between the three armies. To this extent the plan may be considered as presented by the Commander-in-Chief, A.E.F., as a measure of military action affecting the immediate rear, and therefore as only necessary in this particular phase to be discussed in its relation to the several existing military as distinguished from civil authorities.

The plan in its more general application, involving the coordination of activities now under civil control, must be first approved by the Government of the United States as well as by England and France. But since the first conference on this subject of prime importance has developed some hesi-tation as to their authority on the part of members of the conference, I deem it my duty as General Pershing's representative at this conference to place on file the following statement as applying simply to the coordination of the immediate activities of the Allied rear now possible under his plan if approved by the existing military authorities alone.

Before my submission to the conference of General Pershing's plan looking to the military unification of the services of the Allied rear to match the military unification at the front, he had obtained the verbal acceptance of the principle by M. Clemenceau and Mr. Lloyd George. The duty of this conference, therefore, was to devise a plan, not to suggest obstacles to its consummation — to which most of its time was devoted at the first meeting. The letter of General Pershing, addressed to myself and submitted to the conference, considered together with the detailed statement of his plan, indicated that his desire is such to secure military unification of the Services of Supply of the Allied rear, that while he would prefer final authority to be located in one man he would acquiesce in an agreement by which the military authority of the proposed committee could be set in motion only by the unanimous consent of its three members. This suggestion should of itself sweep away the objections raised at this conference to this procedure. General Pershing's contention is that if British and American lives can be trusted to French control so can British and American material. This military central control of Supply Service is as essential to maximum effectiveness of effort against the enemy as unified military control of the front. The recent reverses during the first days of the last offensive were sufficient to sweep away the arguments against Allied military unification suggested by national pride and prestige for the last four years. With the difficult months ahead of us, and the urgency of unity in action and mutual cooperation, minor considerations should not now be raised against a plan involving a principle so indisputably correct that it is immediately adopted upon presentation by those first in authority and committed to us to work out and not to combat.

Given a military control committee of three, one each representing the British, French, and American armies, with authority through military channels to collect full information and then with power to put into effect by military order a unanimous decision improving the coordination of the rear, what harm would result? If it did nothing else this military committee would be a clearing-house of information, thus facilitating the now clumsy efforts, born of overwhelming necessity, to coordinate the activities of the Allied rear. Each Government retaining its control over its member could, through his veto power, save from any possible alteration its entire system of intermingled civil and military control so jealously exploited in the discussions of this conference. So vast are the possible accomplishments of good from the military unification of the Allied Services of Supply, under one man or military committee, extending throughout England, France, Italy, and the United States, properly to be regarded as the "rear" in this effort, that we are instinctively prone to dwell constantly on the impossibility of obtaining it, overlooking the possibilities of obtaining most important advantages in the immediate rear of the armies without necessarily cutting any governmental system of internal red tape and using only existing military authority.

As charged by General Pershing with the duty of making recommendations to him looking toward the coordination with our allies of the army activities of the American rear, if this military committee is formed, and even if contrary to his advice its military authority could not be set in motion except by unanimous consent, I would ask and expect from it unanimous action resulting in the transmission of the necessary orders as follows:

(1) Ordering information from the departments concerned of the three armies as to the status of the present warehouse capacity of the three armies in France, and if it is found sufficient to provide for the present and future requirements of the Allied armies considered as one, an order to the American army not to waste tonnage, material, work, and men in building new warehouses where sufficient empty warehouse space exists.

(2) Ordering information from the concerned departments of the three armies as to the total present unloading capacity of the docks of France (including transportation from the docks to the front of the unified Allied army) and the amount of material now being transported to the front from these docks so that it may be intelligently determined whether the American army is building unnecessary docks and thus diverting material, work, and men from more important service.

(3) Information ordered from the three concerned departments of the total amount of civilian and militarized labor now at the disposal of the three armies, so that if it were ascertained that the present supply, if used in proper coordination, is sufficient, orders be issued for its proper use and for the A.E.F. to cease the continued importation of civilian labor from adjoining countries, thus putting a further tax upon the local resources of France.

(4) Ordering information from the concerned departments of the three armies as to the present status of motor transports in France, and, upon the development of the situation, the issuance of immediate orders preventing any one army from consuming shipping space by bringing camions to France when sufficient are available or can be manufactured here for the unified army at the front.

(5) Information with appropriate orders as to whether central distributing depots for the joint use of the three armies do not now exist to that

extent which will render possible an intelligent reduction of American construction projects in this connection.

(6) Information with appropriate orders as to the collective situation of freight cars and locomotives, the use to which they are being put at present, whether economical to that effect as would render it impossible for us to cut down requisitions of this nature from America.

(7) Obtaining information regarding normal supplies common to the three armies with a view to their equitable distribution as needed, in order to prevent unnecessary use of tonnage, to accumulate unusual quantities during the present crisis in shipping.

(8) And many more subjects of importance — the above being only a few important illustrations.

That the members of this conference, instead of devoting themselves to a discussion of the methods necessary to carry out a plan accepted in principle by the Prime Ministers of England and France and proposed by the Commander-in-Chief, A.E.F., confined themselves chiefly to the suggestion of the obvious difficulties in the way of a complete international application of the idea, resulted in this first conference in a comparative lack of discussion of certain practicable steps of greatest importance related to the immediate rear of the armies. General Pershing has made this proposition in no spirit of distrust. It must be realized, however, that if as suggested at this conference the partial pooling of supplies and resources now going on under the pressure of necessity is continued through subordinate or separate controls as distinguished from a military central control, an insuperable obstacle is raised to a fair and complete solution of the problem. This insuperable obstacle to complete perception of the necessities of a common situation and the application of the necessary remedies in connection with it lies in the fidelity of the subordinate in charge of a particular supply to the unit which he supplies. The conception of such a subordinate of a common necessity is determined primarily by its effect upon the need with whose satisfaction he is charged as a matter of military duty.

While the disposition seems to exist to combat the logical extension of the idea of authority in this time of emergency and war to a military dictatorship of the entire Allied Service of Supply, as suggested by General Pershing, it is well to point out that if that idea was accepted by the three Governments, the central authority being charged with the responsibility for the whole would conceive and carry out these responsibilities in terms of the whole and not in terms of three separate armies. Is it possible that France, England, and the United States will trust under French command their men and hesitate at trusting their material? This question must not be discussed except upon the assumption that if the central control is established it will be impartially administered. Objections to it must be upon the ground alone of the impossibility of creating the machinery.

If I have wrongly interpreted the conservatism in this conference it is not because of any lack of appreciation of the spirit of cooperation, as evidenced by the treatment which the Americans have received from Services of Supply in France. Generosity and quick response to our suggestion of any necessity have ever marked the attitude of our allies. All freely bring to the common cause the limit of resources in wealth and precious lives. The people from the highest to the lowest are one in complete self-sacrifice. The question, therefore, is only one of natural steadfastness and conservatism. But this conservatism and steadfastness should not now be allowed to interfere with the consummation of the common victory. General Pershing has placed his authority over his military Service of Supply at the disposal of the Allies for its proper coordination and to insure the maximum effort against the enemy. This action on his part is the highest expression of his confidence in the justice and fairness of our allies and is the best indication of his belief that the plan which he has proposed, notwithstanding all the arguments raised at this conference against it, is possible of accomplishment if it is met in a similar spirit.

In conclusion, let me say that the matters to which I am calling specific attention and which demand coordination, are matters affecting the immediate military rear of the armies. The authority to create the military central control, absolutely necessary to deal with them effectively, exists or can be made to exist in this conference by the delegation of existing military authority alone.

As military men we have no right to screen our responsibilities for a bad situation as regards coordination in the immediate rear of the armies by raising smoke about civil interference and extending unduly the scope of the discussion of a comprehensive and unquestioned principle. It is our fault and our fault alone if we do not correct the situation. Civil governments have delegated us both duty and a full authority with which to accomplish it. Concessions of independent military authority must be made to a central control. The American Commander-in-Chief in his plan places his at the disposal of the Allies. The present lack of military coordination of the Allied Services of Supply of the immediate rear of the armies prevents the maximum use of our military resources against a thoroughly consolidated enemy. If as military men we fail to correct this we are responsible in blood and lives and possibly defeat — and we alone.

Charles G. Dawes
Colonel, Engineers, N.A.

Paris, Sunday night, May 12, 1918

By my letter, revised and improved by General Pershing, to M. Jeanneney, President of the Inter-Allied Conference, called to discuss the military unification of the rear of the armies, I think I have taken away the last ground for English opposition to it. At the conference the English evidently feared to depart from the *status quo.* Any one who desires to maintain the military and economic *status quo* of the Allies has, I notice, a desire to refer the matter under discussion to the Supreme War Council. By the time that august body is ready to apply a remedy, the need for it has generally passed. The patient dies before the doctors can decide as to the medicine he needs. But my letter, it seems to me, makes it impossible for England not to acquiesce.

Cravath[26] came over from England to get information about the General's plan and to ascertain what relation it had to the field of activities of certain civil boards and plans. He asked me to meet him, Loucheur, and Clementel[27] (Minister of Commerce, France) at Loucheur's office yesterday morning, which I did. I explained that while the principle of the plan could be beneficially extended over civil cooperation with the armies, the idea was to inaugurate it in military fields and by military authority alone. It therefore would not interfere with the civil work now going on, but only make it more effective by a more intelligent and proper use of its results. I think — for he so stated — that I satisfied this able and useful man, and turned him from a tendency to question into an advocate of English cooperation under the agreement — or suggestion, rather — that a unanimous agreement of the members of the proposed board be essential to put its military authority into action. Cravath has large influence with the English, and great ability and energy. I value most highly his judgment.

This (Sunday) evening General Patrick,[28] whom General Pershing has asked to assume charge of aviation, dined with me, having stopped on his way back to Tours from Chaumont to ask some questions as to the ability and qualifications of certain men whom he contemplates using in reorganization of the Aviation Department — the best and one of the most serious organization problems of our service. Am glad it is going into General Patrick's hands.

Paris, Thursday, May 16, 1918 (night)

On Thursday afternoon the second meeting of our inter-ally conference on the subject was held. The English were not present, having filed a written statement of their views. I had also filed mine, having previously delivered it to M. Jeanneney and to M. Loucheur, who had it when they prepared the French note which was presented at the meeting of the conference. M. Clemenceau was present and presided, stating that he had come because of the great importance of our subject to his Government. I took Captain Moore, who acts as my secretary, and my nephew Gates with me to the meeting. The principal French ministers, some French military officers, and General Merrone, the Italian Quartermaster-General in France, were present. I sat by M. Clemenceau, who read the French note, which was our plan of a military committee acting by unanimous agreement (in order to bring in the English in the future), and an added plan for extension of the principle as General Pershing had suggested to civil authorities and activities, which, of course, was not possible of authoritative acceptance without the approval of the United States Government. Was very careful not to commit General Pershing any further than his military authority extended. The discussion extended over some two hours. Arranged at the meeting for the French and Americans to proceed on unification of their rear so far as military authority will permit. Also arranged with Loucheur for meeting at which to provide for pooling behind our lines of American and French ammunition and wired Colonel Moseley,[29] of the General Staff, 4th Bureau, A.E.F., to meet Loucheur, the French artillery military authorities from the front, and myself, at Loucheur's office this afternoon. At this conference this afternoon ammunition pooling behind the lines was agreed upon. We also discussed the details of carrying out our general plan which I am to discuss with General Pershing to-morrow. Arranged with Loucheur to hold the announcement by the French to the English Government of the plan as agreed upon by the French and ourselves at the Tuesday meeting until I could revise it to be certain that in its statement to the English it clearly stated the limits and nature of the military authority under which the military control committee proposed to start functioning.

Am in so many important conferences that I despair of making these notes anywhere near complete, but hope to keep up a general outline of the methods by which we proceed.

Nearly 1,000 men gassed and killed and wounded out of one regiment in the First Division the other day — mustard gas.[30] Air raid on Paris last night — not much to speak of. They have become more infrequent. The long-range gun, too, seems to have been put out of commission by the French artillery. The General has been at the front — wires he will arrive here to-morrow. We are located in the Élysée Palace Hotel with the General Purchasing Board and my Staff, having moved from the Mediterranee. General Patrick called on me the other evening to discuss aviation which he will soon take over.

Paris, May 23, 1918

I have not written for some days because I wanted to record the emergence of General Pershing's plan from the fog which, after its adoption by the conference, was thrown around it by the reports of the conference drawn up by the French which did not clearly outline the division between what was adopted and what was simply discussed. Yesterday General Pershing drew up a simple restatement of the plan and took it to Clemenceau and the two signed it. This paper will go to the British and Italian Governments in place of the statements prepared by Loucheur and Lavit, which had been submitted to me for suggestion and revision. As soon as I received Lavit's statement, which it was proposed to send to the English, I realized that in effect it subordinated principles to the discussion of details to carry them out, and that if it went to the English, even corrected so as to make it clear that the American military authority alone as distinguished from civil was being coordinated, it would probably cause serious if not fatal obstructions to their acquiescence. Accordingly in an effort to clarify and simplify things I prepared a report to General Pershing of what actually was agreed upon at the conference, which I submitted to Loucheur, and which in its statements was revised by the General himself. Loucheur at first agreed to my report as being a proper form of statement after some suggestions had been incorporated to make the plan accord with French administrative authority. The idea was to have the report go to the English as simplifying things.

But the next day Loucheur, who had taken the report to submit to Clemenceau, sent me another statement drawn by himself likewise including details which might induce dangerous delay through discussion even to the extent of endangering the adoption of the principle. So I spent an anxious evening with the General (Pershing), and found him even more convinced than myself that the statement which Loucheur prepared might if presented destroy the chances of the plan's adoption by all. The General decided to make an effort with Clemenceau to clear the fog away. On May 21 (day before yesterday) Colonel DeGrailly, representing Loucheur, called on me stating that upon reconsideration Loucheur thought his own statement inexpedient, and that the principles having been adopted we had better leave the details of the method of applying them to our mutual agreement as time developed their need without endeavoring to make a preliminary agreement upon an outline of them. This wise decision made by Loucheur himself lifted a weight of anxiety from me, as the whole plan after this terrible month of effort was hanging in the balance again.

At 4.30 P.M. (May 21) General Pershing called to go over our new head-quarters for the first time, and I had Colonel DeGrailly state Loucheur's suggestion to him.

The next morning, May 22, General Pershing called me to his house and showed me the restatement which he proposed to present to Clemenceau in the afternoon (or late in the morning). It was admirable, as is everything John writes and studies. In the afternoon he telephoned that Clemenceau had signed it with him and sent me a copy.

May 22, 1918

It is hereby agreed among the Allied Governments subscribing hereto:

1. That the principle of unification of military supplies and utilities for the use of the Allied armies is adopted.

2. That in order to apply this principle and as far as possible coordinate the use of utilities and the distribution of supplies among the Allied armies, a Board consisting of representatives of each of the Allied armies is to be constituted at once.

3. That the unanimous decision of the Board regarding the allotment of material and supplies shall have the force of orders and be carried out by the respective supply agencies.

4. That further details of the organization by which the above plan is to be carried out shall be left to the Board, subject to such approval by the respective Governments as may at any time seem advisable.

We agree to the above and wish it to be submitted to the British and Italian Governments.

(Signed) G. Clemenceau

John J. Pershing

What I have gone through this last week has been really the hardest work I have done over here. It has nearly used up my energy — for a few days, anyway. And now must come the building-up of the new and great organization which properly effected should do so much toward bringing us an Allied victory. Real power should be camouflaged by a wise man as is a heavy cannon. To expose it unnecessarily is only to attract hostile artillery. This is the principle upon which I will try to work in forming this new organization. Only when power becomes so great that the unmasking of it demonstrates the futility of any attempt to oppose it is it safe to depart from this principle. Even then, though it be safe, it is not wise. Vanity is often the assassin of a useful career.

Paris, Sunday, June 2, 1918

We are at the height of a military crisis. It is all a question of the ability of the Allies to hold out until we can come in with full strength. General Pershing is here for the Versailles Council. If I had time to write them, it would be interesting some time to read notes of what he tells me from day to day about his matters and the general situation; but I cannot do so and cannot even write as I should of my own work and duties. Everything here including work and duty is for me now on a vast scale.

· One week ago on General Pershing's orders I started for England to endeavor to persuade that Government to join in our plan for military unification of the Allied Supply Service. Took Dwight Morrow,[31] of the Shipping Board, and Sergeant Francis Kilkenny with me. Martin Egan, a friend of the General's who was in England, had wired suggesting that if I went to England I might straighten out some misunderstandings of their officials and remove their doubts about the wisdom of British participation in the plan. Arrived London Monday about noon. Saw Egan; then called on General Biddle, Base Commander, U.S.A., London, who took me to lunch. Went to 10 Downing Street after lunch (they had told me Lloyd George would see me the next day) and caught Lloyd George in the hall. Presented to him there the letter from General Pershing designating me as the representative of the American army and containing copy of the plan which he and Clemenceau had signed. In answer to his statement that "they" — meaning the British War Office — "were against it," I explained that this was a statement of the plan so simple that they could neither misunderstand it nor be against it. He announced himself for it — as he had already done in principle to Pershing. Arrangements were made to call the British War Council together to consider the matter, at which I was asked to be present and present the plan. This meeting was set for 1.30 P.M. the next day. In the meantime Cravath, whose aid has been invaluable in this English end of the matter, had made an engagement for me to meet Lieutenant-General Cowans, British Quartermaster-General, who was the man blocking things. Lord Milner, whose attitude was favorable owing to Cravath's presentation of the plan to him, did not get back from France in time for the 1.30 meeting of the War Council next day, and so I was notified from Cowans' office that the meeting was off until Milner returned.

This proved fortunate, for I then saw General Cowans and General Crofton-Atkins, British D.G.T.,[32] with Cravath and Morrow. We had no difficulty in reaching an understanding and Cowans signified his agreement to the plan. As Lloyd George was already favorable, and also Milner, this settled the matter and made a meeting of the War Council unnecessary.

Cravath and Morrow, after consultation with Milner, prepared the letter of acceptance for Milner to sign which, after he had approved it, was submitted to me for approval. And so was completed a most important step for better Allied operations in the future.

Met my London purchasing office staff for a short time. Left for France Thursday morning. The British War Office (who were very kind) had telephoned Major-General Carter, B.E.F., at Boulogne of my coming. The latter had sent me an invitation to visit British G.H.Q. when he heard I was going to England. He met me with his motor and went with me all the way to Paris, stopping for thirty minutes at his headquarters.

Saturday presented the matter to General Pershing, who was pleased and so expressed himself. Milner's letter to Pershing sent in my care I delivered to him last night and he is preparing letters to Milner and Clemenceau. Asked him to include suggestion to the French Government to put the Belgians on the committee as the English first proposed. This heroic little army which made the Marne possible, and therefore all possible, must never be forgotten as the larger armies march to the battle they commenced.

And now my larger work begins. It will require great patience and tact, for at first, operating as we do under a conceded authority, reluctantly granted, we must proceed by degrees; but if this war continues a year this Board, or what springs directly out of it, will, next to the three military commanders, be the chief factor in eventual Allied success. This comes not because of self-confidence (of which I have no small degree), but because we can officially clear the way for common sense — the ultimate king of all successful wars — to have its day in the rear of the armies.

I have many, many plans. But to gain power to execute them for the good of the Allied Supply Service our Board must remain humble and work very hard. This afternoon (Sunday) had a conference on the general A.E.F. dock programme with Langfitt, Colonel Townsend, and Raymond (U.S. Shipping Control Committee), Sherman and Morrow (U.S. Shipping Board). Spent part of the morning with General Pershing. Am very busy.

Paris, Tuesday, June 4, 1918

Yesterday I received a request from the French Minister of Armament to arrange for use of American ammunition depots by the French, who must hurriedly remove ammunition from certain depots endangered by the German advance. Communicated with General Wheeler, who came to Paris, and gave him details. This morning at my office General Wheeler met the French officers and gave them the needed space. Was pleased with the way our people were prepared to act immediately and the way General Wheeler handled the matter. We are working closer all the time with our allies, and we must if we are to win.

Saw General Pershing yesterday afternoon. He had just returned from the War Council. Clemenceau brought up the matter of our plan and it was confirmed. We were a little afraid the War Council might mix in, but they did not. This is no day for advisory committees — only for action.

Am sorry I have time only to write of the general events and cannot make a picture more in detail of what is happening. One lives a lifetime in a month in time of war. The next sixty days are the critical ones. If our allies hold, we shall win.

Our Board becomes naturally the link between ourselves and the two other armies in all coordinated supply activities. The General, however, wants me to hold the position of General Purchasing Agent for a time until he can have me promoted based on my record in that position and then formally transferred to my new work, at which I am now engaged under his official designation to our allies.

Paris, June 8, 1918

At General Pershing's suggestion I attended the conference yesterday between Colonel Logan and General LeRond, Deputy Chief of Foch's Staff, relative to the horse situation. In order to put American artillery into action 80,000 horses are immediately necessary, and 100,000 horses in all are needed to see us through the next sixty days. Later in the day the French notified Logan that they would furnish the 80,000 horses as rapidly as possible. Am busy with matters relating to the coordination of the rear of the army with our allies. Already we have arranged for coordination of munition depot plans. There is so much to be done, and it is so important that I am not waiting for the appointment of the other members of the Board by the French and English, but going ahead along general lines. Have conferred with both French and English military authorities. Am doing it constantly. Why on earth some one was not doing this on a comprehensive scale three years ago, between the French and the English, I do not know. But their present acquiescence in any plan for improvement is indicative of a useful future for our effort.

Our work will not involve on our part excessive attention to detail. It is only necessary to get the proper independent heads of the three services to conduct their efforts with one common purpose in mind. To bring them into proper contact and have them evolve the procedure is wiser than to attempt primarily to suggest procedure to them who have first contact with actual conditions. My experience in these first important matters is convincing me of this. The result of my calling General Langfitt and General Wheeler here indicates also that to men so intelligent and energetic as they there is little need of doing anything but bring them into contact with conditions. We must introduce the active heads of the supply services of the three armies to each other, point out the common necessity, and rely chiefly on them to suggest the steps to meet it. My experience in working for coordination teaches me that the coordinator must himself coordinate his mental activities with others. To seek to display authority is to embarrass progress. Reason must be king. A good reason carries one farther than a General's stars. Where one must enforce authority he cannot be too patient in explaining the reason for its particular exercise. This, of course, applies to the great changes we are endeavoring to effect in army policies of the three Allies. It is all just a matter of common sense.

General Pershing has talked over with me his wish to found a great band for the National Army.[33] Colonel Boyd called me by telephone to say the General was sending to me for suggestions the report of a board recommending the instruments to be used. While time is precious, am going to take occasion to help in this matter, for little is of greater importance to an army than its music. My idea is that we should get a fine bandmaster to visit every regimental band in the army, and select from them the personnel. The way an organization of this kind starts determines largely its career. If it is started, not with the idea of making it a good band, but the best, it will probably become such. There should be in the formation of this great organization no concession to mediocrity; for it will some time march before one of the greatest armies the world has seen — an army sanctified by suffering, glorified by victory, and first in the love and pride of every true American.

Paris, June 12, 1918

Am still struggling to get our Military Board in operation. When I think of what one in military command of the rear of the three armies could accomplish for their greater strength in only one month's time, the delay is taxing my patience. We are waiting for the French to name their man. Shall have a conference with Tardieu and Ganne to-day and urge their immediate action. In the meantime the heavy arrival of our troops makes imperative greater cooperation in the rear. Am in daily conferences with our services as to their necessities. Kernan called on me yesterday. He is an able officer and a fine soldier as well as executive. Had a conference on Monday with General Pershing who explained his plans of fighting our American troops. He believes in keeping the men in motion.

Paris, June 13, 1918

I am thankful that when we started nearly sixty days ago this effort to coordinate the rear of the armies, we did not realize the enormous obstacles in the way of it having their root in individual selfishness and ambition. When a man looks at a proposition involving the common interest only from the standpoint of how it will affect his own authority, he is a hard man to persuade — in fact, you cannot persuade him. The only way you can move him is so to expose his opposition to reason to all those about him in official position that his self-clogged soul suddenly realizes that if it longer opposes reason it will be hurt more than by acquiescing in it.

It has been my long, weary, and ungrateful task during the past few months to state the necessity for certain great steps of Allied self-preservation over and over again so clearly that selfish opposition to it has to unmask itself and put off the disguise and pretense of an opposition based upon sincere purposes.

The French were delaying their appointment on our Board — and seemed undecided on the man. This was explained to me by them as caused by the fact that several men wanted the place. Yesterday I had appealed earnestly to M. Tardieu and M. Ganne stating the folly and wickedness of delay, and this morning was invited to a conference which they had succeeded in having called. Present were Ministers Vilgrain and Lavit, M. Tardieu, M. Ganne, and Colonel Payot, of Foch's Staff, and myself. I think sometimes that it is fortunate I cannot speak French, for in a crowd of Frenchmen I stick to the text better. I have no temptation to digress, for I can't understand anything.

All I have the patience to record here is that somehow, some way, they all agreed to do as I asked, after about two hours "go" at it, and stated that they would unanimously recommend to Clemenceau to appoint Payot. I want also to record appreciation of the help of Tardieu and Ganne. It was effective, unselfish, and most opportune.

This afternoon the representatives of the Belgian Government called, as I had suggested to Van de Vyvere to have them do, and I explained the plan to which they acquiesced.

No wonder the Allies have not coordinated better on the battle-fields! No wonder it took terrible defeats to bring about military unification at the front! To achieve real leadership in the army, intelligence, energy, and ambition must (with other things as well) be united. The soldier in high position is often consumed with an intense pride. Everything contributes to inflate his egoism. Suddenly an emergency requires him to submerge himself for the common good. If he has a Commander-in-Chief over him, his will is bent as needed through military discipline. But when the soldier to make a sacrifice is one in independent command!!! John Pershing is about the only one over here who is big enough to do this — and he has done it. Because there are no more like him my task is so hard. But once we are started we shall make rapid progress.

Paris, Sunday, June 23, 1918

Am writing this, 3 P.M., upon my arrival in Paris by automobile from Tours.

Last Monday morning General Pershing called me by telephone to come immediately to Chaumont. I took Captain Jay with me for company. Left by motor and arrived at the General's house in time for dinner. In the evening in his room he outlined his plan of action and programme for the American military effort. This was in effect a preliminary statement to me of the announcement he made to the conference of his officers the next morning. But to me he gave his reasons more in detail. The General believes that just as the present — since it is the moment of the Allies' greatest weakness — has called for Germany's supreme effort, so the time immediately following the collapse of the German offensive is the period of greatest weakness for them, and the time for our supreme effort as quickly as it can be delivered. He fears reinforcement next year for the Germans from western Russia. He feels that he must fight vigorously all along the line, utilizing against a worn foe the fresh and eager army which he commands. From the standpoint of enemy morale and our own, vigorous movement will lower theirs and increase ours. He desires to keep the war one of movement as far as possible.[34] He believes in a constant harassing by raids in the intervals between larger attacks, thus in every way keeping the enemy nervous and on the defensive. Therefore he has determined to demand that America continue until next April a schedule of shipment of 250,000 troops per month, which by April 1 will give him an army of 3,000,000 (or more exactly 2,850,000 men). But in the meantime he will begin to fight with the men he has along the lines above mentioned. He will take command under Foch — or, as he has told Foch, under any one Foch may name — of the American field army. He has notified the Secretary of War that he will take care of the men asked for over here. In other words, he purposely burns the bridges behind us in order to win victory by insuring our maximum effort as soon as possible. By August 1 we shall have 1,250,000 troops here. He called the conference of his leading officers to announce the plan, and to notify them of the tremendous burden of effort it will impose upon them in connection with the supply service. Asking my opinion I heartily approved. I told him that I believed the supply service could make good.

Much will depend upon how we can make our Military Board of Allied Supply function, for to support this programme coordination of the rear of the armies becomes imperative. Told the General that emergency, more than anything else, compels unity of Allied action; that this was illustrated by Great Britain furnishing sea transport for American troops when defeat threatened if she did not; that the emergency in supplies which he would create by the execution of his programme would operate to compel greater unity in their handling; that troops in the line would not be allowed to starve; that in emergency all warehouses, all supplies, everything, would be treated as a common store; that coordination, impossible to a proper extent between allied armies not under great pressure, was unavoidable in matters of food supply when under great pressure; to sum up that he had a right in making this programme to assume that behind a united front were all the resources of supply of the armies of France and Great Britain and our own army supplies to be handled as one. In the accomplishment of this our new Board must be made a great factor. This Board makes it possible if it is properly handled.

Next morning at his headquarters the General announced formally his plan of campaign to the officers he had invited to meet him. There were present, besides the General, the following: McAndrew,[35] Chief of Staff; Kernan, Langfitt (Major-Generals), Atterbury (Brigadier-General), Connor (Fox), Logan, Moseley (Colonels of the General Staff), and myself. With the General's consent I brought Jay to the meeting. Sherman, of the Shipping Board, was also present. The plan was approved by all, and we committed ourselves as representing the supply service.

The General devoted much of his time in the afternoon to the preparation of the announcement to the army of the establishment of the Military Board of Allied Supply and my appointment thereto as the representative of the A.E.F. He directed McAndrew, Logan, and me to submit a proposed draft. We did so, and the General promptly proceeded to write an entirely different and better one. Care is necessary in announcing to the army this important step so as not to have it misconstrued by either it or our allies.

In the evening at his house, the General read me the letter announcing his plan for the war to Secretary Baker and asking the approval of the President and the Secretary of War. This we discussed at length as well as the whole situation. As illustrating the completeness with which the General makes his plans, and the force with which he presents them, not one thing was suggested to be changed by any officer after the fullest discussion. He had prepared the plan some days before, as well as the letter to Baker. This is the kind of a leadership that wins — to be willing to submit to reason, but to reason so well that the submission involves neither delay nor difference. I am sure my love and admiration for John is not interfering with my cold judgment when I say that I consider him the ablest man in both action and reason in time of emergency that I have ever known or shall ever know.

Jay and I left the General's house Wednesday morning for Paris via Provins and Meaux. (Less than one hour, thirty minutes by motor from Chaumont to Troyes, 55 miles: quick travel.) Stopped at French General Headquarters and called on Payot, and talked over plans for our new Board. Foch and Pétain have combined in recommending Payot to the French War Office for promotion to Brigadier-General as he takes on these duties. Payot succeeded General Ragueneau, who commanded the rear of the French army under Nivelle. He is one of the ablest men in the French army. He had his supply system — both ammunition and rations — so well thought out that the recent great German advance covering so much territory did not disarrange it. We are good friends and both feel we shall work well together. We agreed on headquarters for the Board at French G.H.Q. with an office also in Paris.

At Meaux, where I had gone to see my friend Harbord, was greatly disappointed to find him away. Stopped on the way and took mess with some soldiers (company) of the 2d Division temporarily out of line. Arrived at Paris in the evening.

Yesterday morning (Saturday) I left by motor for Tours taking with me Colonel Sewell who was visiting me in Paris. Am anxious to see this fine officer and able man called more into the center of things than he can be at a base port. Went to Tours to talk with Kernan on the methods of cooperation between him and myself in connection with the new Board. Had full and satisfactory conference. Asked him to appoint a member of his Staff to centralize information on all our army warehouse situation (all services), as this is the first thing I want to get started. Expect in this first step in coordination to effect an enormous saving in our army construction with the aid of the French. Kernan's man under our direction will match up information with the French and English and thus give our Board the basis for an order of coordination. Discussed other matters with various members of the Staff. Was entertained at dinner by my friends Smither and McAdam, of the Staff C.G.S.O.S.

Paris, June 29, 1918

Yesterday afternoon (Friday) the new Military Board of Allied Supply met at my office for the first time marking in my judgment the beginning of an inter-Allied Staff which, if the war lasts, must be the chief factor in the intelligent use of the resources of the rear of the Allied armies for the benefit of the front.

Payot now has charge of the French rear, and this fact adds greatly to our opportunity for immediate beneficial action. Beadon,[36] the English army representative, is a good man, but so handicapped by his superiors, who are still nervous about the way in which the Board may exercise its powers, that he acted (as every man must who is not expected to exercise authority in the company of those who do) as an obstructionist. Still we got through everything which Payot and I regarded as important.

Before the meeting talked with General Pershing on the telephone in Payot's presence and explained Payot's ideas. The General approved them, as they were along the lines which we have so long been earnestly striving for.

Nothing is slower than an Englishman to move in matters involving a possible loss of authority. But when he does move, and when he gives his word, he stands by it through thick and thin. Since England is now represented in the plan, her full and complete sympathy with it is only a matter of time. The purposes of the Board are such that, as its action develops, all will put their shoulders heartily to the wheel. Least of all will England be backward in the time of greatest emergency which is still before us. Unless this Board can coordinate the Allied rear, I doubt if in France we can handle the 3,000,000 men who, if the General's plan is carried out, will be in the American army by April 1. That is why I have been so anxious to get started. Payot and I are in complete accord. As he expresses it we have "two heads under one hat." As the chief measures of coordination are first to be taken between the French and American armies, we hope to move rapidly, and the full measure of English constructive cooperation will come a little later when the influx of our troops makes more pressing the food situation.

As it is now we are all too prone to think in terms of surplus instead of deficits, which latter we must do to bring to bear our maximum effort against the enemy at his time of greatest weakness Pershing's insistence on troops and his general plan have been determined largely by his confidence that the rear can be made to support properly the front. And it will.

Thursday night had a narrow escape in the air raid. Two bombs dropped near the hotel. General Winn, Junior Ames, and I were watching the raid from my window on the fourth floor of the Ritz about midnight. When the appalling explosion occurred, found myself half across the room from my window sitting in an armchair. The hotel was not directly struck, but its glass was shattered everywhere. One man on our floor severely cut.[37] The wounded in the hotel and vicinity were not numerous, but some were severely hurt, and on the street some were killed. Junior took a wounded woman to the doctor's in a taxicab. This makes about my thirtieth air raid — or thereabouts — but it has given me an added respect for a bomb. It is certainly a case where "familiarity does not breed contempt." We have had raids for the last three nights.[38]

Paris, July 3, 1918

The usual meeting of our Military Board was held at my headquarters yesterday. The English are cooperating like the thoroughbreds they are. Consulted with General Pershing relative to the machinery to be installed in our own army to give me, as a member of the Board, the authority over our own services necessary to enable me to coordinate our rear with the French and the English. Am in too much of a whirl of work to write details. Subsequent events will develop a record of them in official papers.

General Pershing is daily conferring with the Allies. He wants to give them enough American troops to keep their defense lines stiffened, without unduly delaying the accumulation of his army of the offensive. Meantime he is daily harassing the enemy. Thank God for this great man of action. The French made ceremonial calls on us at my headquarters this afternoon. But in the life of this particular individual at this particular time there is no time for extended ceremonies. Harbord sent me a bayonet with the "compliments of the Marine Brigade."[39] This division saved Paris. Air raids nearly every night. Since my narrow escape the other night in the bomb explosion near the Ritz am a trifle "gun-shy."

Paris, July 8, 1918

Yesterday (Sunday) went for first time to the headquarters established by the French Army for the Military Board of Allied Supply. Was accompanied by General Jadwin and about eight of my personal staff of assistants. Colonel Smither arrived at night, having been delayed. Cannot spare time to describe at length our magnificent headquarters. They consist of a chateau (modern) at Coubert,[40] where the members of the Board will live (when at Coubert), and an old castle for our Staff about a quarter of a mile away, built in the year 1550 and occupied at one time by a sister of Louis XIV (so they said).[41] The French have outdone themselves in providing impressive and convenient surroundings for us. At the meeting of the Board Payot presided. He came in from Foch's headquarters angry. At Versailles the other day Lord Milner, in the presence of Lloyd George, said to Clemenceau that it was clearly understood that Foch had no control over our Board. Clemenceau repeated this to Foch, who was irritated over it. He called Payot to his headquarters yesterday morning and forcibly expressed himself in the matter — hence Payot's attitude. Payot proceeded to take it out on Beadon. We all in reality clearly understood that Foch does not have a military control of us. It is logical that he should—Pershing recommended it — but after a long contest with the English, who opposed it, our compromise of a unanimous consent provision was reached. Everything was and is understood — but the English keep "rubbing it in," and the French kick back every time. However, somewhat through my efforts we finally settled down to business and took up warehouse and construction coordination. Have asked G-4, G.H.Q., and G-4, S.O.S.,[42] each to name a man for my Staff. We shall rapidly collect the information from the three armies necessary to base our decisions upon. We must proceed wisely and firmly. Unquestionably we have in our hands the power if we but act with wisdom.

Payot saw Pershing Saturday and the General told him that anything Payot and I recommended would be ordered into effect by him in the A.E.F., which makes it possible for Payot and me to coordinate the French and American rear even if the English do not join. I know, however, that on the essential and important things the English will cooperate to the limit. No one could ever make me believe to the contrary. They, however, are very cautious.

To-day received a telegram saying the Commander-in-Chief desires me to take up the horse situation (artillery) immediately through Tardieu. Am pressed by an emergency somewhere every day owing to the immense increase in our army. Am trying to do my best, which is all any one can do.

Jadwin is demanding more laborers. Am simply putting on a little more steam—plugging away—and not being "rattled."

Stayed all night at our palace called by courtesy "field headquarters," and came to town this A.M., about fifty minutes' ride. Stopped at the Roman ruins of an amphitheater[43] (*Rue des Arènes*) for a few minutes.

Am determined that by means of our Board, Foch's needs shall be met from the rear as they are interpreted by Payot. This is common sense. While the English will not concede the theoretical general authority necessary to make one army — with a single command covering the front and rear — they will, I am sure, when the individual propositions come before our Board, follow the dictates of common sense and agree upon remedial action rectifying present conditions. However, in any event Payot and I can put over two thirds of the rear in shape to satisfy Foch.

Paris, Sunday, July 14, 1918

Matters and time move so swiftly that it is difficult to keep track of either. As the practical mediator between the French Government and army and the A.E.F. in supply matters, the burdens of my position are growing heavier. The division of an insufficient supply between two imperative necessities is never easy. In artillery horses, lumber, transportation, munitions, warehouses — in almost every department the difficult situations exist. But one by one they must be met. To deserve the confidence of both sides — really to deserve it — is my constant effort. As far as possible in anticipation of decisions and actions I try to keep the French officials and the heads of our own services advised of the real conditions confronting each other. The thorough appreciation of another's necessities lessens the blow when it comes. Each must make concessions. The common purpose demands it. An attitude toward the French dictated alone by our own necessities without reference to the satisfaction of theirs is fatal to the common cause. It is very difficult for me sometimes to make our officers see this, struggling as they are under the tremendous load of our military programme.

Friday night General Pershing and I spent the evening together, taking dinner by ourselves in a little restaurant near the *Arc de Triomphe*. Here we discussed the best method of handling our supply problems. If it was not for his thorough understanding of the difficulties of my situation and his ever loyal and sympathetic aid, I fear I could not keep myself at times from discouragement, which is generally equivalent to a paralysis of effort. But his words of commendation are a stimulus, equal almost in their force to the combined sense of duty and fear of failure. That is a tribute I can justly pay to his character and personality.

Saturday I visited the 164th French Division in the line, taking Colonel Byllesby[44] and Captain Dyar with me. French G.H.Q. sent a liaison officer with us. At the front the French Colonel commanding a brigade accompanied us also, besides another French Commandant from Division Headquarters. Interesting trip — front comparatively quiet; some artillery firing back and forth. Coming back saw General Bullard at the headquarters of General Degoutte,[45] the latter being in command of the 6th Army. General Degoutte insisted on our staying to dinner, although it was after he had finished — about 9 P.M. He wanted me to stay all night, as he was sure the Germans would attack before morning and thought it would be interesting for us to watch events in his office. He showed us all his maps, location of troops, preparations, etc. In the 6th Army now there are about 300,000 troops, one half of whom are Americans.[46] Bullard, who is under Degoutte, tells me he has great confidence in him. As General Harbord was waiting for me in Paris had to leave for there.

At French G.H.Q. they tell me they have located six railroad tracks behind the German lines which they believe are to carry the big guns for the bombardment of Paris. This they expected last night or this morning to commence with the German offensive. They expected the German attack on a front of sixty kilometers, especially heavy at three different points. Passed a brigade of French cavalry on our way back.

To-day Major-General Harbord is with me. He has received his promotion as commanding in the recent actions the famous Marine Brigade. [47] His casualties during thirty days of fighting were about 3,600 out of 8,000.

At Major Collins's suggestion saw Walter Damrosch,[48] and he agreed to go to Chaumont to help out the reorganization of army bands, and to assist in forming the headquarters band along the line of my suggestions to Boyd, which have been adopted, providing for its selection by competition. General Pershing's desire for a fine army band will now be realized.

Witnessed the 14th of July military parade this A.M. — or part of it — from the top of my automobile on the way to my office. Have a good automobile — a Cadillac — which takes the French roads easily and continuously from thirty-five to fifty miles per hour without shaking us up much, notwithstanding the roads are now a little rough in spots owing to the heavy army transports.

Inspected a French battery of 280 mm. guns (3) yesterday which was camouflaged better than any I have yet seen. Nothing improves on Nature's own fresh foliage for camouflage.

Worked at office this morning. Lunched and took a walk with General Harbord, who has left me for a time to visit two of his wounded Colonels in a hospital. This is a holiday.[49]

Paris, Sunday, July 21, 1918

The great counter-attack of the French and our army keeps bringing almost hourly emergencies to be dealt with.[50] Have just returned from British Headquarters at Montreuil. This is noon, and am called to French Headquarters this afternoon on the ammunition and transportation situation. Received letter from Payot by messenger this morning saying Foch wants immediate pooling of French and American ammunition. This we shall arrange by to-morrow afternoon at our Board meeting then. If we can get the men and supplies to keep up the present counter-attack the German salient toward Chateau-Thierry can be pinched off. Great questions press. We need space in schoolhouses or other buildings for 45,000 beds along the front. Am trying to arrange this. Have been at Coubert (Field

Headquarters Board of Supply, Allied Armies) at our meeting Wednesday, 17th. Stayed all night. We shall on next Monday have a map — the first one made during the war — of all installations in the rear of the three armies. When I consider the past lack of coordination of the Allied rear I wonder that the Allies have held out against the consolidated Germans. But from now on all will be changed in the rear — just as the arrival of the Americans and the unified command of Foch is changing the situation at the front. Victory — sure and complete — is in the future.

Was the guest of Lieutenant-General Travers Clarke at G.H.Q., B.E.F. Was invited to dine with Sir Douglas Haig last evening, but could not wait owing to important matters waiting for me at Paris. Major Bacon (Robert) rode back with me. On way back called on General Bell commanding 33d Division[51] (Illinois troops). Went through deserted and bombarded Amiens.

Travers Clarke wants to—and should—go on our Board in pride that I had helped some, though the sight of the wonderful accomplishments of others must keep any one of us humble if honest in mind.

On Friday was at Coubert where we had a meeting of great importance. The great composite pictures we are making for the first time of the needs of the three armies are already profoundly affecting our plans and activities. The great experience and high authority of Payot — his wonderful ability — are invaluable assets to the Board. I like him very much. We are good friends. Every morning of a meeting he sends his representative to Paris to consult as to our prospective work at the meeting. We cooperate most intimately.

We shall secure a reduction in the forage ration[52] of the A.E.F. at our next meeting. We are working on the mobile automobile reserve for Foch. We have already pooled ammunition at the front, but no less important is the effect upon individual army policy, in the line of practical cooperation, of the wonderful pictures of common needs for the three armies which we are now making and furnishing to those whose departments are involved. From common knowledge arises coordinated effort. I marvel that the necessity for this cooperation in the rear did not force its adoption years ago before the United States entered the war in France.

At Paris Herbert Hoover, the U.S. Food Controller, sent for me and we had a long conference Saturday. This morning I took breakfast with him. Shall meet him again to-morrow in an endeavor to assist him in securing concessions of food from England (which has accumulated a large stock) for the benefit of France. He wants a letter from Pershing indicating the importance from a military standpoint of the immediate relief of the people of Bordeaux. I like him very much. He is a wonderful executive — a man inspired only by the principles of true and unselfish devotion to duty.

Am leaving for Coubert this afternoon (and Provins afterward) after meeting General Pershing, upon his arrival from his trip, by his direction. Am taking Sam Felton with me. The Staff of Payot is giving him a dinner at French G.H.Q. to-night on the occasion of his promotion to officer of the Legion of Honor, and he has asked me to be present.

Paris, August 8, 1918

Important matters press hourly. This week with Loucheur, Tardieu, Ganne, General Chevalier, and others of the French, General Jadwin and I arrived at an agreement on the railroad-tie situation through which there will be assured the maintenance of the reserve of ties behind the lines necessary to support an advance of the Allied troops.

This morning Harjes called at my rooms before I was up to warn me of Payot, whom he believed from French information to be untrustworthy and who had said to others, according to Harjes, that he (Payot) "could lead me by the nose." I replied to Harjes "that any one could lead me by the nose, provided he knew the road better than I did, and it led in the right direction." This leads me to make a few notes concerning Payot and our relations. In every possible way I encourage Payot to initiate and suggest methods of coordination for the rear of the armies because he is the best informed man on conditions of the rear and its needs in France. In all sincerity I create in his mind a feeling of my dependence on him, for he has the knowledge and experience while I am only in the process of acquiring it, and never shall acquire it as he has it. In every way I encourage the use by the French of our Board. I declined the suggestion of my Staff that we have an American version of our meetings made as they thought the French did not include in our minutes of proceedings a sufficient record of our own part in them. It was only a non-essential and the suggestion would imply distrust as well as vanity on my part. That anybody should think they could hurt Payot in my estimation for asserting his influence, when for over a month General Pershing and I fought to transfer entire control of the rear of the three armies to the French command, shows that they have little conception of how in earnest we are to secure proper coordination. As a matter of fact Payot is entirely trustworthy. He only wants to win the war. Naturally he is ambitious — and this is no crime. Close cooperation with him by me means I can get useful things done. If I let others influence me to unwise attitudes suggested by personal vanity I shall fail to be of high service to the common cause. I have a good sense of direction. No one can lead me down a wrong road. And Payot, least of all would, if he could, deceive me as to wise military measures.

Received telegram from Harbord to-day saying that the Commander-in-Chief is issuing orders reducing A.E.F. forage ration to the English basis. Thus again our Board, by making a picture of a coming crisis, lessens the danger by compelling economy in time to help meet it.

This noon was the guest of General Sackville-West[53] at Versailles, where I went to please my friend [R. H.] Beadon of the Military Board of Allied Supply. Had a pleasant time.

Deauville,[54] France
Friday, August 16, 1918

For the first time in fifteen months I am taking a few days' rest — vacation. Harbord asked me to take an inspection trip with him, but I wanted more quiet than is possible on a trip with an active General like Harbord. I came, therefore, to Havre on Wednesday, spent the day and night with my friend Van de Vyvere, and came to Deauville yesterday accompanied by one of Van de Vyvere's clerks who acted as my interpreter. Find I am not as tired as I thought and a few days of sunlight — out of doors and sea bathing — will put me in the fittest shape again.

Last Sunday we had an important meeting of the Military Board of Allied Supply at Coubert. Took my friend Colonel Sewell, McRoberts, and Mr. Walcott and Mr. Bell, of the Commission,[55] with me; also Major Fairchild, a friend of McRoberts's. After our meeting we stayed all night at our headquarters at Coubert, and on Monday morning, under the guidance of Commandants Brault and Lescanne and Lieutenant De Sieyes, all of whom are on Payot's Staff, we left for the front. Our first stop was to call on General Mangin,[56] commanding the 10th French Army, at his headquarters in the field. Like the most of the successful French Generals he is a man evidently of intense nervous energy. When I told him of the gratification of the American people, as expressed in the American press, at his praise of the brave American troops under him in his last successful drive, he went to his desk and gave me a printed copy of his order citing our troops. He said he could not over-praise their battle qualities and the record they had made. Our next call was on General Munroe, who like Mangin was most cordial. He also said he could not speak too strongly in praise of our American soldiers. We then went on toward Soissons,[57] taking lunch in a battle-ruined chateau at Longpoint [*sic*].[58] We went over the battle-field of Corsy and the St. Paul farm. My nephew Charles, whom I had with us, gathered up helmets, a gas-mask, and a rifle as souvenirs. Thousands of unexploded hand-grenades remained; wreckage of battle was everywhere. At points the dead were still being buried. Demolished tanks were much in

HEADQUARTERS MILITARY BOARD OF ALLIED SUPPLY, COUBERT

evidence during the day. The St. Paul farm was a mass of wreckage. It was at the point of the turn in the line. It was a point of crisis.

We reached the line of Soissons in the afternoon. A French Colonel and some of his officers went with us to the brow of the hill overlooking Soissons. We reached the brow of the hill through an underground passage, but upon reaching there emerged in view of the valley and of the Germans as it proved. We watched the effect of our shells on the German positions. Our troops occupy a part of Soissons and the Germans are in the outskirts. We walked back to the Colonel's dugout and when we were there the Germans opened fire, dropping four large shells within one hundred and fifty yards of us. The French Colonel and his officers insisted on our drinking toasts of champagne in tin cups, which we did to the sounds of the guns and the explosion of shells.

After our visit with them we went back to General Munroe's, where they had prepared tea for us. I cannot state my appreciation of the courtesy with which we were everywhere treated.

We then returned over the recent battle-field, through Chateau-Thierry, past the "Wood of the Marines" (*Bois de Belleau*),[59] where Harbord and his men fought at what I think will prove the Gettysburg of this war. Great stores of German ammunition were taken. I have not time to describe what we saw. History will describe all such things. We returned to Paris through Meaux, our French escorts leaving us there. The wreckage of one of these modern battles is immense. From the effect of the shell-fire in villages, fields, and forests I wonder anybody comes alive out of battle.

1   CGD: As I saw these young men there came to my mind the following words from Gen. Sir A. W. Currie's order to the Canadian troops who were about to go into action: "To those who fall I say, You will not die but step into immortality. Your mothers will not lament your fate but will be proud to have borne such sons. Your names will be revered forever by your grateful country, and God will take you unto Himself." [Ed. General Sir Arthur William Currie (1875-1933] commanded several divisions in the Canadian Expeditionary Force during the war.]

2   Robert "Bertie" McCormick (1880-1955). McCormick covered the war in 1915 as a correspondent for the *Chicago Tribune* (the paper founded by his maternal grandfather, Joseph Medill). He later joined the Illinois National Guard and served alongside General Pershing during the Mexican Expedition. His unit was mobilized for service overseas in the war. McCormick served on Pershing's staff, and later became a colonel in the field artillery. He took part in the battle of Cantigny, after which he would later name his farm (now a museum in Wheaton, Illinois). After the war, McCormick assumed control of the *Tribune* and, with his cousin, Joseph Medill Paterson, founded the Medill School of Journalism at Northwestern University in 1921. For more see: Thomas B. Littlewood. *Soldiers Back Home: The American Legion in Illinois, 1919-1939*, Southern Illinois University, 2004, 15-16. For more see, Richard Norton Smith, *The Colonel: The Life and Legend of Robert R. McCormick, 1880-1955*. Evanston, IL: Northwestern University Press, 1997.

3   Lieutenant Vivian B. Mayo, son of architect Ernest Mayo, was from Evanston. He attended Yale University and was a civil engineer. He was wounded twice during the war.

4   Pershing and the A.E.F. were criticized by some European leaders for failing to move more quickly to deploy troops. Pershing, backed by President Wilson and Secretary of War, Newton Baker, believed that the American troops had to be properly trained before going in to war (using different tactics than those that had been used by the French and British armies). Although the first American troops arrived in 1917, it would not be until 1918 that their numbers would swell. In June and July 1918 alone, over half a million American soldiers arrived in France, and by August 1918 there were 1.5 million American soldiers "over there." By the time of the Armistice, two million American soldiers were overseas, out of an American force of roughly 4 million.

5   Sir Alfred Milner (1854-1925) was a highly influential member of Lloyd George's war cabinet. Dawes' mention of Milner here was made at the very moment that Milner had been appointed British Secretary of State for War, a position he held until December 1919. Milner would also serve on the British delegation at the Paris Peace talks.

6   See Appendix D, Cablegram from Pershing to the Adjutant-General, Washington, D.C., April 19, 1918.

7   The First Battle of the Marne was fought from September 5-12, 1914. The battle pitted the French and British forces against the advancing German Army, which came through northeastern France and Belgium and reached the outskirts of Paris. What looked like an inevitable defeat and subsequent occupation of Paris turned into a "victory" for the Allies, and French and British soldiers pushed back and held off the invading German Army. However, the battle ended in the entrenchment of all forces and the beginning of the more than four long years of stalemate and trench warfare.

8   Ironically, it was Pershing who would "tell on" Dawes. In April 1925, at a reunion dinner in Chicago, Pershing told an audience the story of his meeting with Foch. He looked over at Dawes, who not only had all but one of his coat buttons unbuttoned, but was also smoking a cigar. He told Harbord to "command" Dawes to button up and throw away that "d---" cigar. "Pershing Tells on Dawes," *New York Times,* April 25, 1925. Pershing and Dawes often joked about Dawes' lack of military decorum: He greeted Pershing as "John" in front of other officers, failed to stand when Pershing entered a room, and generally appeared in less than regulation form. As is clear from this entry, Dawes himself admitted that he was lacking in the manner of a true military man, but used his casual nature to his advantage many times.

9   Industrialist and arms manufacturer, Louis Loucheur (1872-1931) served as France's Minister of Armaments from 1917 though November 1918. He was an advisor to Clemenceau during the 1919 Peace Conference. He would go on to serve in various government posts after the war.

10   James Addison Logan, Jr. (1879-1930), Assistant Chief of Staff, G-1, Administration, G.H.Q. Logan had served in the military since enlisting to serve in the Spanish-American War. He was sent to France in 1914 to head up the American Military Mission to Paris and later assisted with planning for American deployment in France. After the war, Logan assisted with the food relief programs in Europe, and later served as U.S. representative to the Reparation Commission, established by the Treaty of Versailles. From 1925-1930, he was affiliated with the investment bank, Dillon, Read and Company. Michael McCarthy, "Logan, James Addison, Jr.," in *The United States in the First World War: An Encyclopedia,* 352-353.

11   A slang term that refers to a thrashing with switches or rods; a severe working through.

12   The original manuscript includes the full passage, which reads: "In reply to a vigorous statement by General Pershing of the views he would like to present to our inefficient, from our view, Ambassador to Italy, who should be aggressive instead of pathetically mild in time of emergency. Col. Mott who had been to Italy and knows Page, said, 'You might as well throw baseballs at a feather bed.' We will try sending Cutcheon again with Crosby's agreement." Dawes, Manuscript, np.

13   On April 25, 1918, the French suffered staggering losses at the town of Mont Kemmel (also known as Kemmelberg) in Belgium. The German Army bombarded the French soldiers, gassing and shelling them for hours straight. The French suffered more than 5,000 men killed in just a few hours and the Germans would take the position that had been held by the Allies for years.

14   Raymond Stephens (1874-1942), a former Congressman from New Hampshire, was the U.S. Representative to the Allied Maritime Transport Council (an advisory body created in December 1917) and vice-chairman of the U.S. Shipping Board, 1917-1920; George Rublee (1868-1957), also a member of the Shipping Board and the council, was a lawyer and political adviser; Dwight Morrow (1873-1931) was a partner at J.P. Morgan and Company. He was one of the chief negotiators of the 1916 Anglo-French loan, to which Charles G. Dawes subscribed. (See the introduction for more on the 1916 loan.) Initially, Morrow came to Europe as an American advisor on shipping matters, but soon joined the Shipping Board full-time. Morrow later served as U.S. Ambassador to Mexico. Marc Eric McClure, *Earnest Endeavors: The Life and Public Work of George Rublee*. Westport, CT: Greenwood, 2003, 143.

15   Colonel Henry Carpenter Smither (1873-1930). A graduate of the United States Military Academy, Smither had many years of military experience. He received the Distinguished Service Medal for his work with the S.O.S. Dawes mentions Smither several times below.

16   Most likely T[homas] Bentley Mott (1865-1952), liaison between Foch and Pershing. Mott would later translate Foch's 1931 memoir.

17   Moore (1883-1966) was the great grandson of Clark Clement Moore, author of the "'Twas the Night Before Christmas." Moore had a degree in forestry from Yale. He served with the engineers in World War I, and helped organize operations to secure lumber and other material for the Allies. In 1919, he was awarded the Cross of the Legion of Honor by the French government. He later worked for the American Museum of Natural History and served as the president of the Ecological Society of America. *The National Cyclopaedia of American Biography*. Vol. XVIII. New York: James T. White and Co., 1922, 18.

18   Sir Travers Edwards Clarke (1871-1962) served as British Quartermaster General from 1917 to 1921.

19   Henri Varaigne, chairman of the French Mission attached to the headquarters of the American General Purchasing Board. A few days after the above meeting with Dawes, Dawes received a letter from Varaigne in which he expressed gratitude to him and to Caro Dawes for the sweaters they had "generously placed at [his] disposal." Henri Varaigne, *Le Commandant Varaigne, Chef de la Section près Les Services Américains, de L'Office Central des Relations Franco-Américaines*, letter to Charles G. Dawes, no date, Dawes Archive, Northwestern, Box 71. See the essay "Homecoming" at the end of this volume for more about Caro Dawes' work

during World War I.

20 Jules Jeanneney (1864-1957) French Deputy Secretary of State for War.

21 During the war, German prisoners of war were organized into labor companies and put to work on various projects, including the construction of barracks and the repairing of roads.

22 Sir John Cowans (1862-1921).

23 Quartermaster General.

24 Alban Randell Crofton Atkins (1870-1926) was British Director of Supply and Transport.

25 See below for Dawes' July 11, 1919 entry when he refers to his "former differences" with Cowans. According to Major Griscom, the U.S. representative in the British War Office, Dawes and Cowans did not hit it off upon this first meeting. When Cowans responded to Dawes' presentation with the statement, "We'll think about it," Dawes (reportedly) "got very angry and got up and banged the table and said. . . 'Let me tell you an effete monarchy like England will never win this war without our help and we have come here to win it for you.' Sir John Cowans could not believe his ears and rose and passed out of the room and said, 'I have had enough of this man.'" It was up to Griscom to repair the damage. Eventually, Dawes and Cowans ended as the 'best of friends." Quoted in Gary Mead, *The Doughboys: America and the First World War*, Woodstock, NY: The Overlook Press, 2000, 122-123.

26 Paul Drennan Cravath (1861-1940) was a corporate lawyer, and member of the firm known today as Cravath, Swaine and Moore. Cravath was decidedly pro-British and urged the U.S. to enter the war. He was a founder of the Council on Foreign Relations in 1921.

27 Étienne Clémentel (1864-1936).

28 Mason Mathews Patrick (1863-1942) was Pershing's classmate at the United States Military Academy. Pershing appointed Patrick to command the Air Service in May 1918. After the war, Patrick was instrumental in establishing the Air Corps, the precursor to the Air Force, established in 1947. In 1921, at the age of 59, Patrick learned to fly and obtained the rating of Junior Airplane Pilot. That same year, Patrick attained the rank of Major General and was appointed Chief of the Air Service. "Mason Mathews Patrick," Arlington National Cemetery, Accessed June 5, 2015, http://www.arlingtoncemetery.net/mpatrick.htm.

29 George Van Horn Moseley (1874-1960) graduated from the United States Military Academy and served in various military posts. He commanded the 5th Field Artillery of the First Division in France and joined the General Headquarters staff in November 1917. In April 1918 he was appointed to head the supply section and was promoted to brigadier general. In 1921, Moseley served as an assistant to Charles G. Dawes during Dawes' tenure as the first Budget Director. Moseley later became infamous for his anti-Semitic views.

30 The attack took place overnight on May 3-May 4, 1918 in the Villers-Tournelle sector, near the town of Cantigny. In the course of three and a half hours, roughly 1,500 high explosive and mustard gas shells rained down on a battalion of the 18th Infantry, American troops of the First Division. An estimated 850 casualties resulted. This was a prelude to the battle for Cantigny which would engage the First Division in the coming weeks, resulting in many more casualties, but also in a significant boost for the Allies after the American troops captured Cantigny. The Society of the First Division, A.E.F., *History of the First Division During the World War, 1917-1919*. Philadelphia, PA: John C. Winston Company, 1922, 74.

31 CGD: Dwight Morrow was a man who without accepting a military commission performed work of the greatest military and economic value to the A.E.F. and to the Allies. Members of the British General Staff requested me to ask Mr. Morrow to visit them at G.H.Q., Montreuil, because, as General Travers Clarke said, they wanted to meet the man whose clear analysis of the Allied shipping situation had profoundly affected the Allied policy finally adopted. His unusual work with the General Staff of the A.E.F. during the war was generally recognized. He received the Distinguished Service Medal of the United States.

32 Director General Transportation.

33 The band would become known as "Pershing's Own." The United States Army Band, officially created in 1922, bears the same name and has its origins in the band Dawes helped organize during the war.

34 This was one of Pershing's signature tenets: in order to be victorious, he believed, American soldiers had to wage "open warfare," engaging in a war of movement, rather than one of attrition and stagnation with soldiers remaining entrenched. Mark Ethan Grotelueschen, *The AEF Way of War: The American Army and Combat in World War I*. Cambridge: Cambridge University Press, 2006, 31-34.

35 Major General James William McAndrew (1862-1922) was a United States Military Academy graduate with many years of military service. He served in France with the A.E.F. from June 26, 1917 until June 8, 1919. In May 1918, he succeeded James Harbord as Chief of Staff, American Expeditionary Forces, after Harbord took up a military command. McAndrew served as Chief of Staff until May 26, 1919. See the essay "Homecoming" at the end of this volume for more about McAndrew.

36 Roger Hammet Beadon (1887-1945).

37 CGD: It afterward developed that this man—a waiter at the hotel—was struck by shrapnel in two places and severely wounded.

38 On the evening of June 29, 1918, Paris was struck by fourteen shells. At the Ministère de la Justice, three people were killed. The Hôtel Ritz next door was damaged and "lost nearly all its windows." Alice Ziska Snyder and Milton Valentine Snyder, *Paris Days and London Nights*. New York, E. P. Dutton and Co., 1921, 210-211.

39   In June 1918, Harbord took command of the 4th Marine Brigade (nick-named-supposedly- "Devil Dogs" by the Germans) of the 2nd Division. From July 15 through August 1918, Harbord would command the entire division.

40   Roughly 30 miles southeast of Paris.

41   *Château de la Grange-le-Roi.*

42   The General Headquarters (G.H.Q.) of the A.E.F. was divided into five sections. G1 (Administration), G2 (Intelligence), G3 (Operations), G4 (Coordination), and G5 (Training). The Services of Supply operated with only the G1, G2, and G4 sections. Isaac Frederick Marcosson, *S.O.S. America's Miracle in France.* New York: John Lane Company, 1919, 39-40.

43   *Arènes de Lutèce,* the ruins of a 10,000 seat amphitheater in the Latin Quarter of Paris, built c. 200 AD.

44   Henry Marison Byllesby (1859-1924) was an electrical engineer. In 1917, Byllesby was commissioned as a major and served in the Signal Corps. Later, he served in London as the purchasing agent for the American Expeditionary Force.

45   Brigadier General Jean Marie Joseph Degoutte (1866 -1938) commanded Moroccan troops in the French Army prior to assuming command of the 6th Army. From 1919 to 1925, he served as commander of the French forces in the Rhineland.

46   Dawes is not accurate in stating that American troops were a part of the French 6th Army. U.S. units fought alongside the 6th Army, but not within its ranks.

47   On July 11, Harbord was promoted to Major-General. The promotion came soon after the Battle of Belleau Wood, which took place from June 1-26, 1918, during the German Spring Offensive. U.S., French and British troops took part in the battle. Harbord was in command of the 4th Marine Brigade, a unit that was noted, in particular, for bravery. The battle ended in an Allied victory. About 1,811 Americans were killed in the battle that counted a total of roughly 9,777 casualties. *The Illustrated Encyclopedia of Warfare.* London: Dorling Kindersley, 2009, 462.

48   Walter Damrosch (1862-1950) was a famous composer, conductor, and director of the New York Symphony Orchestra (founded by his father in 1878). Later, he would conduct the world premiere of George Gershwin's "An American in Paris." In 1918, he toured U.S. camps for the Y.M.C.A. Dawes asked him to meet with him in Paris and suggested that he talk with Pershing concerning American military bands. Damrosch and Pershing met and it was agreed that Damrosch would work with the roughly 200 U.S. bandmasters in the army. He opened an 8-week training program in Paris, recruiting well-established French musicians to help train the Americans. The musicians studied conducting, harmony, and orchestration, and were also schooled in the playing of instruments which Damrosch saw

as decidedly lacking among the American bands, namely, oboes, bassoons, French horns and flugelhorns. James A. Keene, *A History of Music Education in the United States.* Centennial, Colorado: Glenbridge Publishing, Ltd, 2009, 323-235. The band Damrosch helped create would be called "Pershing's Own." Before leaving for France, Dawes had supplied instruments for a brass band for the 17th Engineers.

49   Bastille Day.

50   On July 18, 1918, the Allied forces launched the Aisne-Marne Offensive, a major counterattack in response to the German military's effort to attack the Allies on a grand scale. Roughly 270,000 American troops were involved. The weeks of fighting that followed and the numerous battles involving both French and American soldiers would ultimately conclude "the Second Battle of the Marne" with a victory for the Allies.

51   The 33rd Division, a U.S. National Guard Division, nicknamed the "Prairie Division," arrived in France in May 1918. General George Bell, Jr. commanded the division overseas.

52   Feed (hay, oats, et al) for horses and cattle.

53   Major-General Charles John Sackville-West (1870-1962) served on the Supreme War Council after being wounded in battle during the war.

54   Deauville is a seaside resort in northwestern France, about 120 miles from Paris. During the war, many of the resort's hotels were converted into hospitals and wounded soldiers were sent to Deauville to recover.

55   The Commission for Relief in Belgium (CRB) founded by Herbert Hoover in London in October 1914. Mr. Walcott was F.C. Walcott, and Mr. Bell was Golden W. Bell, members of the commission. "Register of the Commission for Relief in Belgium Records, 1914-1930," Hoover Institution Archives, Stanford University, Stanford, California. Online Archive of California, accessed March 10, 2016, http://www.oac.cdlib.org/findaid/ark:/13030/tf6z09n8fc/entire_text/.

56   General Charles Mangin (1866-1925) was known by French troops as "the butcher" because of his penchant for commanding with a reckless disregard for their lives. *Encyclopedia of World War I: A Political, Social, And Military History,* Spencer C. Tucker and Priscilla Mary Roberts, eds. Santa Barbara, CA: ABC-CLIO, 2005, 743.

57   The Battle of Soissons took place from July 18-22, 1918.

58   The abbey at Longpont was almost entirely destroyed during a recent battle. Only a single wall remained standing. "A Pilgrimage to the Battlefields," *La France,* June 1920, 425. See photograph on page 382.

59   On June 30, 1918, General Degoutte, commander of the French 6th Army, renamed Belleau Wood the "Wood of the Marine Brigade." American Battle Monuments Commission, "Belleau Wood Marine Monument and Chateau-Thierry Monument," Visitor Brochure, nd., www.abmc.gov/cemeteries-memorials. Accessed March 17, 2016.

Section 4

August 25, 1918 - November 12, 1918

DOOR AT CIREY-LE-CHÂTEAU

Paris, Sunday, 4 P.M.
August 25, 1918

Everything seems to contribute to the heaviness of my burden of responsibility. Spent all day yesterday with Harbord and three hours to-day with the Commander-in-Chief. I should be well-nigh discouraged were it not for the confidence of these dear and loyal friends supporting my authority in every way, and encouraging me by words of praise and sympathy. The very extent of the powers they place in my hands is in one sense an embarrassment, for I have constantly to watch myself in my relations to others lest my usefulness be interfered with by latent opposition to them.

Foch requested of Pershing increased power over the rear in supply and transportation. Through Payot, General Foch keeps in closest touch with our Board. He naturally desires to put Payot in supreme command of the rear, but John cannot safely part with the control of the line of communications to his own command now that the segregation of the armies has been accepted as best from a military standpoint. John so notified Foch's emissary, stating that through our Military Board the necessary measure of central control over the Allied rear could be maintained without interfering injuriously with the control of his own rear in other essentials by himself.

In the meantime on last Wednesday I made the first draft (dictated) of a letter[1] to the Commander-in-Chief designed to set out clearly the importance of the present work of the Board, and the necessity of guarding against possible divergence of view in the future between the General Staff and myself as the American Member of the Board. In my first draft of the letter I advocated the appointment of the Chief of Staff as the member of the Board in place of myself; but upon telling Payot of my intention that evening at Coubert after the meeting of the Board, he so strenuously objected to my leaving the Board that I had to promise him I would not do so of my own volition. He stated that it was through my relation to the Board that he could secure the cooperation of the departments of the French rear under civil control, which they would not accord to him as a member of the Board unless associated with myself who have conducted in the past a large part of the negotiations of the A.E.F. with the French civil government; and gave other reasons, among them — strange to say — was his idea of my influence with the English. He stated if I left the Board he would immediately ask to be relieved and that the Board would no longer exist; that the Board was regarded as my creation and my separation from it would destroy its prestige with the French and English. I don't think any one was ever more surprised than I was to hear this from Payot.

So on going to Paris next day I altered my letter to a recommendation that a member of the General Staff be made an additional member with me. To-day I gave the letter to General Pershing. This afternoon he will see Foch if possible on his way to Chaumont, and among other things take up with him this letter and the subject of strengthening the authority and machinery of our Board. The Commander-in-Chief (John) realizes what the Board means just as I do who am a member of it. It is fortunate that this is so, for if he did not I should despair of the proper settlement of many of the supply crises of the future. Experience has taught me that in the last pinch, whenever they cannot be present to attend to a supply crisis themselves, both John and Harbord turn to me, and practically to me alone, either to conduct or to supervise the conduct of the negotiations with the French and English. The more acute the crisis the surer they are to do it. Yesterday and to-day are examples on the hay and potato situation at Is-sur-Tille[2] involving the army policy. Upon my negotiations with the French to-morrow must rest the final decision of the hay question including the question of American importation. The crisis is acute. There is no hay at Is-sur-Tille — there the telephone rang and my office tells me Payot has telephoned me he is coming to Paris to see me to-morrow. I had appealed to him for help for our army by wire.

The question of the establishment of a proper fiscal system for the army is receiving our best attention. I have recommended that this matter be made independent of me; but as is usually the case the difficulty is to convince others (i.e., the C.-in-C.) that it should not be under my jurisdiction.

I never saw General Pershing looking or feeling better. He is sleeping well. He is tremendously active. He will soon strike with his field army. I know he will succeed. He is not letting anything get on his mind to absorb it from the all important question of how to get a military victory. He tells me how much confidence he feels in Harbord and myself, and that he sleeps well at night because we are in the S.O.S.; and that this is why he does not worry over problems which it is for the S.O.S. to solve, to an extent to divert his mind from the plan of his approaching fight. All of which only shows that John realizes the best way of getting all the best that is in us enlisted in the work. He is a very great man — and a very dear friend.

Paris, August 28, 1918

Was interested yesterday when Bacon (liaison officer at British Headquarters) telephoned saying that, as General Travers Clarke, in command of the British rear, could not come to Paris on account of the battle going on, he wanted me to come to British Headquarters to talk over the demand of Foch that Payot be put in charge of the rear of the three armies.

As it was impossible for me to go, I sent copy of my letter to General Pershing, dated August 25, for Bacon to read to General Travers Clarke, and told Bacon to tell him that Pershing had notified Foch that he could not accede to the suggestion because the organization of the American field army made necessary final control of its line of communications in its commander. However, I pointed out that Pershing and Foch would use the Military Board, of which Payot is a member, to get the necessary central military control over the Allied rear without interfering with the right of the unit to the essential measures to self-preservation. If military experience had not shown that the men fight better with their own armies kept separate than when commingled by regiments or battalions, or even divisions, the complete military unification of the rear for which I contended so strenuously in the past would now be conceded, in my judgment.

Shall be interested to see if the British will not now cause their command of the rear to be directly, instead of indirectly, represented on our Board, as I have always urged. Everything tends to increase the power and usefulness of our Board, and my part in its conception and formation is my chief satisfaction in my military service.

Received letter from Pershing saying he had discussed matter with Foch and explained some of the difficulties of the situation of which Foch had not been informed.

In his endeavor to assist in the hay crisis at Is-sur-Tille, Payot came to Paris to see me. He responds to my every suggestion for assistance to our army to the very best of his ability. By our extremely close cooperation and understanding we are much relieving the common situation in a time of common crisis. He tells me that he will meet me prior to every meeting of the Military Board of Allied Supply or whenever called for. Payot has many enemies, for with his great force he lacks patience in his dealings with the civil departments and ministers of the French Government in contact with him. He told me the other day that he was very tired and very much overworked, as is natural with our lines of battle advancing. "I am working sixteen hours a day," he said; "four hours fighting the Germans and twelve hours fighting my own people."

My Saturday with General Harbord and my Sunday (last) with General Pershing enabled me to get settled several important policies and my mind is much more quiet, though my work was never greater.

I certainly resent the attitude of some of our chiefs of services who try to excuse their own shortcomings by blaming the French whenever there is a shortage of supply. I wish I could let these officers of the French civil government and army so nobly working to help us — this people almost bleeding to death and still giving — giving — giving — know of how strongly, and to their faces, do I resent this attitude on the part of very few of our officers. In this strong feeling of overwhelming obligation to the French, I find our splendid Commander-in-Chief as decided as I am, and as stern in his attitude toward their critics who cannot know the difficulties under which they labor as do the General and myself who are more closely in contact with them.

Paris, August 29, 1918

Yesterday afternoon General Travers Clarke, through Bacon from British Headquarters, telephoned he would come to Paris to see me Sunday and go to the Board meeting with me Monday. He wanted to know what the A.E.F. had done in connection with Foch's request that Payot be placed over the Allied rear. I told him that General Pershing, in declining acquiescence, urged the greater use of our Board in military coordination of the rear as the only effective agency possible at present, and had seen Foch in this connection.

Foch yesterday ordered the French army to give us the horses we need. Thus as time proceeds the truth is apparent of my constant contention that military necessity will properly apportion insufficient supplies as we enter the critical period of the war. Am glad to note greater interest in the Military Board of our hesitant friends the English.[3]

Paris, Monday, September 2, 1918, 10.30 P.M.

I am just arrived from Coubert from a meeting of the Military Board of Allied Supply this afternoon which was important and interesting. General Travers Clarke accompanied me to Coubert; also my old friend Samuel McRoberts[4] (who has just been made a Brigadier-General for his fine work in the Ordnance Department) and Colonel Smither and Colonel Harry Nut whom I knew as a boy in Lincoln. While the meeting was in progress General Pershing and General Pétain arrived, and both thanked the Committee for its work.[5]

The subject of the mobile automobile reserve being under discussion both Pershing and Pétain emphasized its importance as well as that of the treatment by rules, etc., of the motor transport system from the standpoint of the inter-Allied armies. The new rules are nearly completed for adoption by the armies. The completeness and thoroughness with which they have been prepared by our joint sub-committee, General Pershing said he wished, too, to express his appreciation of the work the Committee were doing. The idea of the pooling of resources, he recalled, had been initiated by the

Americans in connection with the sea tonnage. They had always considered it to be a most important factor in economy of tonnage; one that should enable the Allies to take advantage of any excess in available shipping for the general prosecution of the war. Starting from that basis, the Americans had always encouraged the principle of unification in all branches of resources and effort. He wished to state that in his opinion the object of the activities of the Committee was not to take away resources belonging to an Allied army to turn them over to another army. Their object was chiefly to establish practical rules and methods enabling the Allied armies, when it was decided to be necessary, to use the common resources in the most intelligent and effective manner. He finished by thanking the Committee for the work they were doing.

Their great importance from a military standpoint in connection with our approaching offensive, the great necessity underlying them, all will contribute to their lasting usefulness. This visit of John's was made on the eve almost of our first great military attack on the front, the consequences of which are sure to be extremely far-reaching.

General Moseley, Assistant Chief of Staff G-4, G.H.Q., also came to the meeting. (Smither is Assistant Chief of Staff C-4, S.O.S.) Moseley feels we are well prepared for the attack of the first field army upon which the hopes of our cause so greatly depend. Pershing and Pétain came with Payot from a conference [6] with Foch at his near-by Headquarters, which was also attended by General McAndrew and Fox Connor, of our G.H.Q.

The English attack of to-day is proceeding well as Travers Clarke is informed by wire.[7] General Travers Clarke had completed the arrangements of the British rear before leaving British Headquarters — so he stated — so that, though the English attack would take place in his absence, his machinery would run through three days all right notwithstanding. In contrast to the attitude of some of the English high officials toward our Board, General Travers Clarke took this trip at this important time to ask me to ask General Pershing to make a request of Lloyd George for additional representation on the Board for British General Headquarters along the lines of my letter of August 24 to General Pershing regarding our own army which I had sent him through Major Bacon. I am to see General Pershing early to-morrow morning in this connection just before he starts for the front where so many important events are impending. Everybody has been doing his best to get things ready, and General Pershing will lead into battle a magnificent and well-equipped army.

My days pass in a succession of tasks which must be accomplished. It would be interesting if in these notes I could describe our gatherings in the old and historic rooms of *La Grange du Roy* [*sic*][8] and our dinners at the chateau. Now that the Belgian Army is represented, there gather around the table officers of five different armies. We are great friends. The French officers especially are considerate. But the beautiful and impressive surroundings somehow I seem to see only when I have left them, for the hard burden of difficult and perplexing decision is upon one's mind all the time. When the war is long over and I am far away from all the cares of the present and from this beloved country, there will come to me pictures in detail which now I hardly notice. Now above and overshadowing all is the atmosphere of tragedy unspeakable.

Paris, Tuesday, September 3, 1918

While I am waiting at his house for General Pershing this morning it occurs to me to make a note of something that happened at our meeting yesterday as illustrating negotiation from an inter-army standpoint. Pershing and Pétain had both discussed the great necessity of the motor reserve. Payot had stated with great emphasis the necessity for the American army to furnish its quota of camions. The matter of the failure by the French to deliver us hay as agreed had been the subject of our earnest discussion before Pershing and Pétain arrived. I had stated that because of that failure Harbord had just requisitioned 16,000 tons of hay from America — three shiploads. So I interrupted Payot to say, with the emphasis with which he was demanding camions from us, that if he would deliver us 16,000 tons of hay as a reserve we would give him these three ships full of camions for the inter-Allied motor reserve. I had been demanding, in view of the importance of saving tonnage, that the French withdraw their order preventing us from buying hay locally. Now Payot and Pétain work as closely together as Pershing and myself. Immediately that he saw that I was to expose a shortcoming of the French— which, Heaven knows was excusable enough — he winked at Pétain, who suddenly arose, thus putting an end to the entire meeting. Pershing, Pétain, and Payot left the meeting, and as soon as they were out of the building Payot sent for me to join them, and told me he would come to Paris to-day to get the French (through Vilgrain) if possible to agree to our buying hay in France. — Here comes the General.

P.S. 5 P.M. I resume after a long conference (up to 1.30 A.M.) with General Pershing who is on his way to his army.

In the evening Beadon came to me to express his indignation because Payot's wink, which closed the meeting, prevented an exposition on my part of a partial failure of the hard-working French which I was only resorting to in order to compel action as important to them as to us. I told Beadon that he had a wrong impression of Payot; that he had only done what I should have done; and that by agreeing to do what he knew was right had proved that any further argument on my part was unnecessary. When Beadon, who is a very fair man and nice fellow, heard what Payot had said to me afterward, he agreed fully that I was right. The incident only shows how easy it is for people to make trouble when there is a lack of full knowledge of all the circumstances, and how careful we should be at all times not to criticize or misjudge others. I am very very fond of Payot and trust him. He is an invaluable aid to the American army and a superb officer.

To-day Payot is here laboring to get the civil French authorities to agree to our buying hay direct which they yesterday refused Colonel Krauthoff. He brought me this afternoon a complete German grenade-thrower which he had himself taken and with a brass plate attached with an inscription to me, which I shall have translated and file with these notes. [9] Took lunch (very late) with Ganne, Tardieu, and others.

The main purpose of my visit with General Pershing, among others, was to have the General write Lord Milner urging that the English create a direct representation of the British General Staff on our Board in addition to the representative of the English War Office. The General wrote the letter, attaching my letter of August 24 as explaining in detail what was desired. General Travers Clarke is anxious to have this done and to come on the Board himself. I hope finally that our long siege against English conservatism will now be completely successful. My letter of August 24 to General Pershing was largely written for English consumption. It brought General Travers Clarke to Paris and Coubert. Now we shall see if it does not bring around the War Office. If it does our Board is entirely equipped. An Englishman always defers to a sound reason in time, though it must be firmly, almost violently and continuously, presented under some circumstances. I attach a copy of the General's letter. [10]

At Coubert General Moseley told me he had advised General Pershing to send him to the front and put me in charge of the 4th Bureau of the General Staff in his place. General Pershing this morning also told me that Moseley suggested this. No higher tribute could be paid me than this by Moseley, but I know what my training fits me for and I stated that this would be a mistake of a very serious nature. General Moseley is a most able officer, and his commanding ability and long experience with our own Zone of the Advance render him indispensable in this place. Like all unselfish and overworked men, he occasionally, working at such great tension, becomes discouraged. But he never falters. Much of our coming success will be due to his work. General Pershing told me of his violent interview with Marshal Foch of last Saturday. [11] While notes were taken of the interview, they will never indicate how important and intense was the issue. At one time Foch told Pershing he would appeal to the President of the United States. It ended with John's success. But I will say here that if any weaker or less able man than John Pershing had been confronted with this crisis, the American army, which is the pride of our nation and will ever be in history, would have been dissipated and a common victory rendered less certain. And yet Foch and Pershing are great friends and will always be so. Each admires the other. Unusual men take unusual methods of expression at times, but they never misunderstand each other. The sincerity of both Foch and Pershing, their common and sacred purpose, their common ability, bind them closely together. But when General Foch said, "I accept," he had yielded the American army its proper place in history.[12] This was due to General Pershing, and to him alone, under circumstances which no other man in any of the three armies in my judgment could have mastered. Pershing is incomparably the strongest character I have ever known.

Paris, September 5, 1918

Have just returned from the British aviation field where I saw my friend General Sam McRoberts start on his trip from Paris to London by airplane, and now have a few minutes' quiet.

At my request the Labor Bureau has been transferred to Tours to get it in closer contact with the operating construction chiefs. Received a fine letter of commendation from S.O.S. for my accomplishment. When I took over the task of recruiting and organizing militarized civil labor for the A.E.F. in addition to my other work, it was with some misgivings. But with the able help of Jackson, Smith, Estes, and others the Labor Bureau of the G.P.A. has made good, and that task is done. We started about February 25 with nothing. Our task was to recruit, officer, feed, transport, discipline, and maintain laborers under organization, turning them over to the control of construction officers only when they were actually at work. On March 25 we had 6,000; on April 23, 14,000; on May 23, 23,000; on June 25, 30,000; on July 23, 37,000; and on August 26, 45,251. Of this number 8,000 are prisoners of war operating under the Labor Bureau. Our actual recruiting amounted to about 26,000. The other laborers we took over from others for organization and control. When we started, Europe had been thoroughly combed over. Spain, Italy, and Portugal all embargoed our recruiting. I do not understand yet how we did so well. But thank Heaven! it is done. I will attach letter from Smither conveying commendation of General Harbord and his own.[13]

Our laborers consist of Spanish, Italian, Chinese, IndoChinese, Portuguese, French, Senegalese, Cabyles [*sic*],[14] Moroccans, Tunisians,

Germans (prisoners of war), and some others under the caption "mixed," which may sound like piling Ossa on Pelion[15] in the matter of designation. And then — and this should have been mentioned first — we have some 6,000 to 7,000 women, including "W.A.C.S," whom we brought from England.[16] I still, however, must help recruit as per my orders.

The retreat of the Germans continues. We are straining every nerve to get the S.O.S. in the immediate rear ready for the advance. Harbord arrives this evening.

Paris, Monday A.M.
September 9, 1918

Arrived from visit to front 1 A.M. and leave for Coubert in a few hours, but had such an interesting trip shall make a note of it. Arranged the trip for McFadden, of War Trade Board, through our Military Board French officers. He has been a faithful and effective worker of great ability for the A.E.F., and had not as yet been to the front. Arranged to have the party, including Dr. White and Mr. Darrow, of Chicago, go to Coubert for dinner and the night at our headquarters, meeting me at Meaux yesterday morning, to which point I went (Sunday morning) with General Harbord, who stopped there for a celebration of the Battle of the Marne. Mr. Stettinius[17] accompanied us. Went to Soissons, where we saw Mangin at his new headquarters near there into which he had moved that morning. Went about eight to ten kilometers beyond Soissons, where we looked at the artillery action. A French deputy who had preceded us at this point two hours before was killed by a shell which burst in his party. Looked at the shelling of the Chemin-des-Dames road. Brought back a French bayonet as a souvenir of this spot. It was lying near the body of a French hero—a private soldier. Went through Soissons — bombarded and deserted — and stopped for a minute in the deserted and ruined cathedral. Took the road as Mangin directed and got to the Oise by Noyon, but the bridge was blown down and we could cross only on a temporary footway. Noyon, like Soissons, is a stark ruin. The Germans are just out of it. The Noyon-Soissons road was somewhat rough from occasional shellcraters. Came back through Compiegne and then to Soissons again. Took dinner with General Mangin and his Staff. Clemenceau had been there in the afternoon on his way to visit the wounded deputy, who later died.

It was an interesting trip, as there was action everywhere in progress on the front, though comparatively light, owing to the rainy weather. We came into sight of it, however, only east of Soissons. Mangin again and again expressed his appreciation of the American troops. We traveled some

LIEUTENANT-COLONEL JOHN PRICE JACKSON, CHIEF OF LABOR BUREAU, AND STAFF

two hundred and fifty to three hundred miles during the day according to McFadden's estimate.

At Military Board meeting this P.M. I expect to receive for the A.E.F. authority for it to buy hay locally in France, which we have desired so long and which should save us much tonnage. Have not heard of the results of Pershing's letter to Milner, which I am awaiting with interest. When General Travers Clarke came to see me in Paris he brought with him and showed me the correspondence between Foch and Haig in connection with the former's request for the central command of the Allied rear. Considering this correspondence, considering the wisdom also of such a step, and the general situation, I do not see how the British can decline to accede to General Pershing's suggestion.

Discussed with Harbord Saturday evening the question of a central financial organization for the A.E.F. He and Kernan dined with me.

Paris, September 10, 1918

At Coubert for meeting of Military Board yesterday afternoon. Long and weary session. Got permission for the A.E.F. to buy hay in France along its line of communications which should help out our acute hay crisis. We have now only ten days' supply on hand.

Discussed the 60 c.m. railway situation and accepted principle of an inter-Allied Staff study and treatment of it including a school such as the M.B.A.S.[18] has established at Rozoy for the Allied motor transport.

At the château in the evening Major-General Buat (Pétain's Chief of Staff), General Woodruff, English liaison officer at French G.H.Q., and Colonel Mott, our American liaison officer at Foch's Headquarters, dined with us. All are much interested in our work. Stayed all night at Coubert and then motored to Rozoy with the other members of the M.B.A.S. to see the inter-Allied Staff school we have established there in connection with the system of unification of the motor transports in the rear of the Allied armies. In the school there are thirteen American officers, ten English, ten French, five Belgian, and two Italian. We listened to the morning lesson. Payot addressed the school. Prepared a telegram to Pershing asking his ratification of the inter-Allied system of motor transport which we are putting into effect, as Foch desires to promulgate it immediately.

Had a sense of satisfaction in attending this meeting and seeing some of the results of the tremendous efforts which we have made to establish and empower the M.B.A.S. Its immense usefulness is at last generally recognized and I no longer have to apologize, threaten, or explain. It speaks for itself. It has been no light task to fit the yoke of a common purpose upon the necks of the proud and independent chiefs of the services of the three armies, but with the wonderful aid and upon the initiative of our great Commander-in-Chief, General Pershing, it has been done. For all my trials and disappointments and work in getting this inter-Allied agency started — and they have not been inconsiderable — I felt myself repaid this morning as I sat before the school engaged in a meditation made practicable by my inability to understand the lectures in French delivered by the instructors.

Returned to Paris as usual at forty miles per hour. I often wonder at my peace-time conservatism in regard to speeding. It makes a difference when you have to do anything. Theoretically nothing mapped out for our Services of Supply is possible considering the increasing importation of troops, but practically we will take care of them. Dwight Morrow's story is applicable. A father was telling his little boy a story. He said, "The alligator had his mouth open and was about to close it on the turtle, when the turtle suddenly climbed a tree and hid himself in the foliage." "But, papa," said the little boy, "a turtle can't climb a tree." To which papa replied, "But *this* turtle *had* to."

Paris, September 14, 1918 (11 A.M.)

General Pershing and his army are winning a splendid victory, having wiped out the St. Mihiel[19] salient.[20]

When I appeared at Coubert at the Board meeting yesterday afternoon all praised the first field army and its commander. Payot brought over a French field map from his headquarters with the American advance platted up to the last hour and the other members of the Board signed it and presented it to me as a remembrance of the occasion.

Beadon notified me that the English Government had agreed to comply with General Pershing's request to have the British General Staff represented on our Board, and that General Ford[21] had been appointed.

Ford is one of the ablest men in charge of the British supply of the army rear. I think in our long fight for English cooperation he has constantly approved our plan. My recollection is that Lloyd George told General Pershing long ago that Ford favored rear coordination and suggested in our early efforts a consultation between Ford and myself. At any rate, England is now squarely "in for it" — and the world knows what that means for the success of any great effort.

At the meeting I was enabled to state that the American motor transport system was being reorganized as a result of the work of the Board and along French lines. Payot said Commandant Doumenc was at St. Mihiel then, and that our motor work was being carried on there under the more elastic plan of central control which the French follow. As our lines advance the subject of motor transport behind the lines is becoming of vast importance. The work which our Board has accomplished already in unification of circulation and general regulation of motor transports will be ever remembered. Then if we get our mobile automobile reserve of 24,000 camions, to operate under Foch, completed — and we shall if the war lasts a time longer — it will be a tremendously effective weapon in his hand. We established the Staff school for 60 c.m. railways at our meeting. I gave the Committee what the A.E.F. could contribute in time of emergency to Foch in light railway material, equipment, and personnel; also estimate of motors available for his reserve in October.

The great victory which John and his army is now winning will live in the history of the ages. It is difficult for me, however, to keep my mind from dwelling on the fact that it renders secure in every way my dear friend in the continuance of his great work. I think my nephew William must have been in a heavy tank in this fight, but am not sure.

Paris, September 15, 1918

General Pershing's victory is upon the minds and in the hearts of all. His military success will be that which appeals to the imagination and for which he will probably receive his greatest praise. And yet really his greatest achievement is the organization built up and held together during the past year under enormous difficulties. The great number of investigators and official visitors now among us are telling us how we can improve this and that in our system. They forget the difficulties with which we have been confronted. Results were always first in our mind — system second. As fast as we could apply system without lessening results, we did so. And upon results we asked to be judged as well as upon our system which we have evolved under the entirely new circumstances of an allied warfare. I therefore keep my patience when the young men from the War and Treasury Departments tell us what we should and should not do. Much of what they say is useful — much is nonsense.[22]

Stettinius, however, who is extremely efficient, has a clear, logical, and helpful mind. Sent here to report on us, he is showing every appreciation of our past difficulties and his criticisms are always constructive and helpful. We have been trying to devise a central financial organization for some time. He has given every assistance in this work. It is a pleasure to have him here. Both Pershing and Harbord, as well as I, feel this way about him.

Harbord spent much of yesterday with me. We had a conference with the French on the hay situation in the afternoon. John is biting into the

S.O.S. for motors and personnel for the emergency at the front and Harbord is bearing a heavy load. But he is a great man and his shoulders are strong enough to carry it. He is a dear, faithful, and loyal friend.

This morning received a telegram saying that General Pershing had wired General Foch, as I suggested, indicating his acceptance of the motor transport organization behind the Allied lines. I certainly am rejoiced that John and I did not yield to discouragement in our long fight to establish our Board.

Received telegram saying Portugal had granted our request to recruit 5,000 laborers there. "To him who hath shall be given." Victory is making our great task easier — though it is hard enough yet.

Paris, Wednesday September 18, 1918 (9 P.M.)

Started for Chaumont (G.H.Q.) Monday afternoon by automobile with Logan. My purpose was to expedite the settlement of the differences on the minor details of the Allied motor regulations which still remain and which the General Staff has appointed a board to consider. When this is done, Pershing will approve and Foch issue the rules to the Allied armies. Everything is settled except a few details, and the delay is annoying. Hope to have the matter settled so that the order can be issued by Foch to the armies next week. As our lines advance farther from the railheads nothing is more important than this motor transportation system. While what I say here does not apply — thank Heaven — to Moseley and G-4, who are concerned in motor transportation, my patience and forbearance are at times strained to the limit by the narrow and bigoted attitude of some of our American officers toward the French. So thoroughly is General Pershing in sympathy with, and possessed of knowledge of, the magnificent efforts which the French are making for us that in justice to these officers I feel that it would be unfair to them for me to indict them before the General, without their presence. This feeling alone keeps me from making a serious issue with some of them. However, since supply relations and negotiations with the French are largely in my hands, I am able to see that justice is done in almost every case. But it is exasperating, with knowledge of the sacrifices that these people are making and have made to help out the Americans, to hear prejudicial expressions from small natures reflecting upon them. Of course these men speak from only limited knowledge of our dealings with the French army and Government. Again to blame the French for an actual or alleged failure to do what they promised often serves as an excuse for their own dereliction or lack of energy. I state here that the record of French cooperation with the A.E.F., when it is understood, will ever be remembered to their credit. The attitude of a very few officers is something of a handicap to us at times in our inter-army and A.E.F. governmental negotiations.

The instinct of property universal in mankind makes difficult all questions of coordination in supplies. I have reflected on the comparative ease with which military cooperation is secured as distinguished from supply cooperation. Perhaps the answer is this: that military cooperation is dictated not only from motives of self-preservation, but as well because in the broader sense it works for the protection of supplies and property, and the property instinct therefore supports instead of opposes it. But it is curious to see an officer cheerfully acquiesce in the sending of men to lose their lives in the battle-line of an ally — as he should — and then favor a narrow policy in supply contribution.

Logan and I started late Monday afternoon, and took Colonel Mott with us as far as Foch's Headquarters. From there Mott telephoned to Cirey-le-Château[23] that Logan and I would be there for dinner. We lost our way and at 1.30 A.M. reached the chateau. We found Madame (Vicomtesse) Salignac-Fenelon and her daughter, Countess de Castres, sitting up for us. I had never met these charming representatives of French hospitality nor seen the wonderful chateau in which Voltaire lived and worked so long.[24] But I put here a word of appreciation of these women who have turned over the use of this beautiful and historic home to our officers and aviators. The husband of Countess de Castres is wounded and a prisoner in Germany. It is significant of the devotion of all of France to this cause that the delicate, sensitive, and refined Countess de Castres left this beautiful place to become a nurse, and for the first three months of her two years' work felt honored to wash the feet of the wounded and suffering *poilus*[25] as they were brought to the hospital. After this preliminary experience and further training she became a regular nurse.

At Chaumont I spent a busy day. Took lunch with General McAndrew (Chief of Staff) and General Davis at John's château. John is at the front preparing for what I cannot here write. Logan and I left Chaumont Tuesday evening and went as far as Cirey-le-Château where we spent the night. General Frank McCoy also spent the evening there.

The plan of campaign being carried on by Foch is that which General Pershing used so strongly to advocate in his talks with me long before the July offensive started. But his plan of striking with the maximum force at the time of the enemy's greatest weakness, *which is now*, involves a policy of the rear as well as the front. It involves a policy of tonnage and sea transportation as well as troop movements. How few realize the full weight of responsibility which General Pershing carries! How many after the war will realize that in carrying out his plan he has to risk all in one sense. Suppose in carrying out this plan in order to get a blow of the maximum force possible this fall, he jeopardizes by his tonnage policy supply reserves necessary for his army next winter and spring. Suppose he does not thus jeopardize supply reserves, but plans for another full year of war and this makes it impossible to strike the *maximum* blow and end the war before Christmas! John is going to strike his maximum blow. He is taking his chances on his supply. He believes a reserve is meant to be used in emergency. This is why John Pershing is fit to command the finest army in existence. He carefully considers, and then acts without hesitation and with the sublime confidence in his power to achieve which is ever the mark of genius. May God be with him and his army during the next month.

Paris, Saturday night
September 21, 1918

During the course of a conference yesterday over transportation (rail—in Zone of Advance), General Rageuneau, of whom I am very fond, gave a lunch to those concerned and invited me. As Moseley and Payot were both present I took an unfair advantage of a social occasion, called Hodges and and Roop[26] by telephone to the restaurant (*Voisin*),[27] led Moseley and Payot out of the lunch-room into an adjoining room, and there we settled a form of approval to be given by General Pershing of the motor transport regulations of the Allied armies which will enable General Foch immediately to promulgate them. While I subordinated etiquette to take advantage of the opportunity afforded by this accidental juxtaposition of powers, my friend General Ragueneau agreed with me that the end justified the means.

Since our army motor transport system is in course of reorganization under the plan to the M.B.A.S. no working time has actually been lost in the unreasonable delay in getting this matter of form settled. Such delays have their roots in human nature. In any large association of men engaged in a joint effort certain individuals in authority will be found whose narrowness of vision and personal selfishness of power, associated with extreme competency in the administration of their particular unit of the machine, makes their unreasonable opposition to general measure of coordination difficult to deal with at times.

This afternoon took lunch with Payot and De Siéyès. Payot feels deeply the great injustice done by him by the French War Department in not promoting him to Brigadier-General in accordance with the recommendation of Foch and Pétain. He is exercising powers equal to those of a General of an army like Mangin, but because these powers must be exercised in the rear they do not attract public imagination, and therefore poor Payot can be safely treated with injustice by civilian authority where the victorious army commander could not be. The history of this war will be written around achievement—not shoulder straps. But this does not comfort Payot.

Sent Colonel Hodges to Pershing's field headquarters with the copy of the motor regulations for his approval and signature to-day. These regulations are to govern, first, road traffic in the zone of operations; second, the hauling of material by mechanical transports; third, governing troop movements by mechanical transports. I think our new system will be in operation to a sufficient extent when our next advance occurs as to prevent some of the motor transport jams which occurred in the St. Mihiel offensive. However, Doumenc helped out the situation materially according to my present information. Instead of ten American officers as at present at our motor transport school Pershing has told McAndrew to send one hundred if possible.

Paris, September 23, 1918 (12.30 A.M.)

I have not written anything about our new offensive,[28] which starts to-morrow, because I did not dare trust it even to a paper which would remain on my person. But now there is not time enough left to have such an accident happen as to lose it. We shall have twenty-five divisions on hand under General Pershing available for the drive. Instead of striking at Metz — which we hope the Germans expect — our left flank, as I understand, will be in the neighborhood of Varennes, west of Verdun. We are bombarding Metz, but the General's eyes are elsewhere. St. Mihiel was but a preliminary effort. The next is our great movement.

Spent a very busy forenoon on supply and transportation matters. Prospects better for 60,000 animals from Spain.

11 P.M.

At my room after spending evening with Major General Ford, the new English member of our Board, and Lord Pembroke. General Ford reports three days' steady rain around Verdun which will probably delay our offensive. Ford has aggressive plans for the Board evidently. I no longer am apprehensive of a lack of British interest. My nephew William Dawes is in the 301st Heavy Tank Battalion, A.E.F., with the British Army. Am anxious about his welfare in the recent fighting. General Ford offered to telephone British G.H.Q. to have them look him up and will do so in the morning.

Paris, September 25, 1918

Returned last night from meeting of our Military Board at Coubert. Delivered to the Board General Pershing's signed approval of the three sets of regulations governing motor transport of the Allied armies. The reorganization of the motor transport system of the American army for which the Board is responsible will in my judgment almost double the effectiveness of the transportation in the rear of the First American Army in the coming offensive. The Board is rapidly becoming what I always felt was inevitable — the coordinator of the Allied rear. Major-General Ford, of the British General Staff, who attended his first meeting, is an ideal member — experienced as a soldier, possessed of authority, and having a keen, alert, and practical mind. Throughout all the delays of the English I have never lost faith in the idea that finally they would become enthusiastic cooperators in this great work. That time has now arrived. Ford, acting upon an expression in my letter to Pershing, transmitted by him to Milner, suggests the changing of the name of the Board more nearly to express its coordinating military power. He complains that the word "supply" creates the impression that we are dealing simply with something to eat. Being long habituated to covering military authority under civilian camouflage, and avoiding the encouragement of opposition in the effort to establish usefulness, I am more or less indifferent to names, but I agree that the Board is now so powerful and well recognized that its name makes little difference. As a matter of fact I am responsible for the English name.

Ford has proposed to the Board the consideration of railroad transportation. We established the sixty-centimeter school. The record of our meetings will indicate our growing activities.

While writing this received a code message from General Pershing asking me in person to make another appeal to the French for additional animals to help him in his operations at the front. Will do this later in the afternoon to M. Tardieu.

General Ford was kind enough to telephone British G.H.Q. and found that William is still all right.

Paris, September 29, 1918

Events move so fast I cannot note all of them. I will detail one of the more important of them.

Pershing wired me on the 24th to make an appeal in person to the French for more horses for his army. I did so and Tardieu took up the matter with his customary energy. To-day I have wired Pershing that the

French expect to send him 30,000 additional horses cutting them out of the French army. Marshal Foch is meeting the emergency. As I have always maintained, emergency is after all the greatest coordinator. Motor trucks and horses are the essential things for the hour.

Our lines advance. The army must follow closely the enemy. Delay in pursuit is disastrous. But the requirements in transportation facilities for a modern army are simply overwhelming. This is why what the French have done for us in the horse supply is so vital. I wired Pershing this morning, telling him that the French would furnish 30,000 more horses (they have already given us 136,000) and that the 30,000 was a reduction from the French army: "While this instance of extreme cooperation on the part of our noble ally is but one of many, it evidences her high confidence in your personal ability to effectively use in a crisis her most essential military resources."

General Harbord spent most of yesterday with me. Our lines advance everywhere. Foch is bending every energy to following up the enemy's slow retirement under pressure.

Paris, Thursday night
October 3, 1918

Just back from a day at Coubert — two meetings of the Board. General Ford, the new member, is ideal — cooperates in every way, ignores irrelevant detail and has an eye always on results. He understands the relative importance of things. Railway transportation problem was the principal one under consideration. Arranged for a committee of officers representing the three armies to visit all fronts to report on the car unloading methods with a view to their improvement. Committee will meet at my office Paris Monday morning and start immediately after a short consultation.

Discussed matters at rear of American First Army with Payot, who is coming to Paris to-morrow for a further consultation with me. If second conference confirms my impressions derived from the first, am thinking of going to General Pershing's Headquarters to make suggestions to him looking toward improvement. French claim that confusion of transports in our rear makes our rapid advance impossible. The problems of the rear in modern warfare are infinitely more difficult than those involved in simple military strategy. Thus it is that General Pershing's mind has been, and is now, so much on the rear.

The military situation steadily improves, though the fighting has been terrible the last few days. We have now about 72,000 in hospitals. May the Lord bring this war to a close soon, provided its close marks an enduring peace! May all this sacrifice insure for centuries a peaceful world! But this war must be fought to a finish — not negotiated to one.

Payot goes from Pétain to Foch this month.

At my office Jay is doing splendid work in tightening down our system of coordination through purchases by category. He is an administrator and executive of the highest order of ability. Besides this he is a lovable character, a strong man and a faithful friend.

The longer I am connected with our Military Board the more I realize the tremendous advantage its earlier organization would have been to the Allied armies even before America entered the war. The lessons as to our own rear which we are now learning under such difficulty could have been mastered much sooner. We have not yet mastered them. I have no disposition to underestimate the difficulties of the handling of the rear in the Zone of the Advance. But some of our Staff officers are not ready enough in profiting by the experience of our allies, in keeping in that humble state of mind which does not regard the seeking of the knowledge of the experienced as derogatory to military dignity. This emphatically, however, does not apply to poor Moseley who has about the hardest and meanest task in the war. He learns where he can, and does the best he can.

Paris, October 4, 1918 (1 P.M.)

After a morning of conferences too many to be enumerated — of crisis after crisis involving action, of long-distance telephoning, of a crowded office, one of those mornings in which one crowds a month of normal experience (even a normal month over here) — I find the room suddenly empty, and after a lunch on my desk have an inclination to make a few notes.

In the flush of victory after the war when only the more spectacular things or strategical things are remembered by the many, the memory of mornings like this will recur at least to me; for they indicate the quicksands that are ever under the feet of those in high responsibility. If they cross them, the world acclaims them. If they sink, the level landscape of the future will be unmarked by the evidence of their fruitless and heroic struggle. So in the advance, so in the rear. So with life and in battle; so with reputations both at the front and in the rear which must support the front.

Unquestionably the French and English desire to dissipate the American army to a large extent. While John is at the front, an attack is being made on his management of the rear. If he cannot advance his army farther because his rear is disorganized, they say, then why not let the French and English take over more of his troops in their sectors. The danger in the argument is that they are right—unless they are wrong about the state of the rear of the first field army. I believe they are wrong, but my idea is to be certain of it; and if they are right to make redoubled efforts to help straighten out the rear. That, of course, will be the General's view: for mixed armies do not fight as well as single armies provided that in military control they are in effect one army, and from every standpoint the solution — if the trouble really exists to the extent the French claim — is to make the rear stronger instead of the front weaker. But Clemenceau and Lloyd George seem to feel differently. I may be wrongly informed as to the depth of their feeling, but I believe it exists based upon reports they have received from our front.

Telephoned Harbord the situation fearing that in the interview Baker is to have to-day with the French this view would be pressed upon him without our side being represented. Harbord tried to get Pershing on the telephone, but he is in the field. Harbord is coming to Paris this P.M. at Baker's suggestion and will see him. In the meantime I expect to meet Payot and develop the full strength of the French military criticism of our rear in the advance zone. This, of course, is not under Harbord. But as friends of the General as well as a matter of duty we are trying to develop the exact situation for his information and action. What I fear is that an effort will be made to attribute to bad management in the rear a situation chiefly created by natural obstacles and which no amount of good management could have avoided, and thus injure unjustly the reputation for efficiency which the army has so well earned by its wonderful work under its great leader.

I am jotting down the thoughts of the minute — they must not be considered as records of permanent opinion. One changes his mind as information changes, provided that information alters the foundation of correlated facts upon which opinion must always be builded. But we must be guided by facts. If we are justly criticized, we must do better. It is never helpful to waste time resenting criticism which is needed to discover whether it is well founded. Nobody cares about us — only how the thing comes out.

And now to work again.

Souilly,[29] *October 8, 1918 (4 P.M.)*

Received orders to come to Souilly in accordance with my own suggestion, though I found on arriving that General Pershing had already written me of his own initiative to come. Arrived at Souilly from Paris with General McAndrew (C. of S.) by motor Saturday evening, October 5.

Have a few minutes now to record what I am working at this afternoon. Our general attack takes place to-morrow. Am trying through Payot at General Pershing's order to get ballast delivered by to-morrow for the normal gauge railroad nearly completed to Varennes — to be delivered from St. Dizier to Aubreville where the completed road ends. It is immensely important to hurry the railroad. At Varennes (which I visited yesterday) several wagon-roads diverge which can supply our divisions if we can get the material there by rail as well as by camion. It has been raining hard this morning, though it is clearing now. Ballast must be had if possible. The French engage to deliver eighty cars to-day. Am asking for two hundred by to-morrow. Payot telephones he is after them. Germans are shelling Varennes this afternoon, but are missing the wagon-roads by about a hundred yards at last accounts. We will attack heavily to-morrow between the Meuse and the Aire; also in other places. Was in St. Mihiel this morning for a short time. Will try and write later as to occurrences between Saturday night and the present time.

Souilly, October 8, 1918

On Sunday, having heard the General explain in detail (on Saturday night) to McAndrew and myself the plan of the coming attack of our troops, I went with Colonel Boyd, the General's aide, a man of great ability and military knowledge as well as personal charm, to look at the expected field of the action which will take place to-morrow (October 9). On the way to Montfaucon we called on General Bullard commanding the First Corps. Found camion transports being well handled everywhere. Found the town of Montfaucon under fire, so had to leave the automobile at the bottom of the hill on which the town — or rather what is left of it — stands. Troops were repairing road through the town, breaking stone by hand. Wounded were being carried down the hill as we passed. Boyd and I went on foot through the town and partly down the slope on the north side. There behind some signal corps camouflage we had a fine view of the country ahead. Our first line before us was being heavily shelled. Looked at the hills to the right, left, and ahead and realized as never before the extent of the task which has been allotted General Pershing. His men must go forward fired on from heights on three sides. Much of the fighting in the Argonne Woods and other woods is as severe as in Belleau Wood.

Instead of trying to describe his plans, after the attack is over I will attach the order of movement.[30]

Returned over the road via Cheppy and Varennes, as the General wanted a report on the bridge work being done over the two mine-crater holes which are now being by-passed. At and around Montfaucon we were in the midst of the artillery, and a battery of 155's — four in succession firing within fifty feet of me — well-nigh burst my ear drums. This was after our return from our observation post. Much aerial activity and heavy anti-aircraft and machine-gun work directed at Boche[31] machines was going on. My heart was

BATTERY C, 108TH FIELD ARTILLERY, 28TH DIVISION, FIRING ON THE GERMANS FROM VARENNES

ST. MIHIEL AND THE MEUSE

A CROWDED ROAD THROUGH ESNES NEAR THE MEUSE-ARGONNE FRONT

BELLEAU WOOD

heavy with pity for the wounded in the long lines of ambulances swaying along over roads so rough that at times their agony must have been excruciating. It was less difficult to look upon the dead. Some mother's son lay sleeping the last long sleep near our observation post. In the frightful noise all around he looked strangely peaceful and rested. Reached the train where we live and spent the evening with the General alone. Went over all Payot's suggestions as to our rear with him and discussed them fully.

Am not going to try to write about what happened in our long conferences until I get to Paris. On the way back saw General Summerall[32] commanding First Division at his P.C.[33] He was having hard fighting that day and had the same yesterday and to-day.

Souilly, October 9, 1918 (10.40 A.M.)

Am here with General Pershing, and as I am through with my work of getting information as to the rear in Zone of Advance, and of expediting a little part of it, make these notes. After a bombardment of nineteen hours (about) of the hill to the northeast of Montfaucon in which it was expected to use 500,000 shells, our attack started at 8.30 A.M. The news from the front will soon begin coming in.

As usual Payot made good, and at 9.30 last night received a telephone from him on the General's special train, where we live, that he would deliver at the rate of four trains of ballast to-day and to-morrow at Aubreville instead of two — (train 35 cars each, making 140 cars per day, instead of 80 as before arranged). I did this at General Pershing's direct order confirmed afterward by General Drum, Chief of Staff, First Army, although the order of General Pershing was delivered to me in Drum's presence. I make this note, as the Engineers complain this morning, I understand, that the ballast may be more than they can handle. How I wish I could put on boots and take charge of the pushing through of those few miles of vitally important railroad construction as in my old days at Big Run, Athens County![34] But I have done all I am ordered, and therefore able, to do. I found generally in the rear that Moseley has made splendidly good. Was especially pleased with the work of the M.P.'s, graduates of our school M.B.A.S., in handling motor supply trains at the crossroads at Varennes — a difficult spot. Good work is being done also at the difficult spots in the road. Hope the Germans are not getting the range of the vital crossing spots at Varennes. Then with the railhead brought there, as it will be soon, a supply basis for a considerable advance is provided if our attack to-day makes it possible.

On Monday, on my trip along the front and supply lines with Major Quekemeyer (an aide of General Pershing's), I went through the part of the Argonne Forest we have taken and over the supply road there. On that day went to La Forge and in the midst of active artillery again. Later in the day went over to Verdun and the supply roads there. Everything was in good shape, and I am convinced that as our lines advance the necessary supplies can be brought up. But right here I again want to pay my tribute to the French for their wonderful cooperation. While they criticized a little, because for a day or so immediately after the victory at St. Mihiel things were somewhat blocked owing to the condition of the roads as well as to other temporary causes, they are now generous in their commendation of the way in which those things were mastered. Americans recognize no impossibilities in warfare. This army of ours is a wonderful organization. Pershing's attack last Saturday had already answered any criticism, as to the effect of which I had had some concern.

Drum like myself is wearing his stars for the first time. Am much impressed with his ability. Pershing is going to make another request of Clemenceau to do our friend Payot justice and promote him as he has so long justly deserved. Will stop here and read the messages from the attack.

Paris, Saturday night
October 12, 1918

Reached Paris Thursday afternoon. Came by motor from Souilly, stopping at Chalons all night. As during my stay at the front I lived with the C.-in-C. on his train, and was with him much of the time, these impressions of him in action will be of interest hereafter, as the fighting he is now directing is the hardest which the American forces have yet done — barring Belleau Wood which equaled it. General McAndrew and I arrived in time for dinner Saturday evening, October 5. After dinner General Pershing explained to General McAndrew and myself his plan for the coming attack in detail. His grasp of the situation is in general and as well in exact and specific detail. Every foot of the ground over which the attack was to occur he knew. He is intensely concentrated mentally. Every unit to be engaged was at his tongue's end. Carefully and in detail he explained the method of attack and the reasons for each step. So exact is his knowledge of the topography of the region that when on the next morning at his office he was further explaining his plans to me by reference to an elaborate and colored profile map, he suddenly challenged the accuracy of the map in which investigation sustained him. Extreme mental concentration and tension, combined with firmness and mental calmness and coldness, marked the great commander. As he finished his long exposition he said he thought everything was well and would go right. "But," he continued, "when my wife and I were in the

OBSERVATORY OF THE GERMAN CROWN PRINCE AT MONTFAUCON

MONTFAUCON
Observation Post of Crown Prince in foreground

243

MONTFAUCON: VIEW FROM THE SOUTH

Philippines she would ask, 'Jack, how do things stand?' I would say, 'Very well at present.' Then she would reply, 'Look out! Something is going to happen.' And," said the General, "something always did happen." Late at night, as the General and McAndrew and I were still sitting around the table in the observation car, Boyd walked in with a telegram stating that Germany had asked for an armistice.[35] I remarked to the General, "Here is the 'something' that has happened." The news which we are now receiving shows that the General's plans have succeeded. His gallant army responded to the demand as only the brave can do. Their precious blood is sealing the final and complete victory which now seems but a question of a short time.

Paris, Wednesday, October 16, 1918

Many important happenings as usual the last three days. Yesterday was at a lunch given by Stettinius and Logan. Loucheur, Clementel, Tardieu, Ganne, General Bliss, General Harts, McFadden, and others present. Bliss brought in the text of President Wilson's reply to Germany which he had just received. Was interested to note the great satisfaction of the French ministers present with the President's note.

Monday was at Coubert at a most important meeting of the M.B.A.S. — two sessions morning and afternoon. The work of this Board is becoming so varied and important that I will not try to cover any of it in these notes.

Yesterday (Tuesday) General Moseley called me up in distress over an order of Foch's through Payot taking away camions from the first field army. He wanted to keep me advised of the situation. Large questions are involved. The C.-in-C. bears heavy burdens. If events prove this is an effort of Foch to assume command of the rear as well as the front, it will cause complications with both British and Americans. If so he is asking a control over the rear of the American and British forces which in his own army even he divides with civil authority. Until, however, I know all the situation I am in no position to judge of what is involved in this request or its propriety.

This I know: that John Pershing is being attacked in the rear while fighting at the front by those who would like so to divide the American army as to destroy largely its entity — something inconceivably unjust considering its great accomplishments and apparently without the excuse of military necessity.[36] I cannot believe Payot desires this. Nor do I wish to infer that Clemenceau and Foch desire anything that does not advance the common cause in their judgment. It is only another one of the interminable succession of inevitable conflicts and compromises between the interests of the whole and the units composing it. Each is dependent on the other. As in the case of a wounded man, it is sometimes necessary to amputate an arm to save the body. But no reputable physician cuts off the arm without endeavoring to save the arm first if it seems possible. Thus also in military matters must decision be left to those in best position to diagnose what is and what is not indispensable in the relation of a unit to the whole. Therefore I refrain from further comment. In nothing is Pershing showing greater ability and wisdom in his handling of his army than in its relation to Foch and the Allies. In nothing is he confronted with more difficulty. His attack of October 4 silenced the French military critics.[37] Now they are beginning again. Pershing has been given the hardest part of the line. The most difficult in topography to attack, it has the greatest and most determined concentration of the enemy behind it now existing in France. That concentration has drawn much strength of the enemy from in front of the English and French lines and made their great advance of the last week possible. Our army with the hardest fighting is making possible great and gallant victories of the others while slowly, obscurely, and painfully forging ahead itself. Its work is not spectacular, but magnificent in its effects. But to-day John has men north of the Bois de Forêt, and I am hopeful that events will soon crown our devoted army with its proper reward and recognition and make their position and that of the C.-in-C. less difficult.

Paris, Thursday night
October 24, 1918

Have just returned from Military Board meeting at Coubert. For the last three days have been trying to find time to make these notes while the important events were fresh in my mind, but events themselves and not myself are masters of my time.

Last Friday noon, at the request of General Travers Clarke, B.E.F., I left for B.E.F. Headquarters at Montreuil, taking Dwight Morrow and McFadden[38] with me, as questions of tonnage as well as matters within my more direct province were to be discussed. It is no longer possible for me to take time to describe many of the important matters in which I am engaged, for they are too numerous to permit of it. The particularly bad one just now is horses to put artillery into action, and General Pershing has notified me that he places primary responsibility on me to get them. Today General Travers Clarke telephoned me of the first five thousand which have resulted from our efforts. But that is but an incident of the last week, and the report of my daily activities to General Harbord must supply the details of my work.

Just a word about our visit to our English comrades. Their entertainment of us was that of brothers meeting in time of mutual dependency and with a mutual affection. After our important conferences were over Saturday morning, McFadden and I went back (by motor, of course), via Arras, Bapaume, and Peronne, through the devastated district. Passed the Scotch marching through Arras with their bagpipes playing, and somehow it always brings tears to my eyes to see them. We reached Paris in the evening traveling as usual at "breakneck" speed. Sunday morning (October 20) my office was full of officers, General Moseley among them. Talked with him about his trip to Foch's Headquarters to see Payot and Weygand and the importance of maintaining the present agreeable relations with them. I then suddenly decided to leave for General Pershing's Field Headquarters to put before him the reports as to our rear supply system emanating from some French sources, which reports were unfounded but making trouble; this with a view to having him in touch with the real situation, which was a simple one as follows:

After the St. Mihiel attack and when our army was being hurriedly moved over to the west for the next attack, there occurred, owing to the condition of the roads and other ordinary causes, a congestion of supply trains which was not fully relieved for about a day and a half. Clemenceau happened to be at the front and saw it. Somehow the impression got abroad that the Americans could not renew their attack because of this temporary congestion, but such criticism immediately ceased from any responsible source when the Americans did attack on October 4. They have been attacking and advancing ever since. However, unfounded criticism having started from high sources, their ceasing it did not prevent the miserable gossips from causing us some annoyance. On my trip took with me my friend Lieutenant-Colonel Cushing, of my old regiment. We arrived at Souilly about 9.30 P.M. The General has moved some war maps to the office in the car of his train so as to have them before him there as well as at the staff building in Souilly. The terrible battle is at its height and will probably remain so for some time. Our casualties so far in this movement have been 75,000. It is a greater Battle of the Wilderness.[39] Some officers and Generals are weakening — but not so the Commander-in-Chief.

Paris, Saturday, October 26, 1918

Interrupted last Thursday by callers, one of them Colonel Milton J. Foreman;[40] also M. Ganne, who came from Clemenceau with the word that for the present he could not see his way clear to requisition additional horses for our army from France. I do not wonder at this, as France has already given us over 125,000. Lest I forget it, will say here that General Travers Clarke telephones me to-day that we can now hope for up to 13,000 horses from the English. So I am getting a start on horses to get which I am turning heaven and earth. In this war quantities are so enormous and needs so critical all the time that I wonder how normal business conditions will seem to me after it is over.

After being at the front and looking at a German barrage laid on our first line, I know what artillery horses mean to our men. That is why I keep everybody on a tension of nervous effort and keep myself there. Ever since I have been here I have tried to visualize military emergency needs to keep myself at the highest pitch of effort. I have tried to see always a private soldier holding out his hands to me, and my beloved Commander-in-Chief smiling when I filled them. Now to resume:

Spent the evening when at Souilly with General Pershing alone. We stayed up until nearly one o'clock in the morning. He is in the midst of his greatest work, his most difficult test. After our talk he decided to go to Paris and see Clemenceau and to Foch's Headquarters. He started by his special train Monday evening while Cushing and I started by motor Monday morning, October 21, as I wanted to see how our supply trains, etc., were functioning at the front. Took the road from Souilly to Varennes — everything running finely. We went up from Varennes as far as Fléville, near Grandpré — everything running smoothly. The reorganized transport system, A.E.F., is in partial effect and the graduates of our Military Board Motor Transport School are at work on the roads guiding traffic, although the orders actually authorizing the reorganization have not yet been issued by G.H.Q.

Moseley deserves great credit for the way our supplies reach our troops. He makes a great Chief of G-4, G.H.Q. To occasionally visit the front and see his work and that of our organization there always encourages me.

At Fléville, where we took lunch with the soldiers, the town was under shell-fire and Cushing had his first experience with it. It was very mild. But what our own batteries there were giving the Germans was another matter. We reached Paris Monday night. Tuesday General Harbord arrived in the city. I have been so busy on horses and everything else that I cannot remember — and have no time to try and fix the time — whether it was Tuesday or Wednesday night, but on one or the other General Pershing telephoned to us and we three took dinner at Fayot's[41] (that is not spelled right, but the name sounds like that), where General Pershing often takes us. We had an interesting time. John was entirely satisfied with his trip. He feared, from what Clemenceau told him, what has since happened, that the former would not requisition additional horses for us. Am writing very hastily, for callers are waiting, but I want to record my admiration for my nephew, Lieutenant William Dawes, who commanded a tank in the recent attack of the British and Americans upon the northern Hindenburg line. His ride in his tank, as I cabled his father, should become as much a matter of pride in our family as the ride of his great-great-grandfather with Paul Revere. Rockenbach tells me in our American tanks our percentage of casualties among officers is very heavy. And here I also want to record what I have often meant to do before, that is my new admiration for my father and my Uncle Eph.[42] Interrupted here — but will complete this later.

Paris, Sunday P.M. October 26, 1918

To have taken the 6th Wisconsin through its charge upon and capture of the 2d Mississippi Regiment at Gettysburg, where every other man of the 6th was killed or wounded, and to have been in eighteen battles of the Civil War besides skirmishes, means something more to me now about my father. I have seen war as it is. To the memory of my brave Uncle Eph, shot through the jaw at Dallas, I also uncover. My experiences on the line are nothing as compared to theirs, but enough to give me knowledge of what a long continuance of such an experience entails in physical and nervous strain. Before the front-line private soldier and the front-line officers, the aviators and the tank men, a Staff officer, no matter how essential his work or high his rank, feels like standing at salute. At least I do.

I suppose peace is near at hand. General Pershing and all are here to-day. The conference on the terms of armistice to be offered by the Allies will be held at Versailles Tuesday. But like the runners at the end of a race, our heads are down in the effort and we cannot stop to concern ourselves with that which is not our business. To do one's own part is privilege enough.

If the German army breaks before the armistice is declared, Foch notifies us on the Board through Payot that the potential inter-army motor transport reserve which we have organized will be needed in pursuit. I think we can furnish 12,000 camions at least. We ought to have 24,000.

I am just as hard after horses as if the war was just commencing. It is our duty to keep at our maximum efficiency until the fighting actually ceases and peace is declared.

Paris, Monday (noon) October 28, 1918

Have just come from General Pershing's bedroom, where he is slightly ill of grippe or a cold. When I got back from the theater with Covell and

Griscom[43] last night received a note to call up the General's house immediately, which gave me a shock for fear he was seriously ill. He had wanted me to come there — and so I went this morning. His purpose was to talk over the attitude he is to take at the Versailles conference Wednesday which is to settle the Allies' terms for granting an armistice. He has made up his mind that his position will be that the only thing to do is to demand unconditional surrender. He told me what he had suggested at Foch's Headquarters last Thursday when he, Foch, Haig, and Pétain held a conference at St. Lys to compare notes on what the military terms of the armistice should be. The General after the conference carefully wrote out his personal suggestions and submitted them. Foch has a copy. He made his suggestions verbally at the conference and reduced them to writing afterward. Will not go into detail as to these terms, as all these things will be better recorded elsewhere, but was impressed with Pershing's suggestion in his proposal as to terms that the Allied armies should take possession of the east bank of the Rhine. At the conference Haig spoke of the French and English armies as somewhat tired. Foch took issue with this. Haig also made some slight reflections on the organization of the American army which John let pass without comment. But Foch, on the other hand, paid our army and its command the highest tribute.

What is forming in General Pershing's mind now is the form of his statement at Versailles. This he discussed at length. He will make a review of the military situation in connection with it. He is convinced that if civilization is to receive the full benefit of this terrible war it must end only with the unconditional surrender of Germany. The military situation is such that in his judgment there can be no excuse for not obtaining unconditional surrender. Not even the quagmires of a Versailles conference can impede in my judgment its ultimate acceptance of the General's position as correct. I think the General will be able to get out of doors by to-morrow.

Paris, October 29, 1918 (2.30 P.M.)

Have spent the last two evenings with General Pershing who is still confined to his room with the grippe. He is, however, working as hard as ever. He read me the first draft last night of what he is to say at the Versailles conference, which has now been postponed to Friday. Told me of Major Robert Bacon's good work in connection with Haig's reflections on the A.E.F. made at the Foch conference. At that time General Pershing made no comment on them, but felt them deeply, which fact Bacon communicated to Haig. Sir Douglas did not really mean what he said at the conference, and sent General Pershing through Major Bacon a three-page letter saying so. Inasmuch as he had left a memorandum with Foch in which this slight criticism appeared, he sent a Staff officer and withdrew it substituting another statement. This is only another indication of the essential fairness and high-mindedness of Sir Douglas — and of all the English. They are stubborn and outspoken in argument, but at all times essentially helpful and cooperative. Bacon did a good service to Pershing and the A.E.F. and a greater one to Haig himself, who is justly honored by us all, and who last of all would wish to make a serious reflection on our advancing army which has already lost over 75,000 men engaging German forces on our front, some of which otherwise would have been fighting Haig and his troops.

The Commander-in-Chief (J. J. P.) seemed much better last night. He is preparing a brief and strong statement.

At noon yesterday I went to La Morlaye, about one hour distant by motor from Paris. [44] There I took lunch with Payot and his staff, who are quartered in Baron Rothschild's fine country residence. [45] Discussed with Payot important matters now before our board. Was absent from my office only about four hours, but had to work pretty lively the balance of the day in consequence. Am very fond of Payot. It is in times of greatest trial that the most enduring friendships are born.

Paris, Wednesday
October 30, 1918 (10.15 P.M.)

Have just returned from General Pershing's house. He leaves to-night for the front. He will resume the general attack with his armies day after to-morrow. The conference at Versailles Friday will not be held. Am glad things are being settled without a Versailles town meeting. The General attended a conference of the Prime Ministers at Quai D'Orsay this afternoon. House was there. The armistice terms for Austria-Hungary have been agreed upon and will be announced. Austria-Hungary has surrendered. The armistice terms of the Allies for Germany are still under discussion.

At the Foch conference at St. Lys, Pershing and Pétain handed their suggestions to Foch. He has handed his to the ministers. The General said they did not differ much from those suggested by him, which were drastic. Notwithstanding there will be no general conference Friday, General Pershing to-day sent to the Supreme War Council at Versailles his views as to the armistice. [46] He argues against an armistice and for peace—that it may be enduring—by the sword rather than by negotiation. These are his views as a military adviser. He gave House a copy of them. Pershing's statement is a series of numbered paragraphs, clear, concise, and to the point, devoid of any attempt at rhetoric and designed only at clear presentation. He has worked hard in his sick-room. To-night he was dressed and feeling fit. Besides the armistice and peace conditions we discussed imminent supply situations, notably horses. The General thinks it will be nearly a year before he and I can go home, even though an armistice is declared immediately which he thinks very likely.

Have had a very busy day. Payot came to the hotel and gave me a signed photograph of Foch this evening.

Paris, Friday
November 1, 1918 (1.30 P.M.)

Notice by the papers that meetings at Versailles are being held after all. Although Foch and Haig were present, with others for their Governments, the United States was not represented except by House and the navy chiefs. Owing to his care not to catch the grippe or others reasons, the Colonel has not leaned, and evidently does not intend to lean, heavily upon the General in connection with advice as to peace negotiations. The General's views are on record, however, as those of a military adviser. [47]

Not that the war is about over, I am resigning myself to the inevitable future in which the critic and the politician take center stage. If there is any way in which General Pershing *can* be attacked, they may be trusted to find it.

Attended Military Board meeting at Coubert yesterday. Took Stettinius and Colonel Dudley, of the Gas Service, with me. Senator Béranger, head of the French Gas and Oil Service, was present and we reached some agreements.

Am making some headway in the horse and mule supply. My work was never more exacting since entering the service, but my health keeps good.

Paris, Sunday
November 3, 1918 (morning)

Yesterday General Pershing was in the city. Attended the conference. Says Foch and Lloyd George have commended highly his written statement to the Versailles Supreme War Council. However others may think of it, it nevertheless expresses not only what should but what will happen—a peace by victory, not by negotiation. Germany will soon be in a state of complete military and governmental collapse. Since peace terms under these conditions mean negotiation simply among the Allies between themselves, the so-called peace conferences are comparatively unimportant as shaping results. The troops at the front are furnishing these. Last night the telephone from Souilly to the General announced the splendid advance of our troops, which have at last broken through. How pitifully cheap now sounds the pessimistic chirp of the fireside crickets who have maintained that lack of organization in our rear, and not the fierce resistance at the front, has made our progress slow and painful up until yesterday when our break-through commenced. Let the casualty lists answer this lie. I am not going to concern myself with it further. Reports having come to General Pershing that House was repeating such views, he asked House about it and the latter denied it. At 5.30 last evening James Keeley brought Lord Northcliffe[48] to my room at the hotel. The latter said Grasty,[49] of the *New York Times* (who had proved a loyal defender of the General and a valuable one since he has been in personal contact with him the conditions at the front), desired him to make a statement to the American people through the *New York Times* which would assist in quieting this unfounded criticism of our rear. He asked my opinion about the matter and the situation, and I gave it emphatically. As a result he went to his room, wrote a splendid article, which he submitted to me, and I in turn to General Pershing later in the evening. It had therefore gone forward.[50]

Reported to the General that in my judgment we had established a weekly flow of animals to the First Army of about seven thousand. Hope this will be the last emergency work put upon me, as peace seems imminent.

John is well—very tense, very energetic, very determined. He made up his mind that the American army would break through and they and he accomplished it. Six new German divisions were put in against him in the last few days. Got him to sign approval of the inter-army regulations for secondline telegraph and telephone system adopted by the Military Board of Allied Supply.

Smashed up in the automobile coming back from the General's train, on which he left at 11 P.M., and bumped my head, but not enough to prevent it working as usual.

Paris, Friday, November 1, 1918 (9.30 P.M.)

Colonel Mott has just told me that our attack has attained a depth in the center at last reports of seven to eight kilometers with 1200 prisoners. It started at 6 A.M. to-day. Germany internally seems in a bad way. Realizing that prophecy is generally unprofitable I have nevertheless been predicting for the last six months that finally the Allies in peace negotiations will have in Germany no better form of government with which to deal than Germany formerly had with Russia after the collapse of the dynasty. That enduring results for the good of humanity should arise out of this terrible war it will be best so. Have had a busy day as usual.

To the future student and historian of the methods of allied warfare:

Largely for your assistance as well as because the information is of practical use at present for our armies, I am taking steps to have the Military Board of Allied Supply gather information as to the present military status of the three armies in regard to their supplies, transportation, lines of communication installations, etc., as of date October 31, 1918. I hope one or more of you will be able to clearly demonstrate from these data the overwhelming advantages in allied army cooperation of a military unification of supply as well as of combat operations. The work of the Board, of course, has already demonstrated many of these advantages. But you should be able to show that if from the first the Allies could have united their rear activities as well as those of the front the war would have been won long ago. To fully understand the situation you must thoroughly go over France itself. And you should also be able to show that the central control of the rear of any allied armies is as important as a central military control of their combat movements. The work I have done, with the splendid support of my able and generous Commander-in-Chief, in forcing the international consent for such unification of the rear as we have been able to effect through our Military Board, has been the most difficult of my varied experience here.

As you point out many things which could have been done in improvement of our allied military position — some of which I have fruitlessly labored for and of some of which I probably have never thought — it will be difficult for you, in considering their self-evident importance, to realize the enormous obstacles in the way of this kind of improvement, which we here to-day confront and have confronted from the first. You will realize them better when I state that if at the next meeting of the Board I should ask for an order to issue to the three armies requiring a report of the three Quartermaster Departments as to food supplies on hand, it would be impossible to get the unanimous consent necessary. Therefore I have asked for information on munitions first. So fearful are the Quartermaster Departments, especially the English, that a superimposed authority exercised for the common good might interfere in their separate control, that in my judgment they would veto even the gathering of information which might lead to a discussion of a betterment of conditions. The defeat of the English in front of Calais brought about the control of Foch, brought about the transport of the bulk of the American army by British ships, brought about a desperate struggle on the part of our proud and independent army elements to get together in many ways. In those dark days in April with their ominous outlook was born my own effort to contribute to the effectiveness of the Allied armies by securing unity of supply and supply movement to match the unity of the front under Foch. Had the Allied armies been confronted from a supply standpoint with a situation as critical as their military position after the March offensive of the German army, my idea of a central control of the rear would have been adopted. It takes more than reason to bend national pride. Necessity must also exist.

But I persevered in my efforts, and General Pershing, intervening at a critical time by securing the Clemenceau agreement, rendered possible the partial adoption of the principle of proper inter-army Allied cooperation by the establishment of our great Board whose work even with its handicaps should ever make it remembered in history.

Paris, November 11, 1918 (6.15 P.M.)[51]

The greatest struggle of humanity ended to-day with the signing of the armistice by the Germans. Colonel Robert Bacon called me by telephone at eight in the morning saying it was signed at 5 A.M. After breakfast, on my way to my Headquarters at the Élysée Palace Hotel, was met by my faithful aide, Lieutenant Kilkenny, who said General Pershing wanted me to call him up immediately on the telephone at Chaumont. For the first time since being over here I did not anticipate an emergency, but thought his mind might be on the victory. It was characteristic of the Commander-in-Chief that he was hard at work, and what he wanted was to talk over the plan for a financial section of the General Staff. During our conversation I suggested that he should issue to the army chiefs of services an order relative to stopping immediately construction and purchases not essential to the A.E.F. under the new conditions created by the armistice. While the C.-in-C., Harbord, and I have all had this matter under consideration and have taken action therein as far as possible up to this time, it seemed to me that a statement by the C.-in-C., issued on the very day of the armistice, would not only result in a great saving through the prompter action of the chiefs of the services, but would indicate to the American people that the A.E.F. appreciated its duty to save everything possible in view of the enormous self-sacrifice which our nation had made in order to supply us.

At the request of the Commander-in-Chief I later dictated over the telephone such a suggested statement, first telephoning it to Harbord, who approved it. Am anxious to see how the Commander-in-Chief will finally issue the statement.[52] In anything important he usually writes out the matter in long hand, then gives it careful revision. As a result Pershing's individuality is so apparent in his orders that I can generally tell from reading the ones he has personally prepared. He is a great master of English. When I congratulated him on his success he said he would not regard that he had succeeded until the army was safely back in the United States.

Went to lunch given at the Inter-Allied Circle by George McFadden at noon; present, Ambassador Sharp, Ganne, General Harts, Dwight Morrow, Auchincloss,[53] Stevens of the Shipping Board, Atwood (who came with me), Stettinius, and others. Worked at office in the afternoon. The city has gone wild. Great crowds are everywhere. People are singing and cheering and carrying up and down the streets the flags of the Allied nations. The Place de la Concorde is jammed, especially in front of the Metz and Strasbourg statues. Clemenceau was to make the announcement of the signing of the armistice in the Chamber of Deputies to-day, but I made no effort to go.

Somehow — and I think it is true of almost every one else — I keep thinking of what I have seen and of those who made all this possible, but themselves cannot know of it as they sleep buried in the wheat-fields and by the roadways of northern France. I could not cheer to save my life, but I have to try hard all the time to keep from crying. Am waiting now for my dear friend Harbord who is coming by motor from Tours to spend to-morrow with me. We plan to see General Pershing on Wednesday.

Last Tuesday I went by motor to Tours, spent the night and Wednesday there, staying at Harbord's house. Went with him on his special train on a partial tour of the ports. At St. Nazaire on Thursday, also at Nantes, at La Pallice on Friday in the morning and Bordeaux in the afternoon and evening. We arrived at Tours again Saturday morning. I reached Paris Saturday night. The achievements of the S.O.S. cannot be described by me here. General Walsh, General Jadwin, General McCawley, Colonel McCaw (Chief Surgeon, A.E.F.), Colonel Smither (A.C. of S. G-4, S.O.S.), and Colonel Wilgus were also on the train. Took Francis Kilkenny along with me at General Harbord's suggestion. Harbord has made good in the S.O.S. and that statement means something to any one who has seen the work accomplished.

General Pershing has asked me to go with him when he decorates Sir Douglas Haig with the "Distinguished Service Medal" of the United States. Will try hard to get things in shape to do it. To-night the General told me how much he had come to think of General Pétain, and of how stanch and able a soldier and good friend he was. The General has recommended McAndrew and Harbord for promotion to Lieutenant-General, but Baker replies that while he would be glad to do it, under the law they must be in command of line troops. It seems too bad that Harbord, who commanded the Marine Brigade at Château-Thierry and afterward the 2d Division, should now, because he has been placed at the head of 400,000 men in the S.O.S., be deprived of the rank which belongs justly to him. But history will take care of him.[54] And so — as Pepys says — to bed. [55]

Paris, Tuesday, November 12, 1918 (11.15 P.M.)

So much has happened since last night it seems as if it were a week ago. Others will tell of the world activities, but I am near the center of the situation as it confronts our supply situation. The tremendous change in army supply policy, made necessary by the armistice yesterday, brings to us a series of questions so numerous and varied and at the same time of such far-reaching importance that there is not a minute's relaxation, which would normally follow a victory.

Taking up only one of the great questions considered today: General Merrone[56] called at my office with a telegram from his Government saying that they (Italy) had 1,000,000 prisoners and 200,000 Austrian horses and were practically without food or hay for them. He asked immediate aid from the A.E.F. General Pershing had arrived this morning, but had gone to see Foch. I got General Rogers and took him and Merrone to the General's house where we met General McAndrew (C. of S.) and General Harbord. I proposed that the A.E.F. take over 100,000 Austrian horses in order to cut off the necessity of our Spanish purchasing now going on. At five o'clock General Pershing having returned, we all met again with him and went over the situation. He will help Italy with flour from our stock at Marseilles. After outlining about what we could do, he instructed me to handle the matter if possible through the Military Board of Allied Supply.

Germany is in revolution and appealing for food.[57] Reports are that Switzerland is becoming disorderly. Washington is wiring us to be careful — not to sell to our allies, etc. We have got to act in the great emergencies which confront us as best we can, make decisions as best we can, and come out for better or for worse as we may, trying only to do our duty and act as far as possible under the highest authority at hand.

The day of the civilian is approaching, but it is not quite here. Since the Allied armies and governments always approach our army and General Pershing through myself in supply matters, the crisis which confronts all Europe is reflected in the daily happenings of my office.

As a result of the call of the Belgians and the conference I arranged for them, Rogers sold them about $3,000,000 worth of foodstuffs to prevent starvation. It was an emergency. But Washington through various channels is manifesting opposition to the army dealing with civilian or alien army relief. I feel that Washington is right on general principles and that these matters are properly for inter-Allied boards to handle, but we cannot wait while people may be starving for such machinery to start operations. The crisis, however, should soon be tided over.

The General (Pershing) had Davis (Adjutant-General) issue the order I suggested yesterday and had it wired to Washington showing that on the day of the armistice we had acted. To-day came a cable from the War Department suggesting what we had already done and instructing Stettinius to cooperate with us as representing the War Department. Harbord also to-day sent a comprehensive order to the chiefs of the Services of Supply so that we are getting the tremendous machine reversed.

To-night to get a little relaxation for all, I had General Pershing, General McAndrew, General Harbord, and Colonel and Mrs. Boyd for dinner at the Ritz and we afterward went to see "Zig-Zag"[58] at the theater. We had a box and the General thought he was hidden, but somehow the audience must have learned he was in the house, for they did not leave at the close of the performance. Our party was taken by the stage entrance to our automobiles in the street, but a crowd had gathered at the side entrance to cheer the Commander-in-Chief. The streets are still packed with people. All day they have been parading and singing in the streets.

Had McAndrew and Harbord at lunch, as usual talking over the problems in which we are submerged. Last night Harbord and Atwood and I went to the same theater as did our party to-night. Then it was like a night in a madhouse, the audience and performers were so enthused with the victory announced yesterday morning.

1   See Appendix E for Letter from Dawes to Pershing, August 24, 1918.

2   Is-sur-Tille was the location of a major supply depot for the U.S. military. William Chakin, "Quartermaster Supply in the A.E.F., 1917-1918," *Quartermaster Review*, May-June 1950, np.

3   One objection to the idea of coordinating supply among the Allies was that there would be too much standardization of items. Different countries had different strengths and by establishing the board, those strengths would be diluted. "British hospitals were better than the French," historian Elizabeth Greenhalgh wrote, explaining the British's initial hesitation toward establishing the board, "and the French did not like British bread, and vice versa." *Victory through Coalition: Britain and France during the First World War.* Cambridge: Cambridge University Press, 2005, 234.

4   Samuel McRoberts (1868-1947) oversaw procurement in the Ordnance Department of the U.S. Army. McRoberts was a lawyer and banker who worked for Armour and Company before working for several banks, including American Trust and Savings Bank and National City Bank of New York. After the war he became president of Metropolitan Trust of New York.

5   See Appendix F for Memorandum, Military Inter-Allied Committee at Coubert, September 2, 1918.

6   CGD: At this conference the employment of the American army as a unit was definitely conceded. [Ed. Here Dawes directs readers to the *Final Report of General John J. Pershing*, 70.]

7   On August 21, 1918, the British 3rd Army launched an attack south of Arras and the 4th Army continued to attack at the Somme, pushing the Germans back from the positions they had taken during the Spring Offensive.

8   *Château de la Grange-le-Roi.*

9   CGD: *Granalenwerfer Pris pres Epieds (10 Km. N.E. de Château-Thierry) le 23 Juillet, 1918, sur le champs de bataille où s'illustra la 26ième Division, U.S. Rapporte au Colonel Charles Dawes en souvenir de l'activité et de l'intelligence remarquable avec lesquelles le Colonel Dawes a constitué le Comité Inter-allie des Ravitaillements, dans le but de cimenter l'union des armées françaises et américaines et de rendre plus forte leur action commune, par son devoué collaborates et ami le Colonel Payot, Aide Major-Général. Au G.Q.G. 24 juillet, 1918. (Signé)* Ch. Payot [Translation: Granatenwerfer (Grenade-thrower) Taken near Epieds (10 Km. N.E. of Château-Thierry) July 23, 1918, on the battle-field where the 26th U.S. Division made itself illustrious. Brought back to Colonel Charles Dawes, in remembrance of the remarkable activity and intelligence with which Colonel Dawes formed the Inter-Allied Committee of Supplies, with the aim of cementing the union of the French and American armies and of strengthening their common action, by his devoted collaborator and friend Colonel Payot, Aide-Major General. At G.H.Q. 24th July, 1918. (Signed) Ch. Payot.]

10   See Appendix G for Letter from John Pershing to Viscount Milner,

British Secretary of State for War.

11   CGD: The General was referring to his conferences of August 30 and September 2, both of which were devoted to the issue of the unity of the American army. [Ed. Here Dawes directs readers to the *Final Report of General John J. Pershing*, 39 and 40.]

12   At the time Dawes wrote this entry, Pershing was preparing what would be the largest American offensive of the war, the Meuse-Argonne Offensive. Along with French troops, the U.S. troops launched a coordinated assault on a line that had remained relatively unchanged since 1914. The offensive began on September 26, 1918 and was fought in three phases until November 11, 1918. Comprised of a series of important military engagements designed by Pershing and his generals using their "defense in depth" tactics, the offensive effectively constituted the end of the war. During the campaign, 1.3 million U.S. troops fought in the battles that occurred along the entire Western Front. The newly created U.S. 2nd Army fought, along with British and French troops. In the end, 26,277 American soldiers were killed and 95,786 wounded. Germans losses numbered 28,000 killed and 92,250 wounded.

13   See Appendix H for letter from H. C. Smither, Commanding General, S.O.S., to Colonel Charles G. Dawes, General Purchasing Agent, August 31, 1918.

14   Kabyle, an ethnic group of people originally from Algeria.

15   "Piling Ossa on Pelion," from Homer's *Odyssey*, meaning making something big bigger.

16   The Women's Army Auxiliary Corps was established in Great Britain in 1917 and deployed many thousands of British women to France for work. The U.S. Army also employed French women, with a total of 12,000 French women employed by the Americans during the war. Tammy M. Proctor, *Civilians in a World at War, 1914-1918*. New York: New York University Press, 2010, 130.

17   Edward R. Stettinius (1865–1925) was Dawes' friend from Chicago. He worked for J.P. Morgan and Company before going to work for the U.S. War Department during World War I, where he oversaw procurement and production of supplies for the U.S. Army. On April 6, 1918, he was appointed Assistant Secretary of War. After the war, he returned to his work for J.P. Morgan and Company. His son, Edward R. Stettinius, Jr., would serve as U.S Secretary of State, 1944-1945, and as U.S. Ambassador to the United Nations, 1945-1946.

18   Military Board of Allied Supply.

19   The assault on St. Mihiel took place from September 12 -13, 1918. The A.E.F., along with French troops, waged an attack on an area that had been held by the Germans since 1914. The attack was designed by Pershing, using a "combined arms" approach. Infantry, tanks, artillery, and air planes all took part in the battle. The Americans achieved their goal of taking the St. Mihiel salient and the battle was considered a great victory for the Allies, but in particular, for the Americans.

20   See Appendix I for telegrams exchanged between General Harbord and General Pershing on the occasion of the St. Mihiel victory, September 1918.

21   Major-General Reginald Ford (1868-1951).

22   See Appendix J for Charles G. Dawes' note on Edward R. Stettinius.

23   *Le Château de Cirey*, located in Cirey-sur-Blaise, about 150 miles southeast of Paris. The château was built in 1643.

24   Voltaire lived at *Le Château de Cirey* from 1734-1749.

25   *Poilu* is a term for a French soldier, meaning, literally, "hairy." It was used as a term of endearment. At the time, many French soldiers wore mustaches and were characterized as being rather earthy and rustic.

26   Lieutenant Colonel J.C. Roop, Assistant General Purchasing Agent.

27   Located at 261 rue Saint Honoré in Paris, *Voisin* had been a staple of French cuisine for decades, run by chef Alexandre Étienne Choron (1837–1924). The restaurant was expensive and known for its spectacular wine cellar. *Voisin* closed in 1930. John Baxter, *Chronicles of Old Paris: Exploring the Historic City of Light*. New York: Museyon, 2011-2012, 74, 77.

28   CGD: The beginning of the Battle of the Argonne. The attack was actually delivered September 26. [Ed. The Battle of the Argonne was part of the Meuse-Argonne Offensive.]

29   The headquarters of the newly organized American First Army was established at Souilly, southwest of Verdun, on September 21, 1918. Pershing arrived the next day. He was not only in command of the A.E.F., but also in command of the First Army. Paul F. Braim, "Meuse Argonne Campaign," *The United States in the First World War: An Encyclopedia*, 381.

30   See Appendix K for Secret A.E.F. orders, October 7, 1918.

31   *Boche* was a derogatory term for a German. The term originated with the French and Germans considered it a terrible insult.

32   General Charles P. Summerall (1867-1955) was a United States Military Academy graduate with years of military experience. For his command of the First Division during World War I, Summerall was awarded the Distinguished Service Cross, the Distinguished Service Medal, and the Silver Star. After the war he served as Army Chief of Staff from 1926 to 1930, and from 1931 to 1953, he was president of the Citadel.

33   Post command.

34   In 1886 or 1887, Dawes served as chief engineer of the Marietta Mineral Railway Company which ran a line from Big Run in Athens County, Ohio, near Dawes' hometown in Marietta, Ohio. His father and other relatives were also involved in the railway business. *Annual Report of the Commissioner of Railroads and Telegraphs to the Governor of the State of Ohio for the Year 1886*. Columbus, OH: The Westbote Co., State Printers, 1887, 531.

35   From October 1918 until the official armistice was declared on November

11, 1918, representatives of the German government, President Wilson, and the Allied leaders communicated multiple times concerning the nature of an armistice. Bullitt Lowry, "Armistices of 1918," *The United States in the First World War: An Encyclopedia,* 48. The first overture towards peace was sent by Germany's new chancellor, Prince Max of Baden, to President Wilson on October 5, 1918. Godfrey Hodgson, *Woodrow Wilson's Right Hand: The Life of Colonel Edward M. House,* New Haven: Yale University Press, 2006, 206. Allied leaders later met at Versailles to discuss the matter.

36   Dawes does not reveal the incredible drama that was unfolding behind the scenes at this time. The Allied leaders, headed by Foch, were attempting to remove Pershing from his command and wrest control of the American troops from their American commander to be used as they saw fit. Foch first attempted "to divide the American army among the Allies," but when Pershing rejected this, he then worked to "dilute Pershing's operational control," going so far as issuing an order, presented to Pershing by Foch's assistant, Weygand, relieving Pershing of his control of the First Army and sending him to a "quiet sector." Other attempts were made to place a French general in every American division to act as an 'advisor.'" (Lacey, 1, 167-168) Pershing was relentless in his opposition to all of these attempts to push him out; he firmly believed that the American army would fight as its own force, commanded by American officers. In this he was backed by President Woodrow Wilson and Secretary of War Newton Baker.

37   The second phase of the Meuse-Argonne Offensive was launched on October 4, 1918.

38   George McFadden, representative on the War Trade Board. Working from Paris, he worked closely with the General Purchasing office. He was later awarded the Distinguished Service Medal.

39   An American Civil War battle fought May 5-7, 1864 in Virginia.

40   CGD: Foreman was a friend from Chicago, a former Republican alderman on the Chicago City Council.

41   The Café Foyot, most likely. Located at 33 Rue de Tournon, near the Palais du Luxembourg, it was a stylish restaurant frequented by Americans for many years, particularly in the post World War I era.

42   During the American Civil War, Dawes' father, Rufus R. Dawes (1838-1899) served as an officer of the 6th Wisconsin Volunteer Infantry (part of the famed "Iron Brigade") and his uncle, Ephraim Cutler Dawes (1840-1895) served as an officer in the 53rd Ohio Volunteer Infantry. Both fought in many important battles. Uncle Eph was severely wounded (but would recover). Both men were honorably discharged in 1864. (See the introduction for more about Dawes' father.)

43   Major Lloyd C. Griscom (1872-1959) was a lawyer and a career diplomat. During the war he served as Pershing's liaison in the British War Office.

44   Lamorlaye, a city roughly 30 miles north of Paris, where General Payot's headquarters were located.

45   Most likely the Château des Fontaines in Gouvieux-Chantilly, located about four miles from Lamorlaye. It was completed in 1882 for James Edouard Rothschild (1844-1881), a member of the French branch of the famous Rothschild family, and his wife Laura Thérèse Rothschild (1847-1931).

46   In his statement, Pershing outlined his views, including this final point: "I believe the complete victory can only be obtained by continuing the war until we force unconditional surrender from Germany; but if the Allied Governments decide to grant an armistice the terms should be so rigid that under no circumstances could Germany again take up arms." General John Pershing, letter to the Allied Supreme War Council, October 30, 1918, in *Understanding U.S. Military Conflicts through Primary Sources*. Volume 1. James R. Arnold and Roberta Wiener, eds. Santa Barbara, CA: ABC-CLIO, 2015, 112.

47   Pershing sent his statement directly to the Supreme War Council, bypassing Wilson's appointed advisor on peace negotiations, Colonel House (although Pershing did give House a copy). This was, in House's view, inappropriate. Pershing should have given his statement directly to House. Further, House objected to Pershing's "meddling" in politics. (Lacey, 174). House notified President Wilson that he believed Pershing had "strayed well outside his assigned military responsibility in writing his statement." *Understanding U.S. Military Conflicts through Primary Sources*. Volume 1, 111. U.S. Secretary of War Newton Baker agreed with House and drafted a letter reprimanding Pershing for his action, but President Wilson would not approve sending the letter to the General. For his own part, Pershing did perceive his error in offering political advice, and did not repeat his mistake. (Lacey, 174-175).

48   Lord Northcliffe was Alfred Charles William Harmsworth (1865-1922), a newspaper publisher and founder of the *Daily Mirror* and the *Daily Mail*. He also acquired the London papers, the *Observer*, the *Times*, and the *Sunday Times*. His opinion pieces were said to exert tremendous influence on public opinion. In 1918, Lloyd George appointed Northcliffe as British Director of Propaganda in enemy countries.

49   Newspaper editor and publisher, Charles H. Grasty served overseas as a war correspondent for the *New York Times* throughout the war.

50   On November 7, 1918, Grasty's piece, "Northcliffe Praises Work of U.S. Troops," appeared in the *New York Times* and numerous other papers. The article consists of a statement from Northcliffe as he praises Pershing and the American troops, saying, "Many critics wondered when Ypres would be in our hands. Often great impatience was manifested." But, he asserted, the "American effort in the Argonne. . . has been one of the finest of the American successes."

51   At 5AM, Paris time, an armistice was signed. It went into effect at 11AM, Paris time, effectively ending World War I, although the actual peace treaty would not be signed until June 28, 1919. The armistice was the result of negotiations that

had taken place in the weeks prior to an agreement being reached. In the United States, November 11 would be known as "Armistice Day" until 1954 when the day was changed to honor all war veterans and re-named "Veterans Day." Critics of the armistice, including Pershing, argued that it constituted a cessation of hostilities and not a complete victory for the Allies. Complete victory, he believed, would have been achieved with a continuation of the offensive and the occupation of Germany. And only then, as Pershing later stated, would the Allies have established a "deterrent against possible future German aggression." John J. Pershing, *My Experiences in the World War.* Volume 2. New York: Frederick A. Stokes Company, 1931, 369.

52   Pershing issued his statement on November 12, 1918. It read, in part, "The enemy has capitulated. It is fitting that I address myself in thanks directly to the officers and soldiers of the American Expeditionary Forces who by their heroic efforts have made possible this glorious result." "General Order 203," November 12, 1918, quoted in Pershing, *My Experiences in the World War.* Volume 2, 390.

53   Gordon Auchincloss (1886-1943), the son-in-law of Edward House, was a lawyer who served as House's unofficial secretary and confidant during the war. Later, he was director of Chase National Bank, among other positions.

54   Harbord would not be promoted to Lieutenant General until 1942, two decades after he retired.

55   Samuel Pepys (1633-1703) kept a now famous diary chronicling his life in London over a nearly ten year period. It was published in 1825.

56   General Enrico Merrone served on the M.B.A.S as the representative of Italy.

57   Germany was in the midst of the "November Revolution" which would persist in phases through 1919 when the Weimar Republic would be established. Civil unrest, revolt among troops, the abdication of Emperor Wilhelm II (the Kaiser), coupled with severe shortages would prove to create a chaotic situation in the postwar period.

58   "Zig Zag" was a wildly successful musical revue performed at the Folies Bergère at 32 rue Richer in the 9th Arrondissement. The revue included the song "Over There" by American composer George M. Cohan. The show ran for 648 performances at the London Hippodrome prior to its Paris opening.

Section 5

November 25, 1918 ~ August 2, 1919
(beginning with correspondence, November 2, 1918)

A PART OF THE ARGONNE FOREST WITH ITS BARBED-WIRE ENTANGLEMENTS

Mount Ephraim,[1] Faversham
November 2, 1918

My Dear General Dawes:

Thank you so much for your letter and for sending me [a] copy of your telegram to Lieutenant-General Travers Clarke and his reply to you. These telegrams will be preserved as a family heirloom, as I am proud to realize that through Ambrose our families are from the same root. The family which moved to America over three centuries ago is so honorably represented by you in the office of such great responsibility which you hold, and the next generation by William in the Heavy Tank Battalion.

My brothers Edwyn, Bethel, and Halford, and my son have served more particularly in Palestine. Halford has had some adventures; wounded Gallipoli, twice submarined in Mediterranean, he is now with the Murman Expeditionary Force.[2] My uncle's son was a soldier before the war, so was out with the original expeditionary force and was badly wounded on the Aisne. As soon as he was patched up he was out again, then badly gassed. At present he is doing home service. When we look back to that awful period in March and regard the position to-day, what thankfulness we feel to America. America has brought a complete transformation. We all realized American strength, doggedness, energy, etc., but results are far beyond our greatest expectations. Then the President — what a wonderful man, the greatest statesman in any time! How grateful the world is that in these awful times there is one outstanding man to speak for the peoples and carry them with him unitedly. Our gratitude to the American arms and American statesmanship is greater than words can express. People have suffered since August, 1914 — their spirit was not broken — America has come forward with both arms and we see the wrong being paid for and a glorious end in sight and our hearts are uplifted and our gratitude is very great.

I was in Scotland in August and September — London and here since — and the feelings I have tried to express are the feelings on all sides. Governments try to express these feelings, but they are deeper down with all than words can satisfy. In replying to my American cousin's kind letter, I have ventured in a poor way to add my thankfulness and gratitude. With best wishes,

Believe me

Yours very truly

William C. Dawes

P.S. If there are three or four convalescents — or on leave — you will personally train or send here, we will do our best to make their stay at

Mount Ephraim as pleasant as present conditions allow.

November 14, 1918

Mrs. Mary B. Dawes
508 Fourth Street
Marietta, Ohio

My Dear Mother:

It was a year ago in October, after my return from the Belgian front, that I wrote you the one and only descriptive letter in which I have had time to indulge since coming to France with the army. Not alone the pleasure it gave you, but the interest which one is sure to have hereafter in details liable to pass from memory unless recorded, both make me regret that I have not written you more often in this way. However, one cannot live a life of action over here and do much writing. My secretary, Lieutenant Mulloney,[3] is taking this letter by dictation and in it I will describe something of the happenings of the last three days, covering those personal details which I am sure will interest the family as my ordinary short and hasty letters cannot do.

The armistice was declared, as you know, at about 5.30 Monday morning, November 11. At eight o'clock Colonel Robert Bacon, who has come to be a very good friend and whom you will remember as former Secretary of State and Ambassador to France, called me on the telephone at the hotel and announced the news. On my way to the office Lieutenant Kilkenny met me to say that General Pershing wanted me immediately on the telephone from Chaumont. For once I did not anticipate an emergency call and supposed he simply wanted to talk over the great victory. It was characteristic, however, of General Pershing that he was hard at work at his desk and wanted to discuss certain prospective changes in our General Staff organization covering a finance section and also the tremendous change of policy with which the American Expeditionary Force was immediately confronted as a result of the armistice. Under his direction my day was given (as was his and General Harbord's, we three being in constant telephonic communication) to reversing suddenly the tremendous business engine of the American Expeditionary Force. One does not know how many tens of millions of dollars saving to the people of the United States depended upon prompt and intelligent action. I only noticed casually the singing and cheering crowds on the streets and gave myself over unreservedly to the consideration of orders and instructions to the purchasing services under the authority of the Commander-in-Chief and the Commanding General,

Services of Supply. General Harbord left Tours by motor at noon and arrived in time to take dinner with me in the evening. General Pershing left Chaumont for Paris, arriving Tuesday morning November 12.

As I have told you practically all supply negotiations between the American Expeditionary Force and the Allied Governments, as well as many other governmental negotiations, center in my office. On the morning of the 12th my friend General Merrone, of the Italian army, who represents that army on our Military Board of Allied Supply, called with a telegram from the Italian Government stating that they had on hand one million Austrian prisoners and 200,000 horses with nothing to feed them and appealing to the American Expeditionary Force for help in the crisis which they feared might possibly precipitate them in a revolution. General Pershing in the transportation crisis at the front had put upon me the prime responsibility of animal supply. I had managed to get horses moving from Spain, and through a trip to British General Headquarters and by sounding "the call of the blood," had induced the English to rob their own home divisions of about thirteen thousand horses which were arriving. The Treasury Department is strongly objecting to our securing horses in Spain because of exchange conditions. I immediately put the proposition for consideration to the Italian Government, through General Merrone, that they loan us 100,000 of the Austrian horses if we could find transportation. I then secured a meeting between the Chief of Staff, Quartermaster-General, General Harbord, and myself, and got the situation ready to present to General Pershing upon his arrival from Pétain's Headquarters at five o'clock in the afternoon. As a result, just as we have recently let the Belgians have $3,000,000 of food supplies, we are now in shape to furnish from our A.E.F. stock of flour at the Marseilles base enough to feed the one million Austrians for twenty days, to which General Pershing has given his approval, but asked me as a member of the Military Board of Allied Supply to conduct the negotiations if possible under the international authority possessed by it. I cite this as simply one of probably ten similar questions of policy, each as important, under consideration during the three days.[4]

Again on the 12th it was in a dim and indistinct way that I was conscious of the tremendous celebration on the streets, and it was only when the conference between General Pershing, General McAndrew, Chief of Staff, General Harbord, Commanding General, Services of Supply, General Merrone, of the Italian Army, and myself had terminated at 6.30 P.M., with things pretty well cleared up, that I began to take more notice of things. I took General Pershing and the other American officers to dinner at the Ritz and then to the theater, where we had a box. We thought we had slipped the General in unobserved. He had been recognized in his automobile during the afternoon on the streets and there was such a demonstration of enthusiasm that his safety was really endangered. That night, however, when the curtain went down, the audience remained, and it was evident that in some way they had found out the General was there. It was necessary for us to go through a side entrance in an effort to get the General away, and even then the crowd had filled the side street cheering for him and making progress slow. This will give you a little indication of the scenes which have been going on.

As the General desired me to take the trip of which I am about to write you, I put in yesterday in getting all important matters in shape so that I could spend to-day away from the office. Last night I left with General Pershing on his special train for the Field Headquarters of Marshal Haig where the General was to decorate the Marshal with the American Distinguished Service Medal, acting under the authority and by the direction of the President of the United States. Other officers on the General's train were Colonel Quekemeyer, his aide, and Colonel Bacon. We left at eleven o'clock at night and reached the ruined town of Cambrai at about eight o'clock this morning. English officers waiting for us there took breakfast with us, and at 9.15 the General, Colonel Bacon, and I got into an automobile and started for Marshal Haig's Field Headquarters which were on a special train near a little town called Ewey,[5] situated about eight kilometers distant from Cambrai. Before going the General told me that if I landed smoking at Marshal Haig's, he would not only invoke upon my head the combined maximum military penalties for capital offenses, but in addition would endeavor to apply personal chastisement on the spot.[6] After this discussion the machine suddenly stopped in the fog and Field Marshal Haig appeared at the door on one side and General Lawrence, his Chief of Staff, on the other. The morning was quite foggy and one could not see a very great distance ahead. Haig and Pershing walked a little ahead of General Lawrence and myself, and in a few minutes turned off into a field where a large American flag attached to a pole made of a tall sapling was planted. Drawn up in a square around it was a brigade from the most famous division of the English army, the 51st Highlander Division,[7] who presented arms. Then Marshal Haig and General Pershing stepped to the middle of the square, Marshal Haig being accompanied by General Lawrence and General Home, Commander of the First British Army, and General Pershing being accompanied by Colonel Quekemeyer and myself. The General then briefly conferred the medal, pinning it on Sir Douglas Haig's coat, and Sir Douglas responded. Standing on the far side from us were General Davidson, head of the Operations Section of the British General Staff, and General Lord Clive, head of the Intelligence Section.

Captain Demarenche, of the French army, Captain Thornton (who used to manage the La Salle Hotel and is now Quartermaster in charge of the General's train), and four or five English officers were present, and this was the entire audience save the magnificent Scottish Brigade. This ceremony took about five minutes, and then the American flag was moved about one hundred yards to the left and planted in the ground and we took up our stations for the review of the Brigade. The mist had cleared away enough to give a full view of this famous organization. The first battalion to pass was from the Black Watch and the fifty bagpipes which were stationed opposite Marshal Haig and General Pershing played the Black Watch air. All the troops were in the regulation Scotch kilts and held their heads high in the air as they turned "eyes left" in the customary salute when passing the High Command. They were followed by the Argyll and Sutherland troops. Then I knew "the Campbells were coming,"[8] for the bagpipes suddenly started that air. As these magnificent and battle-worn troops passed, it was not of them that I thought, but of the Sixth Wisconsin Volunteer Infantry marching down the Emmitsburg Road on that Second of July with Father at their head, his fife and drum corps playing the same air with which, because of this, as you know, I had been familiar from my earliest childhood. I thought of the sudden order which came to him to stop the music and of the famous charge which followed in which he led his regiment on foot and captured the Second Mississippi Regiment in the railroad cut. He lost every other man killed or wounded in that charge over a space of only one hundred and seventy paces. Before no braver set of men was this Scotch air ever played than before the Sixth Wisconsin and those who were then passing before me in the mist. After the brigade had passed, we went back to our automobiles.

Before we left, Sir Douglas Haig stepped over to me and told me what he had heard of me and my work and invited me to make him a visit when he returned from his Field Headquarters. I greatly missed seeing my good friends Lieutenant General Travers Clarke, and Major-General Reginald Ford of his Staff, who are absent, and of whom I have come to think so much. General Ford represents the English army on the Military Board on which I represent the American Expeditionary Forces.

We returned to Cambrai and left at 10.30 A.M. And this reminds me that the moving-picture operators of the Signal Corps were present, and not being able to take pictures as usual of the ceremonies, took pictures of us as we returned to the train and as we were seated at dinner. They also took a picture of General Pershing at his desk in his fine new office car which has recently been added to his special train. The progress of the train was very slow, as the track had been recently relaid, the Germans having destroyed the old track in their retreat. This gave me a fine opportunity to see the general ground over which Lieutenant William M. Dawes fought in his tank. And here I want to say something of William, who knew the great dangers of the Tank Service before he entered it and before the attack in which he had persuaded his commanding officers to allow him to participate. Colonel Bacon, who was on the train, had been with the 27th and 30th American Divisions at the time of their first attack on the Hindenburg Line on September 29, and at the time of the second attack on October 8, just over the line, in which William participated in command of a tank manned by Englishmen. The old canal, after having been an unfinished project for many years and finally completed by Napoleon in 1802, runs through a tunnel between the villages of Bony and Bellecourt for a distance of about six thousand yards. It was across this ground that our divisions attacked under the concentrated fire of massed German artillery. On this first attack, September 29, to give you an idea of tank mortality, not one of the eleven tanks which progressed beyond Bony but was destroyed. I suppose I saw twenty demolished tanks from the train window. Judging from William's letter he must have started with his tank, October 8, from somewhere near Bony, and proceeded in the attack to some village to the north, the name of which he does not state. I understand there are several villages not far to the north of Bony. If you can corkscrew the further details of the operations from this modest young man, what I write here may be of more help to you in explaining his part in that tremendous and successful fighting on account of which the English so praise the bravery of their American cousins in the 27th and 30th American Divisions and the Heavy Tank Battalion.

I arrived in Paris this evening at 6.30 and am dictating this at my room to-night. I know I shall always be glad that I took the time to do it, especially because I know it will give you pleasure, to whom I owe so much. I think I wrote you when I was at the front between the Argonne Woods and the Meuse, in the midst of those terrible scenes, of how my mind reverted constantly to what Father and Uncle Eph had gone through in the Civil War. I could not at that time write of such experiences as I had along the line, and I am glad on some accounts that I could not do so. General Pershing and his troops fought here a greater Battle of the Wilderness, and history will, I think, record it as the greatest of American battles. To have been with him the time I was and where I was marked an epoch in my life. As you know I have been a number of times along the lines at the front, but the fighting before that, in the particular spots in which I was, consisted for the most part only of artillery activity. To see, however, the German shells put down on our front lines and to see the effects of them gave me my first true idea of what this war has been. There on the forward slope of Montfaucon in early October far in advance of our own artillery, I felt as far in the rear of our thin line ahead as the United States of America was in my rear. And so I take off my hat to Lieutenant William Mills Dawes who advanced in his tank in the face of similar artillery.

The service of Beman and Charles has been as honorable as that of William, although despite their efforts they did not succeed in getting so much service at the front. Charles, after his service in the Advance Zone with the Engineers, made the endeavor to get into Aviation, and finally succeeded, despite his youth, in getting into the American Expeditionary Forces Artillery School at Saumur where he is now stationed. The war has ended, however, before his course is completed. Beman's service at the front was before his enlistment when he was at the head of a motor transport unit for the French. At Beman's request I had about completed arrangements with my friend General Harbord to have him transferred to the Marine Brigade, when Harbord left that organization to take command of the Service of Supply, which prevented their consummation. While to both these young men it has been a disappointment that their service has not been more on the line, they have both made very fine records. Beman has been promoted for merit and has been recommended for still further promotion, although I am afraid that the order recently issued by the War Department against any further promotions after November 11 in the American Expeditionary Forces will prevent his receiving his second promotion. He had been in charge of most responsible work and is at present at Marseilles, where, as I understand it, he is supervising part of the unloading and transportation system. The only reason that I am not writing more of the achievements of these two nephews is because I have not been recently in contact with them. What I say in praise of them is reported to me by their superior officers who have stated that their work has been noteworthy. Returning again to myself: Those things for which I shall be best remembered in this war when its history is written will not be those which I shall remember best. In all the reviews, celebrations, and gatherings which may be before me in the future there will always be in my mind the picture of what went on to make them possible and the wonder whether the millions buried in the wheat-fields and along the roadsides of Northern France can know of them. There is no tie like the tie of blood, and while in our international deliberations the English and I have at times almost fought, it has all ended in our loving each other as brothers because we were sincerely united in a common purpose. I was touched to learn inadvertently that my good friend Major General Ford, representing the British army on our Board, had been especially instructed by the English War Office to defer in every way possible to my suggestions in Military Board relations. This was not necessary, for I do not think General Ford and I could find any subject on which we did not agree. But I must not speak of my regard for the English without speaking also of my regard for the French. Out of struggle, danger, and difficulty rise the enduring friendships. I find that General Pershing is deeply attached to General Pétain and regards him about as I do Pétain's great assistant, Colonel Payot. Payot recently brought me in, together with a picture of himself, a picture from Marshal Foch inscribed to me. These, together with a picture of the fight of the Marines in Belleau Wood, which General Harbord who commanded them gave me, I sent home by an American officer yesterday.

I do not know when I shall be through my army service. For the present I am needed here and General Pershing says he wants me to remain and return with him. I shall still have some months of work. The way my Staff Department of the army has been built up is something like this. I started in a single room doing things largely with my own hands. In this way I became acquainted with every detail and method. This was possible when the business of the American Expeditionary Forces was starting and comparatively small. When I had completed the machinery for coordinating and increasing the supplies of our army, General Pershing began to call on me in cases where great emergency existed. The first emergency was the organization of coal shipments from England and the distribution scheme in France. This I carried on simply to such a point as met the existing crisis in coal supply. Then came the emergency call for labor and a consequent building up by me of a Labor Bureau organization which I turned over, with nearly 50,000 militarized employees, to the Army Service Corps on the 1st of September. Because of similar emergencies referred to me I created the organizations of the Board of Contracts and Adjustments, the Technical Board which coordinates the electrical power of the American Expeditionary Forces in France, the Bureau of Accounts and the Bureau of Reciprocal Supply, all in addition to my original work as Chairman of the General Purchasing Board and General Purchasing Agent. In addition, with General Pershing's powerful assistance, I had much to do with the creation of the Military Board of Allied Supply. With the dwindling load upon the General Purchasing Board, incident to the reduction of the army, as soon as I can get rid of these other organizations I feel that I can properly leave the service since the General Purchasing Board work is well organized. A financial officer of the General Staff is being named now that the war is over to take over two of my bureaus. As fast as possible those organizations which have been built up, under the pressure of emergency, around my personality and because I was the only executive Staff officer in Paris, will be thrown back into the regular army organization where they properly belong, leaving me with only the General Purchasing Board, my membership on the Military Board of Allied Supply, and my duties in connection with inter-army supply negotiations as representing General Pershing and General Harbord; with the latter I must necessarily be engaged somewhat as long as I am in France. But I must complete my work and remain as long as duty requires. My deep attachment for General Pershing if nothing else would impel me to stay here until he is completely convinced that it is all right for me to go. The General has now become one of the first figures in the history of our nation, but to me he is as always the faithful and affectionate friend and congenial associate of twenty-four years' standing. His head is not turned in the least. Every accession to his popularity arouses in him the fear of a reaction which may hamper him in that work which is nearest his heart—the proper handling, care, and return of his army to America.

In the length of this letter and the variety of subjects covered, you must not think I have forgotten after all my chief purpose in writing it, and that is to evidence to you, as I would try to do to Father if he were living, my desire that you know now as always my impulse is to lay at your feet whatever accomplishments may be mine in grateful recognition of what you have always been to me in life.

Your affectionate son,
Charles G. Dawes

Paris, Monday, November 25, 1918 (9.40 P.M.)

General Pershing has just left my room at the hotel where we took dinner together and spent the evening. The pressure of the situation is lessening, and we have no longer the emergencies involving human life hanging heavily over our heads. He arrived in Paris this afternoon from the trip during which he entered Luxembourg with his army,[9] and also went over to Brussels when the King of Belgium entered that city. At his home this afternoon I telephoned General Harbord to come to Paris to-morrow bringing Colonel Hull[10] with him for a conference with the General on our policy of contract cancellation and methods of general liquidation. The bulk of the liquidation of material property left by the army in France we agree should be left to a civilian commission — at least, that is our present judgment as to the wise course to pursue.

Have been quite busy at important matters since my last note. A part of my work and experiences I covered in a letter to Mother dictated to my stenographer at length. My cousin Junior Ames (K. L., Jr.)[11] visited me at the hotel. He has been in the fighting from St. Mihiel to the end and has done himself great credit. He is a Lieutenant in Colonel Foreman's old 1st Illinois, now an artillery organization.[12] He, William, Gates, and Charles have all done well in the service.

Colonel Boyd told me this afternoon that the French Government, on the instance of the Chief of Staff, French Armies of the North and Northeast, had notified General Pershing of its desire to name me a Commander of the Legion of Honor, and that the General had expressed his approval of the decoration. I appreciate greatly this action on the part of the French.[13]

I am pushing my organization built up at such effort back into the regular organization of the army as fast as I can now that the war is over, and the emergency is lifted. It was built around my personality and because I was the only executive staff officer in Paris and therefore in constant contact with the French Government whose attitude in regard to all our army matters was so important. Still it will probably be some months before I can leave the army for my old life. I want to stay until I have fully completed my work which I ought to do — and then get home as soon as possible.

At the Military Board of Allied Supply meeting next Friday, now that at the last meeting I secured the issue of orders to the three armies for a report of their condition as of October 31st in regard to men, supplies, ammunition, munitions, transportation, etc., I propose to ask for additional information to be preserved for the future consideration of military students of the war. While much of interest is transpiring around me, I have to force myself to keep notes. The merely spectacular in life will never lack description. What my notes have recorded for the most part is the current of that great river of effort, so far as I have had part in it, which has made possible all these spectacles. I long for peace and quiet for a time.

Paris, Tuesday, November 26, 1918 (9.30 P.M.)

I am very tired after a day spent largely in conference with General Pershing, General Harbord, E. R. Stettinius, Special Representative of the Secretary of War, Colonel Hull, Judge Advocate and new Finance Officer of the A.E.F., in which was settled the plan to be recommended to the War Department and, so far as the A.E.F. is concerned, followed, in liquidating the immense property and plant of the American army in France. Was personally squarely up against the question of my duty to stay and help in the more prosaic but no less necessary work of liquidation. Much as I desire to return to home and business and to comparative rest, there was no alternative but to cheerfully acquiesce in the feeling of my associates that I must stay until I am clearly not needed. Accordingly General Pershing had Harbord and me prepare an order in which Stettinius (ex officio), Colonel Hull, and myself were detailed as an Advisory Settlement Board of the A.E.F. "to consider and recommend policies connected with the disposition of war supplies, material and equipment pertaining to the A.E.F., etc.," under command of the Commanding General, Services of Supply. The liquidation of fixed property was recommended by cable to the War Department by General Pershing to be undertaken by a commission of five. Considered myself fortunate to have escaped the draft on the latter proposition.

I wish selfishly I could stop my military work at this juncture. Personally there is nothing to gain by success and much to lose by mistake. However, I did not enter the army as a pastime.

Late in the afternoon General Pershing, General Harbord, and myself and others went to the Signal Corps photographic plant and saw some wonderful pictures, including those taken of the trip when the General decorated Marshal Haig.

Harbord, Hull, and Lieutenant-Colonel Collins dined with me at the hotel.

Paris, Thursday, December 3, 1918 (9.30 P.M.)

At the last meeting of the Military Board of Allied Supply, which was held at my office, I secured the issuance of orders to the three armies—also Belgian and Italian armies in France— for the preparation of the record of their respective Services of Supply from the beginning of the war, covering questions of policy, changes in policy and the reasons therefor, etc., for preservation in the records of the Board. General Ford, of the English army, demurred somewhat, maintaining that this could be done better after the war, to which Payot and I took the contrary view. Ford, with his customary good humor and spirit of helpfulness, then agreed. He states that it will take the English army six months to complete its record report. General Harbord, who was present and addressed the Board, has already started the work for our own army, as has General Moseley of G-4, G.H.Q. I am sure that no literature of the armies will exist after the war so instructive and illuminating as this which I have been instrumental in having prepared — that is, from the standpoint of the Service of Supply and its relation to the conditions at the front and its military strategy. I think I have covered all the points upon which information will be chiefly desired — though, of course, I have probably omitted something.

In the great press of work of the last week my visits and work with Herbert Hoover remain in memory. He outlined his plans for feeding Europe so far as it has been possible to formulate them.[14] His present liaison with our army is through my office. He shared my frugal lunch on the office desk the other day. General Pershing called me by telephone the other night. He is very much annoyed by the newspaper talk about him as a candidate for the Presidency and was contemplating a statement about it, strongly denouncing such gossip. He desired my opinion about making a statement. I advised it was not worthy of notice — at least at present. John will never be rushed off his feet. He sincerely deprecates anything of political kind. His future lies in his chosen work as he views it. I do not wonder, however, that he is talked of for this position. Many American statesmen in recent years have spread their sails for the popular winds. John, in any gale however severe, always lays his course by the compass.

My friend John McCutcheon[15] is here and brought me a picture of my new grandson — now three months old.[16] I am afraid it will be a long time before I see him, much as I should like to do so. William, Charles, and Gates, my three nephews — fine boys — have also visited me this last week.

Paris, Sunday, December 8, 1918 (10 P.M.)

During the last week, at the suggestion of our Advisory Liquidation Board of three, prepared a plan for the A.E.F. to follow, subject to the modifications which the War Department may hereafter impose, in liquidation of current supplies and assets. Read the plan over the telephone to General Pershing and to Harbord, both of whom approved it. The Board afterward approved it without change and it will therefore pass into orders. It is based upon the plan originated by General Pershing covering the acquirement of property, modified to provide for disposition of property.

The French Government has informally submitted to the A.E.F. for discussion the question of that Government taking over all our property, either to liquidate with concurrence of an American representative, or to pay a lump sum for it. We are considering this on both sides. Am in favor of something of the kind for many reasons. Attended many conferences, including one with Stettinius (who has done wonderful work) and Tardieu and Ganne.

I feel the load lifting and am no longer under a strain. General Harbord spent two days here this week. McFadden left to-night for the United States after a wonderful record of usefulness to the A.E.F. as the representative in France of the War Trade Board.

Paris, Thursday night, December 19, 1918 (10.15 P.M.)

Am just in from a four days' trip over the Services of Supply. Last Saturday President Wilson arrived.[17] My headquarters office was filled to see him pass on the avenue where he received a very great ovation from the French people. Harbord, General Ford (B.E.F.), John McCutcheon, and I spent that evening together. Sunday morning Harbord, Hull, and I conferred with General Pershing upon the situation created by the Comptroller of the Treasury, who has made a ruling making it impossible for our country to settle its business in France honorably without a change of law.[18] General Pershing decided upon a policy and cables were prepared for transmission to the War Department by Colonel Hull. Harbord, General Ford, Mr. Hurley of the Shipping Board, John McCutcheon, and I then left for Coubert to attend the last meeting of the Military Board of Allied Supply to be held at those headquarters. Hoover had expected to go with me, but Wilson called him into conference just as we were about to start. However, at the meeting I made the inquiry of Payot as to how much the French army could assist in transporting relief supplies to the devastated districts and arranged for conference between Payot and Hoover upon statement of former that the French army would assist.

Am meeting with some reluctance on the part of the English to immediately furnish information as to their rear service for reasons which they gave me in confidence and which I cannot disclose. However, in time we shall get it. They are anxious to cooperate in every way.

We arrived in Paris again Sunday evening. General Travers Clarke and Major-General Ford met us there. They dined with us and at midnight we took General Harbord's special train for our trip. In the party were Harbord, Travers Clarke, Carter, Ford, Colonel Maud, John McCutcheon at the start. At different points some fell out and new ones came in, including Senator Wadsworth of New York, E. N. Hurley, General McCoy, General Jadwin, and others. First day at Gievres; second day, Bordeaux and surrounding installations; third day at St. Nazaire and Nantes; fourth day, Tours. The trip was arranged in honor of our British guests. It was a success. Enjoyed visiting the officers of my old regiment still at St. Nazaire.

General Ford brought an artist with him who is employed by the British Government. He started my crayon portrait for the British War Office collection, which I considered an honor.

While visiting the staff at Tours I received a tonnage statement showing that during the whole first six months of the existence of the A.E.F. in France, from June to December 31, 1917, only 347,653 tons of material were shipped to us from the United States. Last month alone (November) 639,659 tons were shipped. What the A.E.F. would have done without the General Purchasing Board may be inferred from the fact that the United States shipped us only 4,826,516 dead-weight tons from June, 1917, to December 31, 1918, whereas we secured on this side during that period at least 8,300,000 ship tons and I think my final figures will raise this latter estimate to nearly 10,000,000 ship tons. I had not fully realized, myself, how dependent upon my organization the A.E.F. had been for its supplies until I received these figures from the staff to-day as to shipments from the United States. The shipments from England amounting in the same period to 1,725,105 tons (June, 1917, to December 1, 1918) were secured during a critical period, and are in addition to the shipments from America. These latter shipments, however, were under the General Purchasing Board.

It can be inferred from the above how important has been coordination with our allies and good understanding with them in the matter of their aid in meeting our continual crisis in supplies. No wonder we had to "work on our toes" in the General Purchasing Board and the General Purchasing Agent organizations. While at times encountering among our own and the Allied representatives some distrust of each other and a tendency among subordinates to sometimes befog their true situation in supply dealing in order to get the best of a negotiation, I have always found the highest authority honest in statement. Thus I have always relied, in times of difficulty and supply emergency, upon this principle for comfort and inspiration for perseverance in effort: In supply negotiations between allied governments in war to understand is to agree. I therefore never feared to reveal at once our exact situation whether strong or weak.

July 22, 1919
Memorandum: For General Dawes.

I have collected the following approximate figures concerning the amount of money expended by the A.E.F. for supplies procured in Europe. Exact figures cannot be obtained at the present moment, as many matters are still in suspension, in some cases amounting to very large sums, but the estimate is intended to cover the amounts properly due which have not yet been definitely fixed.

The figures are based primarily upon reports to you from the individual purchasing officers, which have recently been checked up again with these officers.

The following approximate estimate is submitted:

Quartermaster Corps	$362,000,000
Ordnance Department	308,000,000
Engineer Corps	208,000,000
Air Service	65,000,000
Medical Department	50,000,000
Chemical Warfare Service	12,250,000
Signal Corps	10,750,000
Motor Transport Corps	8,000,000

$1,024,000,000
J. C. Roop
Lieutenant-Colonel, Engineers

Paris, December 23, 1918 (10.30 P.M.)

General Payot (he was made General to-day), Herbert Hoover, and Lieutenant De Sieves (interpreter) have just left my room, where we have spent the evening discussing means of transporting supplies to the devastated regions of France. Hoover is going to ask Pershing to allow me to be made the chairman of a military commission to take charge of the relief of the German civilian population. I do not know whether this task will come to me or not, but I have made up my mind that it is no time for me to shirk continued work in the face of the present need for action, and so I have given up thought of a return home for many months. I am impressed greatly with Hoover. He is clear, direct, intensely practical, fearless, and possessed of the widest perspective. He is essentially a man of action. In bringing him into contact with Payot I bring together the ingredients of immediate results.[19]

I note by American papers received to-day *(Chicago Tribune)* that the Ordnance Department of the War Department is under criticism for not having supplied us with American ammunition.[20] The great trouble was that America had not prepared for war and that she was not in the war long enough for her to get her stride. What was true as to ordnance was true as to airplanes and as to ships, and as to everything directly related to the supply of an army operating in a foreign country. One development of history will be the results achieved by our Services of Supply, A.E.F., and through the splendid cooperation of the French and English, which as yet are not fully appreciated. But the United States after all turned the tide of war. The support given our army by our Government was all possible for it to give. Again it will be developed to the credit of our governmental authority that, not being able to ship supplies as rapidly as needed, it gave the Allies that immediate financial and moral support that enabled them to continue until we could furnish the men. I cannot approve of the *ex post facto* criticism of the Administration. Granted that it erred in not forcing preparation long before the war, yet when the war came it did everything it could to forward it.

It was a vast undertaking which confronted America when she entered the war, and Rome was not builded in a day.

Paris, December 27, 1918 (11 P.M.)

Spent much of to-day with the Commander-in-Chief, who arrived from Chaumont this morning, and left for a much needed rest in the South of France this evening. Herbert Hoover saw him this morning and suggested my detail for duty in Berlin. In calling this morning upon him (Hoover) with General Long of the British Army (Director-General, Supplies and Transportation, B.E.F., at Saloniki), I learned that the Commander-in-Chief was non-committal as to my detail for this work. This afternoon and evening the Commander-in-Chief took up the matter with me. Am inclined to think he will not let me go, regarding my knowledge and experience in inter-army and inter-government matters as still needed by the A.E.F. In view of the disturbed conditions in Berlin and the interesting nature of the work, my sense of adventure is somewhat involved and the comparative inactivity in my office since the armistice makes the detail more attractive. However, I am in the hands of higher authority.

Harbord is here and we took lunch with Harjes. President Wilson has gone to England, where he is being received with the honor due him and our nation. My son-in-law, Captain Melvin Ericson, is here on his way with Major Cotchett to Bulgaria.[21] He brought me some pictures of my new grandson whom I would much like to see in person.

Paris, Tuesday, December 31, 1918

Returned last night from a trip with General Harbord on his train to Neufchateau, the advance headquarters of the Services of Supply and to Chaumont. We took Lieutenant William Dawes, my son-in-law, Captain Ericson, and Sergeant Bob Wallace with us. Left Paris Saturday night. At Chaumont yesterday I heard for the first time the headquarters band at guard mount. This band has been created by the competition and combing-out process of our army bands aided by the bandmasters' school established in connection with the plan by Damrosch. I was delighted, though not surprised, at the splendid results of the effort as evidenced by this great band. General Pershing, Collins, and Boyd have all taken a great interest in the matter of army music and the reorganized band owes its existence to General Pershing's first suggestion and continued attention. I think the band ought to be named for him. It should have a distinctive insignia and be known as the official band of the A.E.F. Yesterday called on my good friends of the General Staff at Chaumont. Discussed with General Davis policy of Distinguished Service Medal awards to our allies.

Paris, Sunday January 5, 1919 (9.15 P.M.)

General McAndrew, Chief of Staff, called on me yesterday morning and said one of the purposes of his trip to Paris was to talk to me about Hoover's request for my detail to Berlin; that from what General Pershing had written him he feared that the General's warm friendship for me might result after all in his letting me go; that John was not sure he was doing right by me if I wanted to go; that John did not think I could be spared and that he (General McAndrew) and Harbord were agreed that it was not right for me to leave my present service at this time. I was touched by the way he spoke and his reference to what the General called "my career." Told him, "Career be damned; that if they felt that way about it they could not drive me away with a club." Called up Hoover on the telephone and asked him to drop the matter. I know I should stay here if only to complete my Report upon which I am at work.

When I leave the army my great department with all its files is an orphan. Superimposed on the regular army organization— the creature of temporary (during the war), but while it lasted a continual and overwhelming succession of emergencies— the ending of the war ends all but its record. And its record will be appreciated, remembered, or forgotten according to the way I now compile and complete its elements.

Now that the pressure of emergency is over I have to spur myself to work. I believe I am naturally inclined to indolence when off a red-hot stove, where I have sat for the last two years at least. Am enjoying the visit of Tiffany Blake[22] and the keen and able appreciation he has of our army situation and the problems it has involved.

Paris, Saturday, January 11, 1919 (11.45 P.M.)

John McCutcheon, Tiffany Blake, Percy Hammond,[23] and Floyd Gibbons[24] have just left my room, where its atmosphere has been rended for three hours by post-bellum discussion immodestly led by myself. As I am too much awake to go to sleep for a while I shall resume these neglected notes.

While measured by pre-war standards my present life is made up of incidents suggesting the propriety of their preservation in writing, they all seem trivial compared to anything that happened prior to November 11, 1918. However, spurring myself constantly I am working daily a little on my Official Report covering the last sixteen months. One of the most difficult things for a man to do is to refrain from accepting undeserved credit. Notwithstanding experience and reflection confirm the dangers of silence when over-praised, and the specter of merited reaction haunts the inner soul, still it is hard to pursue the path of duty and wisdom and be loyal to the truth to the extent of so holding the minds of others to it that undeserved halos drop from one's own head. But in my Report that is what I must do — and be careful in doing it thoroughly. The whole thing is so important. When John named me "General Purchasing Agent, A.E.F.," he seems to have created the idea that I bought everything of the 10,000,000 odd tons which we secured on this side of the ocean, whereas I never even bought a lead pencil. However, in such a statement I go to the other extreme in creating a wrong impression. My Report must show what the independent services did, and what my control of them did and did not do. It is not an easy task. Again, my Report must not be construed as reflecting upon the splendid accomplishments of the War Department. It must also pay the tribute due to our allies. My best efforts will be given to give a true picture. I received to-day the notice of the award to me, by the President, of the Distinguished Service Medal of the United States in accordance with the recommendation written by the Commander-in-Chief himself.[25]

Not being in an especially modest frame of mind, therefore, I may as well proceed to extremes and tell of an occurrence to-day which appealed to my amusement and pride as much as anything that has happened for a long time. I took Charles M. Schwab[26] over to call this noon on General Pershing, who has just returned from a few days' rest at Nice. In the anteroom we met General Fox Connor, of the General Staff, a regular of regulars, a most able and efficient, albeit precise, officer.[27] Schwab in his remarks said, "Well, I notice one thing over here, and that is that Dawes does not seem to be thoroughly disciplined." "No," replied General Connor, "and in the early days a number of regular general officers got ready to hand him something, but after looking him over once decided not to do it." General Connor, I may add, did not give the impression that this decision was based altogether upon motives of personal consideration for me. It amuses me to think of what must have been the first impressions of me of these splendid officers and dear friends — so used to conventional military methods of statement and address — when, breathing fire and brimstone, I made my incursions into the system after results, my mind fixed upon the red hot poker of dire necessity pressed against the lower part of my back and oblivious to nicety of expression or conventional forms of military salutation. Well, it is all over. And now I am by degrees relapsing into more placid and dignified ways befitting the banker and business man of the old days. But shall I ever get quite back?

To impress Schwab with two things—first, the terrible supply emergency with which the A.E.F. contended, and, second, what he and his Shipping Board had done to help us — I told him, what is the fact, that in the month preceding the armistice he had shipped us from America over twice as many tons of supplies as had been shipped us during the entire first six months of the existence of the A.E.F.

And so, as Pepys says, to bed.

Paris, Thursday, January 30, 1919

On Friday noon, January 17, started to Tours with my friends John McCutcheon and Tiffany Blake, both of whom returned to Paris on General Pershing's train Saturday. At Tours at General Harbord's house all night. On Saturday morning, January 18, was decorated with ten other Generals, including General Harbord and General Kernan, with the Distinguished Service Medal. General Pershing gave the medals and the ceremony took place before troops in the Headquarters enclosure. Balthasar Gracián made a remark several hundred years ago to the effect that it is not the applause which greets one on entrance, but on exit, which is important.

The anticlimax which the inexperienced and over-vain bring upon themselves by encouraging newspaper self-exploitation upon assuming important duties is one of the chief causes of a subsequent failure. The censor happily protected the A.E.F. from much of this sort of thing, but many in the United States were destroyed, or destroyed their own usefulness themselves, by it. I have been so accustomed to associating ceremony with non-accomplishment, since in civil life it is the chief resource of those desirous of publicity whether deserved or not, that I confess I was not over-impressed on this occasion. To be sure, this was a case of applause on exit, but the receiving of conspicuous applause at any time should be avoided on principle as dangerous and involving one in a mental trial as to his comparative merit by every disappointed competitor. The court being prejudiced and the decision therefore against him, one accumulates prejudices which endure, while from the minds of those not directly concerned remembrance of the distinction soon vanishes.

The value of ceremony as a social power is unquestioned. It cannot be dispensed with without destroying one of the great incentives to human effort, and one of the useful agencies of proper governmental and social discipline. At times the individual must use ceremony as the best means to noble ends. But let every wise man beware of too much ceremony whether it is directed toward the submerging or toward the exploitation of his own individuality. In all my negotiations as an army officer in inter-Allied conferences I have fought it as a bar to progress and quick understanding. In proportion as men are right-minded and intelligent, ceremony is unessential in their relations.

Left Tours Saturday night for a visit to the Riviera. My son-in-law and Major Cotchett, on their way to Bulgaria, through General Harbord's kindness went on the special train with us to Marseilles, stopping at Bordeaux. General Harbord, General Langfitt, General Rockenbach, and General Russell were in the party beside myself. This all-star aggregation landed at Monte Carlo Monday night. Every day except two it exhausted itself in a chamois-like game of golf on a rough portion of the Alps. The first two days, after five hours' hard exercise on each day, I was pretty stiff, but by the end of the week got well limbered up. We had a delightful time, though the discipline under which we moved could not have been stricter. We could not even visit the Casino, being in uniform.

Returned to Paris last night. While writing this received a telegram from Harbord that I had received the decoration of Commander of the Legion of Honor. I certainly am pleased. How difficult it is to keep vanity under the harness of the intellect.

Paris, Friday February 14, 1919 (10 P.M.)

We buried Colonel Carl Boyd to-day.[28] Only a week ago he was in good health. His loss is a heavy one to General Pershing who relied upon him greatly. He was a noble character. He leaves a wife and daughter with whom we all mourn.

Am somewhat depressed as I force myself to these notes. Secretary Baker having suggested that I be the military member of the Liquidating Commission, General Pershing, who had the matter already in mind, bore down irresistibly, and here I am head over heels in a mean and thankless task, but one which I have no honorable right to decline. Had I not long ago decided to sink personal considerations in this war service, I should have avoided this position as I would smallpox. The "going is good" for me to leave the army now, but to stay as a member of a commission to sell its assets is to work hard without the incentive of a war purpose; to be away from my family and business; to run the risk of making serious mistakes which will result in attack upon one's motives; in other words, to risk the reputation for success which I now have for no adequate personal purpose. However, the way the thing has been put up to me I should feel like a skunk if I did not do it. There is no patriotism in what I am doing — only a desire not to shirk what I really am qualified to do and that I ought to do. Somehow it is not so inspiring to work at saving money for one's Government as to work at helping to save its life.

Am working hard at my Report as General Purchasing Agent; next must come my Report as American Member of the Military Board of Allied Supply. In the meantime am working already as a member of the commission. And this is the time I looked forward to as that when I should be about leaving for America.

And so to bed.

Paris, February 16, 1919

The continued deaths and dangerous illnesses of my army friends and associates depress me greatly. This morning Webster Otis is critically ill and I have had to wire his father that the outcome is very doubtful.[29] He is a dear fine boy and has done his part well. Have been in daily communication about him with the doctors for a week.

Spent the morning trying to catch up with some of my personal mail, and also worked on my Report.

Last night at a dinner given to Hoover was decorated formally as Commander of the Legion of Honor by Clementel, French Minister of

GENERAL JOHN J. PERSHING WITH COLONEL JAMES L. COLLINS AND
COLONEL CARL BOYD

Commerce, who inexpressibly horrified me by kissing me on both cheeks before a large audience of which the American part must have been tremendously amused. Hoover made a telling address. This man has earned the highest possible place in history. As we sat at the table together I told him our old friends in Cedar Rapids, Iowa, and Marietta, Ohio, who knew us better, would never have made the mistake either of making us so prominent or of kissing us.

Paris, February 28, 1919 (10 P.M.)

I to-day finished my Report to the Commanding General, Services of Supply, as General Purchasing Agent and Chairman of the General Purchasing Board, A.E.F. This has been an absorbing and difficult task. Now that it is over I wonder whether anybody will read it. Impressed myself with a sense of its public and historical importance, I have exercised great care and given the best there is in me to its preparation. Owing to constant interruption in my office I have done much of the work in my room at night. The final figures of tons of material secured on this side of the ocean, from the beginning of the A.E.F. to the date of the armistice, stand at 10,000,000 ship tons as against 4,400,000 dead-weight tons shipped us from the United States. If any one had told us at the beginning that this task confronted us, we should not have believed it possible of accomplishment. As David must have kept his mind upon his sling-shot instead of on the size of Goliath, so it was with us.

And now in extra hours I must prepare my Report as the American Member of the Military Board of Allied Supply.

Two of my colleagues on the Liquidation Board[30] of the A.E.F. — Senator Hollis and Mr. Homer Johnson — have arrived. After talking with them I am impressed with their breadth of view and their competency. I feel sure that within a very few months it will be possible for me to make way for General Krauthoff as a member and complete my army work. It is only because I felt I might help a little, through my long experience in general Allied supply negotiation, in getting the Board more rapidly acquainted with the real environment in which its work must be performed, that I became at all reconciled to the idea of becoming the military member. Now after meeting them I know that they have every personal quality I possess, and after giving them whatever information I have, it will be possible for me to go without embarrassing the work. I really should not stay long, for I find it increasingly difficult to be patient with others when my will is crossed — as of course I should be. It is only that I have worked under pressure so long. But after an explosion is over — and they are only

GEORGE WEBSTER OTIS, 17TH ENGINEERS

Died in France

He represented all that is cleanest and best in the young
American soldier and his memory is enshrined
in the hearts of his comrades

occasional — I force myself to humble apology for whatever is improperly personal in my reflections.

The Commander-in-Chief and I are occasionally given in our close friendship to shutting the door and indulging in strong comments upon a hostile world — after which it is always easier to deal meekly with it.

I regret the gradual but increasing neglect of these notes, the interest of which hereafter I realize. Since starting them I have never read any of them over.

The General Headquarters band from Chaumont, which they now call "Pershing's Own," delights me. Because of the method of forming it I believe it to be unique in the world today. It is the most virile and stirring band to which I ever listened. Including the 26 trumpeters and the accompanying drums, there are in all 106 in the organization. Collins and I (who with Damrosch worked over its plans) went to hear it the other night. It should be kept alive after the war as a national asset, and if the people of America ever are allowed to hear it there is a possibility of arousing enough sentiment behind it to secure the legislation necessary. On the spur of the moment I think I shall suggest to some public spirited citizens to start such a movement right away.

Paris, Sunday, March 9, 1919

A week ago to-day I left for Tours to meet the Commander-in-Chief on last Monday. The purpose of my trip was to get action on the delayed promotions in my old regiment, the 17th Engineers, as it sails in a few days for the United States. Am glad to say I was successful — General Pershing telephoning to General McAndrew about it. Lieutenant-Colonel Coe becomes Colonel and takes the boys home.[31]

Spent Sunday night with Harbord. Read him my Report as General Purchasing Agent which I left with him. General Pershing arrived Monday. I left with him on his special train at noon on an inspection trip of the troops. Monday afternoon we were at Saumur. Was with him until Thursday morning when we reached Paris. He inspected troops at Gièvres, Is-sur-Dun, Chateaureaux,[32] and other places in their general vicinity. Troops inspected numbered about 25,000. Part of the time as we walked between the lines we were in mud so thick that we had trouble in pulling out our feet. No heels were "clicked" this trip. Reviews were held at some places. The General made short and effective addresses after inspection to the men at all places. At Is-sur-Dun, just before we took our motors to leave for the next point, the General said that he had not asked for the aviators to fly, as when he and Baker were there before one of the men lost his life in exhibition flying. But our young eagles came out notwithstanding and flew for a long distance over and beside our automobiles. It was not until evening on the train that we learned that one of the boys who flew alongside our machines made a dive and was killed. It seemed so unnecessary. We were greatly grieved. I did not learn the name of the aviator.

The Peace Conference moves slowly along.[33] McFadden, whose work with it naturally grows more important with time, complains that when Wilson is away our delegates, since there are several of them, generally remain comparatively silent during important discussions, since in Wilson's absence leadership is not established among them.[34] The foreigners, therefore, shape the trend of things for the time being. I do not know how the peace conferences are conducted, for I have too much to do to concern myself with securing information about them. As time passes and public opinion presses for a conclusion, it will operate to hasten agreement. During the war in our inter-Allied conferences, whenever I happened to represent our Commander-in-Chief and our army, which was frequently, I soon came to employ certain methods to secure early decision. Where the conference was confronted with the necessity of agreement on something involving a sacrifice to one of the parties and a bitter difference was inevitable, I always endeavored to precipitate immediately the issue in the clearest and most distinct way. By smoking cigars, by great emphasis, by occasional profanity no matter how dignified the gathering or impressive the surroundings, I generally got everybody earnestly in discussion of the very crux of the question in the first half-hour. My disregard of the conventions was studied and with a purpose. It was not only to save precious time by dissipating that atmosphere of self-consciousness in which men so often commence their negotiations, but by having the session start in comparative acrimony the foundation was laid for a natural reaction to good feeling later in the session which would cause every one to leave the conference in comparatively better humor than if the fight occurred just before the ending.

If the difference between conferees is vital and important enough, it will be strongly contested. A perception of this at the beginning of a conference and a courageous meeting of the situation creates rough sailing for a time, but steadily smoother until the end; whereas weak men, or vain or conventional men, or even strong men at times, by over-politeness, by over-deference to a non-essential environment or strange and dignified surroundings, carefully avoid ruffling the waters at first only to ride later into the inevitable storm. In such cases all leave the conference annoyed, some by the decision and some by the others. In a common cause and a common emergency men should come out of a conference not only with a decision, but as friends. Among sincere and honest men in an emergency involving the common interest, the quicker disagreeable truth involved in decision is met, the surer will be an honest and quick settlement of respective duty.

In the above I am not speaking of ordinary conferences among ordinary men, but of vital conferences upon which hang great events.

Paris, Sunday
March 30, 1919 (10.30 P.M.)

To-day I handed to General Pershing my Report as the American Member of the Military Board of Allied Supply. We read over the more important parts together and he seems satisfied with the Report over which I have very carefully worked. We had a meeting of the Board during the week. I regard the Report as my most important contribution to the military literature of the war, and the most important document which I have ever prepared. However, it may be years before anybody digs it up and appreciates it for what it is. The world is in a crisis and Europe will remain in one indefinitely, so that the minds of this generation will not largely concern themselves with retrospect.

My prediction of a year ago that if the Allies won they would have no more of a government in Germany to deal with than Germany had in Russia, bids fair to be realized within sixty days. The war has broken up the central control of the Continental Empires, and left the alien peoples to define their own relations, which they will proceed to do by the usual process of wars. The phrase-makers, politicians, idealists, and pacifists may now realize that whether democracy is safe or not depends upon the people in question, and that in parts of Europe self-government is as impossible in certain stages of development in the life of a particular people as in the Philippines.

Self-government in our own dear land is safe, but right minded people, and not alone the demagogues and timeservers, must be active to keep it so. The ultimate judgment of the American people is sound, provided the checks and balances of our Constitution are kept in existence so that ultimate and not hasty or temporary judgments may pass into law.

My two Reports are now finished. My work on the Liquidation Commission is important, but as responsibility is divided and life and death for others is not involved, the mental strain under which I have been so long is lifting.

On Friday, for the first time in my army service over here, I faced an American audience at a banquet given to a delegation from the Cleveland Chamber of Commerce by Homer Johnson, of our Commission. General Pershing, Secretary Daniels, M. Loucheur, and others spoke.

Last night (Saturday) I entertained at dinner at the Ritz and afterward at the Olympia Vaudeville[35] the Generals of the First Army whom Harbord had taken over the S.O.S. General Pershing was present; also Lieutenant-General Liggett,[36] commanding the First Army; Major-Generals Warner, Bailey, McNair, and Smith, Brigadier-General Hulit, and in addition Major-General Harbord and myself and aides of the party — in all twenty-six. My friend General Payot was present. Before dinner General Pershing conferred the Distinguished Service Medal on George McFadden, which he certainly has brilliantly won.

During the week, under the direction and delegation of General Pershing, I pinned the Distinguished Service Medal of the United States upon the uniform of my associate, Major-General Reginald Ford, of the English army — a brave and successful officer of the line on the Somme and afterward a most efficient member of the British General Staff.

Paris, Friday
April 11, 1919 (10.30 P.M.)

I regret that the disinclination to write has prevented me from commenting on the many interesting and historical characters whom I constantly meet. To-night I have been so interested in my talk with the Grand Duke Alexander of Russia[37] that I will try to make a few notes of it. The Grand Duke lives here at the hotel and met me because of his interest in an interview of mine in the *Stars and Stripes*[38] in which I spoke of the cooperation of the French with our army supply efforts.[39] He has had me at dinner with him twice this week, to-night having also Mr. and Mrs. McFadden and Countess Olga. Alexander is a brother-in-law of the late Czar. Three of his brothers have been murdered by the Bolshevists. He told me seventeen of his family had met this fate. His son-in-law, Prince Yusopoff, murdered Rasputin.

Alexander is in a position to know what he is talking about, and to-night being in distress of mind about the Crimea where the Bolshevists are advancing,[40] and where a number of his children are living still, he opened his heart freely to me. He is outraged because the Allies are taking no steps to restore order in Russia. He says that while the Germans were there they at least preserved a semblance of order. He says that the abandonment of Russia by the Allies means only one thing—the future cooperation of Germany and Russia; that within a year or so the old regime must be established in Russia by the force of events and the reaction against the present terrible anarchy. He is an intelligent, forceful talker. Wilson declined to see him; England will not allow his family to go there. He thinks America would not receive him if he asked permission to take his children there. His property has been confiscated, and he is tired of "Grand Duking." He is an extremely likable man, and though my short acquaintance with him does not enable me to pass judgment upon him as a statesman, I would trust him as a man.

The home papers announce the arrival in America of my old regiment.

We are hard at work on the Liquidation Commission. Warren Pershing, the General's boy, is on his way here. I am so glad for John's sake. Tardieu has cabled a resume of my *Stars and Stripes* interview to America. If it is published there it will be the first time the fact has been made public that we secured two thirds of the tonnage consumed by our army on this side of the ocean. Harbord asked me to give the interview and same was first submitted to him.

Coblentz, [sic] Germany,[41] *April 24, 1919*

Have been on a trip with General Pershing since Sunday.[42] In the party besides the General are the Secretary of War, General Harbord, Leopold, the Crown Prince of Belgium,[43] the General's aides, and myself. General Harbord and I left Paris Sunday morning, April 20 (Easter), and arrived at Chaumont in the afternoon. Dined with the Commander-in-Chief and the Secretary and left for Is-sur-Tille Sunday night with the party.

Of the events of this unusual trip I will mention the march past of the 33d Division (chiefly from Illinois) which took place in a magnificent natural amphitheater near Die Kirch. It took about six or seven miles of walking to complete the inspection which the General made, his party including myself accompanying him. After the decorations were conferred — among them one to Colonel Sanborn,[44] of Evanston — the review took place. The ground was so level that the entire division in movement could be seen at once. The setting sun shone upon the blue steel of the bayonets of the twenty-three thousand men as they approached us, and at a distance it gave the appearance of a bluish mist just above the brown of the helmets. The massed regimental bands played well. It was unquestionably the most impressive and inspiring sight of my life. The review next day of the 89th Division was also very wonderful, but not so many men by about one half were in line.

This trip is the first the young Prince Leopold has ever been allowed to take alone. He is seventeen years of age — a very natural, modest, dignified, and altogether likable boy. He is greatly enjoying himself and tells me he is writing all about it to his mother.

Am finding the Secretary of War an extremely agreeable companion.

His speeches to the men are admirable. His critics will pass into oblivion, but his accomplishments under great disadvantages will always be remembered in our history.

The week before I started on this trip at Paris was a busy one. Spent much of two days with General Pershing. Went with him to the studio of Jo Davidson,[45] an American sculptor who is making a bust of the General. Was so pleased with it that I purchased the first one finished. I think it will become the standard bust of General Pershing, as it is by all odds the best yet made of him — especially when looked at in profile.

One night last week dined with General Botha,[46] the Prime Minister of South Africa. We were both guests of General Bethel of the English army.

Our great army is rapidly being reduced in numbers. This sojourn on occupied German soil, however, may continue some time for the Third Army.[47]

Paris, Sunday, May 4, 1919

Outdoors this morning for the first time in three days, having been down with a mild but exasperating case of ptomaine poisoning. Took lunch with Generals Harbord, Drum, and Hagood, Grand Duke Alexander, and Mrs. George McFadden.[48]

The early part of the week was at Tours, where with other officers of the A.E.F. was made a Companion of the Bath[49] at ceremonies, Lieutenant-General Henderson, of the B.E.F., conferring the decorations. Harbord was made a K.C.M.G.[50]

Our Liquidation Commission is immersed in its difficult problems. Am much impressed with the abilities and high characters of my associates. They are high-minded, practical men, and influenced only by the highest motives. Am much impressed by their earnestness and sincerity.

On our return from the trip to Germany I had the party on the train — excepting General Pershing and Secretary Baker — at dinner and afterward at the theater. General McAndrew and Colonel De Chambrun were also with us, as was the young Belgian Crown Prince Leopold.

At Tours on Tuesday at Harbord's house, where I stayed, Julius Kahn,[51] the new Chairman of the House Committee on Military Affairs, was a guest. He is able and constructive and should be a great asset to our country in the new army reorganization which should follow the war.

The peace treaty is about ready for the signatures of the Germans which probably will be forthcoming, since if they are not our armies will march forward. But when the peace treaty is finally read the world will know that peace-treatymaking is not an exact science.

Received cable that my brother Beman will be here this month. Shall be rejoiced to see him, as I should be the other dear members of my family from whom I have been separated now for nearly two years. Have been worried about my dear mother's health, but a letter this week from her reassures me.

Paris, Friday, May 9, 1919

The Liquidation Commission is struggling with its great task. Roughly estimated at the heavy war costs, we have on hand army supplies and installations of a nominal value of $1,500,000,000. It is scattered all over France. Our nation is pressing for a return of our soldiers. The United States has also a surplus of war supplies at home estimated at $2,000,000,000. Great Britain has about $2,000,000,000 or over in France. France itself has a tremendous stock. Transportation facilities are limited. The value of the stocks is lessening with time. France as a government is in financial straits, and yet it is the only logical purchaser of our property. Our negotiations are rendered more difficult by the complicated inter-governmental credit situation. It is necessary to deal upon the highest plane and with great energy. Whatever we do will be criticized, but I want to be criticized for doing something rather than nothing.

Johnson, Hollis, and I met Tardieu last night. Tardieu is now over his hardest work with the Peace Conference and can put his powerful shoulder to the wheels of our cart. He fully agrees with us as to the necessity of a sale of the whole to France both for the interests of his country and our own. The member of our commission who has shown the earliest and clearest appreciation of the wisdom, indeed necessity, of dealing with France in bulk has been Johnson, for whose abilities I have a constantly increasing admiration. The country is fortunate in having three such able and clean men on the commission as Parker, Johnson, and Hollis. I do not pretend to take the laboring oar; but am trying to be of some help to my associates who are doing most of the work. General Pershing called me by telephone yesterday about the liquidation situation. It concerns the question of the time when we can release all our troops. Earlier in the week the General gave me a sword which he had personally selected— and had duly engraved — which I shall always value, it is needless to say.

On Wednesday I dined with Major-General Thwaites, of the B.E.F., at the Hotel Majestic.[52] After dinner I met Lloyd George. I told him that when after a few months he got time to read it, I wanted him to look over my Report on the Military Board of Allied Supply which he had helped to create. Told him he would be interested because it was, with its

GENERAL JOHN J. PERSHING
(Clay model by Jo Davidson)

unanimous-consent provision, practically a "League of Nations" operating just behind the Allied line of battle. If anybody hereafter (and this is probable) maintains that the League of Nations has no real power because unanimous consent must be the basis of its effective action, the record of what our military "League of Nations" actually did do and was about to do will refute them.[53] He agreed. I now reflect that if I had allowed him to do more of the talking these notes would be of greater moment.

The peace terms have been handed to the Germans. They are certainly stiff enough to satisfy the extremists.[54] But I am free to say that this commission has probably done the very best it was possible to do in the environment in which it acted. When the environment is forgotten and the unconquerable necessities of an actual situation do not confront the critic, there will be much international literature devoted to the demonstration of how much better a treaty would have resulted if the nations had summoned the critics to the conference instead of their greatest men. The highest art in criticism as a rule is developed only in those personally incapable of constructive accomplishment.

Paris, May 23, 1919

These notes have become a more or less perfunctory matter with me, but I realize that hereafter I shall regret it. Harbord and I were talking last night about the "after the-war" adaptation of ourselves to the usual environment of humanity, and he referred to having used the expression to General Pershing, "only eight hundred thousand troops now left in France." His idea of size in armies has altered in two years. The fact of the matter is that we all are passing every day through intensely interesting situations and experiences which, measured by our old pre-war mental attitude, would have been engrossing. But this after-the-war reaction makes people and things seem relatively unimportant. When in a year or so we "come to," so to speak, we shall regret not having made a better record of these armistice days.

Harbord has again become Pershing's Chief of Staff, much to his gratification and that of all of us. W. D. Connor becomes Commanding General, Services of Supply. There are no better men made than Harbord. A great soldier and a great man, he is a faithful, loyal friend to those in whom he believes, and the waning fortunes of a friend only make him his stronger advocate. The world is filled with fawning sycophants these days, and they only emphasize the natural majesty of sincerity and naturalness. The true friend is always the most active in our greatest need of him. General Pershing has been here most of the week. Have taken lunch nearly every day with him and his aides at 73 Rue de Varenne.

Owing to the fact that peace is still hanging fire the General had to cancel the trip to England on which I was to accompany him. Accordingly had to telegraph Mr. William C. Dawes, at Mount Ephraim, Faversham, Kent, postponing the date of the christening of my English godson.[55]

We are struggling away on the Liquidation Commission with one of the big business trades of all time. General McAndrew, the old Chief of Staff, has had a wonderful career of usefulness in his position. He is respected and beloved by us all. He leaves to take up work in the War Department — head of the War College, I think.[56] Everybody hates to see him leave.

Paris, Sunday
June 1, 1919 (10.30 P.M.)

Beman and Bertie arrived last Wednesday from the United States.[57] General Pershing telephoned from Chaumont to bring them there for the Decoration Day[58] exercises at Beaumont and Romagne. Bertie was too fatigued to go, but Beman and I went by automobile Thursday to Chaumont, dined with the General and Harbord, and left with them and others of his Staff by train that night for the Argonne battlefield. The General did not intend to speak at Beaumont in the morning, but after the impressive ceremony conducted by Chaplain Moody ended, and the infantry had fired the three volleys over the long row of newly made graves marked by their white wooden crosses, he stepped down from the platform into the little gathering of French people before him. An old French civilian, the Mayor of the little near-by village, surrounded by a group of French children carrying wild flowers, then spoke to him in a simple way saying that the people of the neighborhood would always care for the graves of the lads sleeping so far away from their homes who had given their lives that the village might remain under France. The tears rolled down the General's face as he said, as near as I can remember: "It is very hard for us to say 'Good-bye' for the last time to our dear comrades whom we now leave forever. But since they cannot go home with us, there is no land save their own in which we would rather have them rest — no people with whom we can more surely leave their ashes to tender care and lasting memory than the dear people of France. I thank you in the name of their bereaved and in the name of our whole people who are mourning them to-day and whose hearts are here."[59]

Somehow this incident overshadowed in my mind all the more formal ceremonies both at Beaumont and later at Romagne, where the General made his formal address before a great assemblage of soldiers.

Beman and I left the party at Romagne and returned to Paris by motor, arriving about midnight. I took him to Montfaucon where I found the observation post on the north slope of the hill, where on October 6 poor Boyd and I watched the battle from a spot near the Crown Prince's old dugout. We returned through Varennes, Chalons, Rheims, Chateau-Thierry. They are rapidly cleaning up the terrible debris at Rheims.

Our troops are rapidly leaving for home. The curtain is falling on this great episode over here.

Paris, June 7, 1919

By July 1 our understanding with the French Government as to our cession of material to them and the settlement of reciprocal accounts will either be completed or in such agreed state that I can no longer be kept as indispensable to their proper completion. After long negotiations we are now practically in accord with the French on everything and await only the completion of certain inventories. The work has been most responsible, but others have borne the heaviest burden of it. Many hundreds of millions of dollars are involved and I have been at times concerned as to the outcome. I feel, however, that we have considered the situation from every angle, and that the conclusion reached will be the fairest and best possible under most difficult conditions. Have kept closely in touch with all matters of policy and decisions relating to it, but have not attempted detail work.

My associates on this commission are most exceptional and strong men. They have worked hard and honestly and shown great ability.

Will leave for Brussels to-morrow for a day or so to say "Good-bye" to Van de Vyvere, my faithful friend, who helped our army so much last year. He is no longer in office.

Paris, June 13, 1919

Arrived in Brussels last Sunday night with Colonel Cushing. Next morning Colonel Sewell came over from Antwerp where he is Base Commander (also at Rotterdam) and remained with me during my visit. My friend Van de Vyvere came over from Ghent and we three took lunch together. My trip was taken chiefly to indicate to Van de Vyvere my personal regard and respect. Tuesday went by motor to Antwerp with Sewell and after an interesting day left that night for Paris arriving Wednesday morning.

The balance of the week rather busy. Conferences with Liquidation Committee and others. General Pershing is here and we spend considerable time together in pleasant visiting in contrast to the old strenuous days.

This morning (Saturday) took part in the ceremonies in court of the

Invalides,[60] with which General Lewis, representing the President, and the Commander-in-Chief decorated my friend Varaigne and other French officers with the Distinguished Service Medal before French and American troops. Beman and Bertie were present. In addition to keeping up with the Liquidation Commission, the plans for final demobilization of the Military Board of Allied Supply and of my own office require thought and careful attention. Am experiencing exasperating delays in securing from the Allied armies the detailed information desired and ordered as to their condition on October 31, 1918.

Made Commander of the Order of Leopold [61]

Royaume De Belgique
Ministére De La Guerre
Bruxelles, June 17, 1919
Direction Des Voies de Communication
From: Major Hainaut, *D.V.C., War Office*
To: General Dawes, *American Member of the Inter-Allied Supply Committee*
Élysée Palace, Paris

Dear Sir:
I beg to inform you that, in agreement with the American authorities, His Majesty the King of the Belgians has decided to confer upon you the Commandery of the Order of Leopold.

You will only receive the necessary chancellery documents in a little time, but I hope to have the great honor to bring you the jewel myself at the next meeting of the Inter-Allied Supply Committee.

With my best congratulations
I remain, dear Sir
Yours respectfully
Hainaut

Letter to my mother
June 30, 1919

Owing to the fact that our negotiations with the French Government for the sale of our surplus army property will require a few weeks longer to terminate one way or the other, my departure for home will be delayed until the 20th of July. This is a disappointment to me, but I feel that you would not want me to leave until I had taken my full share of responsibility in this important matter. If I should ask to come sooner it would seem that

I was leaving upon my colleagues the full onus of a very difficult situation and decision, in which it is my duty not only to our Government but to them that I fully participate. What I hope will be the final negotiations with the French Government will commence to-morrow. And so I am dictating to you an account of my trip to England which will be of interest to you during the three weeks' longer delay in my expected return.

A week ago Sunday at Paris occurred the dedication of the Pershing Stadium,[62] which was presented by America to the Government of France. After attending this exercise in the afternoon, I left with General Pershing and his personal aides for Le Mans, where we spent Monday attending the opening of the International Rifle Contest. We left on the General's special train for Boulogne Monday night and took the Channel boat on Tuesday morning, arriving in London about noon. I did not go with General Pershing to Oxford, where he received the D.C.L. degree[63] on Wednesday, desiring to remain in the city and visit my dear friends Lieutenant General Sir Travers Clarke and Major-General Sir Evan Carter, as well as my younger friend Captain Frank Covell. General Travers Clarke, General Carter, and Captain Covell took dinner with me at the Carlton[64] Tuesday and Wednesday evenings, as did also Colonel Beeuwkes,[65] one of General Pershing's aides. In my report as Chairman of the General Purchasing Board and General Purchasing Agent of the American E.F., when you finally receive it, you will find my tribute to English cooperation with my department of the Staff, for which General Travers Clarke and General Carter were so largely responsible. My friend, Major-General Reginald Ford, now in command of the Service of Supply of the British Army in France, had expected to visit London with me, but was detained in France by an important interarmy conference. It is impossible for right-minded and earnest men to be associated for so long and in matters of such vital importance as those which have engrossed General Travers Clarke, General Ford, General Carter, and myself, without having the warmest friendships develop. When General Pershing placed upon me the responsibility of securing animals for our army during the action in the Argonne, I shall never forget the earnest way in which General Travers Clarke, under the authority of Marshal Haig, assisted me. As for General Carter, from the very beginning of our participation in the war he has been an ever-present help in time of trouble.

I spent some time at the British War Office in the company of these men. On Wednesday evening Beman arrived from Brussels and joined me at the Carlton Hotel. The same evening also Captain Sandys Dawes, the father of my new godson, arrived in London to pilot us down to Mt. Ephraim the next morning. At ten o'clock Thursday morning General Pershing and his aides, including Colonel Griscom, our Military Attache at London, joined us at the Carlton Hotel and, together with General Carter, Beman, and Captain Covell, we left by motor for Mount Ephraim, Faversham, for the christening. General Pershing and I went in the first car. My association with the General is so constant and in all his actions he is so entirely the natural and close friend of the long years, that I find myself forgetting how important he is and what a central figure of interest he has become everywhere. We were both surprised as we rode up to Mount Ephraim about 12.30 to note the road decorated with the Allied flags and to find upon our arrival at the house the military band of the 8th British Hussars. We were greeted by Mr. William C. Dawes, the present head of the English family, and his wife; Colonel Bethel Dawes, a magnificent old army officer of eighty years and a brother of the late Sir Edwin Sandys Dawes; Captain Sandys Dawes, his wife and my little godson, together with Betty and Lancelot, Captain Dawes's sister and brother; besides other collateral members of the family. We started immediately for the old Norman church in Hernhill village near by, built in 1120, where generations of the Daweses, probably more pious than the present, have worshiped for centuries and are now buried. I went in the first car with the father and mother of the boy and the grandmother, Mrs. Dawes. General Pershing, Mr. William C. Dawes, Beman, and General Carter followed in the second car. The villagers had gathered in the little church. The old rector in his red robe, Rev. Dr. Springett, who with an assistant performed the ceremony, is the uncle of Captain Sandys Dawes, having married the sister of Mr. William C. Dawes. General Pershing, Betty Dawes, the eighteen-year-old sister of Captain Sandys Dawes, and I, who were the sponsors and godparents of the child, occupied a little pew immediately in front of the rector. Beman sat with the rest of the family and Charles Ambrose William to our right.

We returned to the house for lunch, which was attended by the family and a few of the leading residents of the section of the country, including the Lord High Sheriff of the County of Kent and the Mayor of Faversham. After lunch the school children of the village called to present an address to General Pershing. After that was over, Mr. Dawes asked me to step before the children — about eighty of them — who proceeded to sing "Auld Lang Syne," which Mr. Dawes said was the village custom when a member of a family returned after a long absence. The General and I were much impressed and found ourselves choked up a little several times. The General left in time to catch the four-o'clock boat for France at Dover, which is but a short distance away, and General Carter, Colonel Beeuwkes, Captain Covell, Beman, and I remained at Mount Ephraim for the night. While the surroundings of the family were impressive and magnificent, they were quite simple and unaffected people — as should always be. The grounds were thrown open to the villagers in the afternoon, who came to listen to the military band and walk in the beautiful gardens which surrounded the house. Beman, General Carter, and Colonel Beeuwkes and I remained until afternoon. In the morning the entire family accompanied me around the grounds, the hunting stables, the beagle kennels, the greenhouses where orchid-raising is the great specialty, and over some parts of the estate which sweeps down the hill from the house as far as the ocean, about three miles away, I should say. We passed near the house an oak-tree by which a tablet was placed stating that it had been planted in 1815 by Charles Dawes to commemorate the allied victory in the Battle of Waterloo. Mr. Dawes then took us to a spot where all the family and the servants were gathered by previous arrangement so that I could plant the tree which would commemorate the signing of the peace in the present Great War. This tree must be regarded as having been theoretically, but not entirely, planted by me, for after I had thrown in a certain amount of earth it occurred to me to suggest that the gardeners, of whom there were a number there, could proceed with it more scientifically, a view in which after watching me they thoroughly concurred. Some of the family took a kodak of the tree-planting, which when they send it to me I will forward to you. I hope that the picture of old Colonel Dawes is a good one, as for some reason he did not appear in the first group, which was taken the day of the christening, by the local photographer.[66]

During the morning Mrs. William Dawes, Betty, and I went over to the old church where we looked at the gravestones of the Dawes ancestors. The Daweses came to Mount Ephraim from Westmoreland, where they had lived for centuries, in the early 1600's and have lived there ever since, except for a short space of ten or fifteen years. During this time an iconoclast rector took up three of the flat Dawes gravestones of the seventeenth-century period in the floor of the church, and after imperfectly chipping off the inscriptions placed them in the walk just outside the church. A brass tablet, however, has been placed inside the church above the old graves. I noticed the grave of Major William Dawes, who fought in the English army in the Revolutionary War. So that here was the case of an American William Dawes and an English William Dawes in opposing armies. In one of the old Dawes homes at Westmoreland over a gateway was an inscription, the facsimile of which Sir Edwin placed over one of the gates at Mount Ephraim. I shall always remember it — "Keep your eyes toward the sunlight, and the shadows will fall behind you." Sir Edwin is buried in the old churchyard. Two commemorative tablets on the walls of the old church and the memorial chapel built by his son are a tribute to his memory. It was his interest in the Dawes family which led him twenty years ago to write to me and suggest a reunion of the two branches. The American family has never been interested up to the present generation in old Ambrose Dawes, the father of William Dawes of Sudbury, the founder about 1620 of the American family. I hope that hereafter both the American and the English family will regard his memory as an asset.

The Daweses showed me the Siwash[67] Indian relics which Rufus some years ago sent to the children, who are very proud of them. They referred often to the pleasant visit which Rufus and Helen made them some years ago. The family is a patriarchal one. The old butler has been with them for fifty years and is as much a member of the family as any one of the blood. The servants cheered when the tree was planted and acted and were treated in all respects as members of the family. Mr. Dawes took me to a blacksmith shop to call on a blacksmith whose family for three hundred years have been at the same work in the same place.

On Saturday afternoon, the next day, I drove with General Carter to his home thirty miles out of London to meet his family. Lady Carter was ill in bed, so that I did not see her, but the two children were as unaffected and simple as had been all of the younger people that I met during the trip.

Captain Sandys Dawes has just returned from Palestine where he served with the English army. He is not entirely tamed after this experience. On Saturday night the family came up and dined with me at the Carlton Hotel during the celebration over the signing of the peace that afternoon. At dinner time Captain Sandys Dawes, although naturally quiet and dignified, arose fully in the most energetic Dawes fashion to the exigencies of that somewhat hilarious occasion. When Colonel Beeuwkes, General Pershing's aide, who had remained in England with me, sat solemnly down, after having delivered an alleged toast, he landed in a plate of meat and gelatine thoughtfully placed on his chair for him by the Captain, who then and during the entire evening, while keeping all his faculties, seemed to rise to every occasion. Being over middle-aged and admitting it, I withdrew at eleven o'clock and went to bed, leaving the somewhat worried elder Mrs. Dawes to feebly but continuously cope with the high spirits of the children, including Lancelot Dawes, fourteen years of age, who was present. The next morning Colonel Beeuwkes told me that it was nearly two o'clock in the morning before she could persuade them to leave for the night motor ride back to Faversham. The tremendous celebration of peace in London I shall not attempt to describe, as the papers have informed you of it.[68] On Saturday night the Daweses brought me up photographs which the village photographer had taken of the gathering at the house and of the General and myself with the family. There are a great many of them and I am sure you will be interested in seeing them.

CHRISTENING PARTY AT MOUNT EPHRAIM, FAVERSHAM, KENT

Seated, left to right: Major-General Sir Evan Carter, Hon. Beman G. Dawes, General Dawes, General Pershing, Mrs. William C. Dawes, Mrs. Selby, Mrs. Springett, Lady Harris.
Next to inner left-hand column stands William C. Dawes, on his left his son, Captain Sandys Dawes, and in front of extreme right-hand column Mrs. Sandys Dawes.

I have tried to write this letter in detail in the way which would please you. It was really an occasion which moved me very much at times. Like the two countries in which they live, the two branches of the family have been at times estranged and on opposite sides, but like their countries I hope they have come together not again to be divided in spirit. While William Dawes of Boston, the fourth from William Dawes of England, rode with Paul Revere in the fight against the English, William Dawes of Evanston, the eleventh from William Dawes of England, rode on the Hindenburg Line in command of a tank manned by Englishmen, fighting with them against a common enemy. This fact, as well as because little Charles Ambrose William Dawes is named after William Dawes, the present head of the English family, after Ambrose, the common ancestor, and after myself, your eldest son, would indicate a complete reunion of a fine old stock in common purpose hereafter. I only wish that the old William Dawes and Father and Uncle Eph and the others, who have done so much in America to make the family name stand for accomplishment and earnest purpose, as well as all the old English Daweses, could know of it all.

Your affectionate son.

Paris, July 4, 1919

On Wednesday our Liquidation Commission received the first offer of France for our surplus supplies in France at a conference with Paul Morel, the Minister charged with the matter of liquidation for the French. The offer was 1,500,000,000 francs. This is much too small a price, and we of course rejected it. We have now to continue negotiations, but they should be concluded within the month — at least as to the aggregate price. Our surplus material is worth under favorable conditions in my judgment about $1,000,000,000, less what we have sold and used and otherwise disposed of during the period of inventory. Suppose we assume $750,000,000 as the value we should fix as the starting-point in the trade as against the less than $300,000,000 which the French offer; I think we shall finally agree on about $400,000,000 to $450,000,000 as the proper price under the difficult conditions in which both sides negotiate.

Filed with the Commission a memorandum giving my views as to the absolute necessity of selling to the French Government. Cabled home postponing my departure until later in the month. Very busy with the Commission during the first three days of the week. Am preparing my papers and work preliminary to leaving for home.

Tuesday, July 4, our national holiday is being celebrated as only our

French allies can celebrate.[69] No people surpass them in sincere gratitude and generosity in the graceful and touching expression of it.

Attended the reception to General Pershing given by the City of Paris at the Hôtel de Ville[70] yesterday afternoon — a most magnificent affair. Attended in the evening the dinner given by the French Government to our military and naval representatives, with General Pershing as the guest of honor, at the Pré Catalan,[71] in the Bois de Boulogne. Marshals Foch and Pétain were present and about eighty other officers equally divided between the French and Americans. The speeches of the French Ministers and of General Pershing were perfect in their adaptation to what was really an historic occasion.

To-day is filled with celebrations in honor of our nation. At the Pré Catalan banquet was pleased with the music of the French military *(poilu)* band and engaged it for my dinner to Payot and the Military Board of Allied Supply which I am to give Tuesday night, at which I shall say "Good-bye" to my dear friends on this side of the ocean.

Paris, Sunday, July 6, 1919 (11.30 P.M.)

Am rather depressed at leaving this life of activity, strenuous endeavor, and unusual environment as the time for my sailing draws near. Took lunch with the Commander-in-Chief and his aides. Harbord and Collins dined with me. The week has been one of numerous celebrations most of which I have escaped. In my younger days I suppose they would have appealed to me more. When Harbord brought me this evening the invitation of the Commander-in-Chief to ride as a member of his Staff in the Peace Parade, I experienced the usual internal conflict between vanity and common sense, the latter finally prevailing. No one will regard my being in the parade as an incident of it except myself — and to ride in it means that I cannot see it.

Am pushing the gathering of information as to the Services of Supply of the three armies as hard as possible, having sent Colonel Hodges to the General Headquarters of the other armies. Our own information is mostly in. On Tuesday night, after the meeting of the Military Board of Allied Supply, I shall give a dinner to General Payot and the other members at the Ritz. I certainly shall miss my faithful friend General Payot when I go.

Harbord wants me to go to Armenia with him as a member of his commission.[72] I should like to help found a better condition of things as an agent of our great country in the land where Will Shedd and Uncle John and Aunt Jane did so much for others — Will finally giving his life.[73] To be useful is to find whatever of happiness there is in life — and there is little enough at best. I used to feel sorry for Will Shedd who was spending his life helping people in Persia, and enduring hardships in order to be able to do it. He should have felt sorry for me.

"Vanity of vanities, all is vanity, saith the preacher."[74] As a matter of fact, if we did not have vanity — which is the commonest of human characteristics — and saw ourselves as others see us, we should probably starve to death as a race, not regarding our existence as worth the effort to maintain it. Such is the reflection induced by the antics of individuals during a time of international pomp and circumstance in peace celebrating. Humanity sets out killing each other, and succeeds in filling millions of graves with the best portion of it. Then a good section of what is left of it proceeds to celebrate in champagne and pre-historic dancing. "Vanity of vanities, all is vanity, saith the preacher." And so to bed. If there is less humidity in the atmosphere to-morrow morning I shall probably take a brighter view of things.

If I had not mentioned my coming dinner for Payot, what I have written before would seem more consistent. But, thank Heaven, I never stayed a pessimist overnight in my life!

Paris, July 6, 1919

The heart-burnings among our officers who have not received the Distinguished Service Medal, when they unquestionably deserve it, leads me to question the advisability in our country of any governmental system of decoration even for military or civil accomplishment. Apart from the unwisdom in a Republic of establishing a system tending toward the creation of classes, the disappointment of the unpreferred is apt to be directed toward the Government as well as toward its agent in decoration distribution. The Decoration Board of the A.E.F. is swamped with thousands of requests for reconsideration of disapprovals of the D.S.M. As a matter of fact it has been impossible, and always will be impossible, to discriminate justly in the distribution of awards in a large army — from the very vastness of the task which prevents consideration of all the cases from the viewpoint of the same minds. An officer of the A.E.F. who has succeeded in his task, been promoted, been commended by his superior officers and associates, should not feel himself reflected upon because he has not received one of the few hundred Distinguished Service Medals distributed among millions of men. And yet some of them do, and I greatly regret it. The "world will little note nor long remember" even our names — much less the minor things relating to our personal vanity. I suppose, as one who has received much more recognition than he deserves, it is easy for me to recommend philosophy to those who have been unjustly treated. But when

I find disappointment so keen and rage so blinding that I have to endure patiently an attack on the system and everybody connected with it, including intimations that I have not been duly active for my friends — all because I have failed in a strenuous recommendation to have the D.S.M. awarded where it was deserved — I come to realize that the system is questionable.

How little any one cares to hear of our failures and grievances! If the world was not cold, human vanity would demand all its time and energy expended in sympathizing with grouches. Realizing, especially this morning, that this is a very cold world after a conversation with some officers who did not get the D.S.M., I suggested to them the following paraphrase: "Weep, and the world laughs at you. Laugh, and you laugh alone." This did not seem to comfort them, their sense of humor being submerged along with their other faculties in deep pessimism.

Paris, Friday evening
July 11, 1919

On Tuesday occurred what will be the last, but one, meeting of the Military Board of Allied Supply. It was held at my headquarters at the Élysée Palace Hotel. The representatives of the four armies were present. General Payot presided. I am happy to say that the compilation by the different staffs of the information as to supply systems has so far progressed that the great composite picture of the Allied army supply system in France will be preserved for the military students of all time.

On Tuesday evening at the Ritz I gave a dinner in honor of General Payot and the other members of the Board at which about one hundred guests were present. I paid as best I could my tribute of respect and affection to my dear friend General Payot, whose wonderful ability and experience were given so devotedly to our army whenever required. General Moseley also paid him a splendid tribute, as did General Connor who made his speech in excellent French. Connor always makes good in the army and elsewhere, but I trembled for him when he tackled this job.

I had opportunity to thank publicly some of those present for what they had done to help me in my work — Van de Vyvere for the Belgian locomotives; Davidson for himself and others for the Portugal railroad ties; General Chevalier for saving our wood situation; Ganne, Oppenheim, and Varaigne most important of all, and Doumenc for helping in motor transport work. I made each get on his feet while I spoke to him, like a class at school. But I taught a pleasing lesson. Lieutenant-General Cowans sat at my left and recounted in his speech our former differences out of which a firm friendship had sprung.

Payot announced my citation in the orders by Marshal Foch. The next day I received the notification of the Marshal through a letter of Weygand, Chief of Staff.[75] The Marshal designated Payot to deliver the Croix de Guerre, which he will do at La Morlaye on the 16th. The citation as given in Payot's letter is too comprehensive in my own fair judgment. It is, however, an honor for which it is difficult for me to express my full appreciation.

The French have increased through Minister Paul Morel their offer for our army material in France from 1,500,000,000 francs to 2,250,000,000 francs. This is still somewhat too low.

Bought to-day at a bookstore De Chambrun's and De Marenches's book in French, "The American Army in the European Conflict." Was pleased with their reference to the work of my department of the Staff. They are both men of unusual ability, and certainly no one saw the American effort from a closer view than they did.[76]

I expect to sail on July 26th. Paris is a mass of flags and crowded with people from outside to see the peace parade.[77] Beman and Bertie left for home Wednesday. I have greatly enjoyed their visit.

Paris, Saturday, July 19, 1919

I expect to sail July 28th and so I am entering upon my last week here. What John McCutcheon once said to me, at about the time America entered the war, is true: "This war is so great that everything that happens after it in our lives will be in the nature of an anticlimax." Therefore I feel my usual disinclination to describe the celebrations of the last week.

The Victory Parade, July 14, which I witnessed from the stand reserved for the French General Officers, was of course the most impressive of history and will not lack describers. Its arrangement and execution from start to finish were perfect. Nor did the tribute to the dead fail to reach the perfection of that to the living. In this the dear and noble French people never fail. It has been a privilege to have lived two years among this heroic and martyred people in such relations that one gained an understanding of them impossible to the casual visitor. As I saw them by the tens of thousands quietly dropping the single flowers before the memorial to their dead, there formed in my mind the picture of them which shall last through my own life.

General Pershing and General Harbord left for England Monday night. On Wednesday noon I went to La Morlaye — General Payot's headquarters — where he gave a farewell lunch in my honor. As I drove up to the building General Payot and other French and Allied officers were waiting and several platoons of *poilus* with trumpeters were drawn up in a double line.

The ceremony of decoration was held immediately, several others being decorated, among them the son of Minister Clementel, the latter being present. In the name of Marshal Foch, General Payot gave me the Croix de Guerre with a palm, reading the citation to the Order of the Army. We went to the country residence of Baron Rothschild, in which General Payot and his staff live, where lunch was served. My friend General Ford and a number of other English, Italian, and Belgian officers, besides Payot's Staff, were present, among them General Nation, Lord Pembroke, Commandant Doumenc, Commandant Lescannes, Colonel Hodges, my Chief of Staff as American Member of the Board. Ford had to take a ten-hour motor ride from the British army line to attend the ceremony — an attention which I certainly appreciate.

Last night, Friday, Mr. and Mrs. Homer Johnson gave a dinner at the Ritz for some thirty-five guests which turned out to be in my honor, though I had not been told of it until Mr. Johnson announced it at the table.

The sale of our surplus supplies to the French is about agreed upon. No essential difference longer exists. I shall leave France with a sense of having "stayed through."

Am making every effort to facilitate the gathering of the final information to complete the great picture of the Allied armies in France and their supply systems. No one will ever realize what persistence this has taken on the part of Hodges and myself for the last nine months. At present there are already on file documents covering approximately one million words besides maps, picture charts, etc. Pershing and Harbord will see the thing through in the thirty days they remain after I leave, by supporting Hodges in his work.

Last night received a telegram from Harbord from London saying John wanted me to come over to-day for the parade and return with them Thursday and that Beman and Bertie were still there. It came too late, however, for me to get to London for to-day. John is unquestionably receiving in England the public acclaim which no living American has better earned.[78]

Paris, July 24, 1919

M. Paul Morel, the French Minister of Army Stocks, today formally offered the United States $400,000,000 for our surplus army supplies in France. This offer will be formally accepted by our commission. It is advantageous both to the United States and to France. The offer was foreshadowed by the discussion which took place at M. Ganne's apartments Tuesday evening at a dinner which he gave as a farewell to me. The only other men guests were M. Tardieu, Commandant Oppenheim, Commandant Varaigne, and

CONFERRING OF DISTINGUISHED SERVICE MEDAL BY GENERAL
PERSHING, TOURS, JANUARY 18, 1919

GENERAL PAYOT, REPRESENTING MARSHAL FOCH, CONFERRING
CROIX DE GUERRE AT LA MORLAYE, JULY 16, 1919

AMERICAN BATTLE FLAGS IN VICTORY PARADE IN PARIS, JULY 14, 1919

MARSHAL FOCH AND MARSHAL JOFFRE AT HEAD OF VICTORY PARADE
General Payot is the mounted officer immediately below the second
standard from the right

GENERAL PERSHING AND GENERAL HARBORD PASSING THROUGH THE ARC DE TRIOMPHE, VICTORY PARADE

the members of our Commission — Judge Parker, Senator Hollis, and Mr. Johnson. In the discussion all the cards were laid on the table by both sides. We all took part. For six months we have been engaged in this work. All have participated, but on our side the work of Judge Parker, our Chairman, has been the most laborious and the most effective of all of us. Senator Hollis did a great service under most difficult and embarrassing conditions in his large sales to the liberated and neutral countries. From the start the commanding ability, breadth of view, and eminent fairness of Mr. Johnson, together with his business knowledge and common sense, made him invaluable in the negotiations. All these men were strangers to me — except Hollis whom I knew slightly — at the beginning of our work together. Our views were at first divergent at times, but they were all honest, and as we gained more knowledge of conditions, steadily approached each other, until after the six months' association our opinion is now unanimous on all essentials. I shall always remember my association with Parker, Hollis, and Johnson with pleasure, and I cherish for them the highest respect as courageous, constructive, and sensible men.[79]

My boxes are packed and my office force and I leave for Brest on Sunday. The Commander-in-Chief arrived from London this morning and I took lunch at the house with him, Harbord, and his aides, including Colonel Collins, who is going to sail with me. After lunch the General and I had one of our visits and discussed the near future. Dear old John, nothing changes him from what he has always been. His feet are always on the ground.

Payot came in and took dinner with me last night. We couldn't talk to each other having no interpreter, but we just sat around together and felt bad about separating. I have had Jo Davidson make a bust of him.

U.S.S. Leviathan — At Sea
August 2, 1919

My last day in Paris, Sunday, July 27, I spent mostly at General Pershing's house, taking lunch there and having a last conference with my dear and faithful friend. He has the power and, what is more, the courage, of severe self-analysis and criticism. We discussed the future, of course. Several times during our long visit we both were greatly affected, but it was when we spoke of the sorrows in our life, not of anything material that there may be left in it for either of us. Later in the afternoon Harbord, Frank McCoy, and I went over to the Louvre, where I wanted to show Harbord some Roman antiquities and to see again the Winged Victory of Samothrace, the beauty of which I had never fully realized until I saw the original on the prow of the ship. The figure needs its setting to fully bring it out.

As usual I spent most of the time among the Roman statues. Then Harbord and I went to the hotel, where my faithful and dear friend General Payot met us. We three, with Colonel Ryan of my old regiment, took dinner together. It was the third time during this last week that Payot had come in to see me all the way from La Morlaye. At 8.30, after shaking hands with my friends the waiters at the hotel—the most of them *poilus*, and many of them wounded — we went to the train. Of my dear friends there to see me off were General Pershing, General Harbord, General Payot, General Moseley, Colonel Collins, Colonel Ryan, Commandant and Mrs. Varaigne, Captain and Mrs. Pesson-Didion, George Dept (the assistant head waiter at the hotel), and Captain Frank Pershing.[80] I had with me my faithful and able assistants, Lieutenant-Colonel Roop, Lieutenant Francis Kilkenny, and Lieutenant Dalton Mulloney, who left with me for Brest. Harbord had wired ahead to Brest, and when we arrived there Monday morning our matters were expedited. Besides my personal staff I have a convoy of five soldiers who are taking with them twenty-two boxes of my official records.

Colonel Collins arrived at Brest Tuesday morning. We sailed on the *Leviathan* Wednesday evening. Major-General Biddle, Major-General Lassiter, Brigadier-Generals Craig, McKinstry, and myself are the General officers on board. The 39th Infantry and 12th Artillery of the Second Division, many casual officers and welfare workers, in all about seven thousand, make up the passengers.

Lieutenant Morrill (of Chicago), of the Navy, is in charge of "Boat Drill" which they now call "Abandon Ship Drill." I had a copy of my old "Boat Drill" and we compared the two with interest. There has been an evolution in boat drills so far as I can see only in the preparations for it made by the navy people which, when the 17th sailed, had to be made by the regimental commander of boat drill. For instance, the "Boat Drill" routes from the hold to the decks are fixed permanently and indicated by painted signs on the wall as well as in the Drill Book handed the army officers. But one oversight in the Drill Book of the *Leviathan* I noticed: no provision had been made for oil lamps or lanterns to be strung along the boat-drill routes to be used if the torpedo explosion should put the ship's dynamos out of commission, leaving them in darkness.

Well, it is all over now, anyway.[81]

THE LEVIATHAN

1   A country estate in Faversham, Kent, England, which has been in the (British branch of the) Dawes' family since the 17th century and is today still run by Dawes descendants. Mount Ephraim is famous for its many spectacular gardens. In 1903, William Dawes inherited the home from his father, Edwyn, and focused on making the magnificent gardens what they are today. "Mount Ephraim Country House and Gardens," accessed March 6, 2015, http://www.mountephraimgardens.co.uk/about/history.aspx.

2   An expedition of troops sent by the British government to Russia to defend the Murman railway and port in Russia. In the fall of 1918, the U.S. also sent American troops to Russia in two separate missions: the A.E.F. North Russia and the A.E.F. Siberia. See Robert L. Willett, *Russian Sideshow: America's Undeclared War, 1918-1920*. Dulles, VA: Brassey's Inc., 2003.

3   Dalton H. Mulloney.

4   CGD: Revising the stenographic copy of this later enables me to say that Washington has notified Pershing to turn over the matter of sale of supplies by the army to Mr. Hoover, who is on his way here. The Italian matter, therefore, passes to his hands. [Ed. On November 7, 1918, President Wilson instructed Hoover to create a single agency to oversee postwar relief in Europe. The agency Hoover created would become known as the American Relief Administration, officially authorized in February 1919 and tasked with distributing food and supplies throughout Europe following the war's end. On January 11, 1919, Wilson appointed Hoover to the position of Director General of Relief in Europe. Kendricks A. Clements, *The Life of Herbert Hoover: Imperfect Visionary, 1918-1928*. New York: St. Martin's Press, 2010, 2-5.]

5   Iwuy, France, northwest of Cambrai.

6   There was an ongoing joke between Pershing and Dawes concerning Dawes' cigar. Dawes himself admitted to being a poor example of following military protocol, and Pershing would often tease Dawes about his ever present cigar. While all the officers around Dawes would "snap to" when Pershing entered a room, Dawes greeted him as an old friend. Pershing once facetiously reprimanded Dawes, telling him that he must remember to move his cigar from one side of his mouth to the other whenever a higher ranking officer entered the room.

7   The 51st (Highland) Division fought in numerous engagements during the war, including the battles of the Somme, Arras, and Cambrai.

8   A traditional Scottish song.

9   Luxembourg had been occupied by German forces since 1914. According to the terms of the armistice, Allied forces were to liberate and occupy certain areas formerly held by the German Army. On November 18, 1918, Pershing issued a proclamation to Luxembourg, announcing that roughly 50,000 troops of the newly-formed U.S. Third Army (Army of Occupation) would advance into the country, declaring it liberated. Thereafter, German forces withdrew. Roughly 250,000 U.S

troops also moved into Germany, occupying the Rhineland, and remaining there until January 1923.

10   John A. Hull (1874-1944) served as Judge Advocate for the A.E.F.

11   Knowlton Lyman Ames, Jr.

12   The 122nd Field Artillery of the 33rd Division.

13   See Appendix L for correspondence concerning appointment of Charles Dawes as Commander of the Legion of Honor, November 1918.

14   While in Paris, Hoover lived in a rented house at 19 Rue de Lübeck. Kendricks, *The Life of Herbert Hoover: Imperfect Visionary, 1918-1928*, 10.

15   John Tinney McCutcheon (1870-1949) was a political cartoonist and a close friend of Charles Dawes. McCutcheon worked for various Chicago newspapers, including the *Chicago Record* (1889–1901), the *Chicago Record-Herald* (1901–1903), and the *Chicago Tribune* (1903–1946). In 1931, he was awarded a Pulitzer Prize for cartoons. While in Paris, Dawes sat for a portrait by McCutcheon, whose sketch of Dawes appeared in the *Chicago Daily Tribune* on March 16, 1919. John T. McCutcheon, "Sketching the Generals," *Chicago Daily Tribune*, March 16, 1919.

16   Charles Dawes' grandson, Charles G. Ericson, was born on August 4, 1918 in Evanston, Illinois. He was the first child of Carolyn Dawes Ericson (1892-1981) and Melvin Burton Ericson (1890-1939). Their second child, Caroline Ericson (Maxey) (1922-2011) was born on October 27, 1922. (See the essay "Homecoming" at the end of this volume for more about Dawes' family members during the war.)

17   On December 4, 1918, President Woodrow Wilson sailed for France on the steamship, the *George Washington*. He was the first U.S. president to cross the Atlantic Ocean and visit Europe while in office. On December 14, 1918, President Wilson arrived in Paris. His temporary residence in Paris was at 28 Rue de Monceau, home of Prince and Princess (Louise Plantié) Murat. Prince Joachim Murat (1885-1938) served as a lieutenant in the French Army during the war and was awarded the *Croix de Guerre*.

18   In November 1918, the U.S. Comptroller of the Treasury ruled against the recognition of claims (from war contractors) which did not comply with all legal requirements. Stats, H. E. (1944). "Termination of War Contracts," *Editorial Research Reports, 1944* (Volume I). Washington, DC: CQ Press, accessed March 10, 2016, http://library.cqpress.com/cqresearcher/cqresrre1944051600.

19   Hoover was also clearly "impressed greatly" with Dawes. This was at least the second time Hoover had asked Dawes to take on an appointment. In 1923, he would finally prove successful when Dawes accepted Hoover's appointment of him to the Allied Reparation Commission. Later, Dawes accepted two other appointments from Hoover, as U.S. Ambassador to the United Kingdom and as a member of the Reconstruction Finance Corporation.

20   Beginning in November 1918, a series of articles written by P. H. Whaley

appeared in the *Chicago Daily Tribune* documenting a critical and unmet need for ammunition for use by the A.E.F.. Calls for investigation followed. P.H. Whaley, "Pershing Had No Shell Reserves When Foe Quit," *Chicago Daily Tribune,* November 26, 1918.

21   Melvin Ericson had been a childhood friend of Charles G. Dawes's son, Rufus. He and Carolyn Dawes married on June 5, 1915. On June 20, 1917, Ericson was appointed confidential clerk for the Secretary of War. "Opinion of the Attorney General. Status of Army Field Clerks, Department of Justice, June 21, 1917, in United States Civil Service Commission, *34th Annual Report of the United States Civil Service Commission,* Volume 34. Washington, D.C.: Government Printing Office, 1917, 134. Later, he served as a captain in the Aviation Section, Signal Officers Reserve Corps. In November 1918, he was appointed Assistant to the Military Attaché of the U.S. in Bulgaria. *Official Congressional Directory,* 66th Congress, 1919, 381.

22   Tiffany Blake (1870-1943) was the chief editorial writer for the *Chicago Tribune.* "Tiffany Blake, Tribune Writer 31 Years, Dies," *Chicago Tribune,* September 29, 1943.

23   From 1909 to 1921, Percy Hammond (1879-1943) served as the theater critic for the *Chicago Tribune.* (He later wrote for the *New York Herald Tribune.*) Hammond was in Paris on assignment to cover the peace conference.

24   Floyd Phillips Gibbons (1887- 1939) covered the war for the *Chicago Tribune.* During the Battle of Belleau Wood, Gibbons was injured while attempting to rescue an American soldier. He eventually lost his eye from the injury. He was awarded the *Croix de Guerre.*

25   See Appendix M for correspondence related to the awarding of the Distinguished Service Medal to Charles G. Dawes. Dawes' Distinguished Service Medal is now in the collection of the Evanston History Center.

26   As head of Bethlehem Steel Company, Charles M. Schwab (1862-1939) had a virtual monopoly on contracts with the Allies to manufacture certain types of munitions. In April 1918, he was appointed Director General of the Emergency Fleet Corporation which oversaw all shipbuilding in the United States. After the war, Schwab (among others) refuted serious charges of war profiteering. See Robert Hessen, *Steel Titan: The Life of Charles M. Schwab.* Pittsburgh, PA: University of Pittsburgh Press, 1975.

27   `   `General Fox Connor (1874-1951) was a graduate of the United States Military Academy and served in the Spanish American War as well as on the Mexican border. During World War I, he served as Pershing's Assistant Chief of Staff for Operations (G3). For his service in World War I, he received the Distinguished Service Medal and the *Croix de Guerre.* Connor was known for serving as an influential mentor to Dwight David Eisenhower. John S. D. Eisenhower, *General Ike: A Personal Reminiscence.* New York: Free Press, 2003, 6.

28   Carl Boyd died on February 14, 1919 after contracting influenza, which was a raging pandemic at this time. According to one account, his "constitution, weakened by the constant work and loss of sleep, was unable to withstand the onset of the disease." He was buried in the American cemetery at Suresnes. J. A. Le Conte, "Carl Boyd," *Fiftieth Annual Report of the Association of Graduates of the United States Military Academy*. Saginaw, MI: Seemann and Peters, Inc., 1919, 199-202. Less than a month after Carl Boyd's death, Charles Dawes told his brother Henry Dawes that he had contacted his bank's trust officer and drawn up a contract for Boyd's widow, Annie P. Boyd. It is likely that Dawes created a fund to care for Carl Boyd's widow and daughter. Charles G. Dawes letter to Henry Dawes, March 11, 1919. Dawes Archive, Northwestern, Box 71. See the essay "Homecoming" at the end of this volume for more about Boyd.

29   On February 18, 1919, George Webster Otis (1895-1919), known as Webster, died of pneumonia following an appendectomy performed at a base hospital in Savenay, France. Webster had just finished his sophomore year at Yale when he enlisted with the 17th Engineers on June 5, 1917 and went overseas. During the time Dawes was overseas, Webster's father, Joseph E. Otis served as acting president of Dawes' bank, the Central Trust Company of Illinois. Joseph Otis joined the company in 1912 and would succeed Dawes as president after the latter was elected U.S. Vice President. George Webster Otis had graduated from the Saumur Artillery School in France in December 1918, and his commission as 2nd Lieutenant had just been approved when he passed away. Thomas Furlong, "J.E. Otis Quits as Head of Dawes Bank," *Chicago Tribune*, May 24, 1934. "Trust Companies," March 1919, 314. F.C. Moore, *Phillips Academy, Andover, in the Great War*. Feuss Claude Moore, 1919, 148. See the essay "Homecoming" at the end of this volume for more about Otis.

30   The Liquidation Commission was officially created as a part of the U.S. War Department on February 11, 1919. It consisted of General Dawes, Edwin B. Parker (chairman), Henry F. Hollis, and Homer H. Johnson. The commission's first meeting took place in Paris on March 17, 1919. Lawyer and banker, Edwin B. Parker (1868-1929) had helped organize the War Industries Board. U.S. War Department, *Final Report of the United States Liquidation Commission*, Washington, D.C.: Government Printing Office, 1920; 13. Henry F. Hollis (1869-1949) was a U.S. Senator from New Hampshire who served as U.S. representative to the Interallied War Finance Council in 1918. Homer H. Johnson was a lawyer from Cleveland, OH.

31   See Appendix N for farewell telegram from 17th Engineers to Charles G. Dawes, March 9, 1919.

32   Châteauroux.

33   The Peace Conference opened on January 18, 1919. Representatives from over 32 countries were involved in the negotiations that would conclude on

January 21, 1920. The leaders of the conference were the representatives of the United States, France, Great Britain, Italy, and Japan. There would be a total of 52 commissions formed, with 1,646 sessions conducted. The conference met a total of 145 times. Many treaties and agreements resulted from the conference, most famously the Treaty of Versailles, which officially ended the war between the Allies and Germany. It was signed on June 28, 1919 in the Hall of Mirrors in Versailles, the French palace. The treaty required Germany to accept all blame for the war, pay reparations, disarm, and relinquish specific territories.

34   Along with scores of advisors and experts, the U.S. delegation included Robert Lansing, U.S. Secretary of State, Henry White, Colonel Edward House, and General Tasker Bliss. In mid February 1918, President Wilson left the Peace Conference to return to the United States for the closing sessions of Congress. At least this was his public explanation for his departure; in reality, he left to "deal with the growing opposition to the League of Nations." Margaret MacMillan, *Paris 1919: Six Months That Changed the World*. New York: Random House, 2001, 149. Wilson returned to France on March 13, 1919 and was shattered to learn that his trusted advisor, Colonel House, "had given away everything." MacMillan, *Paris 1919*, 175. By April 1919, Wilson had fallen ill with influenza.

35   L'Olympia or Olympia Hall, located at No. 28, Boulevard des Capucines.

36   On April 20, 1919, Hunter Liggett (1857-1935) took command of the U.S. Third Army (Army of Occupation), serving in that position until 1921.

37   Grand Duke Alexander Mikhailovich (1866–1933) was a member of the Russian Imperial family. During the Russian Revolution in 1917, he and his family were rescued by the British Navy. They settled in Paris.

38   The *Stars and Stripes* was a newspaper published for the A.E.F. in France. The paper was published during World War I from February 8, 1918 to June 13, 1919, by order of General John J. Pershing. The newspaper would begin publishing again during World War II.

39   The *Stars and Stripes* piece profiled the work of the Liquidation Commission and quoted Dawes as he dismissed widespread rumors that the French government was presenting the United States with "unreasonable bills" for a variety of expenses and services, such as the American use of French railways. Dawes stated that the cooperation between the Americans and French had been "magnificent." "Experts Here to Check Accounts of Entire A.E.F.," *Stars and Stripes*, April 4, 1919, 3.

40   Crimea faced a chaotic power struggle in the wake of World War I and the Russian Revolution. It had been occupied by the German Army during the war. After German troops withdrew in November 1918, Bolshevik troops moved in, declaring the Crimean Socialist Soviet Republic. The area would change hands many times in subsequent years as the Russian Civil War played out.

41   The headquarters of the U.S. Third Army was established in Coblenz,

Germany, in December 1918. *Final Report of General John J. Pershing*, 56.

42   Pershing made his first visit to the Rhine in December 1919 and returned several times thereafter. On the April 1919 visit with Dawes, the group was accompanied by Secretary of War Newton Baker. Troops of the Third Army were hosting a five-day carnival at Coblenz, with horse jumping contests, athletic exhibitions, and airplane stunts conducted by U.S. fliers in German airplanes. While at Coblenz, Baker was besieged with questions concerning when the Third Army troops would be allowed to go home. His reply was that it was "up to the peace conference." Edwin L. James, "Pershing at the Rhine," *New York Times*, December 24, 1918; Edwin L. James, "Baker Ends Visit to Rhine Army," *New York Times*, April 27, 1919.

43   Leopold III (Leopold Philippe Charles Albert Meinrad Hubertus Marie Miguel, 1901–1983), son of Albert I (1875–1934), King of the Belgians from 1909 to 1934. Leopold later reigned as King of the Belgians from 1934 until 1951. Like his father, Leopold served in the military during World War I. He was just 14 years old when he enlisted with the British military. Later, under his reign, Belgium was again overrun by the German military, and Leopold would be charged with being a Nazi sympathizer (owing to a number of factors); he abdicated the throne in 1951.

44   Joseph Brown Sanborn was 62 years old when he commanded troops in World War I. He was awarded the Distinguished Service medal for his courage in action. Office of the Adjutant General of the Army, *Congressional Medal of Honor, the Distinguished Service Cross and the Distinguished Service Medal Issued by the War Department, Since April 6, 1917, Up to and Including, General Orders, No. 126, War Department, November 11, 1919*. Washington, D.C.: Government Printing Office, 1919, 183-184. Sanborn's unit reportedly used the word "Evanston" as a password for troops on patrol. Colonel Joseph B. Sanborn, et al. *The 131ˢᵗ U.S. Infantry (First Infantry Illinois National Guard) in the World War*. Chicago, IL: np, 1919, 572.

45   American born artist Jo Davidson (1883-1952) was renowned for his sculptures. Over the course of his career, he created busts of notables such as Franklin Delano Roosevelt, Helen Keller, Dwight David Eisenhower, Charlie Chaplin, and many others. During the war, he had a studio in Paris at 14 Avenue du Maine. After the war, Davidson created 24 busts of Allied leaders, including President Wilson and Charles G. Dawes. In 1920, the busts were exhibited in the American mid west, starting at the Toledo Art Museum and traveling to Madison, Milwaukee, Chicago, and other sites. Eulalia Anderson, "Jo Davidson's Portrait Busts," *American Magazine of Art* (November 1920), 469-472. While serving as U.S. Ambassador to the U.K., Dawes had another bust made by Davidson, this one for the U.S. Senate collection. That bust was completed in 1930. "Jo Davidson Making Dawes Bust," *New York Times*, December 15, 1929. The Dawes House at 225 Greenwood St. in Evanston, IL, has several of the Allied leaders' busts created

by Davidson on exhibit.

46   Louis Botha (1862-1919) would die of complications related to influenza on August 27, 1919.

47   The U.S. Third Army was an army of occupation, commanded by Major General Joseph Dickman, and later by Lt. General Hunter Liggett. It was formed on November 7, 1918, just days before the Armistice. Roughly 240,000 U.S. troops, along with troops from other Allied nations (France, Great Britain, and Belgium) occupied areas of Germany after the war, as dictated by the terms of the Armistice. The Americans were ordered to occupy German territory west of the Rhine. The U.S. Third Army was officially disbanded on July 2, 1919, but troops remained under the title, "American Forces in Germany" (AFG). The final AFG troops (numbering roughly 1,000) were withdrawn in January 1923; some French troops remained until 1930. Ironically, the occupation of Germany would result in a critical military stand-off between German and French and Belgian troops in the Ruhr in 1923, a situation that would lead to the formation of the so-called "Dawes Commission" to find a peaceful solution. Dawes would later be awarded the Nobel Peace Prize for his work on that commission. *Final Report of General John J. Pershing*, 55-57. *United States Army in the World War, 1917-1919*, American Occupation of Germany, Volume II. Washington, D.C.: Center of Military History, 1991, 2. See also: Alexander F. Barnes, "Coblenz 1919: The Army's First Sustainment Center of Excellence," *Army Sustainment*, September-October 2010. Accessed March 11, 2016. http://www.alu.army.mil/alog/issues/SepOct10/coblenz_excellence.html.

48   The wife of War Trade Board representative, George McFadden.

49   The Most Honourable Order of the Bath, a British order of knighthood. "May all companions of your bath be dressed," wrote Dawes' brother, Rufus, in a comical poem he composed for the occasion, "Pride fills the sharers of your early bath." Rufus C. Dawes, "To General Charles C. Dawes," nd, Dawes Archive, Northwestern, Box 71.

50   Knight Commander of the Most Distinguished Order of Saint Michael and Saint George. A British honor bestowed for service to the country.

51   Julius Kahn (1861-1924) was a U.S. congressman representing California. He had a hand in drafting the National Defense Act of 1916 and the Selective Service Act of 1917. He also drafted the odious Chinese Exclusion Act of 1902.

52   The British delegation stayed at the famous hotel at 19 Avenue Kléber during the Paris Peace Conference. During World War II, the Hotel Majestic was used as the headquarters of the occupying German Army.

53   At the time Dawes wrote this, the League of Nations was in the process of being established. Championed by Woodrow Wilson (for which he would be awarded a Nobel Peace Prize in 1920), the creation of the League was included in the Treaty of Versailles. When the League began its work in January 1920, the United States would not be part of it. Opposition in the U.S. Senate meant that

it would fail to be ratified. After the war, Dawes publicly supported the League, arguing that its goal of cooperative diplomacy was something that his own MBAS had achieved.

54   Article 231 of the Treaty of Versailles, commonly known as the "war guilt clause," required Germany to accept responsibility for "causing all [of the war's] loss and damage." It also required Germany to disarm, relinquish territories, and pay reparations that, in current (2016) dollars, amounted to roughly $442 billion.

55   Dawes' godson was Charles Ambrose William (1919- 1982), son of Edwyn Sandys Dawes (1894-1949) and Joan Prideaux (Selby) Dawes (1892-1969) and grandson of William C. Dawes.

56   In June 1919, McAndrew assumed command of the General Staff College in Washington, D.C. In November 1920, the "strain of war had wrought its worst," and he "broke down" and was taken to Walter Reed Hospital. He would never recover and died on April 30, 1922. General Pershing was with him when he was hospitalized and was with him when he died. Pershing said: "He died a casualty of the World War, exhausted in body and soul." He was buried in Arlington National Cemetery. "James William McAndrew," *Fifty-Third Annual Report of the Association of Graduates of the United States Military Academy.* Saginaw, MI: Seamann and Peters, 1922, 104-110.

57   Dawes' brother and sister-in-law.

58   Now known as Memorial Day, Decoration Day began in 1868 as a day to honor soldiers killed in the American Civil War by placing flowers on their graves. The year 1919 was the first year when those killed in the Great War would also be honored on that day.

59   By December 1919, the U.S. Graves Registration Service had record-ed 75,636 graves of Americans in eight European countries. *Location of Graves and Disposition of Bodies of American Soldiers Who Died Overseas,* Washington, D.C.: Government Printing Office, 1920. The fact that so many Americans were killed overseas would create a serious problem after the war. The vast majority of families wanted their relatives returned to the U.S. for (re)burial, and initially, the U.S. government argued that the dead would be repatriated. "Make Plans to Bring Home U. S. Soldier Dead in France," *Chicago Daily Tribune,* March 28, 1919. See the essay "Homecoming" at the end of this volume for more about the issue of American graves overseas in the aftermath of the war.

60   *Hôtel des Invalides* is complex of buildings at 129 Rue de Grenelle in Paris' 7th arrondissement. Originally built to house disabled soldiers, c. 1676, under Louis XIV, the vast complex also contains a museum and the *Dôme des Invalides*, a church with a burial site for notable war heroes, including Napoleon Bonaparte.

61   The Order of Leopold is the highest order of Belgium, established in 1832. Paul F. State, *Historical Dictionary of Brussels.* 2nd Edition. Lanham, MD: Rowman and Littlefield, 2015, 248.

62   The stadium, located at Joinville-le-Pont, was built by Americans on land donated by the French government. It was the site of the Inter-Allied Games from June 22 to July 6, 1919. "Pershing Stadium Ready," *New York Times*, June 17, 1919. It closed in 1960.

63   Doctor of Civil Law.

64   At this time, the Carlton Hotel was one of London's most fashionable hotels. Established in 1899, the hotel was damaged during World War II and closed in 1940.

65   Dr. Henry Beeuwkes was Pershing's personal physician during World War I. He entered the Medical Corps of the U.S. Army in 1909. In 1921 he was appointed by Hoover to lead medical relief efforts in Russia. After retiring from the army in 1925, he came out of retirement to oversee a hospital during World War II. Michael J. Lepore, *Life of the Clinician*. Rochester, NY: University of Rochester Press, 2001, 172-176.

66   The baby, Charles Ambrose William, was named for Charles G. Dawes. His father, Sandys Dawes, asked Dawes to be his godfather. (Letter from William C. Dawes to Charles G. Dawes, May 2, 1918, Dawes Archive, Northwestern, Box 71.) The *Chicago Tribune* ran a story about the visit to Mount Ephraim, accompanied by photographs of Pershing and Dawes holding the newest member of the Dawes family. "No other British youngster can boast of more distinguished American sponsors," the *Chicago Daily Tribune* stated. ("Gen. Pershing and Brig. Gen. Dawes as Godfathers." *Chicago Daily Tribune*, July 23, 1919.)

67   A term for Native Americans in the Pacific Northwest which is now considered derogatory.

68   An official celebration of peace took place in London on "Peace Day," July 19, 1919. Events included a massive victory march of 15,000 troops led by General Pershing and other Allied leaders. Some rioting took place in various locations, as veterans and others expressed their anger toward the government (especially when it came to support and care for veterans). See: Douglas Higbee, "Practical Memory: Organized Veterans and the Politics of Commemoration," in *British Popular Culture and the First World War*. Edited by Jessica Meyer. Leiden: Brill, 2008.

69   Schools and public offices were closed for the American holiday. The day's festivities began at 9 AM and continued late into the night. Along with a parade, receptions, games, dances, and dinners were also held around the city. There was even a "Wild West Parade" down the Champs-Élysées, with American circus performers dressed as cowboys and other "Western" figures. "Paris Celebrates 4th as Her Own," *New York Times*, July 5, 1919.

70   The Hôtel de Ville houses government offices.

71   The still-extant and quite posh restaurant, Le Pré Catalan is nestled in the Bois de Boulogne and includes a grill room, dining hall, and tearoom. It began

as a milk farm in the 18th century. James Roederer and Rob. Mallet Stevens, "Notes from Paris," *Architectural Review*, January-June 1908, 253.

72   In September 1919, a 50-member commission, led by James Harbord, made a 30-day tour and assessment of a variety of countries which had formerly been part of the Ottoman Empire. The committee was created by President Wilson. Simon Payaslian, *The History of Armenia: From the Origins to the Present*. New York: Palgrave Macmillan, 2007, 161.

73   William Ambrose Shedd (1865-1918), Charles G. Dawes' first cousin, was a missionary in Persia, where he died of cholera during the war. His parents, John H. Shedd and Sarah Jane Dawes, were also missionaries in Persia, where William was born. Mary Lewis Shedd, *The Measure of a Man: The Life of William Ambrose Shedd, Missionary to Persia*. New York: George H. Doran Company, 1922, 28.

74   *Ecclesiastes*, 1:2, King James Version.

75   See Appendix O for Correspondence concerning the awarding of the *Croix de Guerre* to Charles G. Dawes, July 1919.

76   Overall, the book provided a very flattering portrait of Franco-American relations during the war. The book was also translated into English by the authors. Colonel [Jacques Aldebert de Pineton comte] de Chambrun and Captain [Charles-Constant-Marie] de Marenches. *The American Army in the European Conflict*. New York: The Macmillan Company, 1919. De Chambrun was a representative of Marshal Philippe Pétain to Pershing, while de Marenches was aide-de-camp to Marshal Ferdinand Foch.

77   The signing of the Treaty of Versailles on June 28, 1919 officially ended the war with Germany. In July 1919, there were numerous victory and peace celebrations in Paris and other European cities. In Paris celebrations took place on July 4, 1919, American Independence Day; on July 14, 1919, Bastille Day in France; and on July 19, 1919, designated as "Peace Day." Peace Day was also celebrated in other countries. The July 14 victory celebration in Paris saw 2 million visitors arrive in the city of 4 million inhabitants to join in the festivities which included a parade down the Champs-Élysées, open air dancing, free matinees and concerts, athletic tournaments, memorials, and ceremonies. Balconies along the Champs-Élysées were rented for a premium since they offered a spectacular view of the victory parade. "Paris Honors to Pershing," *New York Times*, July 3, 1919. Kenneth Adams, "France Thanks Vanishing Yanks on Glory Fourth," *Chicago Daily Tribune*, July 5, 1919. "Victory Day Fetes Have Begun in Paris," *New York Times*, July 14, 1919.

78   Pershing's reception in London was indeed spectacular. He was the guest of Queen Mary and King George at Buckingham Palace; he was a guest at the House of Commons, where he was introduced by Secretary of War, Winston Churchill. Three thousand American troops were brought to London to take part in a victory parade; and Pershing and the Prince of Wales reviewed the troops in Hyde Park. "Pershing Urges Ties With British," *New York Times*, July 18, 1919.

79   CGD: In a letter dated June 3, 1920, Judge Edwin B. Parker, Chairman, wrote me as follows: "On the whole I have heard very little criticism of the work done by the Commission and quite a number of complimentary things said about it." The amounts involved in settlement (i.e., claims against the A.E.F.) aggregated $893,716,093.26, while the amount of all sales totaled $822,923,225.82. [Ed. The criticism would come later. See the essay "Homecoming" at the end of this volume for more concerning the postwar investigation of war expenditures conducted by members of the U.S. Congress.]

80   John Pershing's nephew.

81   The *Leviathan* docked in Hoboken, New Jersey, on August 6, 1919. After a brief stay in New York, Dawes went to Washington, D.C., where he turned over his records to the U.S. War Department. Afterwards, he returned for a brief visit to Marietta, Ohio, before returning to his home in Evanston, Illinois for a few days. He then traveled back to Washington, D.C. While still in Europe, he resigned from his position on the Liquidation Commission on August 1, 1919. "Dawes Returns from Long Duty to US Abroad," *Chicago Daily Tribune,* August 7, 1919. "Two Quit Paris Liquidation Board," *New York Times,* August 2, 1919. Homer H. Johnson also resigned from the commission on August 1, 1919.

Dawes (right) receiving one of many honors for his service during
World War I while a photographer films the ceremony, France, 1919.
Evanston History Center Archives.

Homecoming:
Charles Gates Dawes and the Shadow of World War One

*It now only remains for me to lay aside my pen, as I did my sword,
and again take up my business.* [1]

General Rufus R. Dawes

On August 6, 1919, the SS *Leviathan* docked at Pier 4 in Hoboken, New Jersey. On board were 6,410 men and officers of the A.E.F., including Charles Gates Dawes. [2] The *New York Times* featured images of the *Leviathan* in port, the decks crowded with returning servicemen, accompanied by an oval inset photograph picturing Dawes with his friend Major General William Lassiter. [3] Large crowds were on hand to shake Dawes' hand at his arrival, along with members of the press. [4] More than one journalist would comment on Dawes' "extraordinarily youthful appearance." [5] He "acts and looks like [a] youth," one paper noted. "At sight of him it was unbelievable that the general is in his fifty-fourth year. Hair scarcely gray; a youthful but strong countenance, unmarred by a wrinkle; a resolute yet kindly mouth of colorful lips, back of which are perfect teeth; a firm neck, a body slender and agile as that of a college athlete." [6]

Along with flattering him, the press portrayed Dawes as keen on returning to private life. "[W]e break no confidence when we tell you he is heading straight for that big mahogany desk in the president's office of the Central Trust Company on Monroe Street, in the lower right hand corner of which he keeps my favorite cigars," wrote Spearman Lewis of the *Chicago Tribune*. [7] Reporters also besieged him with questions, namely, would the heralded General make a bid for the U.S. presidency? "I am going to hit the first man in the nose who talks politics at home," Dawes told reporters in Paris when any mention of a future political career came up. "I want a suit of civilian clothes. I want to sit down at my desk and begin dictating letters to the faithful," he said of his homecoming plans. [8] When asked to make comments on the current political scene, he replied that he was "still in the United States army and would make no statements that had political significance." [9]

Waiting for him in Hoboken was his wife Caro. They used part of Dawes' ten-day leave for a brief stay at the Biltmore Hotel in New York City, and then it was on to Washington, D.C. to deliver his 22 boxes of official records, which he and his staff had brought back from France. Afterward, they went to Marietta, Ohio, for an "old-fashioned family reunion at the Dawes Mansion." [10] The reunion brought Dawes together with his brothers, Henry, Beman, and Rufus, and his sisters, Betsey and Mary Frances.

For Dawes' mother, Mary, the reunion was one of the best days of her life. "Charlie's homecoming," wrote one of Dawes' sisters to Caro, "is one of the great events of her life. I suppose perhaps the only other that was greater was Father's homecoming from a great war."[11]

It was raining when the train carrying Charles and Caro arrived in Chicago. "I have been away from my country and from Chicago so long that my impressions are very keen," Dawes confided to one reporter. "What strikes me most deeply is the youth of our country, the abundance of stalwart young manhood on the streets. I have just left a country where old age and sadness are the rule, for the best and bravest men have been taken away."[12]

One of those who had been "taken away" in the war was Webster Otis, who had died in France less than six months earlier.[13] When Dawes and his family members were greeted in Chicago by a delegation of friends and colleagues. Joseph Otis, acting president of Dawes' bank and Webster's father, was among them.[14] Reunited with his old friend, Dawes knew that the two men now shared the most unbearable experience known to a parent: the loss of a child. Dawes understood his friend's sorrow, for he himself had long and deeply mourned the death of his own son, Rufus. And even the grand welcome he received upon his arrival in Evanston could not erase the tinge of sadness he felt, the sense of loss that cast a shadow upon his homecoming.

After a few days at home "getting reacquainted once more" with his family, he returned to Washington, D.C.[15] Again Caro accompanied him to the capitol city, and they stayed at the Willard Hotel where they "entertained at luncheon," with guests including officers who had served with Dawes in France.[16] Then, it was on to Columbus, Ohio, to attend the wedding of their niece, Dorothy Dawes. Her husband, Captain David Harold Young, had served in France as a pilot with the famed 96th Aero Squadron. Wounded in action, he had received the Silver Star for "gallantry in action."[17] The ceremony took place at Beman and Bertie Dawes' home at 840 East Broad Street; the house was decorated simply; the flowers all in shades of red, white, and blue.[18]

"I am mighty glad to get back," Dawes said in the waning weeks of the summer of 1919 when he was back in Evanston again. Now it was time to resume his work and establish himself once more in a daily routine. But this would be a period of re-adjustment, as the long days of war began to recede into the past. "I long for peace and quiet for a time," Dawes had written just weeks after the armistice. "One lives a lifetime in a month in time of war."[19] But even after his homecoming, the memory of the war and its impact would linger.

While Dawes had been in France, one of his friends had made an "observation in connection with you," as his brother Henry later told him, and it applies to "everyone who had been in the war:" "all of the soldiers had gone through a terrific strain which manifested itself in extreme nervousness." Henry advised his brother that "it would take some time after they got back to recover their habitual poise."[20] Dawes' brother Rufus commented in a similar vein, observing that "all those who come back from France show a nervous strain." His own two sons, William and Charles, had returned home from the war "looking well," but they needed several weeks of recovery before showing "remarkable improvement."[21] Both Henry and Rufus urged Dawes to take time off and refrain from "enter[ing] immediately into business activity."[22]

After the intensity of his war work and the stresses of living in a war zone for two years, Dawes knew well that "recovery" came in stages. "I am by degrees relapsing into more placid and dignified ways befitting the banker and business man of the old days," he had written while still in Paris. "But shall I ever get quite back?"[23]

Dawes' question was significant. The immediate postwar period, from 1919 to 1922, would be a critical time for him, a period constituting a process of homecoming, when the war's impact would be revealed in the trajectory of his career. He would emerge, as it were, a new man, saddened, sobered, and strengthened by his war experience. In part, his professional work during the war would frame his point of view, but there were also personal dimensions to his war experience, those he did not elucidate in *A Journal of the Great War* that would add a layer of meaning to his postwar experiences. His feelings of homesickness during the war, the emotional challenges he endured, his family's experiences stateside, and his relationship with his three young nephews who also served overseas, constituted the psychological foundation of his war experience. What happened to him overseas – what he saw and what he lost – are essential to understanding his postwar career. These elements also shed light on what would prove to be a critical period in American history, a time which might well be seen as the country's own homecoming as Americans struggled to return from the war – both symbolically and literally – and achieve a state of normalcy. "Recovery," a return, a homecoming, was something many desired. But although the war had ended, its reverberations were only just beginning to be felt. As people tried to adjust to normal life once more, there was a profound sense that the world would never be the same. There was no going back.

Homesick

It is the irony of fate that Paris, the playground of the travelling American, is, and always has been, for me the place of strenuous endeavor and anxiety night and day, and little else.[24]

Charles Gates Dawes, 1924

In January 1924, Dawes would return to Paris as chair of the Reparation Commission, a body established by the terms of the Treaty of Versailles.[25] This time, he would work on another pressing matter of international import, with war threatening to break out once again between France and Germany. Upon arriving in Paris, Dawes observed that the city remained "the place of strenuous endeavor and anxiety night and day" just as it had been for him a few years earlier during the war.[26]

Dawes' time in Paris during the war had indeed been one of immense strain and intensive daily labor. A typical morning consisted "of conferences too many to be enumerated — of crisis after crisis involving action, of long-distance telephoning, of a crowded office, one of those mornings in which one crowds a month of normal experience (even a normal month over here)."[27] "In war," he wrote, referring to the non-stop action of his demanding workload, "the status quo has the restlessness of a jumping flea."[28]

The most intensive phase of his work came during the period from the fall of 1917 through the spring of 1918, when the German Army launched a massive offensive. At that point he was "simply overwhelmed with work in the day time," as he wrote to his nephew William. "I have to take my lunch on my desk everyday now, not even being able to get away enough to go outside for it."[29]

Along with the pressure of work, Dawes also confronted waves of homesickness. "I miss my dear ones on the other side of the ocean sorely," he wrote on one occasion.[30] By December 1917, he recorded, "I stay in my room in the evenings, and outside of my business endeavor in every way to save my nerves. They have got to last through the war — and then, if we win, I guess they will remain in my possession."[31]

It helped that Dawes had his friend nearby, John Pershing, who was regularly in Paris and maintained a residence in the city throughout the war. Pershing would visit Dawes at his hotel, lunch or dine with him, and attend social events with him, such as dinner parties. The two friends often went to the opera and the circus together. Pershing, a widower, would take up a relationship with a woman he met upon his arrival in Paris, Micheline Resco, an artist who ultimately became his wife in 1946. (Their relationship, including their marriage, was kept secret and would not be revealed to the public until well after Pershing's death in 1948.[32])

Dawes' own homesickness and "nerves" also stirred him to find a companion in Paris. By November 1917, he had two: a piano and a dog. "Have moved a piano into my bedroom at the Ritz, and will get my mind off work a little with it in the evenings," he wrote. "Also got a fox terrier for company which the servants at the hotel take care of for me."[33]

In a letter to his youngest daughter, Virginia, Dawes revealed that the dog's name was Marico. He wrote to her that Marico "only talks and understands French, but he likes Papa. Papa is the only one in the hotel who comes downstairs to breakfast. Marico always takes breakfast with Papa sitting on a chair by the table with him. Here is a picture of us."[34] (A copy of Dawes' drawing is reproduced at the end of this essay.)

As lonely as Dawes may have felt while overseas, he was, in fact, (along with Marico) surrounded by a steady stream of men with whom he worked. And there is no question that Dawes was a man who thrived on relationships. Many of the men with whom he worked in France were those he had known in Chicago, and after the war, many of these friendships would survive, such as the one he enjoyed for decades with his "faithful aide," Francis J. Kilkenny,[35] who had been "associated with General Dawes since boyhood."[36]

Kilkenny was just one of many of Dawes' close associates who rallied to the colors alongside of him.[37] When he enlisted in the 17th Engineers, Dawes received requests from colleagues, relatives, and friends hoping to join his unit too. "There are some young men in Evanston," Henry wrote to him just days after Dawes left for training in Atlanta, "who want to enlist in your unit."[38] He also received queries from relatives and colleagues looking for assistance with their sons' enlistments.[39] Dawes' bank supplied a steady stream of recruits, with employees from tellers to bookkeepers having "caught fever" and enlisted.[40] Neil B. Dawes, assistant note teller in the bank, wanted to join the 17th, but needed help. His father, William R. Dawes, the bank's vice president, turned to Dawes.[41] "You have done a lot of things for me," he wrote upon hearing the news that Dawes had arranged for his son to be discharged from the Illinois National Guard in order to join the 17th, "but this gives me very great satisfaction."[42] Webster Otis had just finished his sophomore year at Yale University when he decided that he also wanted to join the 17th. On June 5, 1917, Webster enlisted with the unit. Ultimately, the bank's service flag had 43 stars and many young men from Evanston were now members of Dawes' unit.[43]

The colonel is "doing big things here," Kilkenny reported from Paris in one of his many letters to Henry Dawes.[44] Dawes' family agreed, even if it was sometimes with a tongue-in-cheek humor so often deployed by the Dawes brothers. Henry told Dawes that his important work overseas is finally "commensurate with your ability, which was hardly the case with your previous work."[45] His daughter, Carolyn, expressed her feelings sincerely: "Someone asked me if I wasn't proud of you and I said not any prouder than I always had been since I can remember. You have always been on a pedestal to me."[46]

There can be no doubt that Dawes' family felt tremendous pride in him for enlisting, especially when most recruits were less than half his age. Still, once he and the others had gone overseas, there was a profound absence. They would be separated not only by physical distance, but also by extreme delays in the mail, as receiving "irregular" letters became commonplace.[47] (In March 1918, for instance, Dawes noted that he had only just received letters mailed to him in December 1917.[48]) Without news coming directly from Dawes, his family was often left to rely on newspapers, whose war reporting was heavily censored. "The air is full of sensational rumors," Henry admitted to Dawes at one point.[49] Dawes' own letters were also subject to censorship. All the names of the Belgian towns he referred to in a letter to his mother, for example, were redacted.[50] Owing to censorship regulations, Dawes himself lamented that he was unable to relate the nature of his work to his family. "I am under embarrassment in correspondence of being surrounded by multiplicity of news items none of which it is allowable to transmit," he wrote to a relative.[51] Sometimes, he was reduced to stating only generalities: "Never in better health in my life," he wrote to Caro in January 1918, "and never found it more use. Happy New Year."[52]

The anxiety concerning his well-being runs like a thread through the family's letters and telegrams. "How are you?" Caro cabled at the beginning of the 1918 spring offensive. "Am much worried. Do be careful."[53] "We are all well," Henry wrote to his brother, and "trying to preserve our mental poise in what we all believe to be the acutely critical period of the war."[54] After his mother received Dawes' letter recounting his visit to the front in October 1917, she wrote: "How can I thank you enough for the happiness [your letter] brought me. But don't go again."[55] "We are naturally nervous," Henry admitted, as reports came forth that Big Bertha's shells had hit Paris. "As long as you are in Paris," he stated, "I must confess that I wish they were attempting to terrorize some other place."[56]

By June 1918, Dawes had undergone thirteen air raids, witnessed a couple of close calls, and had a "narrow escape" one night when two shells exploded near his hotel. He had been "watching the raid from my window," he recounted, when "the appalling explosion occurred." Immediately after the explosion, he found himself "half across the room from my window sitting in an armchair." An experience such as this one, he stated, "has given me an added respect for a bomb."[57] His numerous visits to the front deepened that respect, especially as American troops entered combat. Of the continued air attacks on Paris, he wrote to his nephew Charles, "We are getting some action here for every fifteen or twenty minutes a big shell goes off. Yesterday one struck a church and killed and wounded a large number of people."[58] He also informed his mother of his experiences: "We had an interesting air attack on Paris last night lasting nearly two hours. I had a fine view of the proceedings. . . . the general feeling seems to be that we may reasonably expect them every clear night from now on."[59]

To ease his nerves, Dawes relied on his family to connect him to his former life. Caro was his primary lifeline. Throughout the war, he cabled her to send him the Evanston newspapers, glasses, shoes, books, uniforms, and a bottle of Dr. Walters Medicine—a digestive aid. ("I have not had to use it very much myself," Dawes noted, "but have loaned it to others who needed it badly.")[60] Along with receiving his family members' dilatory accounts of life at home, newspapers also brought him some news of his family and his hometown of Evanston. The city was in full war zeal; a Red Cross Headquarters had opened at 608 Davis Street, a War Council Board had been formed to orchestrate the city's war-related endeavors, and on the first day of "selective service" registration, 3,162 Evanston men registered, a thousand more than officials had estimated would turn out.[61]

From Paris, Dawes read accounts of his family's social life. In the fall of 1917, Caro was organizing the annual charity ball for the Illinois Children's Home to be held at the Evanston Country Club.[62] She also attended the first night of the Chicago Opera season, along with her daughter Carolyn, son-in-law Melvin Ericson, brother-in-law Henry, and his wife, Helen. The night's performance opened with a rousing performance of the "Star Spangled Banner."[63]

Some news from home caused Dawes concern, including reports that his mother was ill. His family, for their part, downplayed her worrisome heart condition, but by the spring of 1919, his sister was in a near panic, urging Henry that Dawes should "come home just as soon as he could," she pleaded. "There is danger that Mother might not be able to enjoy him if he doesn't come home soon."[64] "I was much worried," Dawes wrote to Caro after learning of his children's tonsillectomies,[65] and with the 1918-1919 outbreak of Spanish influenza, his worries only intensified. "[P]eople seem to be more or less hysterical over [it]," Henry informed Dawes, reporting that there had been five cases in his own family, all of whom recovered.[66] Others were not so lucky. Henry provided a list of others who had "died of it a couple of days ago."[67] The pandemic would hit Marietta especially hard; his mother told Caro that it was "not wise" to bring the children for their regular visit since they were especially susceptible to the illness.[68] Henry's bout of German measles also caused concern, although Henry downplayed it with typical humor: "I will appreciate it very much if it should be necessary for you to refer to my illness, if you would refrain from making any pun," he told him. "I have heard them all."[69] There was also a host of more general stories from home that were worrisome, including reports of a serious coal shortage and severe weather during the 1917-1918 winter, and also the news that Beman's 16 year old son Carlos had apparently run away to join the army.[70] "No offense intended," as Henry later told Dawes, "but we too have been through the war."[71]

Indeed. Life on the home front was not business as usual. Although he was worried at times, Dawes was also tremendously proud of his family's ability to keep the "home fires burning," in the words of a popular song. In particular, he was proud of Caro, who was "proving herself as much of a real soldier as anyone I know of," as William R. Dawes put it.[72]

After her husband departed, Caro had risen to many challenges, including managing the Rufus F. Dawes Hotel, a role she found herself "enjoying" a great deal.[73] She also launched an enterprise of her own to help soldiers overseas. Teamed up with Margaret Booker Dawes, wife of William R. Dawes, Caro was overseeing a small industry of knitting sweaters, mufflers, and other items for soldiers overseas.[74] She had assembled a team of volunteers, recruiting everyone she could find, from Emily Otis, the wife of the bank's acting president, to the bank's stenographers and office clerks.[75] She furnished the wool and materials herself and also supplied material to the Chicago Division of the American Red Cross for their own knitting operations.[76] By November 1917, Caro's team had produced $6,340 worth of products to send overseas.[77] Even Rufus and Beman Dawes joined in the effort. "Mother taught all of us boys to knit," explained Beman, who was seen knitting industriously on hotel verandas, in taxicabs, and on Pullman smoking cars." He "knits and talks business," one newspaper noted.[78]

The items supplied by Caro's team were not just welcome additions to the kits of American soldiers; they were critical and, according to Dawes, "much needed," particularly during the bitter cold winter of 1917-1918.[79] Upon receiving one large batch of sweaters, Dawes wrote Caro: "eighteen hundred men will be warm who otherwise would have been cold."[80] In fact, so lacking in warm clothing were American soldiers, that when his nephew, William Dawes, visited him in Paris in January 1918, Dawes "fitted him with a pair of my shoes and a pair of leather leggings which he needed badly, also the chamois skin vest which Henry gave me. He departed in much better appearance and apparently very happy."[81]

Soon after Dawes left Evanston, Caro dispatched her first batch of sweaters to her husband's unit, the 17th Engineers. "Your sweaters were certainly an inspiration," he wrote to her in August 1917. "We all wear them day and night. We do not undress at night as you know. It has been quite cold."[82] Through the fall of 1917, she continued to send out sweaters, as many as nearly 200 in each shipment.[83] "Your sweaters arrived," Dawes cabled her in March 1918, "and will soon be on the backs of American soldiers in the trenches."[84]

By May 1918, Caro's team had produced a total of 2,148 sweaters.[85] At this point, Dawes requested that she shift her industry to the production of socks.[86] By then, her sweaters had been received by all of the men of both the 17th and 21st Engineers,[87] and were now being provided to wounded French soldiers and soldiers of a *Tirailleurs Algériens* regiment.[88] The French commander of the *Office Central des Relations Franco Américaines* wrote to Dawes to thank Caro for her generosity,[89] and soon a flood of letters addressed to "Madame Dawes" arrived in her own hands. Recovering from their injuries at various hospitals such as the *Atelier Des Soldats Blessés* at 16, Boulevard Pasteur in Paris, soldiers wrote to thank her for her kindness. "*Je vous remercie beacoup*," one letter began in an expression of thanks for the gratitude of this unknown American woman. Another gave thanks, signing, "*un poilu.*"[90]

Aside from producing so many garments, Caro produced wristlets and helmets too, and she also sent Christmas packages to "every man in [the] regiment."[91] The "OO La La Times," the newspaper of the 17th Engineers, published an "appreciation of Caro's kindness,"[92] and by the fall of 1917, she had earned the title "Mother of the Regiment."[93]

"I send you my best love," Dawes wrote Caro in November 1917.[94] The couple shared well wishes through letters and cablegrams, marking momentous events with just a few short words: "This is the twenty-fourth [of January]," he cabled her on their 29th wedding anniversary. "Many happy returns of the day."[95] As Christmas 1917 approached, Dawes received her holiday care package. "Especially appreciate things made by you and Carolyn and the dear little fingers of my younger children," he told her.[96] "I wish you all a Merry Christmas," he cabled on Christmas eve. "I wish I were with you."[97]

During the holiday season that first year that Dawes was away, all the stores in Evanston and Chicago extinguished their lights upon closing, owing to a coal shortage and other war-time restrictions. Each night, after the holiday shoppers had gone home, the streets were pitch black. "The large electric signs over the picture theatres are not lighted at all," the *Chicago Tribune* reported.[98] The "war's shadow," as the paper noted, had darkened American cities.

"We all send you wishes for a happy Christmas and miss you very much," Dawes' mother cabled to him on December 24th.[99] "I have often thought that none of my children thought more of Xmas than you did."[100]

Mary Dawes knew something of war's deprivations. She had lived through another war long ago, when she had worried about her husband and brother; and now nearly 60 years later, she was worried about her son. Two of Mary's other sons, Rufus and Beman, were anxious, too, as they prayed for the safety of their own boys who had also crossed the Atlantic, headed for war.

Getting Into the "Real Scrap"

All the Evanston boys in the 17th Engineers are in good health and anxious to get into the real scrap. [101]
Jack Patten, 1918

"This is the greatest war of all time," an eighteen year-old Charles Cutler Dawes wrote to his parents Rufus and Helen Dawes from Marietta College in November 1917. "[A]s you have told me, the men who fought the Civil War ruled the country afterwards, and it will be the same in this war."[102]

This was Dawes' nephew in the midst of pestering his parents into letting him go overseas. He was intent on enlisting and did not ever want to see "the word 'drafted' after my name."[103] Eventually, his parents gave him their blessing. Charles enlisted in the 21st Engineers with his childhood friend, Norman Johnson. By December 1917, the two "chums" were on their way overseas.[104]

When Charles arrived in France, not only was his brother William Mills Dawes already there, but his cousin, Beman Gates Dawes, Jr., known as "Gates," was too.[105] On May 26, 1917, just one day before Dawes left Evanston for training with the 17th Engineers, the two 22-year old cousins enlisted in the American Field Service (AFS), a volunteer organization of truck and ambulance drivers. On June 2, 1917, they sailed for France.[106]

The family relied on Dawes to look after his three nephews the best he could. And this was a task he undertook gladly, not only assisting his nephews while overseas, but also offering comfort and advice to a number of other young men who were also in France, including the sons of friends, colleagues, and distant relatives. Among these young men were Chauncey McCormick, Junior Ames, and also the many members of the 17th Engineers. To his nephews, Dawes would prove to be more than a friendly uncle; he was a surrogate father, providing advice, clothing, credit, and assistance during what amounted to their lengthy time overseas. Dawes also helped their fathers, who were "very anxious" about their sons' well-being, manage their concerns.[107] "He is only a boy," Rufus wrote to Dawes about "little

Charles," "and he leaves a very comfortable home, of which he is very fond, and no doubt will have to experience many discomforts."[108] At one point, Gates' parents were beside themselves with worry at not having heard a word from their son for six weeks. "He is undoubtedly homesick and possibly discouraged," his father Beman told Dawes.[109] Dawes did his best to reassure his brothers and look after his young charges. "Between the [four] of us," Dawes assured his mother, "we will try and leave the family mark on the record. If Rufus were alive he would be with us too."[110]

While overseas, Dawes welcomed his nephews on the many occasions when they passed through Paris, and spent his first "sight-seeing" experience with Gates, as the two visited the Louvre Museum. But his chief concern lay in helping them manage their expectations of their military service. Each was looking to "secure a more arduous service,"[111] and they all wanted to get to the front. William wanted, as he said, "a fighting job,"[112] and Charles was looking "to become a regular 'he' soldier," as his father told Dawes.[113] By the time Charles' unit, the 21st Engineers, reached the front in March 1918, he had developed "aviation fever" and wanted permission from his father to join an aviation section.[114] "Most young fellows want to be either heroes or officers," his older brother William explained to Dawes.[115]

But Dawes was not inclined to help Charles secure his desired aviation training without "direct instructions from your father," as he told him.[116] While he found his nephew's wish "natural and commendable," he encouraged him to stay put. "The trouble is that our best kind of young men are inclined to regard service at the extreme front as the only kind measuring up to their conception of full duty," he wrote to Charles. "This is all very well from the young man's standpoint but those in command of the army as a whole must be the judges of the position in which each of us will be most useful."[117] Eventually, Charles moved closer to his goal of getting into more arduous service: with his uncle's help, he enrolled in the Field Artillery School in Saumur, France.[118] For helping him guide Charles, Rufus was "sincerely grateful to you for your kindness."[119]

Gates also tried on various branches of service, looking for the one which would allow him to play a prominent role. On September 13, 1917, after three months in the AFS and with the help of his uncle, Gates enlisted in the 17th Engineers.[120] "I am sure that it is very seldom that such a high caliber of men is gathered together in one regiment,"[121] Gates observed, but still he wanted something more. "So here I am with no immediate prospects for becoming an officer," he wrote to his parents glumly.[122]

By May 1918, once again with his uncle's help, Gates was honorably discharged from the engineers and received a commission as a 2nd lieutenant in the Quartermaster Corps, much to everyone's delight.[123] He was assigned to Base Section 6 in Marseille, France. Dawes reported that Gates had been "ordered to cut off his moustache as a step in a plan of personal beautification required in staff duties."[124] Despite being happier (and clean shaven) in his new role, Gates still persisted in his desire to do more. "I do want to get to the front," he wrote to his uncle. [125]

Meanwhile, William also wanted to find "some form of hard service." In his role with the AFS, he had "seen the French soldier suffer so much in the trenches that I think he feels the part of the American soldier is to take up that form of service," his father explained.[126] On October 1, 1917, William enlisted with the American Expeditionary Forces,[127] and by November, he was a sergeant in the newly formed Motor Transport Reserve.[128] Still, he wanted to be in action. During a visit he and Dawes made to Chaumont in January 1918, William enjoyed private consultation with Generals Pershing and Harbord, after which Dawes gave him his "approval of his desire to go into the artillery," and Harbord "ordered him to the artillery officers' training school."[129] That month, William enrolled at the Field Artillery School.[130]

In March 1918, William received a commission as a lieutenant and "succeeded in getting into a tank as a machine gunner," as Dawes put it.[131] William joined America's first heavy tank battalion, the 301st, operating under the British Expeditionary Forces. He was sent for training in Dorset, England, before going into battle with the American forces on the Western Front in the fall of 1918.[132]

By September 1918, as the Meuse-Argonne Offensive began, William was living in a dugout near the front lines: "Two other fellows and myself pumped a foot of water out of a dug-out (wooden floor) and made a bed of ammunition cases and corrugated iron sheets," he wrote of his accommodations. He had found himself smack in the middle of war, living in a eerie setting populated by "quite a lot of German sign posts and graves."[133]

"He has entered a dangerous service," Charles wrote upon hearing the news of his brother's frontline role, "and deserves credit."[134] Dawes echoed the commendations for William, telling him: "The great thing. . . is that you are going to see action."[135] He also told him: "I want you to know how greatly I admire you and the spirit which you are showing on the eve of battle."[136] But he was deeply concerned, especially as William's letters tapered off once the American forces engaged in some of their heaviest combat to date. "Am anxious about his welfare in the recent fighting," he wrote.[137] Finally, a letter arrived: "I passed through quite a little danger and had a fine time," William informed his uncle just weeks before the war's end.[138] "A complete allied triumph seems very close," Dawes assured him, "and I am glad to think that one of the family is having the relation to it that you have."[139]

The American press had a field day with the news of young William Dawes' battle front experience. "Rides in Tanks as Did Grandsire Beside Revere," read a *Chicago Tribune* headline, extolling the heroism of the young Dawes. "The Dawes family still has a corner of famous rides," the newspaper explained. "William M. Dawes rode with Paul Revere. Second Lieutenant William M. Dawes, a great-great-great grandson of the revolutionary war hero, for whom he is named, rode over the top the other day in a fighting tank in one of the most sanguinary battles in which tanks have figured." [140]

"I am so proud of you," Dawes wrote to William. Despite his pride, Dawes worried constantly about the well-being of his young charges. He knew far more that their parents about what life was like in a war zone. And their zeal and enthusiasm added an extra edge to his concern. He knew he could not protect them, but he still exercised his avuncular privilege to instruct them. "[C]ut out entirely the use of slang in your language," he wrote to William on one occasion. "It has its purpose in the earlier associations of your youth but as you grow older its use in connection with imparting information only lessens the appreciation upon the part of others of the value of your statements."[141] This was just the kind of advice Dawes might have given to his son Rufus. As he did all he could to help each young man navigate the stormy seas of their war service, he also took it upon himself to make sure that he looked after their character development.

Having helped William and Charles the best he could, Dawes sought to assist Gates further. He had just about "completed arrangements with my friend General Harbord to have [Gates] transferred to the Marine Brigade" when the war ended. Both Gates and Charles, who was still attending his artillery course, were disappointed "that their service has not been more on the line," as Dawes noted. Still, he believed, "they have both made very fine records."[142]

Like millions of young men, William, Gates, and Charles had gone overseas looking to get into the "real scrap." With the war's ending there was relief and happiness, but for Gates and Charles there was also some degree of disappointment. A sense of something lacking emerged after the declaration of the armistice as they prepared to return home. The war's many endings, even after victory had been declared, and Dawes' three nephews were safe, were proving to be comprised of joyous homecomings and bittersweet disappointments.

A Razor Edge

The curtain is falling on this great episode over here.[143]
Charles Gates Dawes, Paris, 1919

On November 11, 1918, Dawes did not join the throngs pouring out onto the Paris streets to celebrate the armistice. He attended a luncheon with his colleagues and then returned to his office, working through the afternoon, as usual. "The city has gone wild," he wrote that day. "Great crowds are everywhere. People are singing and cheering and carrying up and down the streets the flags of the Allied nations. The Place de la Concorde is jammed, especially in front of the Metz and Strasbourg statues. Clemenceau was to make the announcement of the signing of the armistice in the Chamber of Deputies to-day, but I made no effort to go."[144]

Like many who had suffered through the war, Dawes found the war's ending to elicit relief, but also sorrow. "Somehow — and I think it is true of almost every one else —," he wrote, "I keep thinking of what I have seen and of those who made all this possible, but themselves cannot know of it as they sleep buried in the wheat-fields and by the roadways of northern France. I could not cheer to save my life, but I have to try hard all the time to keep from crying."[145]

For ten days after the armistice, Dawes slept for fourteen hours each night. He needed the rest, he later said, since during the preceding months sleep had been a "luxury."[146] Now, what he wanted to do most was to return home, but as the Paris Peace Conference got under way on January 18, 1919, he reluctantly agreed to remain in Paris. He had been asked to serve on the U.S. Liquidation Commission, which was to oversee the sale of surplus equipment and supplies to the French government.

"Now that the war is over," Dawes wrote to his mother, "my appetite for work has very considerably diminished."[147] He admitted that he was "somewhat depressed" at the idea of staying in Paris. But "it seemed only a matter of duty to stay over here for a while," he wrote to Henry.[148] "There is no patriotism in what I am doing — only a desire not to shirk what I really am qualified to do and that I ought to do," he observed. "Somehow it is not so inspiring to work at saving money for one's Government as to work at helping to save its life."[149]

The work of the Liquidation Commission would be strongly criticized, beginning with accusations that the French government had gouged the United States in the sale of supplies.[150] But these reports were counterbalanced by the enormous amount of postwar praise heaped upon Dawes by the American press while he was still in France. Owing to press censorship during the war, Americans knew little about his work (much less about what had happened in the war). But following the armistice, reporters were free to report, and accordingly, they produced profiles of many of the war's leaders. They zeroed in on the Americans who made victory possible, and a key figure in their stories was Dawes, the "no nonsense" American banker with a "genius" for applying business methods to the war's supply side and saving millions of dollars in the process. "We went to war in France as a spendthrift tourist used to make the grand tour of the continent," the *Washington Post* said of American war expenditures before Dawes arrived on the scene, "scattering gold on either side like an intoxicated seafaring man."[151]

Among the members of the American press in Paris were many from the *Chicago Tribune,* including cartoonist John T. McCutcheon, one of Dawes' closest friends, and correspondents Percy Hammond, Floyd Gibbons, Spearman Lewis, and his wife, Virginia Lewis.[152] About this man who had given up pursuit of wealth in favor of service — "the man big enough for one of the biggest jobs,"[153] as Spearman Lewis put it — the press had nothing but accolades. Dawes was "among the Americans who have notably distinguished themselves in France."[154] Along with Pershing, he was "one of the most important Americans in France."[155]

The press now began to circulate rumors concerning his future career. He was touted as a possible candidate for governor of Illinois. For senator. For president.[156] Privately, Dawes expressed his true feelings toward a political future. In a December 3, 1918 entry in his journal, which he later deleted from the published version, he wrote: "When I saw in the Tribune the other day that I was regarded as a candidate for Senator, I felt as if someone had insulted me. It was as if what I had done over here was with an end like that in view. I had a severe case of politics in my time. But it is no longer in my system."[157]

Aside from being cast into the international spotlight, Dawes would also find himself bestowed with a series of medals and honors, including the Legion of Honor, the *Croix de Guerre,*[158] and the Distinguished Service Medal (DSM), for rendering "most conspicuous services."[159] His family and friends had been thrilled at his promotion to Brigadier General in October 1918. ("It goes without saying that the bank feels very 'chesty,' " William R. Dawes wrote on that occasion.[160]) And they shared Henry's pride over "the continued honors which are being thrust upon you."[161] After Dawes was elected to the Most Honourable Order of the Bath, a British order of knighthood, his brother Rufus could not resist composing a comical poem for the occasion: "May all companions of your bath be dressed," he wrote. But even he couldn't conceal his delight: "Pride fills the sharers of your early bath," he noted.[162]

Dawes was indeed honored by the accolades, but he also downplayed their importance, even going as far as to suggest that they could be harmful. "Too many other deserving men were besotted when they did not receive any medals or promotions," Dawes stated, recording his belief that the "history of this war will be written around achievement—not shoulder straps."[163] "The entire medal," he later opined in relation to the DSM, "was a mistake. I have known officers who have been promoted and cited in their dispatches, and who made wonderful records, but because they did not get that little piece of ribbon they went back home with broken hearts as though they had failed."[164]

As Dawes kept up with his work on the Liquidation Commission, he made several trips, including to the French Rivera in February 1919 for a brief vacation, a trip to Coblenz, Germany, with Pershing in April, and another trip with Pershing to England for the christening of his English godson in June. In May, he received his first civilian visitors in Paris, his brother Beman and sister-in-law Bertie.[165] And he delighted in welcoming Pershing's 10-year old son, Warren, when he arrived in Paris to be with his father.[166]

Still, this was a time of trial for Dawes as he watched many of his colleagues depart for home. In March 1919, his former unit, the 17th Engineers, set sail for the United States, returning with great fanfare and reports in the *Chicago Tribune* that the "Charlie Dawes Regiment" was home again. They were just missing one thing: "Charlie Dawes."[167] Dawes' nephews also set sail. In January 1919, Gates returned home, and the next month, he married his fiancée, Janet Newton, in Marietta, Ohio.[168] By March 1919, both William and Charles C. Dawes were back in Evanston; their "reunion," as Rufus wrote to Dawes, "has been the happiest experience of our lives."[169]

After the reporter Tiffany Blake came home from Paris, he told Henry that he had found Dawes to be "in the pink of physical condition." But, as Henry told Caro, "I take it he is getting pretty homesick."[170] By June 1919, there was still "[n]o direct word about the return of Gen. Charles G. Dawes," the *Chicago Banker* reported, "but there is a hunch that another month will see the 'home fires burning' in the big, back office at the Central."

Dawes' final months in Paris were challenging, but they were also a time of necessary transition. "I am in very much better health than I have been for a long time," Dawes wrote to Rufus in the spring of 1919, "due to the lifting of the burden of work and the fact that there is nothing now to get excited over."[171] Having weathered the storms of war, Dawes felt that he had emerged a stronger man. But he also felt the war had changed him in ways that were not fitting to peace time. "The constant succession of emergencies requiring positive action has perhaps given me too much of a razor edge," he confided in Rufus, "but a return to the softer condition of normal life will take that away."[172]

But after the armistice, life did not prove to be softer. On February 12, 1919, Colonel Carl Boyd, Pershing's aide-de-camp, died in Paris of pneumonia after contracting influenza, which was a raging pandemic at the time. Within one week of falling ill, he was gone. Dawes and Boyd had been close, working together throughout the war. Dawes called the 35-year old officer "a man of great ability and military knowledge as well as personal charm."[173] Boyd was buried in an American cemetery in the Parisian suburb of Suresnes, located on Mount Valerien, just across the Seine.[174] The cemetery was a burial ground for 1,100 other Americans — including Red Cross and YMCA workers — who died during and just after the war.[175]

"The continued deaths and dangerous illnesses of my army friends and associates depresses me greatly," Dawes wrote four days after Boyd died.[176] At the time, he was facing one of his worst fears. One of Dawes' young charges, Webster Otis, the 24-year old son of his colleague, Joseph Otis, was seriously sick. He had fallen ill with appendicitis and Dawes was now in touch with his doctors on a daily basis. But on February 18, 1919, less than a week after Boyd's death, Webster died at the American Base Hospital, No. 69, in Savenay, France.[177] He had just graduated from the Artillery School in Saumur, and his commission as a 2nd lieutenant had just been approved when he passed away.[178]

Dawes received the news of Webster's death with astonishment and profound and utter grief. Not only had Webster been part of the circle of Dawes' friends and colleagues, including Francis Kilkenny, Neil B. Dawes, and Eddie Hart, who enlisted in his own unit, the 17th Engineers,[179] but his father was his close friend. Knowing intimately the unspeakable pain his friend was about to endure, Dawes had the sad duty to cable Webster's father with the news of his son's death. "Webster was conscious until the end, and died without pain," he told him, letting him know that all of Webster's associates "mourn with you and your family in your bereavement and grief." Dawes praised young Webster for his service. "Paid him high qualities of manhood. His generous and lovable disposition and fine conduct as a soldier made him inexpressibly dear to his associates," he wrote. "[W]hile his life was short," Dawes struggled to conclude, "it added glory to the family name."[180] On February 19, 1919, Webster was buried with full military honors by his 17th Engineer comrades in the American cemetery at St. Nazaire.[181]

Back in Chicago, the news of Webster's death came as a "great shock" to his family, as William R. Dawes informed Dawes. After hearing the news, Joseph Otis, his wife Emily, and their children, left their home at 1441 North State Street on an unplanned trip out of the city.[182] Webster's father was wracked with guilt. He was "brooding somewhat over whether or not he had acted wisely in urging Webster to go into the service as a private instead of trying for a commission in some of the officers' training schools," Henry told Dawes, "and thought that if his advice had been different possibly the boy would have been alive today."[183] "He had been more or less upset by some untactful friends who had said that Webster had been overworked and was badly run down at the time he was taken sick," Henry continued.[184] Knowing there was very little anyone could do for a family so heartsick with grief, Henry asked Dawes to offer Webster's father some "cheerful news" about his son's accomplishments with the 17th Engineers. Even after Webster's family expressed their gratitude to Dawes for the "comfort" he had given them, he was not assuaged.[185] The loss of Webster was likely the single hardest he had had to bear since the loss of his own son, Rufus. He had been a father figure to so many young men in service, and now, one of his charges would not return home.

In the shadow of Boyd's and Webster's deaths, Dawes found himself grief struck. Carl Boyd and George Webster Otis were two names that were added to the nation's "Gold Star Honor Roll." Now, more than 75,636 Americans lay buried in 2,400 small and large cemeteries across Europe, mostly in France.[186] Back home, families worried that their sons and daughters had been laid to rest with little or no ceremony, and that they lay in graves that were untended, unmarked, or hastily dug. As Decoration Day approached — an informal holiday for honoring war dead[187] — a campaign to place violets on the American graves overseas was launched. On the day of observance in May 1919, President Wilson officially dedicated the cemetery at Suresnes, where Colonel Boyd and thousands of other Americans were buried. The cemetery would be the first given by the French government to the United States, and the "noble women" of Suresnes, President Wilson noted, were caring for its precious graves. "No one without a heart in his breast," the president stated in his dedicatory address, "can stand in the presence of these graves without the most profound emotion."[188]

Just one month later, on June 28, 1919, Paris and other European cities erupted in grand celebration with the declaration of the official end of the war with the signing of the Treaty of Versailles.[189] But Dawes did not have any interest in celebrating. The war's end was welcome indeed, but the whole culture of celebration seemed hypocritical. "Humanity sets out killing each other," he wrote, "and succeeds in filling millions of graves with the best portion of it. Then a good section of what is left of it proceeds to celebrate in champagne and pre-historic dancing."[190]

After the celebrations, Paris changed dramatically. The city now closed down at 9:30 pm each night. Almost all of the American soldiers and civilian personnel had sailed home; those left behind, as journalist Percy Hammond put it, constituted "a depressed and lonely lot."[191] Spearman Lewis concurred: "If there were not a thousand other ways to tell an American from a Frenchman, the lonely look in his eyes as he stalks gloomily through the streets would mark him as an exile." "Paris," Lewis wrote of the city's seemingly empty streets, "has had its day."[192]

Ironically, as his departure approached, Dawes was maudlin. "Am rather depressed at leaving this life of activity, strenuous endeavor, and unusual environment as the time for my sailing draws near," he noted.[193] Most of all, he was heartsick at having to say goodbye to the colleagues with whom he had worked during the war. Numerous luncheons and dinners were hosted for those American officials who were departing and a ceaseless series of toasts were made to and from the many men who comprised the military, political, and administrative leadership class of the Allies.

"It seems such a funny ending for a billion dollar job," Spearman Lewis wrote about Dawes' final day of work in Paris. "He kicked back the chair in his carpet-less office, shook hands with the stenographer, said goodbye to a major or two, slipped into his coat, and briskly stepped along the now darkened hallways of the Élysée Palace Hotel. There were no flowers; there were no bands."[194]

On his last day in Paris, Sunday, July 27, 1919, Dawes paid a visit to the Louvre Museum. He wanted to spend time among his favorite Roman statues and to see the "Winged Victory of Samothrace" again. The statue once graced the prow of a ship, paying homage to the goddess of victory, Nike. It was during that final day in Paris, after victory had been proclaimed in another war, that Pershing and Dawes had lunch together. "[W]e both were greatly affected," Dawes recounted, "but it was when we spoke of the sorrows in our life, not of anything material that there may be left in it for either of us."[195]

Returned to the Rank of Civilian

The quieter and less conspicuous I am after this war, the better I will be suited.
What I am looking forward to the latter part of my life is quiet. [196]
Charles Gates Dawes, letter to his mother, July 1918

"Quiet" would be something that Dawes would claim he wanted many times after coming home from the war. He may have wished to return to private life after two years away, but he would soon find himself cast into the national spotlight; for, his war experience had cultivated in him a desire to continue in public service, and he would gradually emerge as a public figure who seemed to embody something of the spirit of the American postwar era.

Dawes had gone to war with the aim of serving his country, fulfilling a legacy of war service, and combatting his own grief following the death of his son, Rufus. In many ways, he had achieved all of this and far more. Later, he would say that his war work in France constituted the "two greatest years of my life."[197] Those years had given him a new approach to problem solving, and, as he later noted, a "new perspective."[198] It was this new perspective that would not only shape his postwar philosophy, but also his career. The techniques he developed in his work on the General Purchasing Board and in creating the Military Board of Allied Supply (MBAS) would prove useful to him time and again. His skill at achieving coordination among disparate parties and deploying carefully staged "performances" (what he called "breathing fire and brimstone") in order to bring about a desired aim were just two of the techniques, honed in war, that would undergird his postwar career. (See the introduction for more about these techniques.) And, despite his stated wish for quiet, he soon found that he had something to say.

After he arrived home, Dawes was careful to refrain from giving opinions on political issues until he was returned to the rank of civilian. On August 31, 1919, he was honorably discharged, and he wasted no time. On that very same day, he publicly delivered his opinion concerning one of the foremost political issues of the day: the ratification of the Treaty of Versailles, with its important clause creating the League of Nations. He forcefully registered his unwavering support for the League of Nations, arguing that the U.S. should ratify the treaty.[199] For this he went against the Republican party line and allied himself with President Wilson, creator and champion of the League, who was now touring the country in support of ratification. For Dawes, the principles of a League of Nations were precisely the same as those of the MBAS and the Allied unified command that Pershing had championed. The League was a step toward creating cooperation among nations in an effort to avoid future catastrophes.[200] It "embodies the hope for a better future for ourselves and the world," Dawes declared, as he urged Americans to avoid taking the path of isolationism; they should not, he instructed, "cherish the delusion that the problems of Europe and the old world generally do not concern us."[201] America, he believed, had to embrace its new (collective) role on the world stage.

Dawes had been returned to civilian status for less that a month when reporters began to inquire again about his political ambitions. No, he reiterated, he would not pursue office;[202] he would only resume his duties at the bank. When invited by President Wilson to take part in an industrial board roundtable, he declined.[203]

In September 1919, Dawes traveled to New York City to welcome General Pershing home from France. Spectacular crowds turned out to greet the general, and a parade, dinners, and a variety of festivities were held throughout the city. "It was wonderful," Dawes told reporters upon returning to Chicago following such an "enthusiastic reception" for his good friend.[204]

Despite the celebration of the victorious general's homecoming, there was a sense of something other than victory in the country now. The sensations of mourning and loss, along with an increasing feeling of disillusionment, now haunted the American scene; a kind of specter seemed to hang over country as Americans confronted some of the war's long-term implications. Government gridlock over the ratification of the Treaty of Versailles and criticism of President Wilson, who many now judged as an ineffective leader, revealed political disunity.[205] Inflation, strikes, riots, foreclosures, high unemployment, and fears for the future (including another world war, "red scares," and revolution) were now the most immediate concerns of the country.[206] With millions of veterans back home, many seeking "re-employment" in a poor economy, the long shadow of war was still clearly visible on the present landscape.

The American Legion, formed by A.E.F. soldiers in Paris in March 1919, would attempt to address a slate of problems faced by returning veterans, many of whom now grappled with physical disabilities and psychological trauma. "Gold Star" families—those who had lost relatives in the war — lobbied the government to have their loved ones "repatriated" home. But the French government halted any such program, owing to the fact that the country — with its five million "soldier corpses [that] lie in France"[207] — had been decimated by the war, and had neither the means nor the manpower to execute any such a program. The issue of repatriation would remain unresolved for the time being, despite the fact that among Americans there was "a universal and reverential interest that prevails with respect to the graves of the fallen," as Assistant Secretary of War, Ralph Hayes acknowledged.[208] Now, the meanings associated with the war had morphed into something new. With censorship lifted, information concerning the war's costs — both in lives and in money — came forth, and the war itself became fodder for recriminations and investigations. Homecoming was proving more complicated that many had initially believed.[209]

The country now confronted its staggering war debt: 33 billion dollars.[210] Critics charged that those in power had "rob[bed] the Public Treasury" during the war.[211] "Who won the war?" asked William J. Graham, Republican representative from Illinois. "Not the present administration. It has but little ground for self congratulation. It failed in preparedness. It failed in accomplishment. It filled the air with phrases and spent the people's money." Who did win the war? Graham concluded, "[t]he people, whose great heart was stirred to sacrifice and whose funds flowed out in a golden stream." [212]

On June 4, 1919 — the Treaty of Versailles had not even been signed yet — when Graham and other House Republicans launched an investigation into the U.S. War Department's expenditures during the war.[213] "The public is entitled to a careful audit of the accounting of this war," Graham, who would serve as the investigative committee chairman, explained. [214] But House Democrats were "visibly disturbed by the prospect, not because of apprehension that the probes will do permanent injury to the Administration's war record, but because the Republicans, being in charge, can guide the investigations and explode whatever is collected at the right psychological times from a political standpoint."[215]

By the time the investigation's sub-committee members arrived in Paris in August 1919 to hear testimony from Edwin B. Parker, chairman of the U.S. Liquidation Commission, Dawes had already returned to the United States.[216] Although Dawes' name was mentioned in the course of several testimonies, he was not called to testify in front of the Graham committee. He was, however, summoned to testify before another committee, a Senate Subcommittee on Military Affairs, whose members were considering a reorganization of the military.[217]

On November 4, 1919, Dawes was back in Washington to testify, offering his expertise on procurement and supply.[218] His testimony produced little dramatic news, with one exception: senators were stunned to learn from him that the U.S. had purchased more supplies from European countries than from the U.S. during the war.[219] Dawes explained that this had been by design; in fact, it was the very idea behind the creation of the purchasing board in the first place. All U.S. ships needed to be devoted to the transatlantic crossing of what amounted to more than 2 million troops, and not to carrying supplies, as Pershing had argued. Despite the senators' reported astonishment at learning this fact, Dawes appeared perfectly at ease in finally having a public stage upon which to discuss the nature of his work overseas. He happily volunteered to expand on his philosophy when asked, and so talked at length, stating, for example: "when men are so placed in an organization that the interests of the organization and of their own ambitions lie in the same direction they will work better." [220] When the committee members asked that his final report of the General Purchasing Board be entered into the record, Dawes said he was "delighted." [221] "This report of mine — I did not suppose anybody was ever going to read it," he told committee members affably. "I have never yet been able to get anybody to read it, even my mother, but it is a good thing, gentlemen."[222]

Back in Chicago, Dawes was feted by his friends and colleagues with an official "Welcome Home Dinner" for 400 guests at the Hotel La Salle. At the event, Dawes announced 15% bonuses for his bank employees to help them combat the rising cost of living.[223] Festivities and parties, including visits from war colleagues, continued through the fall of 1919, capped off by a visit from Pershing in mid-December 1919. Welcoming the hero-general, hundreds of thousands of people lined State Street in Chicago, eager to catch a glimpse of Pershing waving from an automobile. Half a dozen military bands and scores of military units turned out to welcome him.[224] At Chicago's Auditorium Theater, 5,000 people attended an event held in his honor, and Dawes gave "the speech of the evening" in high praise of his friend's accomplishments.[225]

As the last of these homecoming celebrations took place, it seemed that finally Dawes might have his wish: quiet. It was time now for a new era, a new decade, and just maybe the country could find sure footing and move out from underneath the war's shadow. As the 1920s got underway, the world now seemed very different than it had just a few short years ago.

Dawes now returned to those pages he had written in Paris during the war. They seemed as though they were artifacts from another time long ago. Written during the pressing days of war when nerves and fears and losses and triumphs had come in rapid succession, the pages were evidence of survival, a record of lessons learned. As Dawes began to prepare his war journal for publication, little did he know that his own war experience was still playing out.

Testimony

Stick to it, Buddie. Give em hell.[226]
John P. Foy, letter to Charles Gates Dawes, 1921

"How do you like the suggested title A Journal of the Great War"? editor Charles S. Olcott wrote to ask Dawes.[227] By July 1920, Dawes had entered into correspondence with Houghton Mifflin, publisher of his 1915 collection, *Essays and Speeches*, about publishing his war journal. The publishers were "all very much interested,"[228] and by the fall of 1920, the publishing process was well underway, with the book's release scheduled for the spring of 1921.[229]

That same fall, Republican Warren Harding won the 1920 presidential election and, to many, a "return to normalcy," as promised by his campaign slogan, seemed within reach. From his position as an interested spectator of

the nation's political scene, Dawes continued to offer his advice: the same
kind of strategies to achieve coordination which he had used in France
should be applied to the American government, he argued. At a Boston
Chamber of Commerce luncheon in January 1921, Dawes "advocated the
reorganization of government" into a "highly centralized business organization." What was needed, he advised, was the elimination of "the disgraceful waste and extravagance" and the abolition of "duplicate installations
doing the same work." Furthermore, he was against any cabinet members
"clogging team work," adding that those who obstruct coordination should
"have their heads chopped off and sent out in disgrace."[230]

Dawes' advice was straight out of his wartime playbook. Already widely
known and admired, he now seemed an obvious choice for a presidential
cabinet position. Upon Harding's election, a rumor surfaced that Dawes —
who had "made a good war record" — was a sure thing to be appointed
Secretary of the Treasury.[231] As Harding undertook the process of assem-
bling his cabinet before taking office in March 1921, Dawes would have a
chance to deploy another of his tried and true methods: "breathing fire and
brimstone" in a carefully staged "performance" that would be heralded by
Americans all over the country.[232]

In January 1921, Dawes was finally summoned to testify before Graham's
committee investigating war expenditures. By that time, the committee's
investigation, which had been going on for nearly two years, had assembled
thousands of pages of testimony. It had also become expressly political, as
critics of the Republican-dominated committee charged it with conducting
a lengthy, expensive investigation for purely political ends. The investigation was costing "people many thousands," as one newspaper reported, and
Republicans were seen as having overstepped their boundaries in order to
"find something to criticize."[233] Some even offered the opinion that the
investigation itself should be investigated. For Graham, however, the investigation had been fruitful, uncovering numerous cases of over-charging
or delivery of faulty products.[234] In their frustration, minority Democratic
committee members complained: "Had the committee desired to ascertain
the truth as to the method of purchase of supplies in Europe, it would
have called Charles G. Dawes."[235]

At the end of January 1921, Democratic committee members finally
got their wish. Charles G. Dawes would be "quizzed" as to whether he
"approved the huge purchase of army supplies under frequent criticism in
Congress."[236] On February 2, 1921, Dawes arrived in Washington to appear
before the committee. He had a little time before the committee was to
convene, and so he walked alone for an hour or so in Capitol Park, thinking "over the work we had done in France." In doing so, as he later stated,

"my indignation that it should be attacked steadily increased."[237]

Upon his arrival at the U.S. Capitol he was besieged by the press, looking to confirm his rumored appointment in Harding's cabinet. Dawes "indicated rather emphatically that he would not be in new cabinet." [238] "You don't need my picture," he told the photographers. "I'm not a candidate for any office; I do not intend to become a public officer and I'm not going into politics."[239]

Soon, however, pictures of "Gen. Dawes" would appear in papers nationwide. This was to be Dawes' most dramatic performance of his postwar moment.

Over the course of three days and for seven hours, to a standing-room only crowd, Dawes answered the committee's questions and gave his opinions on a range of subjects, from supply and ship tonnage, to military command and purchasing.[240] He was articulate and thoughtful, but he also made it clear that he was thoroughly offended by being asked questions concerning the making of "extravagant purchases," overspending, graft, and financial mismanagement of the war.[241] In a blunt and profane manner, Dawes testified as members of the committee, the press, and various onlookers watched in absolute shock as he "strode up and down the floor," as one reporter noted, "swearing like a trooper without apologizing." [242] In a "recital [that] was dramatic at times,"[243] Dawes was riveting, as he paced and yelled, swearing profusely and making frequent use of his hallmark cuss words "damn" and "hell-and-Maria" (a phrase that soon became a nickname for Dawes).[244]

"What the H[ell] did we go into war for?" he yelled at one point, "to steal money?"[245] Claiming that not "a dollar was wasted in France," he stood strong in front of the committee, refuting each and every one of their charges. Declaring that "the army was clean in all of its purchases and business methods,"[246] he stated that "there was some comfort even at this late day finding now a desire to set down an honorable record of its work."[247] "Your committee can not put a fly speck on the American army," he said emphatically at one point. "And yet you want to criticize what it did, and you want to investigate."[248] Defending the A.E.F., the Purchasing Board, and all branches of the war effort, Dawes stated that the men who served were "honest men, capable men [who] did great service. There were mistakes, or course, lots of them, and some very absurd things happened. You are finding out, I suppose. But that was only a fly speck on the whole thing, only a fly speck."[249]

Dawes went even further than defending the work of the Americans overseas. He focused his wrath on the committee itself. Accusing the committee members of conducting their investigation purely for "political purposes," he denounced the investigation as partisan and charged the committee members with practicing "peanut politics."[250] Further, he capitalized on the feeling that the investigation had gone on too long, was too costly, and ultimately did more harm than good. And so he offered a little advice: "You could use your time investigating to a better advantage right here trying to save disgraceful government waste," he fumed, as committee members reportedly squirmed in their seats during Dawes' performance.[251] "You could save more money for the people," he told them.[252]

"Mr. Dawes did not conceal the feeling that he was having a good time," one reporter noted of his sensational appearance that soon caused a stir nationwide. "At times the room was in an uproar of merriment and the echo of oaths swept down the long corridor as he turned his wrathful language upon critics of the war who stayed home."[253] "You can give me all the hell you want to," Dawes told the committee at one point. "I like it."[254]

The swearing may have gotten the public's attention, but it was Dawes' message that brought them to their feet. Defending the hard-won American victory in France, Dawes seemed to stand for every single American who had fought or supported the war. Dawes later said he came before the committee ready to "put an end in this country to the official effort to blacken American military achievement for political and partisan purposes."[255]

Soon, accounts of his testimony, accompanied by photographs of Dawes, were on the front pages of newspapers nationwide. "Gen. Dawes Roasts Congressmen For Doing Politics With War," read the front page story in the *Reno Evening Gazette*, while a *Washington Herald* headline announced: "Dawes Scores Politicians in Praising Army."[256] Dawes "struck back today at critics who he said had attempted to belittle the American Army's achievements in France," another paper reported,[257] while another giddily observed that Dawes "spoke as if he were back in an army camp in France."[258] Reporter William Allen White approved of Dawes' "profane indignation over the attempts of Congressmen to investigate the waste in the prosecution of the war." White noted: "The business of killing does not breed the most reformed instincts. So of course in every war there are rascals — thieves, crooks, rapacious persons." But, he wrote, General Dawes is "right in swearing hot, passionate oaths at those who, demanding war, gag at its consequences."[259]

Whatever criticism for the committee there was in the United States — in what many believed to be its political aims, its waste of time and money, and its efforts to undermine the war's victory and the service of millions of Americans — it found its articulation in "General Dawes." And once again Dawes had successfully deployed his tactic of "breathing fire and brimstone" to make his point, just as he had done during the war. "If I was not standing around here swearing," Dawes had acknowledged to the committee, "there would not be any interest in this."[260] Later he admitted that he had gone into the testimony vowing that "either the Committee or I would go out of business" after he was through.[261] He was intent upon putting an end to what he considered to be an attempt to sling mud at the "glorious banner of American achievement,"[262] and "his use of such language was deliberate with the object of attracting attention to his statements, which, he feared, would not obtain sufficient publicity unless he colored them with picturesque terms."[263]

The committee chairman, Graham, called Dawes' testimony a "carefully staged performance" that provided a "smoke screen" behind which "thieves and grafters go unwhipped of justice and pillage the public treasury."[264] But Dawes had struck an indelible note; his no-nonsense declarations not only rang true to many people, but appeared wholly non-partisan, since Dawes, himself a Republican, had directed his attack at a committee led by members of his own party. And soon, hundreds of letters of support poured in from across the country.[265] Some were from colleagues and friends ("Oh, God Bless you!" wrote his friend General Bullard, who had commanded troops in France. "You are a man."[266]) But the vast majority were from strangers, people who wanted to thank him for his "patriotic outburst" for the "small fry."[267]

Government officials, veterans, women who had served in France, fathers and mothers of soldiers, heads of banks and insurance companies, small business owners, presidents of rotary clubs and American legion posts, and even the city clerk of his hometown of Evanston[268] were among those who wrote to Dawes, thanking him for "his manly defense of the American Army in France."[269] "Good for you!" one champion wrote. "That is the best American speech since the war."[270] Dawes was, according to a member of the American Legion, one "'h—' of a good general,"[271] and his swearing, according to another admirer, was a welcome use of "plain but pure Mississippi Valley English.[272] "Thank you for swearing," wrote James W. Vallintyne, minister at the Unity Church of Oak Park, Illinois. "I have not been able to do it in public."[273] Another supporter, a veteran, wrote: "Thank you for speaking in a language that cannot be misunderstood."[274]

Many people expressed support for a future run for the presidency. Dawes was "refreshing," a "real man," and "a red-blooded American" who was standing up for what America had done in the war. One writer thanked Dawes, saying he was "sick and disgusted with the disposition and tendency of our people to discredit our great victory in France."[275] And another wrote: "Everyone I have talked to is rejoicing because a man was found who was big enough to go before this committee and tell them a few things, and brave enough to do it in an emphatic manner."[276]

Dawes' testimony became a bestseller. "Everybody, including dignified members of the Senate," the *New York Times* reported, "sought to read the lurid remarks of Gen. Pershing's former purchasing chief in the original."[277] The Government Printing Office reported that its initial run of Dawes' testimony had been depleted, and a new "edition" would be necessary to fulfill an unprecedented number of requests. But readers might be disappointed, the *New York Times* noted further, since "the official blue pencil had operated on the 'damns' and 'hell-and-Marias' and similar illustrations General Dawes employed."[278]

"I've lost the art of moderate speaking," Dawes later explained. "I had it before I went to France."[279] In fact, his use of expletives seemed to be one of the most welcome and refreshing aspects of his performance — perfectly suited to the postwar era that had done away with the formalities of an earlier age. For weeks following his testimony, newspapers carried accounts of groups assembled to hear Dawes speak, with many in the audience eagerly awaiting his liberal use of expletives and "whose ears were all set for a few good 'damns.'"[280] At one point, Dawes was invited to speak at a dinner where the organizers were hoping he would make an "address interspersed with cuss words," and for this, one newspaper noted, guests "paid up to $100 for a soup dinner."[281]

Just days after Dawes testified, Graham's committee announced that it had ceased hearing witnesses and would issue its final report on March 2, after nearly two years of inquiry at home and abroad. The final report asserted: "The American soldiers fought nobly and well and while they fought ignorance and inefficiency at home wasted their national resources and fattened the profiteer."[282] After Democratic members filed a dissenting minority report, the investigation was closed. "No action was ever taken by the House on a resolution to investigate the investigating committee," the *New York Times* noted wryly.[283] Two days after the committee issued its report, President Harding took office. With many people as weary of investigations as of the war itself, the new administration promised a sense of moving forward, finally. At this point, some felt, "almost everything has been investigated," as one newspaper observed.[284] And anyway, "[t]here is nobody interested in this war now," as Dawes had told the committee. "You put Douglas Fairbanks and Fatty Arbuckle and Mary Pickford on the south side in Chicago, and you put Gen. Pershing and the Army on the north side, and everybody. . . will be on the south side. There isn't any news in it any more."[285]

Dawes was not entirely correct. There may not have been any "news" in the war per se, but plenty of people were still interested in it. And the

Dawes at the U.S. Capitol, 1921. Library of Congress.

one man who had articulated the feelings of millions of Americans was "Hell-and-Maria Dawes," the "champion cusser."[286]

"Anything pertaining to Charles G. Dawes these days is news," the press declared,[287] and compilations of the "sayings" of Charles G. Dawes and "the Wisdom of Charley Dawes" were printed in newspapers across the country.[288] As Dawes rode his crest of fame, reporters looked around for any other tidbits to report about this new American hero. They soon found one: Dawes was "a musical composer and can play the flute, cornet, and violin."[289] In July 1921, world-renowned violinist Fritz Kreisler recorded one of Dawes' compositions, "Melody in A," which was, one enthusiastic reporter declared, "considered a masterpiece by critics."[290] "Why, I play a little," a humble Dawes was quoted saying.[291] His fans delighted in this knowledge, even going as far as suggesting: "Maybe Harding and Dawes could get out a cornet and a violin, respectively, and put a little jazz into Congress."[292]

Dawes had orchestrated his performance well. He knew how to wait, to listen, and then to act. A brilliant public relations coup, one might conclude. And in fact, this masterful orchestration of the contours of his career was not coincidental. As much as Dawes touted his "common sense" approach to problems and his outsider status to political chicanery, he was a savvy political figure who knew his way around Washington, both figuratively and literally. Despite his wish for quiet and claims to be uninterested in seeking a political career, he had entered the public arena with a bang. And Americans were now primed to hear what more the pipe-smoking, no-nonsense General had to say. Thus, Dawes rode his postwar wave of popularity straight into the halls of power in Washington, D.C.

A "Hustling, Roaring, Do-It-Now America"[293]

In politics it is often the unexpected that has the most important results. There's Gen. Dawes, who overnight became a national hero.[294]

After his testimony in February 1921, Dawes took a trip to St. Augustine, Florida, where he met with President-elect Harding. The two men enjoyed a round of golf and were in private conversation concerning, some members of the press surmised, Dawes' imminent appointment as U.S. Secretary of the Treasury. But soon it was reported that Dawes would not join Harding's cabinet. "He thinks he has performed his service to the public in his war work," one paper reported, "and that he is now entitled to sit on the side lines and cheer or criticize."[295]

Despite the fact that Dawes declined the position, he had not given up his desire to be of use in public service — a desire that was, no doubt, cultivated by his experiences in the war. Thus, he continued to apply his skills to issues related to the war's lasting effects, serving, for example, as chairman of the Illinois committee to raise funds for his friend Herbert Hoover's commission on food relief for Europe.[296] His continued focus on war-related issues would also be heavily influenced by the experiences of his wartime friends and colleagues.

In November 1920, news reached him that Pershing's former Chief of Staff and one of Dawes' close friends, Major General James McAndrew, had suffered a nervous breakdown. After celebrating his own homecoming from France, McAndrew had taken command of the General Staff College in Washington, D.C. But the "strain of war had wrought its worst," and he "broke down."[297] McAndrew would be cared for among other veterans at Walter Reed Hospital and there he would remain until he died on April 30, 1922. General Pershing was with him when he was first hospitalized, and would be with him when he died. "He died a casualty of the World War," Pershing later said, "exhausted in body and soul."[298] "It is believed that the great strains under which he labored during the closing days of the war," one paper noted, "when much responsibility for the stupendous operations of the American forces in France fell upon his shoulders, hastened his untimely death."[299] McAndrew was buried with full military honors at Arlington National Cemetery.[300]

Dawes knew well the strain and exhaustion wrought by war, and he knew that the world had not yet recovered from either. When, in March 1921, President Harding asked him to chair a special presidential commission investigating the treatment and care of veterans, he accepted without hesitation. The commission would be charged with inquiring "thoroughly into 'the failures to care for these men,' and 'abuses' which may have arisen."[301]

In April 1921, Dawes returned to Washington, D.C. to commence his work. There, the press was delighted to find that he had "lost none of the ability for sulphuric eloquence." As the commission members assembled to begin work, Dawes told a photographer: "Hell, no; we won't pose. Damn it, we're here to work, not to get photographed. So get the hell out of here and let us work."[302]

Dawes ran his own investigation in a manner that was judged as a "novelty" in Washington. Stating that a "deplorable situation exists" in relation to veteran services, he pledged that members of the commission would "find the remedy and stay in continuous session until we do." "No adjournments, no recesses, no traveling, no loitering!" one paper reported. "Can you beat it? And in Washington, the traditional home of leisure, deliberation, procrastination, and long draw[n] out investigation of all places."[303]

Dawes was true to his word. The commission only needed three short days to complete its investigation. On the final day, Dawes reportedly told members that they could not break for lunch until they had finished their final report. "In three days the commission did more than the average government commission does in three months," one newspaper observed.[304]

The final report bears the mark of Dawes' belief in the efficiency and economy of coordinating efforts under a single entity.[305] Ultimately, the commission found that there was "much confusion and inefficiency" in the overlapping duties of the various agencies that administered to veterans.[306] And it recommended that a single organization be established to oversee their needs. "It cannot be too strongly emphasized," the report stated, "that the present deplorable failure on the part of the Government to properly care for the disabled veterans is due in large part to an imperfect organization of governmental effort; there is no one in control of the whole situation."[307]

Many agreed, and in an effort to better serve veterans and control costs, the U.S. Congress passed a bill creating a single "Veterans Bureau" which would combine the Bureau of War Risk Insurance, the rehabilitation division of the Federal Board for Vocational Education, and sections of the Public Health Service. On August 9, 1921, President Harding signed it into law, appointing Charles R. Forbes[308] as director, although it was reported that various government officials had "tried for two days and two nights to induce Gen. Dawes to take charge" of the new bureau.[309]

Dawes had declined the position, still carefully selecting his postwar work, but in each task, the signature theme of his philosophy was apparent: a focus on coordinating efforts, streamlining operations, and eliminating waste. At one point he even proposed coordinating all the military branches into a single "ministry of defense."[310]

And now, with the war debt and faltering economy foremost on the minds of many, the efforts to combat spending, reduce taxes, and focus on matters other than war and foreign entanglements would create the very position that seemed to be tailor-made for Dawes. On June 10, 1921, Harding signed into law the Budget and Accounting Act which required the president to submit an annual federal budget for congressional approval. Harding again approached Dawes, who had supported the budget act, this time asking him to take charge as the first director of the newly-created Bureau of the Budget.[311] Dawes agreed, and on June 21, 1921, his appointment was formally announced.[312] But Dawes was clear that he was not entering politics per se. For this stay in Washington, D.C., he announced that he would serve for only one year on the job of "showing Uncle Sam that his business can be run as economically as a private enterprise."[313]

In the summer of 1921, during an "enervating heat wave," Dawes again returned to Washington. As he took up his new post, he was said to have "waked up the city from end to end with his vigor."[314] He took with him several men who worked with him in France, including Francis Kilkenny, who would serve as his personal assistant, and two former members of the General Purchasing Board, General George Van Horn Moseley and Colonel Henry T. Smither.[315] He furnished his office in the Treasury Department with secondhand furniture, in a not-so subtle statement of his intentions, and also had on hand two brooms which he often deployed dramatically to illustrate his intention of sweeping Washington clean.[316] He was quick to make it clear that he had no time for the "busybodies and mischief makers, of which Washington had its full quota, [who] flutter around those in public positions like birds of ill omen."[317]

Once again he applied his principles of coordination to the question of the U.S. budget, recommending consolidation of efforts and the elimination of waste. It was, in effect, a "simple and natural application of sound business procedures to a mismanaged private organization," he explained.[318] And once again, he evaded photographers who wanted to get a picture of him seated at his desk in the Treasury Department. " 'Young man,' " Dawes said when a photographer "for the one hundred and fifty-seventh time ventured into his office. 'If you want to live to a ripe old age you had better get out of here.' " The photographer, the paper noted, "got."[319]

The press, it seemed, could not get enough of Dawes. He was the man of the hour, the no-frills man of business, perfectly suited to the modern day, with new skills and clear thinking. Even his signature pipe, with its clever design that made it appear to be upside down, was a novelty. "He is determined, dogged, and has an eye for the phycholgy [sic] of crowds and the effect of bombastic methods," one assessment of him read.[320]

Dawes had only just taken up his new position when *A Journal of the Great War* was published in the late summer of 1921. Dawes' "ever growing prominence," noted the publicity pamphlet for the book, "as one of the potent forces of American public life" meant that his war journal was "especially timely."[321] And indeed, the book was widely reviewed and universally praised. "General Dawes makes a unique contribution to the war story," the *Boston Herald* stated.[322] The *New York Tribune* wrote that the journal was "full of shrewd observations, of sound philosophy, of picturesque portrayal, of mingled humor and pathos, and withal giving such an intimate and vital picture of many of the chief acts and actors in the great drama as we may despair of finding elsewhere."[323] "This book. . . may be called the epic of Charles Dawes," another reviewer wrote, "for though it is mainly a somewhat hurried record of day-to-day activities, a record often detailed and technical to a degree, the greatness of the theme, the tensity of feeling

Dawes, with his signature pipe, in Washington, D.C., July 1924.
Library of Congress.

aroused by crisis after crisis, the heroic exertions described, make it a kind of epic in the rough."[324]

Dawes' hometown *Chicago Tribune* declared his journal to be a "real book by a real man." It was, the paper asserted, "written with large authority and deep stimulation on what is — superficially — the least spectacular phase of war making, but is intrinsically its most vital, most difficult, and, in the final adjudication on campaigns, its most thankful problem — the problem of supply."[325] According to *The Outlook*, the journal was "brimming over with energy and vitality,"[326] and, Americans "shall always be thankful that in those 'times that tried men's souls' afresh the direction of America's war effort was entrusted to men whose Americanism was so rugged and thoroughgoing that none could call it in question."[327]

In this "hustling, roaring, do-it-now America,"[328] Dawes was a figure that seemed larger than life, his public image burnished by the stories, caricatures, and cartoons that filled the nation's papers. Dawes was pictured as the champion of efficiency, a man who can get a job done without pomp or circumstance and without excess of any kind. He was the embodiment of "common sense," of plain American values, and people delighted in his capacity to seemingly place fear into the hearts of the government time wasters, leisure lovers, and fat cat politicians. One cartoon pictured stout politicians, dressed in dapper suits and top hats, cowering behind sandbags as the "General" went "over the top," leading a charge and wielding a comically large pair of scissors aimed at cutting waste from government.

Such an image of Dawes was shaped in large part by his own savvy handling of the media. In the modern postwar era, which was only just beginning to embrace new media such as radio and film, Dawes knew that one's public image needed to be managed in front of a press hungry to report any little detail. His own personally crafted media strategy involved exercising strict control over the use of his own image, something he learned through the discipline he exercised during the war. "Much to your regret no doubt I have just declined to allow my picture to appear in the *Saturday Evening Post* and receive the kind of advertisement which leads to family satisfaction but inevitably incites the attacks of the jealous," Dawes wrote to his mother during the war. "The anticlimax which the inexperienced and over-vain bring upon themselves by encouraging newspaper self-exploitation upon assuming important duties," he observed, "is one of the chief causes of a subsequent failure."[329]

Of course, Dawes knew just when to turn up the volume and attract media attention. He later quipped that he was one of the few politicians who had sworn his way *into* office. Sometimes, though, his efforts to control his own portrayal failed. He tried to stop people from calling him "General," saying that he was no longer in the military, but use of the sobriquet persisted. Upon being returned to the rank of civilian after the war, he wanted, in true American fashion — and just as General Washington had desired after his own war service — to become a private citizen once again, whose only title was "Mister."

Fields of Honor

In October 1921, just after the publication of *A Journal of the Great War*, Dawes traveled to New York City. He was looking forward to seeing General Payot, the former chair of the Military Board of Allied Supply who had been one of his closest friends during the war. In preparing for Payot's visit, the U.S. War Department had instructed that he should be received "in a manner befitting his rank."[330] Dawes had been the key figure in organizing the various events surrounding the American welcome of the famous French general and his wife.

After arriving on the *Lorraine*, Payot and his wife dined with Dawes and took in a performance of the musical comedy, "Tangerine," starring Jeanette MacDonald, at the Casino Theater.[331] Over the course of the next few days, various events were to be held, including a reception at the newly-opened Army Navy Club at 112 West 59th Street, followed by a lavish dinner at the Waldorf-Astoria Hotel in honor of Payot and various former members of the Military Board of Allied Supply, who would also be in attendance.[332] Notable guests would include General Harbord, Charles Schwab, Paul Cravath, Grayson Murphy, and Edward Stettinhouse.[333] Dawes was particularly looking forward to taking the stage at the dinner to deliver remarks in appreciation of his dear colleague, but he would never make the event.

On the day the dinner was to take place, he received an urgent summons from Marietta, Ohio. Dawes was at her bedside when his mother Mary Gates Dawes passed away on October 28, 1921.[334]

"In this community, who was better known, or more respected and looked up to than 'Gen Dawes'?" Mary Dawes had written to her son upon his promotion to brigadier general. "And now his son is 'Gen Dawes' and I am this minute crying for joy. If only he was here to lay his hand on mine and rejoice with me."[335] Dawes' closeness with his mother had only deepened throughout his life. At the close of a lengthy letter he wrote to her from Paris, he closed by saying: "you must not think I have forgotten after all my chief purpose in writing it and that is to evidence to you, as I would try to do to Father if he were living, my desire that you know now as always my impulse is to lay at your feet whatever accomplishments may be mine in grateful recognition of what you have always been to me in my life."[336]

"I have thought that if I could only live to see you 'Gen Dawes' I could have nothing more to ask for," Mary wrote to her son just weeks before the war ended, "but now I want to live to see you come home."[337] Mary Dawes had been fortunate to welcome her son home, just as she had welcomed home her husband from another war.

The period surrounding his mother's death was marked by two other important homecomings that would, in many ways, see the final curtain fall upon Dawes' war service. In February 1921, as Dawes was giving his fiery testimony, another hearing was taking place over the question of whether the United States should follow in the footsteps of Great Britain and France in paying honor to an "unknown warrior." On November 11, 1920, both countries had laid to rest the body of an unidentified soldier at Westminster Abby and the Arc de Triomphe, respectively. With America's continued concern over the many war dead still buried in France, the United States began to consider a bill to bring home one of its own "unknown" soldiers. In February 1921, General Pershing urged the bill's adoption: "We have had no national expression of any sort since the war ended that would give the people an opportunity to show their appreciation of the services over there of the young manhood of the Nation," he said, "and it seems to me it would be a very fine thing for Congress to make some provision for a ceremony that would give the people of the country an opportunity to do that."[338]

On March 4, 1921, Congress passed a bill authorizing the repatriation of the body of an unknown American soldier from France. On Decoration Day that year, four unidentified bodies were exhumed from graves in France. A decorated American soldier selected one to be repatriated to the United States. No one knew who the soldier was, but in an outpouring of grief, Americans reverently paid their respects as the body later lay in state in the Capitol Rotunda in Washington, D.C. He was no one's son. He was everyone's son.

"America's unknown dead is home from France at last," reporter Kirke Larue Simpson wrote in November 1921 of this symbolic homecoming, "and the nation has no honor too great for him. In him, it pays its unstinted tribute of pride and glory to all those sleeping in the far soil of France. It was their home-coming to-day; their day of days in the heart of the nation and they must have known it for the heart beat of a nation defies the laws of space, even of eternity."[339]

On Armistice Day, November 11, 1921, the body of the unknown soldier was buried at Arlington National Cemetery. President Harding officiated at the interment ceremonies, stating, "America lays her wreath on the unknown soldier's grave; sure at least that he is her son."[340]

One year earlier, another American son had been laid to rest. A year and a half after Webster Otis had died, his body was disinterred from its French grave and returned to the United States by his family.[341] On Sunday, September 25, 1920, a funeral was held at the chapel of Rosehill Cemetery in Chicago. Several of the former members of the 17th Engineers, including Neil Dawes, Eddie Hart, and Dawes' faithful aid, Francis Kilkenny, were among the pallbearers. Webster was laid to rest in a grave not very far from the spot where Dawes' son Rufus lies.[342] "He gave his merry youth away for country and for God," the inscription on his tombstone reads. Webster Otis had returned home.

Home Again, 1922

General Dawes has placed the government on a business basis for the first time in its history.[343]
Washington Herald, 1922

The results of Dawes' year in Washington as director of the Bureau of the Budget were touted by those who were already enamored with him as no less than amazing. "By exposing the heart of our financial system for Dawes to peek at," the *Literary Digest* reported, "we have saved ourselves in one year a quarter of a billion dollars, or almost $2.50 for each man, woman, and child in the country."[344] Dawes was credited with "saving" $250,134,835.03 through his cuts and recommendations for more efficient operations. And, he was even celebrated for literally banishing "red tape" from Washington, D.C.: The tradition of bundling government documents with bright red tape was ended by Dawes, who announced that a less-expensive "ordinary twine" would now be used.[345] To be sure, Dawes had his fair share of critics, especially among Democrats who charged that his work for the Budget Bureau was all show and decidedly political, despite his insistence that it had been entirely "impersonal, impartial, and non partisan."[346]

During his stint as Budget Director, Dawes had also busied himself with another war-related matter. In February 1922, he supported legislation to create a commission to oversee the European cemeteries where American soldiers were buried and "to erect suitable memorials commemorating the services of the American soldier in Europe."[347] In March 1923, the American Battle Monuments Commission would be established by an act of Congress, with General Pershing appointed its first chairman.[348]

Roughly a year and a half after Dawes had walked into that fateful committee room, he was now famous, known and recognized throughout the country, and even around the world. Since coming home from the war, he had been seeking a return to normal life, and what he had found was anything but normal. But that may have been quite fitting, after all, for the world had changed and Dawes had changed with it. By the summer of 1922, he was back home in Evanston, having, he said, "returned to private life."[349] "They serve coffee with meals at the White House," he told a reporter amiably, as he sat on his veranda chatting as if with an old friend. "That is the way I like it too," he said.[350]

Once again Dawes took up his work at the bank; his family and friends were close by, and a daily routine at the end of a long summer was reestablished. In his home office, memorabilia from the war – the busts of the Allied leaders that he had commissioned, his scrapbooks, his photographs, and his medals – served as reminders of a war that was receding ever more into the past.

"I'm a private citizen now," Dawes announced to reporters.[351]

Epilogue

We can never know what determines one's career in life. Indeed, it may be that these little and forgotten deeds, accumulated, are the most important factors.[352]

Charles Gates Dawes, 1928

In 1949, on his 84th birthday, Dawes was yet again confronted by reporters. He deployed his time-tried tactic of remaining silent. He had, the *New York Times* reported, "no advice to give to the nation and the world today."[353] A wish to "be silent in private life, having 'talked plenty' in office" would be expressed time and again by Dawes throughout his career, only for him to reemerge on the public stage in an ever more influential role.[354] Of course, after his stint as Director of the Bureau of the Budget in 1922, he began "talking" again, as it were. Soon, he would return to Paris, appointed to lead the Reparation Commission, applying his ideals of coordination yet again to a momentous task. For his role on the commission, which was credited with thwarting another outbreak of war between Germany and France, he would receive a Nobel Peace Prize. In 1925, he would assume the office of U.S. Vice President, and later, he would serve as the U.S. Ambassador to Great Britain.

By unearthing the larger story surrounding Dawes' war journal and by examining his postwar career, it becomes clear that the war proved to be a pivotal experience for him; it would shape him, clarify his perspective, remake his sense of self, and ultimately, solidify his power. Dawes himself had said that people had largely forgotten World War I just a few years after it ended. But, in truth, and as his own postwar reception by the American public reveals, it was anything but forgotten. The war's shadow hung over the American landscape despite any desire to forget it and move on. Indeed, as Dawes entered politics in the postwar heyday of the 1920s, he was part of a larger group of power brokers who rose to prominence in an era that was indelibly shaped by the war — its losses, its grief, its politics, and its contested meanings. By the time Dawes assumed the office of Vice President, the war, as he later acknowledged, still exercised tremendous influence: "When Coolidge was elected," he observed, "the world desired tranquility — a reaction of its peoples from the excess of war."[355]

As Dawes achieved fame during that critical postwar period, he seemed to embody a duality concerning the war: a wish to honor the many millions of Americans who served and those who died, and a simultaneous and concerted effort to move forward, to find new ways of doing business (and politics) in a new American epoch. Dawes was a mover and shaker in an era of transition for America. In some ways, he belonged to an earlier age of "innocence." The son of an American Civil War general, he had only the utmost respect for American ideals and institutions and approached the running of organizations, whether military or government, with a deeply engrained conservatism, cautious in spending money and careful to avoid the pitfalls of personal vanity. But he was also uniquely keyed into the modern energy of the postwar period: he was a businessman with flair and pizzazz, who not only knew how to save money, but also how to make it. He knew how to handle people, express his opinions freely, and routinely enjoyed causing an uproar as he spoke his mind. He was a champion of business *and* government, perfectly suited to the 1920s' clamoring for prosperity and the exultation of commerce, typified in Calvin Coolidge's 1924 declaration that "the chief business of the American people is business. They are profoundly concerned with producing, buying, selling, investing and prospering in the world."[356]

What came after Dawes, the Great Depression and another World War, would, in some respects, eclipse his memory. By the 1960s, Dawes' era would seem antiquated, and even foolhardy, and World War I was by then a long ago war in the faraway past. Dawes himself would be nearly entirely forgotten.

By revisiting his story, and in particular by examining the role that World War I played in shaping it, something more of the complicated nature of war's impact on American society is revealed. In all eras, war is one of humanity's most complex, devastating, and inscrutable endeavors. Its narratives are multiple; its stories can be read through numerous lenses; and its meanings shift, transformed over time as they are read anew by each successive generation.

"Never such innocence again," the poet Philip Larkin wrote about the aftermath of World War I.[357] Any understanding of the war can now only be excavated by later generations who have been "instructed on cynicism," as historian Paul Fussell observed in his classic examination of the war and its attendant meanings.[358] That crucial period of history and the choices that were made while the country struggled beneath the war's shadow would in fact shape the 20th century, and onward. Dawes' story is but one of many narratives shaped by the war. And, like many others, he would rely on the lessons he learned in the war in order to shape the way he thought the world should look afterward, to set the country on a new, modern course. In *Exile's Return*, the critic Malcolm Cowley examines the experience of homecoming after World War I, observing that those who came home "didn't come back to quite the same country, nor did they come back as the same men and women." "The country had changed in many ways," Cowley observed, "for better and worse."[359]

During that immediate postwar period, an American homecoming was unfolding, constituting a critical "period of transition from values already fixed to values that had to be created."[360] It was then that Dawes found his footing on the stage, strutting, swearing oaths, and proclaiming "common sense" prescriptions for his country; he performed for an American audience who watched with rapt attention, marveling at this figure of a man who seemed larger than life, who appeared to embody the strength and courage of an America they hoped might emerge out of the shadow of the war.

Jenny Thompson

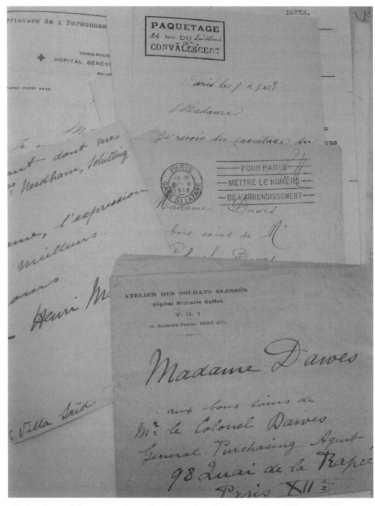

Selection of letters written by French soldiers to Caro Blymyer Dawes,
c.1918. Courtesy of the Charles G. Dawes Archive at the Charles
Deering McCormick Library of Special Collections, Northwestern
University Libraries, Northwestern University.

Dawes' drawing of his dog, Marico, and himself having breakfast at the Hôtel
Ritz, Paris, February 1918.
He included the drawing in a letter to his daughter, Virginia.
Evanston History Center Archives.

Dawes' nephews: Charles Cutler Dawes (above) in uniform, c. 1918. Evanston History Center Archives. William Mills Dawes (below) pictured in the photograph he supplied for his application with the American Field Service, May 1917. Courtesy of the Archives of the American Field Service and AFS Intercultural Programs.

Lt. Beman Gates Dawes, Jr. and an unidentified woman (possibly his wife, Janet Newton Dawes) outside of the Dawes' home in Evanston, c. 1919. Evanston History Center Archives.

Dawes' assistant Francis J. Kilkenny. He served alongside Dawes
for many years. He enlisted in the 17th Engineers and went with
Dawes to France during World War I. After Dawes was appoint-
ed to the General Purchasing Board, Kilkenny was transferred to
Paris to work with him throughout the war.
Evanston History Center Archives.

World War I victory celebration (above) at the Arc de Triomphe, Paris, July 14, 1919. General Pershing (below) in his homecoming parade, Fifth Avenue, New York City, September 10, 1919. Library of Congress.

The war's destruction: Ruins of the village of Longpont, France, with the Abbey visible in the distance (above). Library of Congress. Makeshift burial ground (below) for American soldiers of the 28th Division, killed in France, November 1918. Evanston History Center Archives.

Burial Ceremony of the Unknown Soldier at the Memorial Amphitheater,
Arlington National Cemetery, Virginia. President Warren Harding stands
beside the casket, Armistice Day, November 11, 1921.
Library of Congress.

The man of the hour: Dawes (left) stands before members of the Washington, D.C. press corps. Library of Congress.

Charles Gates Dawes, undated. Evanston History Center Archives.

Notes to Homecoming: Charles Gates Dawes and the Shadow of World War I

1   Rufus R. Dawes, *Service with the Sixth Wisconsin Volunteers.* Marietta, OH: E.R. Alderman and Sons, 1890, 317.

2   "Leviathan Docks with Many Officers," *New York Evening Post,* August 6, 1919. Charles G. Dawes Archive, Charles Deering McCormick Library of Special Collections, Northwestern University Libraries, Northwestern University, Evanston, Illinois, Scrapbook, Box 84. Hereafter referred to as Dawes Archive, Northwestern.

3   *New York Times,* August 10, 1919. Dawes mentions William Lassiter (1867-1959) several times in *A Journal of the Great War.* A West Point graduate, Lassiter served as military attaché at the American embassy in London before being put in charge of American troops in England, overseeing their transport to France during World War I. He then took command of the 32nd Division, and after the armistice, led his troops into Coblenz, Germany, for a temporary postwar occupation.

4   "Hundreds Greet and Welcome Gen. Dawes," paper not recorded, August 14, 1919. Dawes Archive, Northwestern, Scrapbook, Box 84.

5   "Gen. Charles G. Dawes is Welcomed Home," *Chicago Post,* August 13, 1919.

6   Boersianer [Emil Friend],"Gen. C.G Dawes Home; Acts and Looks like Youth," *Record Herald,* August 14, 1919. Dawes Archive, Northwestern, Scrapbook, Box 84.

7   Spearman Lewis, "Dawes Greatest Illinoisan in War," *Macomb Journal,* July 28, 1919. Dawes Archive, Northwestern, scrapbook, Box 84. Spearman Lewis (1879-1954) covered the war in France and scooped the world when he obtained a copy of the peace treaty prior to its public release. The *Chicago Daily Tribune* thus became the first newspaper "to disclose terms of the peace talks to the public." The paper also provided a copy to the U.S. Senate, which, up to that point, had not had access to a copy. "S. Lewis Dies, Won Fame for Tribune Beat," *Chicago Daily Tribune,* February 5, 1954.

8   "Brig. General Dawes End his War Work and is Due in Old Marietta in a Few Days," *Marietta Journal,* August 6, 1919. Dawes Archive, Northwestern, scrapbook, Box 84.

9   "Comment Withheld by Dawes," *Cincinnati Inquirer,* August 10, 1919. Dawes Archive, Northwestern, scrapbook, Box 84.

10   "General Dawes Has Arrived in the Pioneer City," Marietta, Ohio, paper not recorded, August 9, 1919. Dawes Archive, Northwestern, scrapbook, Box 84.

11   Unsigned, letter to Caro Dawes from Charles G. Dawes' sister [Mary Frances or Betsey], June 4, 1919, Dawes Archive, Northwestern, Box 71.

12   "Dawes Home, Glad as Boy," *The Daily News,* August 13, 1919.

13   George Webster Otis (1895-1919), known as Webster.

14   Joseph E. Otis began working at the Central Trust Company in 1912 and would succeed Dawes as bank president after the latter was elected U.S. Vice President.

15   "Dawes Home, Glad as Boy," *The Daily News,* August 13, 1919.

16   "Washington Society," *Tribune,* August 23, 1919. Dawes Archive, Northwestern, Scrapbook, Box 84.

17   GHQ, American Expeditionary Forces, Citation Orders No. 5 (June 3, 1919), Amended by A.E.F. Citation Orders No. 10 (1920). Accessed May 10, 2016. "Silver Star Citation," http://valor.militarytimes.com/recipient.

18   "Dawes' Daughter a Bride," *The Enquirer,* August 17, 1919. "Ohio," *Cincinnati Enquirer,* August 24, 1919.

19   *A Journal of the Great War,* November 25, 1918.

20   Letter from Henry Dawes to Charles G. Dawes, June 18, 1919, Dawes Archive, Northwestern, Box 71.

21   Letter from Rufus Dawes to Charles G. Dawes, April 24, 1919. Dawes Archive, Northwestern, Box 71.

22   Ibid.

23   *A Journal of the Great War,* January 11, 1919.

24   Charles G. Dawes, *A Journal of Reparations*, 15.

25   American, Belgian, British, French, German, and Italian representatives were on the commission. The Treaty of Versailles outlined Germany's payment of reparations, amounting to 269 billion dollars. In 1921, the amount was reduced slightly, but by 1922, Germany defaulted on its payments, its economy nearly in collapse. In response, in January 1923, French and Belgian troops occupied an area of Germany's Ruhr Valley. The Dawes Plan, which came out of the Reparation Commission, was adopted in April 1924. It ordered the evacuation of the occupation troops, the reorganization of the *Reichsbank*, and the loaning of funds to Germany from U.S. banks under the supervision of the U.S. State Department. The immediate crisis was averted. Occupation troops withdrew in August 1925 and the German economy seemed to rebound. And it was for this reason—"for his masterly handling of this crucial international problem"— that Dawes was seen as helping to ensure peace and awarded the Nobel Peace Prize. ("Charles G. Dawes – Biographical," Nobel Prize.org. Accessed June 21, 2016. http://www.nobelprize.org/nobel_prizes/peace/laureates/1925/dawes-bio.html) Ultimately, the Dawes Plan did not stabilize Germany. Once the world plummeted into depression after the 1929 crash, the German economy, now strongly tied to the U.S. economy (and the many bankers whose interests were represented in the economic plans), plunged into financial chaos, and soon Adolf Hitler, who began his political rise in the early 1920s, would take the reigns of power in Germany.

26   Charles G. Dawes, *A Journal of Reparations*, 15.

27   *A Journal of the Great War,* October 4, 1918.

28   Letter from Charles G. Dawes to Henry Dawes, April 15, 1918. Dawes Archive, Northwestern, Box 71.

29   Letter from Charles G. Dawes to William M. Dawes, February 27, 1918. Dawes Archive, Northwestern, Box 71.

30   *A Journal of the Great War,* November 9, 1917.

31   Ibid, December 9, 1917.

32   Jim Lacey. *Pershing, A Biography.* New York: Palgrave Macmillan, 2008, 125. Henry Wales, "The True Story of Famous Generals Romance with a Charming Young Portrait Painter," *Chicago Daily Tribune,* November 30, 1952. Resco (1896-c.1970s) was a naturalized French citizen who was born in Romania. She met Pershing upon his arrival in Paris in June 1917. After the war, she moved to the United States. She married Pershing in 1946 at Walter Reed Hospital, where he was recovering from a stroke. After his death, she returned to Paris. "Donald Smythe Collection of Micheline Resco Materials, Finding Aid." http://jesuitarchives.org/collections/donald-smythe-collection-of-micheline-resco-materials/ Accessed May 3, 2016.

33   *A Journal of the Great War,* November 30, 1917.

34   Letter from Charles G. Dawes to Virginia Dawes, February 9, 1918. Evanston History Center Archives.

35   Charles Dawes first met a young Francis J. Kilkenny (1876-1933) when the latter was working at the check room at the Union League Club in Chicago. Kilkenny, an immigrant from Ireland who arrived in the U.S. at the age of 16 in 1891, caught Dawes' attention. Soon, Dawes took him under his wing and gave him a position at the Republican National Headquarters in Chicago. Later, Dawes took him to Washington during his stint as Comptroller of the Currency. Kilkenny also served as his aide in France and would come to Washington to serve as his private secretary during Dawes's term as Director of the Budget, among other roles. Henry Charles Hallem, "Old Home Year for Ireland," *The World Mirror,* November 1909, 221. Edgar C. Wheeler, "Government Now a Business," *Business.* (September 1921), 7. U.S. Census, 1930, Chicago, Cook County. See also, Leach, *That Man Dawes,* 88-89.

36   Obituary. Francis J. Kilkenny. *New York Times,* January 5, 1933.

37   Other Central Trust Company employees who joined the 17th Engineers included Arthur Knusen, Leo Thory, Herbert C. Johnson, and John D. Hoople. Other Central Trust employees who enlisted included sergeants Wallace H. Waddington and G.W. Freeman, Corporal Adoloh R. Floreen (assistant bank cashier), Private Carl B. Patheal, all of Battery D, 149th Field Artillery of the 42nd Division. "Central Trust Boxes Yuletide Cheer to France," *Chicago Daily Tribune,* November 19, 1917. Dawes Archive, Northwestern, Scrapbook, Box 84.

38   Letter from Henry Dawes to Charles G. Dawes, May 29, 1917. Dawes Archive, Northwestern, Box 69.

39   For example, Dawes helped Junior Ames (Knowlton Lyman Ames, Jr.) the son of Charles Dawes' second cousin, Knowlton Ames, Sr., secure a commission. Dawes mentions Junior in *A Journal of the Great War*.

40   "To Rehabilitate France," *Central Clearings*, June 1917. Dawes Archive, Northwestern, Scrapbook, Box 84.

41   William Ruggles Dawes (1862-1951) was a distant relation to Dawes. His wife, Margaret Booker Dawes (1861-1928) was close friends with Caro Dawes. They lived in Evanston at 1803 Chicago Avenue.

42   Letter from William R. Dawes to Charles G. Dawes, June 5, 1917. Dawes Archive, Northwestern, Box 69.

43   Letter from William R. Dawes to Charles G. Dawes, June 8, 1918. Dawes Archive, Northwestern, Box 71. See also: "Lieut. Col. Dawes to Help Rehabilitate Railroads in France," *Trust Companies*, August 1917, 121.

44   Letter from Francis J. Kilkenny to Henry Dawes, November 7, 1917. Dawes Archive, Northwestern, Box 71.

45   Letter from Henry Dawes to Charles G. Dawes, October 18, 1917. Dawes Archive, Northwestern, Box 71.

46   Letter from Carolyn Dawes Ericson to Charles G. Dawes, February 2, 1919. Evanston History Center Archives.

47   Letter from Charles G. Dawes to Caro Dawes, November 2, 1917. Dawes Archive, Northwestern, Box 71.

48   Letter from Charles G. Dawes to Aunt Frances, [Martha Frances Bosworth Dawes], March 2, 1918. Evanston History Center Archives. Martha Frances Bosworth Dawes (1841-1925) married Charles G. Dawes' uncle, Ephraim Cutler Dawes, in 1866. After his death in 1895, she lived with her sister-in-law Mary Dawes at 508 Fourth Street in Marietta, Ohio.

49   Letter from Henry Dawes to Charles G. Dawes, October 10, 1918. Dawes Archive, Northwestern, Box 71.

50   Letter from Mary B[eman Gates] Dawes to Charles G. Dawes, November 13, 1918. Dawes Archive, Northwestern, Box 71.

51   Letter from Charles G. Dawes to Aunt Frances, March 2, 1918. Evanston History Center Archives.

52   Telegram from Charles G. Dawes to Caro Dawes, January 3, 1918. Dawes Archive, Northwestern, Box 71.

53   Cablegram from Caro Dawes to Charles G. Dawes, Dawes Archive, Northwestern, Box 71.

54   Letter from Henry Dawes to Charles G. Dawes, April 16, 1918. Dawes Archive, Northwestern, Box 71.

55   Letter from Mary [Beman] G[ates] Dawes to Charles G. Dawes, November 13, 1917. Dawes Archive, Northwestern, Box 71. Dawes includes the October 23, 1917 letter to his mother recounting his journey to the Belgian front in *A Journal*

of the Great War.

56   Letter from Henry Dawes to Charles G. Dawes, April 30, 1918. Dawes Archive, Northwestern, Box 71.

57   *A Journal of the Great War,* June 29, 1918.

58   Letter from Charles G. Dawes to Charles C. Dawes, March 31, 1918. Dawes Archive, Northwestern, Box 71.

59   Letter from Charles G. Dawes to Mary B[eman Gates] Dawes, January 31, 1918. Dawes Archive, Northwestern, Box 71.

60   Letter from Charles G. Dawes to Caro Dawes, November 2, 1917. Dawes Archive, Northwestern, Box 71.

61   "Evanston is Loyal," *Evanston News Index,* June 5, 1917.

62   "News of Chicago Society," *Chicago Daily Tribune,* November 4, 1917.

63   "Patriotic Thrill at First Night of Grand Opera," *Chicago Examiner,* November 13, 1917. Dawes Archive, Northwestern, Scrapbook, Box 84.

64   Letter from "sister" [Betsey or Mary Frances] to Henry Dawes, May 29, 1919, Dawes Archive, Northwestern, Box 71.

65   Letter from Charles G. Dawes to Caro Dawes, November 2, 1917. Dawes Archive, Northwestern, Box 71.

66   Letter from Henry Dawes to Charles G. Dawes, October 8, 1918. Dawes Archive, Northwestern, Box 71.

67   Ibid.

68   Letter from Mary B[eman Gates] Dawes to Charles G. Dawes, October 5, 1918. Dawes Archive, Northwestern, Box 71.

69   Letter from Henry Dawes to Charles G. Dawes, March 9, 1918. Dawes Archive, Northwestern, Box 71.

70   Letter to Charles G. Dawes from Henry Dawes, September 6, 1918. Dawes Archive, Northwestern, Box 71. Carlos Burr Dawes (1902-1996) registered for enlistment at the Canadian Recruitment Headquarters in Detroit, but there is no record that he was successful in his efforts to join the military. A boy scout with a zeal for participating in the war effort, Carlos distributed war pamphlets and was decorated by the governor of Ohio for selling the second largest amount of Liberty Bonds in Columbus, Ohio. Carlos would serve as an officer during World War II. Carlos Burr Dawes, membership application for the Ohio Society of the Sons of the American Revolution, 1954, Ancestry.com, accessed on July 2, 2016.

71   Letter from Henry Dawes to Charles G. Dawes, June 18, 1919, Dawes Archive, Northwestern, Box 71.

72   Letter from William R. Dawes to Charles G. Dawes, December 15, 1917. Dawes Archive, Northwestern, Box 71.

73   Letter from Henry Dawes to Charles G. Dawes, June 15, 1917. Dawes Archive, Northwestern, Box 71. By August 1918, Henry and Charles Dawes decided

to turn over occupancy of their men's hotels exclusively to soldiers and sailors. Letter from Henry Dawes to Charles G. Dawes, August 2, 1918. Dawes Archive, Northwestern, Box 71.

74   In a letter to her father, Carolyn Dawes Ericson reported making helmets for the 17th Engineers. Later, Dawes indeed reported having received 55 helmets. Cablegram from Charles G. Dawes to Caro Dawes, November 23, 1917. Dawes Archive, Northwestern, Box 71.

75   "Mrs. Dawes Wins Title of 'Mother of the Regiment,'" no paper listed, November 9, 1917. Dawes Archive, Northwestern, scrapbook, Box 84.

76   "Sweaters for All Boys of Seventh Engineer Corps," *Central Clearings,* August 1, 1917. Dawes Archive, Northwestern, scrapbook, Box 84.

77   The cost of the wool was estimated at $2,115. "Statement showing receipt and disposition of sweaters to Nov. 1st." Dawes Archive, Northwestern, Box 71.

78   "Brothers Knit for Brother in France," *New Cambria Leader* (Missouri), November 2, 1917.

79   Cablegram from Charles G. Dawes to Caro Dawes, January 18, 1918. Dawes Archive, Northwestern, Box 71.

80   Letter from Charles G. Dawes to Caro Dawes, December 22, 1917. Dawes Archive, Northwestern, Box 71.

81   Letter from Charles G. Dawes to Caro Dawes, January 9, 1918. Dawes Archive, Northwestern, Box 71.

82   Letter from Charles G. Dawes to Caro Dawes, August 4, 1917. Evanston History Center Archives.

83   Memo to Charles G. Dawes from Donald Des Granges, 17th Engineers Headquarters, January 8, 1918. Dawes Archive, Northwestern, Box 71. By December 1917, Dawes estimated the value of Caro's sweaters to be roughly $6,340, although he stated that their true value lay in their usefulness. Letter from Charles G. Dawes to Caro Dawes, December 22, 1917. Dawes Archive, Northwestern, Box 71.

84   Cablegram from Charles G. Dawes to Caro Dawes, March 1, 1918. Dawes Archive, Northwestern archives, Box 71.

85   Cablegram from Charles G. Dawes to Caro Dawes, May 1, 1918. Dawes Archive, Northwestern archives, Box 71.

86   Cablegram from Charles G. Dawes to Caro Dawes, April 20, 1918. Dawes Archive, Northwestern, Box 71.

87   Letter from William R. Dawes to Charles G. Dawes, February 5, 1918. Dawes Archive, Northwestern, Box 71.

88   Algerian sharpshooters. These were soldiers recruited from Algeria, a French colony. Many colonial units were raised by the French and English governments. A unit of Algerian soldiers had first been formed in 1840.

89   Letter from Le Commandant Varaigne to Charles G. Dawes, May 13, 1918. Dawes Archive, Northwestern archives, Box 71.

90   Letter signed *"un poilu"* to Caro Dawes, Dawes Archive, Northwestern archives, Box 71.

91   Cablegram from Charles G. Dawes to Caro Dawes, December 21, 1917. Dawes Archive, Northwestern archives, Box 71.

92   Letter from William R. Dawes to Charles G. Dawes, February 5, 1918. Dawes Archive, Northwestern, Box 71.

93   "Mrs. Dawes Wins Title of 'Mother of the Regiment," no paper listed, November 9, 1917. Dawes Archive, Northwestern, scrapbook, Box 84.

94   Letter from Charles G. Dawes to Caro Dawes, November 2, 1917. Dawes Archive, Northwestern, Box 71.

95   Cablegram from Charles G. Dawes to Caro Dawes, January 24, 1918. Dawes Archive, Northwestern, Box 71.

96   Letter from Charles G. Dawes to Caro Dawes, December 14, 1917. Dawes Archive, Northwestern, Box 71.

97   Cablegram from Charles G. Dawes to Mrs. Charles G. Dawes [Caro Dawes], December 24, 1917. Dawes Archive, Northwestern, Box 71.

98   "War's Shadow Darkens City," *Chicago Daily Tribune*, December 21, 1917.

99   Telegram from Mary G[ates] Dawes to Charles G. Dawes, December 24 [no year]. Dawes Archive, Northwestern, Box 71.

100   Letter from Mary [Beman] G[ates] Dawes to Charles G. Dawes, November 13, 1917. Dawes Archive, Northwestern, Box 71.

101   "Jack Patten Anxious to Get into the 'Real Scrap,' " *Chicago Daily Tribune*, April 17, 1918. Jack Patten was the son of James A. Patten (1852–1928), financier and Evanston mayor from 1901-1905.

102   Charles Cutler Dawes (1899-1970). Letter from Charles C. Dawes to his parents Rufus and Helen Dawes, November 18, 1917. Dawes Archive, Northwestern, Box 71.

103   Ibid.

104   "Young Dawes and Chum on Way to France," *Chicago Daily Tribune*, December 22, 1917.

105   William Mills Dawes (1895-1984) and Charles Cutler Dawes lived just up the road from Charles and Caro Dawes in Evanston, IL. They were the sons of Dawes' brother Rufus Cutler Dawes and Helen Palmer Dawes (1868-1941). They lived at 411 Clark Street (the house is now identified by the address 1800 Sheridan Road). William attended Northwestern University, class of 1919. He served 6 months in the American Field Service (AFS) before serving as a sergeant in the U.S. Motor Transport Corps. Beman Gates Dawes, Jr. (1895-1968) was the son of Bertie Burr Dawes (1872-1958) and Charles Dawes' brother, Beman Gates Dawes, Sr. (1870-1953), a former Congressman from Ohio and president of Pure Oil Company.

106   "Spirit of '75," *Chicago Daily Tribune*, June 3, 1917. William joined Northwestern

University's AFS unit and Gates enlisted in the Marietta College AFS unit, which had been organized and financed by his father. "Dawes, An Organizing Genius." *Petroleum Age,* November 1920, 66. Service Record of William Mills Dawes and Service Record of Beman Gates Dawes, Jr., American Field Service, AFS Foundation, http://www.the-afs-archive.org. Accessed March 17, 2016. See also, James William Davenport Seymour, ed., *History of the American Field Service in France, "Friends of France," 1914-1917,* Vol. III. Boston, MA: Houghton Mifflin, 1920.

107 Letter from Rufus Dawes to Charles G. Dawes, April 8, 1918. Dawes Archive, Northwestern, Box 71.

108 Letter from Rufus C. Dawes to Charles G. Dawes, December 10, 1917. Dawes Archive, Northwestern, Box 71.

109 Letter from Beman Dawes to Charles G. Dawes, October 29, 1917. Dawes Archive, Northwestern, Box 71.

110 Letter from Charles G. Dawes to Mary B[eman Gates] Dawes, October 23, 1917. Evanston History Center Archives.

111 Letter from Rufus C. Dawes to Charles G. Dawes, August 13, 1918. Dawes Archive, Northwestern, Box 71.

112 Letter from Rufus C. Dawes to Charles G. Dawes, September 14, 1917. Dawes Archive, Northwestern, Box 71.

113 Letter from Rufus C. Dawes to Charles G. Dawes, September 11, 1918. Dawes Archive, Northwestern, Box 71.

114 Letter from Charles G. Dawes to Sergeant William Dawes, May 1, 1918. Dawes Archive, Northwestern Box 71.

115 Letter from W[illiam]. M[ills] Dawes to "Uncle Charley," ND. Dawes Archive, Northwestern, Box 71.

116 Letter from Charles G. Dawes to Private Charles C. Dawes, April 30, 1918. Dawes Archive, Northwestern, Box 71.

117 Ibid.

118 Letter from Charles G. Dawes to Private Charles C. Dawes, September 24, 1918. Dawes Archive, Northwestern Box 71.

119 Letter from Rufus C. Dawes to Charles G. Dawes, September 11, 1918. Dawes Archive, Northwestern, Box 71.

120 Letter from Beman Gates Dawes, Jr. to his parents, October 8, 1917.

121 Letter from Beman Gates Dawes, Jr. to Charles G. Dawes, September 17, [1917], Dawes Archive, Northwestern, Box 71.

122 Ibid.

123 Cablegram from Charles G. Dawes to Beman Dawes, May 18, 1918. Dawes Archive, Northwestern, Box 71. Gates was honorably discharged from the military on January 25, 1919.

124 Letter from Charles G. Dawes to Rufus C. Dawes, November 14, 1917 Dawes Archive, Northwestern, Box 71.

125   Letter from Beman Gates Dawes, Jr. to Charles G. Dawes, August 29, 1918. Dawes Archive, Northwestern, Box 71.

126   Letter from Rufus C. Dawes to Charles G. Dawes, October 19, 1917. Dawes Archive, Northwestern, Box 71.

127   "William Mills Dawes," *U.S., Department of Veterans Affairs BIRLS Death File, 1850-2010.* Ancestry.com, Accessed February 14, 2016.

128   AFS volunteers were not a part of the U.S. military. Thus, many of them left the AFS to enlist in the A.E.F., especially once the Americans were in France in large numbers. Beginning in August 1917, AFS volunteers formed what would be the corps of the Motor Transport Reserve, transporting artillery and other items to the front lines.

129   *A Journal of the Great War,* January 6, 1918.

130   Letter from Charles G. Dawes to Sergeant William Dawes, January 31, 1918. Dawes Archive, Northwestern Box 71.

131   Letter from Charles G. Dawes to Sergeant William Dawes, September 30, 1918. Dawes Archive, Northwestern Box 71.

132   *World War One: A Student Encyclopedia.* Volume I. Edited by Spencer Tucker. Santa Barbara, CA: ABC-CLIO, 2006, 1771.

133   Letter from William M. Dawes to Charles G. Dawes, September 20, 1918. Dawes Archive, Northwestern Box 71.

134   Letter from Charles C. Dawes to Charles G. Dawes, April 9, 1918. Dawes Archive, Northwestern, Box 71.

135   Letter from Charles G. Dawes to Sergeant William M. Dawes, March 31, 1918. Dawes Archive, Northwestern, Box 71.

136   Letter from Charles G. Dawes to Sergeant William M. Dawes, September 20, 1918. Dawes Archive, Northwestern Box 71.

137   *A Journal of the Great War,* September 23, 1918.

138   Letter from William M. Dawes to Charles G. Dawes, October 17, 1918. Dawes Archive, Northwestern, Box 71.

139   Letter from Charles G. Dawes to Sergeant William M. Dawes, September 20, 1918. Dawes Archive, Northwestern, Box 71.

140   Charles N. Wheeler, "Rides in Tanks As Did Grandsire Beside Revere," *Chicago Daily Tribune*, October 29, 1918.

141   Letter from Charles G. Dawes to William M. Dawes, February 27, 1918. Dawes Archive, Northwestern, Box 71.

142   Letter from Charles G. Dawes to Mary [Beman Gates] Dawes, November 14, 1918, included in *A Journal of the Great War.* Charles C. Dawes' interest in serving would not end with the war's end. Later, he would join the National Guard, eventually rising to the rank of Brigadier General. "Chicago Man Retires From National Guard," *Decatur Daily Review,* April 30, 1946.

143   *A Journal of the Great War,* June 1, 1919.

144   Ibid, November 11, 1918.

145   Ibid.

146   Boersianer, [Emil Friend], "Gen. C. G Dawes Home; Acts and Looks like Youth."

147   Letter from Charles G. Dawes to Mary B[eman Gates] Dawes, February 5, 1919. Dawes Archive, Northwestern, Box 71.

148   Letter from Charles G. Dawes to Henry Dawes, February 28, 1919, Dawes Archive, Northwestern, Box 71.

149   *A Journal of the Great War,* February 14, 1919.

150   "French Did Not Gouge U.S., Says Gen Dawes." *New York Evening Sun,* April 7, 1919.

151   George Rothwell Brown, "Task of S.O.S. Vast," *Washington Post,* February 10, 1919.

152   Virginia Lewis went to Paris in April 1919 and wrote for the *Chicago Daily Tribune.* Her stories were signed "Mrs. Spearman Lewis." Mrs. Spearman Lewis, "Look At France and You Will See Why the Terms," *Chicago Daily Tribune,* May 18, 1919.

153   "Dawes Greatest Illinoisan in War," *Macomb Journal,* July 28, 1919. From a Spearman Lewis story first appearing in the *Chicago Daily Tribune,* Dawes Archive, Northwestern, scrapbook. Box 84.

154   "Charles G. Dawes in the S.O. S," *Seattle Post-Intelligencier,* May 4, 1919, Dawes Archive, Northwestern, scrapbook. Box 84.

155   Carolyn Wilson, "Col. Dawes and His Overcoat," *Chicago Daily Tribune,* October 4, 1918.

156   A preliminary effort, begun in Ohio, had started "to try out [Dawes'] name for the Republican nomination." Walter S. Buel, "Republicans Open Boom for Dawes," *Cleveland Plain Dealer,* March 24, 1919. "Charles G. Dawes for President," read a headline in Lincoln, Nebraska's *The Trade Review,* April 19, 1919.

157   Charles G. Dawes, handwritten original manuscript of "A Journal of the Great War," Dawes Archive, Northwestern, Box 86, np.

158   "Charles G. Dawes Gets War Cross," *Chicago Herald,* July 13, 1919.

159   "Pershing Gives Medal to Dawes and Ten Others," *Chicago Daily Tribune,* January 21, 1919.

160   Letter from William R. Dawes to Charles G. Dawes, October 7, 1918. Dawes Archive, Northwestern, Box 71.

161   Letter from Henry Dawes to Charles G. Dawes, February 13, 1919. Dawes Archive, Northwestern, Box 71.

162   Poem by Rufus C. Dawes, "To General Charles C. Dawes," nd. Dawes Archive, Northwestern University, Box 71.

163   *A Journal of the Great War,* September 21, 1918. Dawes wrote letters to military officials to inquire about the possibility of bestowing Distinguished Service

Medals to at least two officers who were particularly depressed at not having received them.

164   U.S. House, *Select Committee on Expenditures in the War Department, Hearings Before Subcommittee No. 3 (Foreign Expenditures)*, Testimony of Hon. Charles G. Dawes, February 3, 1921. Washington, D.C.: Government Printing Office, 1921, 4513.

165   It is likely that Caro did not travel to France for a visit owing to her small children. When Bertie accompanied Beman to Europe, Caro had reportedly been "pretty sad," but still managed to be "cheerful and full of fun." Letter from Rufus Dawes to Charles G. Dawes, May 14, 1919, Dawes Archive, Northwestern, Box 71.

166   Mrs. Spearman Lewis, [Virginia Lewis], "Hour of Triumph for the Living and for the Dead," *Chicago Daily Tribune*, July 15, 1919. Warren arrived in France sometime in late April 1919.

167   There were casualties among the 17th Engineers, including Private Harry L. Keller, who had been gassed and sent back to the U.S., only to become the "first Chicago solider to die [in the United States] after being invalided home," ("12 Illinois Men on To-Day's List of Casualties," *Chicago American*, July 27, 1918), and Harry Arthur Littlefield, who died from pneumonia on March 16, 1918. New York Adjutant General's Office, *Roll of Honor: Citizens of the State of New York who Died While in the World War*. Compiled by Brigadier General J. Leslie Kincaid. Albany, NY: J. B. Lyon Company, 1922, 135.

168   "Society," *Washington Post*, February 23, 1919. Janet and Gates announced their engagement in July 1917, while Gates was overseas. Janet, a graduate of Wellesley College, worked at Walter Reed Hospital during the war. "Janet Newton to Wed," *Washington Post*, February 23, 1919. One year after Gates married, in June 1920, his cousin William M. Dawes married Nancy Keenan ("Weddings and Engagements," *Chicago Daily Tribune*, June 19, 1920), and the next year his cousin, Charles C. Dawes married Emily McCormick. "Emily McCormick Today Becomes Bride of Charles Dawes," *Chicago Daily Tribune*, January 3, 1921.

169   Upon his homecoming, William was planning to work for Smith and Dunn in the oil business. Letter from Rufus Dawes to Charles G. Dawes, March 4, 1919. Dawes Archive, Northwestern, Box 71.

170   Letter from Henry Dawes to Caro Dawes, February 28, 1919. Dawes Archive, Northwestern, Box 71.

171   Letter from Charles G. Dawes to Rufus Dawes, May 19, 1919. Dawes Archive, Northwestern, Box 71.

172   Letter from Charles G. Dawes to Rufus Dawes, January 9, 1918. Dawes Archive, Northwestern, Box 71.

173   Less than a month after Carl Boyd's death, Charles Dawes wrote to his brother Henry that he had contacted his bank's trust officer and drawn up a contract for Boyd's widow, Annie P. Boyd. It is likely that Dawes created a fund to

care for Carl Boyd's widow and daughter, Anne. Letter from Charles G. Dawes to Henry Dawes, March 11, 1919. Dawes Archive, Northwestern, Box 71.

174   J.A. Le Conte, "Carl Boyd," *Fiftieth Annual Report of the Association of Graduates of the United States Military Academy.* Saginaw, MI: Seemann and Peters, Inc., 1919, 199-202. Charles H. Fiske Jr., "Still Serving Where they Fell," *The New Outlook,* February 18, 1920, 277-278.

175   "Decoration Day Over There," *Lincoln Evening Journal,* May 24, 1919.

176   *A Journal of the Great War,* February 16, 1919.

177   Webster died of pneumonia following an appendectomy. He was likely one of the many casualties of influenza, which was "raging" at the hospital at Savenay where the operation was performed. According to one nurse there, the "big ward [was] full of boys dying." Carol R Byerly, *Fever of War: The Influenza Epidemic in the U.S. Army During World War I.* New York: New York University Press, 2005, 179.

178   Webster graduated from his course in December 1918. Thomas Furlong, "J.E. Otis Quits as Head of Dawes Bank," *Chicago Daily Tribune,* May 24, 1934. "Trust Companies," March 1919, 314. See also, F.C. Moore, *Phillips Academy, Andover, in the Great War.* Feuss Claude Moore, 1919, 148.

179   Beverly Randolph, "War's Workmen Prepare for Battle of Construction," *Atlanta Constitution,* July 1, 1917.

180   "G.W. Otis Dies in France," *Chicago News,* February 19, 1919. "George W. Otis, Son of Banker, Dies in France," *Chicago Daily Tribune,* February 20, 1919.

181   There are conflicting accounts of where Webster was buried in France. One states that he was buried at the cemetery in Savenay, just up the hill from the hospital. (Burials there were constant, with buglers playing taps at regular intervals. Carol R Byerly, *Fever of War,* 179.) But it is also suggested that he was buried in the American cemetery at St. Nazaire, just a few miles away from the hospital, where the 17th Engineers were based.

182   Letter from William R. Dawes to Charles G. Dawes, March 19, 1918. Dawes Archive, Northwestern, Box 71.

183   Letter from Henry Dawes to Charles G. Dawes, February 28, 1919, Dawes Archive, Northwestern, Box 71.

184   Ibid.

185   Letter from Henry Dawes to Charles G. Dawes, February 28, 1919, Dawes Archive, Northwestern, Box 71.

186   United States War Department, *Location of Graves and Disposition of Bodies of American Soldiers who Died Overseas,* Washington, D.C.: Government Printing Office, 1920, 4-5.

187   Decoration Day was first observed in 1868 in honor of American Civil War dead. The day was devoted to decorating their gravesites. Use of the term "Memorial Day" would become more common over the years, especially after World War II. A congressional act in 1967 officially changed the name to Memorial Day.

188   "Shame is Predicted for Foes of League by President Wilson," *Atlanta Constitution*, May 31, 1919.

189   After months of debate, the United States failed to ratify the Treaty of Versailles and would not officially proclaim, through a separate treaty, the end to its war with the Central Powers until June 1921.

190   *A Journal of the Great War*, July 6, 1919.

191   Percy Hammond, "Parisian Scenes Featuring the Homesick Yank," *Chicago Daily Tribune*, February 15, 1919.

192   Spearman Lewis, "Warriors Gone, Paris Fiddles to Empty House," *Chicago Daily Tribune*, July 24, 1919.

193   *A Journal of the Great War*, July 6, 1919.

194   "Dawes Greatest Illinoisan in War," *Macomb Journal*, July 28, 1919.

195   *A Journal of the Great War*, August 2, 1919. Pershing remained in Paris after Dawes left. He returned to the United States in September 1919.

196   Letter from Charles G. Dawes to Mary [Beman Gates] Dawes, July 1, 1918. Dawes Archive, Northwestern, Box 71.

197   Charles G. Dawes, *Notes as Vice President, 1928-1929,* Boston: Little, Brown and Company, 1935, 9.

198   Ibid, 7.

199   Charles G. Dawes, "League of Nations Idea Helped Win the War," *Washington Star,* August 31, 1919. Conceived by Woodrow Wilson (for which he was awarded a Nobel Peace Prize in 1920), the League of Nations was included as a component of the Treaty of Versailles. When the League began its work in January 1920, the United States was not a member. Owing to opposition in the U.S. Senate, the Treaty of Versailles had not been ratified. Dawes had been a vocal supporter of the League, arguing that its goal of cooperative diplomacy was something that his own MBAS had achieved.

200   In particular, Dawes noted that because the United States had now become the "creditor of the world," its obligations were "scattered" all over the globe. As such, the country had much to gain economically from joining the League. Charles G. Dawes, "League of Nations Idea Helped Win the War," *Washington Star,* August 31, 1919.

201   "Common Sense View of the League," *Chicago News,* September 3, 1919. Dawes Archive, Northwestern, Scrapbook, Box 84.

202   "Dawes Says He Will Not Enter Political Game," *Chicago Herald-Examiner,* September 13, 1919.

203   "Dawes Declines to Serve on President's Industrial Board," *Chicago Journal,* September 18, 1919.

204   "Dawes Home; Says Politics Not for Him," *Chicago Journal,* September 12, 1919.

205   In October 1919, President Wilson suffered a stroke. Although he

continued to work to build support for the ratification of the Treaty of Versailles and to take part in the nation's political life, he did not fare well. He died on February 3, 1924.

206   Charles L. Mee, Jr., *The Ohio Gang: The World of Warren G. Harding*, New York: M. Evans and Company, 103.

207   Ralph Hayes, "A Report to the Secretary of War on American Military Dead Overseas," Washington, D.C.: U.S. War Department, May 14, 1920, 12.

208   Ibid, 42. By 1920, a total of 75,636 graves in eight European countries had been counted by the U.S. Graves Registration Service. (United States War Department, *Location of Graves and Disposition of Bodies of American Soldiers who Died Overseas*, Washington, D.C.: Government Printing Office, 1920, 4-5). "Gold Star Mothers" began to campaign to have the bodies of their sons returned to the United States. Of the 75,000 inquires sent to families of deceased soldiers, 59% wanted the bodies returned to the U.S. Ralph Hayes, "A Report to the Secretary of War on American Military Dead Overseas." Washington, D.C.: U.S. War Department, May 14, 1920, 15.

209   Initially, the U.S. government promised to bring home the bodies of Americans who had died in the war. Families of those who had died were asked if they preferred the option of re-burying the bodies in national cemeteries in France, keeping the graves where they were, or bringing them home. (Chris Dickon, *The Foreign Burial of American War Dead: A History*. Jefferson, NC: McFarland and Co., 59.) The French government's ban on repatriating the bodies was in effect from January 1919 to January 1922. After the ban was lifted earlier than the initial dead-line, repatriation began. Many American graves remained untouched, but a sizeable number of the dead were re-buried in official American cemeteries in France or repatriated home. According to the American Battle Monuments Commission, the graves of 30,922 Americans who died in World War I remain in Europe. American Battle Monuments Commission "World War I Burials and Memorializations," https://www.abmc.gov/node/1273. Accessed May 27, 2016. Owing to the vast physical distance separating the "Gold Star" families from their loved ones who were buried in France, the government would later fund pilgrimages to Europe for family members to visit the gravesites. John W. Graham, *The Gold Star Mother Pilgrimages of the 1930s*. Jefferson, NC: McFarland and Co, 2005.

210   Matt Phillips, "The Long Story of U.S. Debt, From 1790 to 2011, in 1 Little Chart," *The Atlantic*, November 13, 2012.

211   "Investigating the War," *New York Times*, June 15, 1919.

212   "Won in Spite of Them," *The Kinsley Mercury* (Kinsley, Kansas), July 1, 1920.

213   C.C. Brainerd, "Republicans to Find Out Just Where 16 Billions Were Spent During the War," *The Brooklyn Daily Eagle*, June 15, 1919. The U.S. House of Representatives Select Committee to Investigate War Expenditures was chaired

by William J. Graham (1872-1937) of Illinois. Graham was elected to Congress just prior to the U.S. entry into the war.

214 "Investigating the War," *New York Times,* June 15, 1919.

215 Ibid.

216 According to Dawes, the committee also attempted to interrogate Pershing and "prevent" his departure just two days before he was scheduled to leave Paris. Charles G. Dawes, *Notes as Vice President, 1928-1929,* 11.

217 U.S. Senate, Sixty-Sixth Congress, Reorganization of the Army: Hearings Before the Subcommittee of the Committee on Military Affairs, Statement of General Charles G. Dawes, November 4, 1919, Washington, D.C.: Government Printing Office, 1919.

218 "Most of Supplies for A.E.F. Bought of European Firms," *Houston Post,* November 6, 1919.

219 "A. E. F. Got More Supplies Abroad Than From U. S.," *Chicago Daily Tribune,* Nov 5, 1919.

220 U.S. Senate, Sixty-Sixth Congress, Reorganization of the Army: Hearings Before the Subcommittee of the Committee on Military Affairs, Statement of General Charles G. Dawes, November 4, 1919, Washington, D.C.: Government Printing Office, 1919, 1714.

221 Report of the General Purchasing Agent and Chairman of The General Purchasing Board, American Expeditionary Forces, to the Commanding General, Services of Supply, American Expeditionary Forces, February 28, 1919.

222 U.S. Senate, Sixty-Sixth Congress, Reorganization of the Army, Statement of General Charles G. Dawes, November 4, 1919, 1722.

223 "Gen. Dawes Guest at Welcome Home Dinner," *Chicago American,* November 21, 1919.

224 "Chicago Throngs Acclaim Pershing," *New York Times,* December 21, 1919.

225 "Pershing and His Men Share Final Tribute," *Chicago Daily Tribune,* December 22, 1919. "Pershing Greeted as 'Chicago's Own,'" *Chicago News,* December 20, 1919.

226 Letter from John P. Foy to Charles G. Dawes, nd, Dawes Archive, Northwestern, Box 95.

227 Letter from Charles S. Olcott to Charles G. Dawes, August 13, 1920. Dawes Archive, Northwestern, Box 90.

228 Letter from Charles S. Olcott to Charles G. Dawes, October 14, 1920. Dawes Archive, Northwestern, Box 90. Dawes' journal was managed mainly by two men: Charles S. Olcott and Roger Livingston Scaife, both of Houghton Mifflin. Ferris Lowell Greenslet (1875-1959), a literary advisor and director at Houghton Mifflin, also had a hand in shaping the journal's publication. Greenslet, the author of several biographies, suggested omissions to some of the notes in Dawes' journal, and told Olcott that the journal "may prove to be of great value." Letter

from Charles S. Olcott to Charles G. Dawes, August 6, 1920. Dawes Archive, Northwestern, Box 90. Dawes had known Olcott for several years, and that relationship may have been behind Dawes' decision to choose Houghton Mifflin as his publisher. Olcott was the author of *The Life of William McKinley,* published in 1916 by Houghton Mifflin. In that book's preface, Olcott thanks Charles Dawes for his "kindness" in granting Olcott access to Dawes' personal diary in which he recorded his experiences working for McKinley. (Charles S. Olcott, *The Life of William McKinley.* Volume I. Boston: Houghton Mifflin Company, 1916, viii-ix.) Via correspondence, Olcott introduced Dawes to Scaife in October 1920, telling Dawes that he should "confer" with Scaife during the production process. Scaife (1875-1951) began working for Houghton Mifflin in 1898, a year after he graduated from Harvard. He was known as an "idea man" with a "flair for promotion." (Letter from Charles S. Olcott to Charles G. Dawes, October 14, 1920. Dawes Archive, Northwestern, Box 90.) Scaife made a visit to Dawes' home in Evanston in October 1920. (Letter from Roger L. Scaife to Charles G. Dawes, October 28, 1920. Dawes Archive, Northwestern, Box 90). In his correspondence with Dawes, Scaife made an effort to secure publication of Pershing's memoirs as well, asking Dawes to "say a good word for Houghton Mifflin" and help arrange a meeting between Scaife and Pershing. (Letter from Roger L. Scaife to Charles G. Dawes, October 29, 1920. Dawes Archive, Northwestern, Box 90). Scaife wrote to Dawes that Pershing "owed [his memoirs] to the American public and to history" and that Houghton Mifflin would "use every effort to try to persuade him to select us as his publisher." (Letter from Roger L. Scaife to Charles G. Dawes, December 6, 1920. Dawes Archive, Northwestern, Box 90). Scaife did meet Pershing at a dinner party of a mutual friend but did not take up the matter with him, since he judged it "not to be an auspicious moment." (Letter from Roger L. Scaife to Charles G. Dawes, November 15, 1920. Dawes Archive, Northwestern, Box 90). Pershing would publish his two volume memoir, *My Experiences in the World War,* in 1931. Frederick A. Stokes and Company was the publisher. The memoir was awarded the 1932 Pulitzer prize for history. In 1934, Scaife left Houghton Mifflin and went to work for Little, Brown and Company. Eventually he headed Harvard University Press. Max Hall, *Harvard University Press: A History.* Cambridge, MA: Harvard University Press, 1986, 105.

229   In November 1920, a contract was sent to Dawes. The publisher received a 20% commission on each book sold, and would promote the book and sell it throughout the country, using "travelling salesmen." Dawes paid for the book's manufacture, which amounted to $6,010. (Letter from Roger L. Scaife to Charles G. Dawes, November 5, 1920. Dawes Archive, Northwestern, Box 90.) Dawes also had 75 copies of special leather bound volumes printed. The publication process seemed to move ahead smoothly, save for a strike by New England printers in early 1921 that delayed the printing, shifting the publication date to the late summer

of 1921. Letter from Charles S. Olcott to Charles G. Dawes, October 29, 1920. Dawes Archive, Northwestern, Box 90.

230 "Need to Arouse People," *Boston Post,* January 21, 1921.

231 "Harding's Choice for Head of the Treasury Department is Splendid," *Greensboro Daily News,* December 31, 1920.

232 See the introduction for more about Dawes' wartime use of the tactic of "breathing fire and brimstone."

233 "An Investigation that Cost People Many Thousands," *The Sun-Journal* (New Berne, NC) June 10, 1920.

234 Later, Graham demanded prosecution for various cases of graft amounting to $78,000,000 uncovered by the committee in relation to contracts approved by the War Department. Graham charged that Secretary of War Newton Baker had been responsible for approving contracts and he also advocated for a Constitutional amendment making war profiteering an act of treason. He also argued that a "secret government" of seven men had overseen war production and "determined all war legislation:" Julius Rosenwald, Franklin H. Martin, Hollis Godfrey, Howard E. Coffin, Bernard Baruch, Samuel Gompers, and Daniel Willard. "Demand Prosecution of Graft," *The Macon Republican,* April 22, 1920. "The Council of National Defense," *Casa Grande Dispatch,* April 30, 1920. In 1924, Graham resigned the House and was appointed by Coolidge as a justice on the U.S. Court of Custom Appeals. He served in that role until his death in 1937.

235 "An Investigation the Cost People Many Thousands," *The New Bern Sun Journal,* June 10, 1920.

236 "House Members Ask Dawes Be Quizzed," *The Evening News,* January 27, 1921.

237 Charles G. Dawes, *Notes as Vice President, 1928-1929,* 10.

238 "Charles G. Dawes Says He's Out of Cabinet," *The Fort Wayne Sentinel,* February 2, 1921.

239 "Not Taking Office Says Gen Dawes," *New York Times,* February 3, 1921.

240 Dawes first served as chairman of the General Purchasing Board for the A.E.F., and then as a member representing the A.E.F. on the Military Board of Allied Supply. After the war, while still in France, he served as a member of the United States Liquidation Commission.

241 U.S. House, Testimony of Hon. Charles G. Dawes, February 3, 1921, 4430.

242 "Dawes Scores His Critics," *Reno Gazette-Journal,* February 2, 1921.

243 Ibid.

244 The phrase "hell and Maria" has its origins in the American Civil War. In December 1864, the steamer, the Maria, loaded with Union Army troops and supplies, was blown up near St. Louis, resulting in numerous casualties. Thereafter, the phrase "hell and Maria" was used as an expletive. H. L. Mencken's Supplement

One of his 1919 *The American Language* (New York: Alfred A. Knopf, 1945) includes a reference both to the expletive and to its use as a nickname for Charles G. Dawes, pps. 308 and 662.

245 "Cuss Congress," *Fort Riley Daily Tribune*, February 3, 1921.

246 "Dawes Scores His Critics," *Reno Gazette-Journal*, February 2, 1921.

247 Ibid.

248 U.S. House, Testimony of Hon. Charles G. Dawes, February 3, 1921, 4492.

249 Ibid, 4459.

250 Ibid, 4500, 4492.

251 "Gen. Dawes Roasts Congressmen for Doing Politics with War," *Reno Gazette-Journal*, February 3, 1921.

252 "Cuss Congress," *Fort Riley Daily Tribune*, February 3, 1921.

253 "Dawes Continues His Bitter Attack on Congress Method of Probing War," *Arizona Republic*, February 4, 1921.

254 "Dawes Storms at War Politics," *New York Times*, February 4, 1921.

255 Charles G. Dawes, *Notes as Vice President*, 9.

256 *Reno Evening Gazette*, February 3, 1921 and *Washington Herald*, February 4, 1921.

257 "Dawes Scores His Critics," *Reno Gazette-Journal*, February 2, 1921.

258 "Dawes Scores Politicians in Praising Army," *Washington Herald*, February 4, 1921.

259 "Overlook the Crooks," *Leavenworth Times*, February 9, 1921.

260 U.S. House, Testimony of Hon. Charles G. Dawes, February 3, 1921, 4506.

261 Charles G. Dawes, *Notes as Vice President*, 10.

262 Ibid.

263 "Dawes Accepts Job of Budget Director," *New York Times*, June 22, 1921.

264 "Hits Back at Gen. Dawes," *New York Times*, February 17, 1921.

265 In the Charles G. Dawes Archive at Northwestern, letters in support of Dawes' testimony far outnumber those "disapproving letters." Roughly 366 letters in support (including one official letter from the city of Evanston, Illinois) are housed in the Dawes Archive, and just 8 disapproving letters (whether or not there were more than 8 received by Dawes is unknown). The disapproving letters include one addressed to "fowl (sic) mouthed Charley Dawes." These letters charged Dawes with taking a "pro British" stance during his testimony, owing to his praise for the British and French, and for his failure to support the war for Irish independence, which was currently being debated within the U.S. Senate. One such letter included the statement: "go to hell you damn lot of English mutts." Another negative letter came from the sculptor Gutzon Borglum (1867-1941), later creator of the Mount

Rushmore carvings. Borglum rallied against Dawes for not revealing the name of a war profiteer to the committee. Dawes had acknowledged the individual and said the A.E.F. had barred him from doing business, but failed to identify him. Letter from Gutzon Borglum to Charles G. Dawes, February 17, 1921. Dawes Archive, Northwestern, Box 95.

266 Letter from [Robert] Bullard to Charles G. Dawes, February 3, 1921. Dawes Archive, Northwestern, Box 95. Pershing also publicly expressed his unwavering support for Dawes' position in front of the committee.

267 Letter from Philip E. Eltoy to Charles G. Dawes, February 4, 1921, and letter from V.G. Severance to Charles G. Dawes, February 4, 1921. Dawes Archive, Northwestern, Box 95.

268 "The people of Evanston should be proud to claim you as one of its citizens," city clerk John Hahn wrote. Letter from John F. Hahn to Charles G. Dawes, February 4, 1921. Dawes Archive, Northwestern, Box 95.

269 Letter from F.A. Burgun to Charles G. Dawes, February 10, 1921. Dawes Archive, Northwestern, Box 95.

270 Letter from Eddy S. Brandt to Charles G. Dawes, February 6, 1921. Dawes Archive, Northwestern, Box 95.

271 Telegram from Walter B. Ellis to Charles G. Dawes, February 12, 1921. Dawes Archive, Northwestern, Box 95.

272 Letter from Jule F. Brower to Charles G. Dawes, February 9, 1921. Dawes Archive, Northwestern, Box 95.

273 Letter from James W. Vallentyne to Charles G. Dawes, February 4, 1921. Dawes Archive, Northwestern, Box 95.

274 Letter from W.H. Harris to Charles G. Dawes, February 4, 1921. Dawes Archive, Northwestern, Box 95.

275 Letter from John Barnell to Charles G. Dawes, February 4, 1921. Dawes Archive, Northwestern, Box 95.

276 Letter from T.S. Webster to Charles G. Dawes, February 4, 1921. Dawes Archive, Northwestern, Box 95

277 "Government's 'Best Seller' is Dawes's War Testimony," *New York Times,* March 18, 1921.

278 Ibid. Dawes himself stated later that the stenographers had a tough time keeping up with him as he yelled and paced and let forth a stream of expletives. He noted that the published testimony was not a verbatim account of what he had said and that many newspaper reporters had a field day embellishing some of his phrases. At the end of his testimony, Dawes himself requested that the profanity be expurgated from his testimony. Although some committee members objected to tampering with the record, the stenographers testified that they had already eliminated them. In their statement, they observed that Dawes' testimony and remarks "were replete with profanity in almost every sentence" and, "that by your direction,

as chairman of the committee, and requests from the other members of the committee, as well as requests of the witness himself, that all profane expressions be not incorporated in the transcript of the proceedings, each of us eliminated such profane expressions from our shorthand notes, and it would not be possible for us at this time to furnish an unexpurgated transcript of the remarks of the witness as given in the committee room." U.S. Congress, House of Representatives, "Select Committee on Expenditures in the War Department," Washington, D.C., U.S. Government Printing Office, 1921, 4515-4516.

279   "Congress Mere Nest of Cowards, Charges Dawes in Speech," *The Washington Times*, October 14, 1922.

280   "Dawes Doesn't Damn, But Opera Folk Grasp Him," *Chicago Daily Tribune*, February 25, 1921.

281   "Willing to Pay $100 For Soup to Hear Dawes Cuss," *Chicago Daily Tribune*, February 7, 1921.

282   "Charge Huge Waste in War Inquiry Report," *New York Times*, March 3, 1921.

283   "War Inquiries Near End," *New York Times*, February 7, 1921.

284   "New Members of Congress All On the Job," *Oshkosh Daily*, April 9, 1921. The Graham committee would not be the last to investigate war profiteering. As public sentiment toward the war debt and war profiteering intensified, especially during the Great Depression, the Nye Committee on the Munitions Industry in the United States, led by Senator Gerald P. Nye, was formed in April 1934. It conducted investigations through February 1936 before being disbanded. Nye's committee revealed details concerning finance, manufacturing, and profit-making during World War I, especially in relation to the loans made to the Allies, and encouraged many Americans' sense that the country should pursue a course of isolationism. (Mathew Ware Coulter, "FDR and the Nye Committee: A Reassessment," in Thomas Phillip Wolf, William D. Pederson, Byron W. Daynes, ed. *Franklin D. Roosevelt and Congress: The New Deal and Its Aftermath*. Vol. 2. New York: M.E. Sharpe, 2001, 26.) Major General Smedley Butler (1881-1940), a two time recipient of the Medal of Honor and a marine with thirty four years of experience, from the Spanish American War to World War I, became a leading spokesman on the issue; his 1935 book *War is a Racket* has since become a classic. Butler was part of the 1932 Bonus Expeditionary Force (aka Bonus Army) of World War I veterans who marched on Washington, D.C., demanding payment of service certificates.

285   U.S. House, Testimony of Hon. Charles G. Dawes, February 3, 1921, 4506.

286   "Dawes a Modest 'Cusser,'" *New York Times*, April 23, 1921.

287   "Dawes' New Book Good War Records," *Chicago Journal of Commerce*, August 4, 1921.

288   *San Francisco Chronicle*, September 4, 1921.

289   "General Dawes, Cusser Deluxe," *Denver Post,* April 15, 1921. Dawes Archive, Northwestern, scrapbook, Box 96.

290   Fritz Kreisler (1875-1962). "Dawes New Role is Music Composer," *The Courier-Journal* (Louisville, Kentucky), July 2, 1921. "Music, Not 'Cussing,' Found General Dawes' 'Ruling Passion," *Philadelphia Public Ledger,* June 27, 1921, Scrapbook, Dawes Archive, Northwestern, Box 96.

291   "Dawes is a Composer, Too," *Chicago Daily News,* July 1, 1921. Dawes Archive, Northwestern, Scrapbook, Box 96.

292   "The Musical Financier," *Bisbee Daily Review,* July 29, 1921.

293   Samuel Mccoy, "General Dawes Revives a Dead Author," *New York Times,* October 19, 1924.

294   "Cabinet Size," *Ironwood Daily Globe,* February 16, 1921.

295   "Dawes Won't Be Cabinet Member," *Daily Arkansas Gazette,* February 13, 1921. Andrew Mellon was appointed Secretary of the Treasury, a position he would hold for more than a decade. It may have been lucky for Dawes that he did not join Harding's cabinet. Several members of the administration would later be embroiled in scandal, with charges of bribery and corruption, especially related to the Teapot Dome scandal.

296   Hoover headed the American Relief Administration, which was authorized in February 1919 and tasked with distributing food and supplies throughout Europe following the war's end. "Hoover Asks Aid for 3,500,000," *Chicago Daily Tribune,* December 11, 1920. In November 1920, at a fundraising event held at the Blackstone Hotel in Chicago, $200,000 was raised. "Let's get their pledges before they leave," Dawes was quoted as saying at the dinner. "Hoover Raises $200,000 Here to Feed Europe," *Chicago Daily Tribune,* November 24, 1920.

297   James William McAndrew," *Fifty-Third Annual Report of the Association of Graduates of the United States Military Academy.* Saginaw, MI: Seamann and Peters, 1922, 107.

298   Ibid

299   "Maj. Gen. McAndrew Dies in Hospital," *The Scranton Republican,* May 22, 1922.

300   "Hold Funeral of General M'Andrew, *News and Observer,* May 4, 1922. "James William McAndrew," *Fifty-Third Annual Report of the Association of Graduates of the United States Military Academy.* Saginaw, MI: Seamann and Peters, 1922, 104-110.

301   "People Are Anxious to Reward All War Heroes," *Times Herald,* (Olean, New York), April 5, 1921.

302   "The Camera Man 'Got,'" *Cook Country Herald,* April 8, 1921.

303   "A Novelty in Washington," *Portsmouth Daily Times,* April 11, 1921.

304   "The Dawes Commission," *Indianapolis News,* April 7, 1921. Scrapbook, Box 96, Dawes Archive, Northwestern.

305   "Dawes Heads Commission on Soldier Relief," *Chicago Daily Tribune,*

March 30, 1921. Dawes and his commission recommended consolidating the agencies that handled aspects of veterans' care into a single entity they initially called the "Veterans' Service Administration." "Wants Single Body for Veterans' Care," *New York Times*, April 8, 1921.

306 "The Dawes Report," *The Independent*, April 23, 1921, 429.

307 "Wants Single Body for Veterans' Care," *New York Times*, April 8, 1921.

308 Charles R. Forbes (1878-1952) was a decorated officer who had served with the A.E.F. during World War I. His tenure as director of the Veterans Bureau was rife with corruption and Forbes himself allegedly embezzled money, took bribes and kickbacks, and did little to nothing with the budget allocated to serve veterans. In 1923, he resigned under pressure when some of his shady dealings became known. He was indicted the next year and convicted for bribery and conspiracy. He served 8 months in prison. David Fahrenthold, "How the VA Developed its Culture of Cover Ups," *Washington Post*, May 30, 2014.

309 U.S. Senate, 67th Congress, Committee on Education and Labor, Testimony of Brig. Gen. Charles E. Sawyer, April 12, 1921, Washington, D.C.: Government Printing Office, 19. See also, *Encyclopedia of the Veteran in America*. William A. Pencak, Ed. Santa Barbara, CA: ABC-CLIO, 2009, 389

310 "Gen. D. Tells of His Plans for Ministry of Defense," *Times Herald*, (Olean, New York), March 28, 1921.

311 The Bureau operated within the U.S. Department of the Treasury until 1939 when it was transferred into the Executive Office. In 1970, it became the Office of Management and Budget.

312 "Charles G. Dawes is Director of Budget," *Democrat and Chronicle*, June 22, 1921.

313 " 'Hell and Maria' Dawes, Job Finished, Due Home Tomorrow," *Chicago Daily Tribune*, July 5, 1922.

314 "Budget Director Dawes is at His Job With a Punch," *Daily Arkansas Gazette*, July 3, 1921.

315 Charles G. Dawes, "Report of Director of Bureau of The Budget," in *Message of the President of the United States Transmitting the Budget for the Service of the Fiscal Year Ending June 30, 1923*. Washington, D.C.: Government Printing Office, LIII.

316 Amity Shlaes, *Coolidge*. New York: HarperCollins, 2013, 226, 236.

317 Charles G. Dawes, *Notes as Vice President*, 33.

318 Charles G. Dawes, "Report of Director of Bureau of The Budget," LIII.

319 "Dawes Prescribes for a Photographer's Longevity," *Chicago Daily Tribune*, July 6, 1921.

320 "Budget Director Dawes is at His Job With a Punch," *Daily Arkansas Gazette*, July 3, 1921.

321 Publicity pamphlet, *A Journal of the Great War*, Dawes Archive, Northwestern, Box 84.

322 "A War Journal," *Boston Herald,* August 20, 1921. Dawes Archive, Northwestern, scrapbook, Box 97.

323 "General Dawes's War Diary," *New York Tribune,* August 21, 1921. Dawes Archive, Northwestern, scrapbook, Box 97.

324 *The North American Review.* November 1921, 711.

325 "A Real Book by a Real Man," *Chicago Daily Tribune.* August 13, 1921.

326 R.D. Townsend, "Behind the Lines," *The Outlook,* September 28, 1921, 144.

327 "The War Experiences of General Dawes," *The American Review of Reviews,* September 1921, 314.

328 Samuel McCoy, "General Dawes Revives a Dead Author," *New York Times,* October 19, 1924.

329 Letter from Charles G. Dawes to Mrs. M. B. Dawes [Mary Beman Gates Dawes], September 20, 1918. Dawes Archive, Northwestern, Box 71.

330 "Allies Supply Chief Due Here tomorrow," *New York Times,* October 23, 1921.

331 Edward Baron Turk, *Hollywood Diva: A Biography of Jeanette MacDonald.* Berkeley, CA: University of California Press, 1998, 347.

332 "Gen. Payot is Guest at Military Dinner," *New York Times,* October 29, 1921.

333 "Gen. Payot Arrives, Met by Notables," *New York Times,* October 25, 1921.

334 "Gen. Dawes at Dying Mother's Bedside When His War Colleagues Celebrate Here," *New York Times.* October 29, 1921. Roughly forty of Dawes' war colleagues attended the reunion dinner. Dawes later did see Payot in Washington, D.C. for a dinner held on October 30, 1921. "Geniuses of War Meet Again," *Washington Post,* October 30, 1921.

335 Letter from Mary [Beman] G[ates] Dawes to Charles G. Dawes, October 5, 1918. Dawes Archive, Northwestern, Box 71.

336 Letter from Charles G. Dawes to Mary B[eman Gates] Dawes, November 14, 1918. Evanston History Center Archives.

337 Letter from Mary [Beman] G[ates] Dawes to Charles G. Dawes, October 5, 1918. Dawes Archive, Northwestern, Box 71.

338 U.S. Congress. Committee on Military Affairs, "Return of Body of Unknown American who Lost His Life During World War." Sixty-Sixth Congress, Third Session, Statements of Hon. Hamilton Fish, Jr., William Tyler Page, Maj. Gen. John A. Lejeune, John Thomas Taylor, Gen John J. Pershing, Maj. Gen. P. C. Harris, and a Letter from Hon. Newton D. Baker, February 1, 1921, Washington, D.C.: Government Printing Office, 1921, 8.

339 Kirke Larue Simpson, "Body of 'The Unknown Soldier' Arrives Home," in *"The Unknown Soldier:" Supplement Service Bulletin of the Associated Press,* December

1921, 2.

340 *Washington Post,* November 6, 1921. The Tomb of the Unknown Soldier is now known as the Tomb of the Unknowns. Unidentified bodies of soldiers from America's subsequent wars have been laid to rest at the same site.

341 The French government authorized the repatriation of American soldiers from their graves within a limited area, called the Zone of the Armies. On March 29, 1920, the first disinterments began. (Ralph Hayes, "A Report to the Secretary of War on American Military Dead Overseas." Washington, D.C.: U.S. War Department, May 14, 1920, 34.) They were completed by March 30, 1922. The French also donated land for several official cemeteries for the burial of the American dead. Constance Potter and John Deeben, "Care for the Military Dead," in *A Companion to American Military History.* 2 Volume. Ed . James C. Bradford. West Sussex, UK: Blackwell, 2010, 1036.

342 "Body of George W. Otis Returned from France," *Chicago Daily Tribune,* September 21, 1920. After he died, Otis was awarded a posthumous degree from his alma mater, Yale University. *Obituary Records of Yale Graduates, 1915-1920.* New Haven: Yale University, August 1920, 1125.

343 "Dawes Claims Government Can Operate Economically," *Washington Herald,* June 29, 1922.

344 "Reforming Spendthrift Uncle Sam," *The Literary Digest,* May 20, 1922, 7.

345 "No More Red Tape," *Times Herald,* (Olean, New York), August 9, 1921.

346 Charles G. Dawes, "Report of Director of Bureau of The Budget," in *Message of the President of the United States Transmitting the Budget For the Service of the Fiscal Year Ending June 30, 1923.* Washington, D.C.: Government Printing Office, 1923, XXXV. Later, the Bureau of the Budget would be seen as anything but non-partisan, but as a tool to exercise executive power. For Dawes, however, complete independence was necessary to ensure the bureau operated fairly. For more on Dawes' work and the evolution of the bureau, see Larry Berman, *The Office of Management and Budget and the Presidency, 1921-1979.* Princeton: Princeton University Press, 1979. Also see Dawes' own record of his year with the bureau: *The First Year of The Budget of The United States.* New York: Harper & Brothers, 1923.

347 U.S. House, Commission to Erect Suitable Memorials Commemorating the Services of the American Soldier in Europe, Statement from Charles G. Dawes, February 23, 1922, Washington, D.C.: Government Printing Office, 1922, 2.

348 The American Battle Monuments Commission (ABMC) operates still. Its purpose is to construct and maintain American memorials and cemeteries in foreign countries where U.S. armed forces have served since April 6, 1917. Pershing would serve as chairman of the ABMC until his death in 1948. By the end of 1919, he had announced that he had purchased a house in Lincoln, Nebraska, and was planning to settle there with his son and two sisters. ("Pershing Buys Home; To Live in Lincoln, Neb.," *New York Times.* December 28, 1919.) In 1921, he was

appointed Chief of Staff of the U.S. Army and returned to Washington, D.C.

349   "Brig. Gen. Dawes Back Home Breaking in a New Pipe," *St. Louis Post-Dispatch*, July 8, 1922.

350   "Harding Like [*sic*] Coffee With Their Dinner," *The Evening Kansan-Republican*, July 8, 1922.

351   "Brig. Gen. Dawes Back Home Breaking in a New Pipe," *St. Louis Post-Dispatch*, July 8, 1922.

352   Charles G. Dawes, *Notes as Vice President*, 51.

353   "General Dawes 84," *New York Times*, August 28, 1949.

354   "Dawes is Through Talking," *New York Times*, July 8, 1922.

355   Charles G. Dawes, *Notes as Vice President*, 33.

356   Calvin Coolidge, speech given before the American Society of Newspaper Editors, Washington, D.C., January 17, 1925.

357   Philip Larkin, "MCMXIV," in *The Whitsun Weddings*, London: Faber and Faber, 1967.

358   Paul Fussell, *The Great War and Modern Memory*. London: Oxford University Press, 1975, 19.

359   Malcolm Cowley, *Exile's Return: A Literary Odyssey of the 1920s*. (1934) New York: Penguin Books, 1951, 296.

360   Ibid, 9.

Gallery of Portraits

SAMUEL M. FELTON

Samuel M. Felton, Director General of Military Railways, accomplished with highest success one of the greatest tasks of the war. He organized the first nine regiments of Transportation Troops which were sent over-seas and, following that, organized all the Transportation and Construction Troops for the Army, amounting to a total at the time of the armistice of 70,000 men in France and 14,000 men in the United States ready to embark.

In addition, he secured and shipped to the American Expeditionary Forces their railroad equipment machinery and supplies amid the greatest difficulties and embarrassments. In this connection, he made contracts involving over $600,000,000.

Declining a military commission as tending to lessen rather than to increase his high powers and efficiency he modestly and quietly rendered his unique and invaluable service.

He was among the first to receive the Distinguished Service Medal, with the following citation:

"Mr. S. M. Felton, Director General of Military Railways, for especially meritorious and conspicuous service in supervising the supply of railway material and the organization of railway operation and construction troops. By his energetic and loyal service, he has contributed materially to the success of the Army in the field."

C.G.D

LIEUTENANT-COLONEL HERMAN H. HARJES

Lieutenant-Colonel Herman H. Harjes, of all my staff, who afterwards became Chief Liaison Officer of the American Expeditionary Forces, rendered the most important assistance in the earlier work of my office with the French Government and Army.

His residence and acquaintance in France as the head of the firm of Morgan, Harjes and Company give him access at all times to those in French authority able to assist us. His advice and guidance were invaluable.

In the matter of cession of the Belgian locomotives and other important supply crises, Colonel Harjes contributed an energy and intelligence that insured success.

In the performance of his duty as Chief Liaison Officer, he suffered a broken hip in an automobile accident, but throughout the last two months of the war, notwithstanding acute suffering, he carried on his army work from his sick bed.

He received the Distinguished Service Medal of the United States.

C.G.D.

GEORGES CLEMENCEAU

MARSHAL FOCH
Taken at the time of crisis, 1918

DAVID LLOYD GEORGE

MARSHAL PÉTAIN

COMMANDANT HENRI A. VARAIGNE

Commandant Henri A. Varaigne, of the French Army, was an invaluable friend and assistant of the American Army in France. An aviator in the battle of the Marne, an experienced staff officer, an accomplished and brave soldier, he became, as chief of the staff of French officers attached to my headquarters, the first interpreter of our supply necessities to the French Army and Government. His devotion to the common cause, his honesty and sincerity of purpose, his great success in securing us needed help in times of acute crisis, his ever-present sympathy and encouragement, endeared him to every American with whom he came in contact. He received the Distinguished Service Medal of the United States.

C.G.D.

MAJOR-GENERAL CLARENCE R. EDWARDS, COM-
MANDING TWENTY-SIXTH DIVISION, AND A. VAN
DE VYVERE, BELGIAN MINISTER OF FINANCE,
NEUFCHÂTEAU, JANUARY, 1918

MAJOR-GENERAL FRANCIS J. KERNAN

FIELD MARSHAL DOUGLAS HAIG

NEWTON D. BAKER
Secretary of War

418

EDWARD R. STETTINIUS

DWIGHT W. MORROW

HAROLD F. McCORMICK
Purchasing Agent in Switzerland

HERBERT HOOVER

LIEUTENANT-GENERAL HUNTER LIGGETT

MAJOR-GENERAL SIR EVAN E. CARTER
Director of Supplies, British Expeditionary Force

ANDRÉ TARDIEU AS CAPTAIN OF ARTILLERY

MAJOR-GENERAL J. W. McANDREW
Chief of Staff, A.E.F.

COLONEL HENRY C. SMITHER
Assistant Chief of Staff, G-4, S.O.S.

LIEUTENANT-COLONEL NELSON D. JAY
Assistant General Purchasing Agent, A.E.F.

LIEUTENANT-COLONEL J. C. ROOP
Assistant General Purchasing Agent, A.E.F.

BRIGADIER-GENERAL H. A. DRUM
Chief of Staff, First Army, A.E.F.

COLONEL HARRY L. HODGES
Chief of Staff of American Member of the Military Board of
Allied Supply

BRIGADIER-GENERAL JOHNSON HAGOOD
Chief of Staff, Service of Supply

422

GENERAL PEYTON C. MARCH
Chief of Staff, U.S.A.

LIEUTENANT-COLONEL EDWARD B. CUSHING

423

LIEUTENANT-GENERAL SIR EDWARD TRAVERS-CLARKE, B.E.F.

MAURICE GANNE

MAJOR-GENERAL SIR EVAN E. CARTER
Director of Supplies, British Expeditionary Force

LOUIS LOUCHEUR
French Minister of Armament

MAJOR-GENERAL H. L. ROGERS
Quartermaster-General A.E.F.

LIEUTENANT-COLONEL F. W. M. CUTCHEON
Chief Board of Contracts and Adjustments, A.E.F.

MAJOR-GENERAL CHARLES P. SUMMERALL
Commanding First Division

COLONEL JAMES A. LOGAN
Assistant Chief of Staff, G-1, General Headquarters

LIEUTENANT-GENERAL ROBERT LEE BULLARD

HOMER H. JOHNSON
Member U.S. Liquidation Commission, War Department

GEORGE McFADDEN
Representative in France of War Trade Board

HON. H. H. HOLLIS
Member U.S. Liquidation Commission, War Department

EDWIN B. PARKER
Chairman U.S. Liquidation Commission, War Department

VANCE C. McCORMICK

PAUL D. CRAVATH

APPENDICES

Appendix A

Principles of Army Purchase and Supply as Suggested by Experience of American Expeditionary Force in France

(Dictated February 24, 1918, and carefully revised March 6, 1918.
For Insertion in War Diary of American Expeditionary Force)

War is the oldest occupation of mankind, and the system of organization for war has been the result of evolution for the longest period of any collective human activity. Therefore, what seems to be in military organization an anachronism must always be considered as to whether our regarding it in that light is due to the different functioning of an army organization in times of peace, as compared with a time of war. The current criticism of army organization is based largely upon the assumption that it ignores certain fundamental principles of normal business organization, which should be applied to the business system of an army notwithstanding the ultimate purpose of an army's existence is military, as distinguished from business, success. The conventional view of the army purchase and supply system, held by the non-military business man, is that the system of independent departmental purchases is a failure, because, while it is susceptible to an outside, coordinating control, this control is not accomplished, as in the normal business organization, by a complete centralization of purchase and supply through one agency acting for the army as a whole. The argument of the business man is that if all purchasing and supply activities were centralized in one distinct army department, created to supply all other branches of the service, there would be obviated competition among the various departments, piecemeal and wasteful purchases, loose methods, insufficient estimation of forward collective needs, and many other objections now incident to some extent to the present system. It is contended that the needs of an army and their satisfaction will be better ascertained and accomplished by a central body, having always the bird's-eye view of the situation, and that equally satisfactory results will not be incident to any method of central control reached through a coordination of independent agencies. It was with this belief that I took up my duties as General Purchasing Agent of the American Expeditionary Force, under a new system of central control devised personally by General Pershing against the advice of a reporting army board to whom the subject had been first referred. This report, attached hereto, with the comments of General Pershing thereon, indicates clearly the legal limitations under which he acted, his entire perception of the business and military principles involved, and the final plan he placed in operation as the best solution possible, in his judgment, under existing law, of the problem of reconciling the existing army and supply system with the fundamental principles of normal business organization without jeopardizing its efficiency from the military standpoint in time of actual war.

I wish I could claim a share in the conception of this plan, but the General had worked it out fully before I arrived at his headquarters and only selected me to put it into effect, and as General Purchasing Agent, American Expeditionary Force, and Chairman, to assemble the General Purchasing Board and direct its operations. My idea, as that of many other business men, had been that the law of the United States, which so jealously guarded the independent right of purchase and supply in departments of the service, was on our statute books as a result of a lack of business knowledge and foresight on the part of legislators, instead of its being, as it is, the logical, legitimate, and necessary evolution of thousands of years of actual military experience. Now, after six months in time of war, in a peculiar position relative to army purchase and supply activities such as does not exist in the British, French, or other army, so far as I know, I am prepared to say that any change in legislation or War Department regulation, designed to bring the organization of army purchase and supply more nearly into accord with the principles of modern business organization, should provide an agency of supervising coordination, which, while it will permit the application of rigid business principles under normal conditions, will not take away from independent departments the right of purchase and supply, especially during the time of actual military activity, the preservation of such independent powers being absolutely essential at times to military success, which of course is the ultimate object of the whole system.

The statement is frequently made that the business organization of an army is the same in its purposes as the business organization of any great corporation. This is misleading. The chief purpose of the organization of successful business is the creation of wealth; the chief purpose of the organization of an army is the destruction of enemy life and wealth. The prime consideration, in the establishment in normal business organization of central control of purchase, is the surrounding of purchasing activity with checks and balances compelling due consideration of every purchase from the standpoint of its relation to a prospective profit; in other words, to compel the deliberate application to every transaction of the test as to whether, if consummated, financial profit or something related to it will, immediately or ultimately, be the result. The first purpose of the army business organization in time of war is the securing of necessary military supplies irrespective of any question of financial profit, yet as cheaply and expeditiously as possible without prejudice to military effectiveness. If the application of all the principles of normal business organization would mean the failure of supply in military emergency, business principles, in the last analysis, must yield, wherever necessary, to military emergency. The principles, however, of normal business as affecting army business organization can be made to apply through a coordinating system as we have done in the American Expeditionary Force, where these principles are applied to any army purchase or supply transaction not involving a preponderating military necessity. I cannot emphasize too strongly that for the preservation of a requisite system of supply for an army in action, the feeling of responsibility on the part of a supply procuring agent must be first to the officers needing the supply. From my experience with the field system of army supply and purchase in this war, the only reason I can imagine why anybody suggests the contrary is because a large portion of the supplies for our army is being collected by the War Department in a country of large resources which, when collected, are shipped from America to the army in France. Business principles, for obvious reasons, can be given a wider application by the War Department in the United States than it is possible to give to the purchase and supply organization of an army in the field. In the business organization of an army in the field, nothing must prevent the immediate application of the greatest possible pressure, directly from the point of military and emergency need, upon an agent of purchase and supply directly responsible to it. Therefore, the central business control of purchase and supply activities of an army in the field, while operating in all normal cases, must not interfere with a perfect device for the operation of a collateral independent system controlled by military necessity. Only in this way can all the needs of an army in time of action be properly met.

Let us assume for purposes of illustration that the American Expeditionary Force in France, at a time when military operations are under way, had an existing central purchase and supply organization for all departments of the army without there being in existence machinery for independent collection of supplies. To that central organization would come a series of demands which we might epitomize as follows: From "A" on the line, two thousand blankets by night-time which if not supplied meant that soldiers would perish from exposure; from "B," one thousand shells for an expected attack the next day; from "C," one thousand cots for wounded soldiers lying on the floors of hospitals; from "D," certain medicines and surgical apparatus with available supplies entirely inadequate, and wounded still coming in; from "E," food for men who had been without it for two days. The central organization, in transmitting to its purchasing and collecting agents these demands, would use an emphatic tone of voice, but that tone of voice would not be the same, nor interpreted by the agent in the same way, as the voice of each officer responsible for the situation at each point of necessity speaking to a man directly responsible to him, and located at a point of possible supply. If a demand came for timber to build a bridge necessary to carry 100,000 troops across a stream for reinforcement of a sorely pressed army corps, questions of the price to be paid, or the manner in which it was to be secured, would not, advantageously, be first referred to a central agency for consideration of the business bearings of the transaction. It is no reply, in such a situation, to maintain that an emergency supply and purchase organization can be created for use in times of war which can function when and where it would be impossible for the central organization to do so. A purchase and supply machine, to function well, must function continuously. In this war the use of troops in restricted localities, the transportation to masses of stationary troops of large shipments of supplies, the fact that the different units of the army, as a rule, are not separated by long distances or isolated by lack of railroad or other means of communication, all make more plausible the demand for the abolition of the great army system of independent departmental supply and purchase. But if any other system is put in its place which does not recognize that the first responsibility of the supply and purchase agent must be directly to the responsible officer nearest the point of necessity, the system in time of military emergency will fail; and the whole object of the military system is not to fail in time of war. In order to give our army organization in France the benefit as far as possible of all the admirable safeguards and advantages of normal business organization, and yet not destroy that which is above all things important, the system which, irrespective of business considerations, supplies most quickly articles at the point of use during military operations, General Pershing originated the idea of the General Purchasing Board, American Expeditionary Force, which, while operating under some disadvantages, has applied to the purchase of army supplies in France the safeguards of normal business. It has insured collective purchasing, prevention of competition, and coordination of effort without interfering with a principle firmly established in legislation and military procedure as a result of thousands of years of evolution.

If nothing is added to the foregoing, it may seem to overemphasize the relative importance of independent agencies of army purchase and supply, as compared with the coordinating and controlling central system, which must function with it. In the American Expeditionary Force certain large conceded and evolved powers of central control, arising out of the exigencies of war and confirmed by the Commander-in-Chief, are being exercised by the General Purchasing Agent, which powers are in effect direct and not negative. It is these direct powers not used to impede, but to regulate, expedite, and widen the action of collateral agencies, which are largely responsible for what results have been accomplished through the organization of the General Purchasing Board.

That the lessons in army supply and purchase taught by this war will find their future legislative interpretation and expression, there is little question. It will be difficult legislation to frame; for unfortunately it cannot be assumed that in the administration of the system in time of peace, it will be characterized by the high degree of cooperation and disposition to subordinate individual interest which exists among the officers of a military force in active operation, welded together by the powerful pressure of military emergency, by strong leadership, and the sacredness of the cause of their common effort. But even though it may not as yet be possible to frame a law recognizing the principles upheld herein without creating some field for bureaucratic dissensions in time of peace, yet such a law in time of war will afford the competent leadership, which always develops on such an occasion, its proper engine of highest effectiveness.

Charles G. Dawes, Colonel, Engineers, N.A.
Chairman, General Purchasing Board General Purchasing Agent, A.E.F.

Appendix B

Report of Lieutenant-Colonel Charles G. Dawes
on Boat Drill on Army Transports
and Information and Suggestions for Officers in Command of Troops

HEADQUARTERS
American Expeditionary Forces
France, September 20, 1917

1. This pamphlet publishes a copy of a report prepared by Lieutenant-Colonel Charles G. Dawes, Corps of Engineers, National Army, who was in command of boat drills for the 17th Regiment of Engineers. The memoranda herewith, intended primarily for the instruction of army officers (landsmen), are commended by experienced ship officers, including Captain J. T. W. Charles, C.B., R.D., R.N.R., the senior captain of the Cunard Line, and formerly one of the captains of the Lusitania.

2. The report is published in full for the information and guidance of all concerned. It is directed that the instructions contained herein be carefully studied by all officers in charge of troops crossing the Atlantic Ocean, and that the most energetic means be taken to carry them out, to the end that the lives of our soldiers may not be sacrificed in case of accident. Copies of this pamphlet will be distributed to all transports entering the ports of debarkation of the A.E.F.

BY COMMAND OF MAJOR-GENERAL PERSHING
JAMES G. HARBORD Lieutenant-Colonel, General Staff Chief of Staff
OFFICIAL: BENJ. ALVORD Adjutant-General

A. BOAT DRILL

INFORMATION AND SUGGESTIONS FOR OFFICERS IN COMMAND OF TROOPS ON ARMY TRANSPORTS

During the near future American soldiers must be transported by sea to France. When they are placed on the transports their officers, although for the most part landsmen with little or no sea experience, are charged with the gravest responsibilities for their care arising out of the new environment. What is written has been submitted for revision to ship officers of high standing who have been on ships when they were torpedoed. To the seaman much here written will seem superfluous, but not to the inexperienced landsman finding himself suddenly invested with new and heavy responsibilities.

The importance of the officer landsman keeping intellectually humble in gathering information from ship's officers cannot be overstated. Instances have occurred where military officers of no naval or sea experience, commanding land forces upon transports, have insisted upon exercising an authority in matters not relating directly to navigation which resulted in such a condition on the ship that if an emergency had arisen it would probably have resulted in great disaster. Hundreds of inexperienced land commanders responsible for the proper conduct of companies and regiments upon ships in times of emergency will, during the next year, march down to the ships with their men and march off on the other side in safety. But such an officer who does not march off with men who have been thoroughly instructed and drilled for a torpedo attack or other emergency will be guilty of criminal negligence.

1. *"Boat Drill."* "Boat drill" is the drill designed to get men in time of emergency from their quarters below deck or elsewhere in the shortest time and by the quickest route to their assigned positions opposite their proper lifeboats and rafts.

The officer in command of "boat drill" for a regiment should, on going on board ship, arrange with the captain of the ship or the chief officer or the naval officers in charge for the earliest possible conference on the matter of "boat drill." At such a conference the landsman in command of troops should state his complete or partial ignorance of ship methods and terms. The deference and courtesy shown his rank by the ship's officers must never lead him to "put on a front." If he knows nothing he should tell them so. They will soon find him out without his informing them, but he will save himself and them time if he will make it clear to them that he does not pretend to know. At my first conference with ship officers, they would occasionally say in connection with advice, "Of course, if you think best, you can do otherwise." If they do this, reply, "Instruct me as if I were here as an under ship officer to transmit and interpret your instructions and suggestions to troops who are simply passengers trained to act in unison at my command." Inexperience and ignorance in its association with experience and knowledge will always profit by humbleness of opinion. The ship officers know what to do in case of emergency; the landsman does not. The ship officers have been through it; the landsman has not.

Notwithstanding this, the landsman is to become practically an under ship officer, partly because he is a military commander on duty with his troops, and in part because all ships are now running short of full crews.

2. Deck Chart. The ship officer should first give you a chart of the decks of the ship from which the men are expected, in times of emergency, to take to the boats and rafts. On this chart there should be marked the position of the boats and rafts, together with the man-carrying capacity of each one. This chart will become the basis of your "boat drill." In general the ship's officers will leave to you, practically without interference, the task of getting the men on deck to their prescribed stations in the shortest period of time. When once your men are on deck the relation of the ship's officers and crew to the situation becomes different and will be discussed further on.

3. Bulkhead Doors. The ship officers will explain the operation and point out the location of bulkhead doors. They will indicate the time when the doors will be closed. This is very important information, as "boat-drill" routes must be determined upon the assumption that bulkhead doors are closed at all times.

4. "Boat-Drill" Routes. After the consultation with ship officers and receipt of the deck chart from them, the officer in command of "boat drill" should carefully explore the holds and stairways leading to the decks, both before and after the companies of his regiment have been assigned quarters. He should consult the captains of the companies for advice as to the best route for their men to the decks. *It seems to be the consensus of advice from ship and naval officers that the formations in which men should move to the deck should conform to the deck chart.* In other words, if you bring your men to deck by companies they will in many cases have to separate after getting there in going to different parts of the same deck or to different decks in order to be opposite the boats or rafts to which they are assigned. This would consume time which can be saved by having the men assigned to the same section of the deck take the same route from the hold, even though it results in the breaking of ordinary military units into new "boat-drill" units in the hold. The "boat-drill" units do not necessarily involve a change in the first location of troops by companies in the holds. Forming them simply means that in some cases the "boat-drill" unit will consist of men belonging to two different companies who have adjoining quarters, and are united into a "boat-drill" unit in reference to a convenient companionway (stairway) or a general route up.

The most of the transport ships are large, having six or seven decks, the lower decks being enclosed by the sides of the ship and constituting the quarters for the men. The way from the lowest quarters in the hold may be by several different flights of stairs not connected by a straight path, but involving the "boat-drill" unit in several turns and twists on the way up. At certain decks through one door all "boat drill" units may converge and then separate. At points where congestion is liable to occur, commissioned officers should be stationed at all times of the night so as to prevent panic and a mixing of the "boat-drill" units in case of a rush in obedience to the agreed-upon signal. If mistakes are made in the selection of routes to the deck, the first drill will generally, but not always, indicate them.

Wherever possible the contemporaneous joint use of staircases by units should be avoided, as should the crossing of routes. In some cases this will be found unavoidable. The commander should ask for suggestions from captains of companies, after the first drill, looking toward the bettering of the assigned routes to the deck. These routes, however, should be settled as soon as possible so that the men may be thoroughly accustomed to them before the voyage has progressed too far. *After they are selected the men composing the "boat-drill" units should be instructed to go to and from their quarters in the hold at all times, day and night, or from one deck to the other, by their prescribed "boat-drill" routes in order that they may take them naturally in case of attack and the sudden giving of the signals.*

In some cases, particularly on the boat deck, it is possible to place a company unbroken before the boats or rafts assigned to them, in which case it is generally possible to move it from the hold to the deck as a company "boat-drill" unit. The selection of the best routes for the different "boat-drill" units from the hold to the decks is a matter of common sense and good judgment.

5. *Lanterns.* Always ask the ship officers to give you lanterns or oil lamps to string along the "boat-drill" routes in the hold, so that if a torpedo attack puts the ship's dynamo out of commission these routes will not be left in darkness.

6. *Meetings of Regimental Officers on "Boat Drill."* Meetings of the regimental officers should be called daily to receive instructions and discuss various features of "boat drill." These instructions in turn should be communicated and explained to meetings of the non-commissioned officers by company commanders.

7. *Portholes.* A detail of two men from each company should be made whose duty it is to see that all portholes are closed at night during the entire voyage, and closed both day and night during passage through the danger zone. The reason for closing portholes at night is to render the ship less conspicuous as an object of attack. They are closed in the danger zone because, if the ship is struck and lists, she will fill more rapidly with water with open portholes, and be less liable to right herself.

8. *Doctors.* Whenever possible a doctor should be assigned to a boat and instructed to precede the men in entering the boat.

9. *Signals.* The general signal of alarm in case of attack or emergency on

the ship is given by five short blasts of the ship's whistle. Through captains all men should be instructed on this point and as to the other signals for "boat drill." They must be made thoroughly to understand that five blasts of the ship's whistle means for them, "Boat drill." For simple drill purposes the "boat-drill" signals should be given at an agreed-upon time in the holds and upon the decks by five short blasts on the bugles and officers' whistles, constantly repeated. The same bugle and whistle signals should be given in real emergency as in drill, for in certain low sections of the hold it is difficult to hear the ship's whistle. At the first sounding of the signal all men should immediately run to their quarters, put on their life-belts and all their clothes (including shoes), and then run by their prescribed routes to their assigned positions on the decks without any preliminary formation into ranks.

Two men at least of each "boat-drill" unit should be a continuing detail to go thoroughly through its quarters after the men are started up to see that none of the men are left behind. They should then join their "boat-drill" unit as fast as possible on the decks.

10. *Mess Drill.* The men gather at mess, and a separate boat drill must be given the men at mess, since an attack is liable to find them there. The men should be drilled in leaving the messroom by prescribed routes to their quarters and to their regular deck positions in "boat drill."

11. At an early stage of the voyage, hold the regiment in "boat-drill" formation on the decks and go before each "boat-drill" unit, accompanied by a ship officer (if he is available) so that he may correct any of your mistakes. Then address the men on the subject of their individual conduct in time of attack or emergency. Remember that whenever with the imposition of discipline the reasons for it can be properly given it is doubly effective. This admonition should cover the proper use of the life-preservers, and other important points which I think will be better remembered if I give the substance of what I said to each of our "boat-drill" units in the 17th.

Engineers:

Attention! What I am going to say is so important that I have brought a ship's officer with me to correct me if I make mistakes. If we are struck by a torpedo, or if any other accident happens to the ship, remember that your main reliance must be your life-preserver. The lifeboats and rafts are secondary in importance. The life-preserver comes first. If you adjust it right, you cannot sink. If you adjust it wrong, it may drown you by keeping your head under water.

Here call a man from the ranks so that all can see him and adjust his life-preserver right, explaining the reasons for each adjustment. The ship officer may be willing to do this for you.

Now listen carefully: We are most of us men who live on inland waters. Our idea is naturally that the less clothes a man has on the easier it is to keep afloat and to handle himself in the water. The ship officers now tell us we must forget all that. We must now put on all the clothes we can — shoes, leggings, and all. It will be all right to put on an overcoat. Then put on your life-preserver. It will float you, clothes and all. If you do not have your clothes on, you may soon perish in the water from exposure. With your clothes and shoes on, the water next your body will not be so cold, and you will last longer and be in better shape when the boats come to pick you up. When we get into the danger zone you will be notified. Then keep your clothes and life-preservers on day and night.

Now listen again! If anything happens, and you are called on deck by the five blasts from the ship's whistle, or the bugles or the officers' whistles, when you get on deck do not interfere with the ship's crew who are handling the lifeboats and rafts'tackle. *Keep away from the ropes. Do not crowd around the boats and rafts so as to interfere with their being launched. Obey any orders given by the ship officer on deck. Give the ship's crew room to work in. THEY ARE DOING IT FOR YOU.*

12. From the time you have got your men on deck, both you and they should be in the hands of the officers of the ship so far as the giving of orders is concerned. The circumstances that may arise cannot be foretold. The boat chart embodies the ship officers' ideas of the best distribution of lifeboats and rafts. But the ship may list suddenly, making impossible the launching of boats and rafts on one side and precipitating the line of men formed on that side on top of the men opposite. The sudden listing forward, backward, or sideways of the boat may entirely disarrange every programme, throw men in a mass into situations where boats or rafts cannot be taken — prevent the launching of boats and rafts and cause great confusion. All men on the open decks, especially those on which the islands are located, should be warned that in any case of emergency, and the sudden listing of the ship, they must keep clear of material sliding along the decks or falling from the islands.

Many other things arising from the explosion of a torpedo may in an instant change the situation. The ship may sink in a few minutes or be hours in sinking. It is because of their actual experience that ship officers do not attach much importance to any use of military commands or programmes after the men are on deck. When they are on deck the situation should be left practically to the ship's officers and to the men themselves. An attitude on the part of a military commander which would discourage individual initiative at such a time might mean unnecessary loss of life.

However, keep constantly in your mind and in that of your men the necessity of not interfering with the ship's crew in their work on the ropes and lifeboats and rafts. The ship's officer may ask for help in handling the boats, and you should have already prepared a detail of men in advance for this emergency. *Keep your men from interfering with the ship's officers and men. Consider yourself practically an under ship officer taking your orders from the ship's officer in charge of your deck.* The above is submitted.

(Signed) CHARLES G. DAWES
Lieutenant-Colonel of Engineers
National Army

Paris, April 13, 1918
From: The General Purchasing Agent, A.E.F.
To: The Commander-in-Chief, A.E.F.
Subject: Military Control Allied Service of Supply.

My Dear General:

From the time that you landed in France you have exerted an influence for coordination of effort and centralization of authority in inter-Ally activity which has had the most far-reaching results. You have exerted this influence among the Allies during the time that you were creating a coordinating and centralizing system in your command. To carry out the purpose of the centralization of purchase and supply in your own army, to become connected with which effort you called me from St. Nazaire, you have as a matter of fact devised the plan the extension of which to the entire Allied operations would seem now vitally essential to Allied success in the war. What I am to suggest to you arises from conclusions based upon knowledge and experience gained in the position in which you have placed me. Even with the conviction which I have of the vital importance of the matter I would hesitate to call it to your attention, were it not for your constant demonstration of the desire to subordinate everything, including your own personal authority as an independent commander, to the common purpose of an Allied victory. To willingly sacrifice individual authority and individual prestige in time of emergency for the sake of a common cause is the highest test of greatness and one which, in all your actions over here, you have stood. The power and influence of the great people of the United States and their assets in men and material with which to secure victory are in the hands of the President and yourself, and you have rightly interpreted their spirit when you notified General Foch to do with you and your army as he might desire. In this offer you have already taken the step, the proper carrying out of which I am going to suggest in this letter. The peculiar position of the United States in this situation, including your own relation thereto, is such that upon the initiative of our Government alone is it possible to accomplish it.

The general proposition is this: that just as there is now a unified military command of the Allies at the front, in other words a merging and consolidation of three distinct independent military authorities into one military authority (General Foch), there must be a corresponding merging of all separate individual authority of the Allies in reference to the Service of Supply into one military authority responsible to the corresponding military authority at the front. One is just as necessary as the other. In fact, for every argument for the necessity of the Foch command at the front, there exist two arguments for a similar authority for supply and transportation in the rear. I mean by this supplies from America, supplies from England, supplies from France, and the land and sea transportation therefor, warehousing and handling thereof. The Foch command at the front necessitates similar control of the rear, and in this case the rear means France, England, the United States, and perhaps Italy. Before discussing the method of accomplishing this let me illustrate in a manner which has no doubt often occurred to you its overwhelming importance. The United States is at this time using an immense amount of tonnage for the purpose of building enormous warehouses and dockage facilities. It is doing this notwithstanding the warehouses of France and England are being emptied and will continue to grow emptier. The French Government has used to a very large extent private warehouses for storing of supplies. Owing to the steadily lessening amount of supplies there is a large amount of French warehouse capacity now idle, and at the same time we are proceeding, at the heavy expense of current tonnage, on plans to immensely increase our warehouse facilities. Who is there, with authority to act, to determine from a bird's-eye view the relation of existing English and French warehouse capacity in France to the present warehousing and transportation projects of the A.E.F.? It cannot be done, except in a haphazard and inefficient way, unless by one man with military authority extending over all the Allies. This man, for the same reason that led to the selection of General Foch, must be a Frenchman and England and the United States must accept him. He must be given exactly the same authority toward the ocean and land transportation, engineering, and supply activities of the entire Allied forces which you have given me in connection with purchase and supply and certain other activities of the A.E.F., his authority being created by the same method. The position of General Purchasing Agent, A.E.F., you built up by a system of compelling the partial cession of independent authority. The weight of your own great powers and personality was thrown into the effort of compelling the creation of this authority, and when any independent head showed signs of not recognizing the necessity for it or bending to it, you broke him on the cross. What has made the success of the organization of my office is its now unquestioned power and authority over independent agencies. I never have had a meeting of the General Purchasing Board except on minor matters such as the distributing of office space or matters relating to the collection of information — never on the determination of action. Our organization is military. The reason why our Allied Boards fail is because action has to be by a board and not by an individual. The organization of the entire transportation and supply of the Allies must be military in its nature and not based upon the principles of either oligarchy or democracy. I do not have to argue this to a man like you. Some time after this war is over get Herodotus and read the discussion of the seven Persian generals when they were riding horseback on their way to Persia discussing the best form of government for them to set up in the place of the monarchy of an assassinated king. If we do not have military management and military control we may fail and a German army at the ports may save us the trouble of unloading some of our engineering material from ships, thus devoted, which should have been bringing men and food to have stopped our enemies where they are now. It may be that our present plans may not have to be abandoned or materially altered, but the point I make is that it is impossible with this great multiplicity of civil boards, crisscross authority between the Allies, and lack of coordination in supply effort to properly determine the matter or properly act after its determination. Take the question of joint supplies. Impelled by the same emergency pressure that compelled unity of command at the front, the French and the English are calling upon me for information as to supplies of our army, with intimations of the necessity of pooling, etc. I am working the best I can in coordination with the French and English in all these matters, but I am in a position where I realize that these questions can be settled, in time to be of avail, only by military authority which, gathering its information, acts, and does not discuss. Who knows to-day, considering the Allied forces as one army, whether or not the great supplies of steel, oil, barbed wire, rubber tires, chloroform, sugar, picks and shovels, forage, clothing, etc., existing in France, England, and the United States are being marshaled in Foch's rear by the quickest routes to proper points, to ware-houses built or to be built, considering both present and future needs and the present military emergency? In this present great military emergency shall we again pursue the timeworn policy of appointing an Allied Board to secure this information, and then, after long delay, subject the self-evident conclusions arising therefrom to the discussion of three separate authorities, influenced by personal or national considerations, personal ambitions, and counter-purposes?

In writing this way I almost feel as if I were insulting your intelligence, who have been the chief leader and have made the greatest personal sacrifice in the effort to apply remedies for this sort of business. If the suggestions herein you cannot force into adoption with the weight and prestige of your country and your own personal power, then we must go back at this time to a new effort to concentrate authority in a new Board of the Allies to do by common consent and town-meeting methods that which should come at once from central military authority extending over all. No one knows better than you what this means in delay, and what delay may mean in a time like this, in a war like this. Can you not force the Allies to agree to adopt immediately the principles involved in the relations of your own Military Purchasing Board to the entire Service of Supply of your own army through which this entire Allied supply and transportation situation shall be placed in the hands of a French military officer with the same kind of authority over the Generals in command of the different services of the rear of the Allies that your General Purchasing Agent has over the separate purchase and supply services of the American army? The authority for the French command of these services could be created by the same method through which you have placed authority in me for our purchase and supply situation in the A.E.F. The three Generals in command of the Allied rear should be coordinated and controlled by French military authority as are the members of the General Purchasing Board by the General Purchasing Agent. As in the case of the purchasing board of the A.E.F., this does not mean the radical interference with the conduct of current activities. It does not even mean the lessening of current activities. It means their proper coordination and intelligent direction, and above all it means that when once a necessity is determined, the authority is in existence to compel its immediate relief. The influence of such unified military command of the service of the rear of the Allies upon the question of tonnage, use of material, economy of construction, and general betterment of conditions, must be self evident. To go with unified military action at the front must come unified military support at the rear. You are the only man that can bring this about. If it was anybody else than you, even under the tremendous pressure of the present emergency, I should hesitate to suggest it; for human nature is weak. Nothing but the weakness and ambition of human nature prevented the unification of military command which you have always advocated until the death of hundreds of thousands and continued military failure brought individual and national ambition under the yoke of a common necessity involving existence itself.

General Harbord took dinner with me last night and spent the evening and I presented these views to him. He did not express himself, but I judge from his demeanor that he was not entirely unimpressed. I understand from Harbord that you may be here within the next few days. I had intended to come to Chaumont to present verbally what I am writing here. There is probably nothing in this letter which has not already been considered by you. However, now that unification of military command at the front has been secured, I am sure that the application of your General Purchasing Board idea to the service of the rear of the Allies is that which will go farther just now in bringing a successful conclusion to this war than any other thing.

Yours,
Charles G. Dawes
Colonel, Engineers, N. A.

Appendix D

Cablegram from Pershing to the Adjutant-General

April 19, 1918
Adjutant-General
Washington, D.C.

Paragraph 1. For the Chief of Staff. No. 953.

The matter of tonnage is so vital to success of Allies that every possible ton is being cut from our requirements during the next three or four months as already indicated by reductions reported. A careful study of Allied demands for tonnage as a whole makes it evident that further reduction can be made if we pool all supplies that are in common use by Allied armies and certain reductions could also be made in supplies for civil populations of Allied countries. We have at last combined military forces under the supreme command of one man and should do the same thing as to supplies and war material. The appointment of many coordinating boards has led to confusion and loss of positive action. Strongly urge that supply question be placed in the hands of one military head with power to determine and decide on disposition and distribution of Allied supplies in Europe and determine what shall be shipped from United States. Much information necessary for prompt action is already available, but no one has power to decide. Supreme War Council comes in the same class with other boards in its lack of power. One man in military control of Allied supplies is necessary. Principle involved is foundation of A.E.F. Purchasing Board. The next three or four months should at least be covered by this arrangement. The class of supplies such as: aviation (which has been taken up in my cable No. 904); munitions (as far as possible considering different calibers); coal, horses, gasoline, oats, hay, meat, flour, shoes, sugar, wagons, tentage, demountable barracks, lumber, timber, supply depots, and warehouses are the principal items that could be pooled. Such pooling would affect material saving in our construction programme including railroad construction. Have presented this suggestion to Mr. Clemenceau, who approves. Shall go to London Sunday to adjust questions relative to handling our troops that go to British. While there shall submit pooling plan to Mr. Lloyd George. Have designated Colonel Dawes, who made this study, to confer with French representatives to be named by Mr. Clemenceau. Shall report progress later.

Pershing

Appendix E

Letter from Dawes to Pershing, August 24, 1918

August 24, 1918

From: The General Purchasing Agent, A.E.F.

To: The Commander-in-Chief, A.E.F.

Subject: Activities of the Military Board of Allied Supply and
Relation of American Member, Military Board of Allied Supply, to the
General Staff, A.E.F.

I. The Military Board of Allied Supply, the formation of which by
the Governments was due to your initiative and strenuous efforts as
Commander-in-Chief of the A.E.F., has now been in existence for two
months. Its activities may be summed up as follows:

First. The first composite picture of the motor transport of the three
armies has been made, the conclusions arising from which are self-evident
and are to-day affecting our army policy. It has considered the question of a
mobile automobile reserve behind the Allied armies, securing the information for the respective Commanders-in-Chief in their determination of it.

Second. For the first time a system for the proper circulation and handling of automobile transports, considering the Allied armies as a whole, is
being studied and arranged and will soon be put into form to be submitted
for your approval.

Third. The first composite study of the forage situation has been made
and in connection therewith you have reduced the American forage ration
to the British standard and issued additional regulations against waste, thus
tending to relieve a later forage crisis among all the Allied armies.

Fourth. Ammunition between the Americans and the French has been
pooled along the front.

Fifth. For the first time a map has been prepared showing complete
installations in the rear of the three armies as to locations. When the final
details of capacity are secured the importance of this map in connection
with the consideration of the construction policies of the three armies is
manifest.

Sixth. The creation of an inter-Allied reserve of 60 c.m. railway material
and personnel is under consideration, which, whether it results in action or
not, will for the first time give such information as to the common situation as to greatly and beneficially affect the individual policy of each army.

Seventh. The investigations of the Board in connection with labor have
demonstrated the impracticability of pooling the same and therefore stimu-
lated the independent agencies of recruiting.

Eighth. The consideration of the general wood and tie situation, while it precipitated coordination in this particular connection with the Ministry of Armament instead of through the Board, unquestionably greatly contributed to the reaching of the recent satisfactory understanding with the French on this subject.

Ninth. It has demonstrated that through it alone can a coming crisis in supply, transportation, and technical military handling of the Allied rear be measured so as to indicate and to justify the necessary and appropriate preparation for it on the part of each army.

Tenth. Lastly, and of great importance, no member of the General Staff or chief of independent service of the A.E.F. has attended one of the meetings of the Board and listened to the discussion of the Allied situation as a whole without having derived in my judgment a more intelligent understanding of how his activities, whether under authoritative direction or not, can be conducted in better coordination with similar activities of our allies.

The importance of its work from a tactical, supply, and military standpoint, in spite of great opposition, is self evident.

2. In some respects the name Military Board of Allied Supply is unfortunate. It is apt to create in the minds of the chiefs of services the idea that it is an organization primarily to pool and divide supplies; in other words, an organization through which somebody is trying to deprive the A.E.F. of a portion of its already inadequate supply or through which the A.E.F. is seeking to secure replenishment from the inadequate supplies of the other armies. Facing an approaching inadequacy of supply, the chief, with this conception of the Military Board of Allied Supply, naturally sees in its existence no possible good and only a menace. We encounter a natural fear in all the armies of a possible authoritative action of any outside body enabled to interfere with supplies. This feeling ignores the useful activities of the Board in connection with the coordinated use of transportation from a tactical standpoint and of construction coordination, to say nothing of other important matters entirely disassociated with any question of pooled supplies. As a matter of fact, however, with each army, confronted as it is by insufficient supplies, a situation is indicated in which in the future the existence of this Board and its powers is rendered of supreme importance not only to the A.E.F., but to the other armies as well. The continued importation of American troops and the present condition of supplies will inevitably create a crisis. Through the force of your personality constantly exercised and through continued and stern admonition, you have taught the A.E.F. already to think in terms of emergency and deficit rather than in terms of surplus, for no one has realized better than yourself that the time is rapidly approaching when a surplus will turn to a deficit and finally

an acute deficit. At such a time the military machinery upon which reliance must be placed is the Military Board of Allied Supply. The continuance of the importation of troops during the fall, unless accompanied by a coordinated importation of supplies — apparently impossible — will unquestionably at times create points and situations along the fighting line where military authority and not common consent must be relied upon to insure such a distribution of supplies as will maintain the troops actually at the front. In the distribution of supplies this Board may not commence to function until the absence of its functioning means in a way that is evident to all that fighting troops must leave the line. We must look ahead. If one feels that there will not be a different situation than exists at present about the division of food supplies when related to the continuance of actual military operations, it is only necessary to recall the attitude of our friends the English in connection with ships up until the time of the German victory around Calais, after which they turned Allied defeat into certain Allied success by the sea transportation of the bulk of the American army. When the time of real crisis arises this Board is the agency through which an intelligent view of the situation is practicable and through which proper measures can be taken. It is also the only body, by reason of its common knowledge, which can give advance notice of approaching emergencies and make the suggestions to the armies useful in the attempt to avoid them. If, from the minds of all, there could be removed the shadow of apprehension that an outside authority was looking with designing eyes upon our insufficient stocks, it would contribute to the feeling of earnest cooperation with the Military Board of Allied Supply. As the segregation of the troops into armies of different nationalities does not affect in any way the desirability of central military control of movement, so the fact of the existence of a large field army of the United States should not be allowed to overshadow the necessity in times of emergency, for the support of that army, of a central Allied control over certain transportation and supplies especially in the military zone. Upon the basis of the retention by the Commanders-in-Chief of the respective armies of the final authority for the distribution and transportation of supplies to their respective armies, it will still be through the machinery of the Military Board of Allied Supply which you have created, and which cannot be set in motion without your approval, that part of the supply and transportation business of the Allied armies which is inseparably connected with general tactical movements will be provided for without interfering with such final authority.

3. Largely because of the personality of such men as McAndrew, Moseley, and Eltinge, with whom I chiefly work, there is between the American member of the Military Board of Allied Supply and the General

Staff the closest cooperation and understanding. The crisis of the present situation from the supply and transportation standpoint will probably be reached within from sixty to ninety days. To properly meet it the Military Board of Allied Supply and the General Staff must practically function as a unit. The authority actually existing in the Military Board of Allied Supply in connection with matters of coordination, under the terms of the agreements which you secured from M. Clemenceau, is great and it is necessary that it should be. Power governing the rear of the three armies cannot be exercised by the staff of a separate army nor can the powers of the Military Board of Allied Supply be set in motion in the way that you intended unless its decisions, approved directly by you and based upon a common viewpoint (impossible to be obtained by a staff not represented on the Board), are accepted by each army as automatically and in as un-questioned a manner as a direct order from a Commander-in-Chief himself. Conflicts having their roots in human nature, which are inevitable between two bodies with concurrent jurisdictions, one acting under one authority and one under another, must be avoided. A very sure prevention for this between the General Staff and the Military Board of Allied Supply is to have the supreme authority of the unit, to wit, yourself or the General Staff, represented authoritatively on any outside board which is created to coordinate and regulate the unit. It is a tribute to your great Staff that as yet the Military Board of Allied Supply has experienced from it only the closest cooperation and understanding. If this does not continue, it will arise out of the fact alone that there cannot be between the General Staff and myself as the present member of the Board continuous juxtaposition and common knowledge of all the elements of a problem. The first view-point of the Staff is properly the necessities of the A.E.F. irrespective of necessities directly counter of the three armies considered as one. With the General Staff in possession of the complete knowledge in detail, derived from the composite pictures of the necessities of the three armies presented by the Military Board of Allied Supply, a more proper military coordination and cooperation will be reached. As you yourself have indicated, the A.E.F. may be in a position under certain circumstances and at certain times where it must subordinate and subrogate its temporary needs for the common good in order to make sure in the long run its own existence through final victory. The General Staff cannot be the judges of what is in the long run for the interest of the A.E.F. until it is put in a position by knowledge of the facts relating to the three armies as to what is essential and what is not essential for the A.E.F. to do as a unit in its own best interest. I therefore suggest that you personally appoint as a member of the Military Board of Allied Supply, either in my place or as an additional member, either the Chief of Staff, General Moseley, or Colonel Eltinge. I am of the opinion that to have the American and French rears properly coordinated, an authority to match Colonel Payot's, who is in command of the French rear in the Zone of the Advance, should exist in the representation of the A E.F. upon this Board. The gentlemen named have had experience arising not only out of military service, but continued contact with the technical rear of our own army, neither of which I have had. They also have the bird's-eye view of the operations of the rear of the A.E.F., which is as essential to a proper understanding of its necessities as is the knowledge arising only out of a membership on the Military Board of Allied Supply of the necessities of the rear of the Allied armies considered as one. An order of the Military Board of Allied Supply thus constituted would produce a mental *status quo* on the part of the chiefs of the American services much more conducive to prompt and efficient action than would otherwise be the case. If the Military Board of Allied Supply was known by the army to be expressing the conviction of the Commander-in-Chief personally, which of course is always the case, since its every action is first submitted to you, attention would be given primarily by the chiefs of the services to carrying out its mandates with less discussion of their wisdom which tends to delay.

Charles G. Dawes,
Colonel, Engineers

Appendix F

Memorandum, the Military Inter-Allied Committee at Coubert, September 2, 1918

In the course of the sitting of the Military Inter-Allied Committee at Coubert, on September 2, 1918, General Pétain and General Pershing made the following statements:

General Pétain said he wished to express his appreciation of the excellent work the Committee had been doing toward the pooling of all the resources of the Allies in motor transportation. He observed that the Allies had been led to the conclusion that such a pooling was necessary by the experience in the French armies since the beginning of the War. In the first part of the war, he stated, every division, army corps, army commander in the French army wanted to have his own motor transportation. The result was a tremendous waste of trucks. Units at rest retained material which was much in excess of their requirements while units engaged in active operations were short of transportation. The total amount of available trucks was inadequate; the Commander-in-Chief had not at his disposal the transportation he required for active sectors of the front. Therefore they were led to centralize the motor transportation,

First, in each army.

Second, for the whole of the French armies.

The results were most satisfactory. He wished to point out that the principle which was true for motor transportation was also true for all sorts of resources, material, and facilities. He pointed out the question of artillery material and recalled the fact that units engaged in active operations required a quantity of artillery far greater than those in quiet sectors. The first thing to study, when large units are to be engaged in such operations, is the amount of artillery that must be given to them in excess of their normal allowance. This has led to the creation of the French General Reserve of Artillery, which is at the disposal of the Commander-in-Chief to be distributed as he sees fit among his armies. He believes in the necessity of extending that principle, and creating a General Inter-Allied Reserve of Artillery, at the disposal of the Commander-in-Chief of the Allied armies. His conclusion was that the pooling principle was the only way to economize all sorts of material, and therefore have the material available when and where necessary. Of course its application is difficult, therefore the Committee are entitled to our gratitude for the very complicated and useful work they are doing.

Appendix G

Letter from John Pershing to Viscount Milner
American Expeditionary Forces, Office of the Commander-in-Chief
Personal
France, September 2, 1918
Rt. Hon. Viscount Milner, G.C.B., Secretary of State for War,
London, England

My Dear Lord Milner:

The attached letter [my letter to Commander-in-Chief, dated August 24, 1918] [See text for the letter] of Colonel Dawes clearly sets forth the importance of the coordination work of the Military Board of Allied Supply in the rear of the three armies, as well as the necessity for the closest touch with it by the General Staff of each army.

Desiring to keep Colonel Dawes as the American member, I have not followed his suggestion to substitute a member of my General Staff in his place, but have given him authority, in his discretion, to call in members of the Staff and chiefs of the services to assist him.

Therefore, in the case of the French and American armies there is the closest contact and cooperation of the General Staffs with the Military Board of Allied Supply. The British General Staff, however, does not have direct representation on the Board, since the British member represents the War Office alone.

Since, for the preservation of final authority of the respective Commanders-in-Chief over the lines of communications of their respective armies, Marshal Haig and I have not acceded to Marshal Foch's desire for central control of the rear under Colonel Payot, and since this Board provides a proper agency for central control, without lessening the final authority, I earnestly request that the British General Staff be given representation on the Board in addition to the War Office in order to further strengthen it in its important work.

If General Travers-Clarke should be directly represented on the Board as is a similar authority in the other two armies, much delay in its work would be avoided and its general purposes be effectively forwarded.

With expression of my high personal and official esteem, believe me,
Respectfully yours John J. Pershing

Incl.P.S. My previous correspondence on this subject was directed to the Prime Minister. J. J. P.

Appendix H

Letter from H. C. Smither, Commanding General, S.O.S., to Colonel
Charles G. Dawes, General Purchasing Agent, August 31, 1918.

American Expeditionary Forces
Headquarters Services Of Supply
   31 August, 1918
   From: Commanding General, S.O.S.
   To: Colonel Charles G. Dawes, General Purchasing Agent
Subject: Labor Bureau

   1. The Labor Bureau has been transferred to the newly organized Army
Service Corps. The efforts of its procurement branch, being confined to
the procurement of labor in Europe, will continue to operate solely under
your direction, in the same manner as do the procurement divisions of all
other Supply Departments in respect to supplies in Europe.

   2. Upon the occasion of this passing of the Labor Bureau from your
direct supervision and control, the Commanding General desires me to
express to you his keen appreciation of the manner in which, under your
able administration, the Labor Bureau rapidly grew from its inception to
its present thorough-going organization. During that period it has been
the agency which has enabled important projects to be continued under
construction. Dealing with laborers of many different nationalities, a mul-
titude of vexatious problems were involved in the successful management
of this organization. All of these you have met and solved in the most
expeditious and capable manner.

   3. Please permit me to add my personal appreciation, as I have personally watched this development from its beginning.

   By order of the C. G.: H. C. Smither, Asst. Chief of Staff, G-4

Appendix I

Telegrams exchanged between General Harbord and General Pershing
on the occasion of the St. Mihiel victory

General Pershing, C.-in-C., AEF.
September 13, 1918
Congratulations on your birthday and your fine work thereon. Nearly three hundred years ago Oliver Cromwell on the 13th day of the month, September, went into battle quoting Psalm 68, now the Episcopal morning prayer for that date, "Let God arise and let his enemies be scattered; let them also that hate him. Like as the smoke vanishes so shalt thou drive them away." Harbord

Major-General Harbord, September 19, 1918
Tours
Many thanks for your birthday telegram. Your old division might well be termed The Ironsides, though I doubt whether they went to battle quoting Psalm 68. - Pershing

Appendix J

Charles G. Dawes' note on Edward R. Stettinius

CGD: Edward R. Stettinius brought to the assistance of the United States Government an unusual experience in connection with munitions of war. Shortly after the outbreak of the Great War, he organized and directed, for Messrs. J. P. Morgan & Co., all purchases in the United States of war supplies for the British and French Governments, which purchases reached an amount not far short of four billion dollars, and, by meeting the Allied deficit of munitions at a critical time, did much to save the Allied cause.

As Surveyor-General of Supplies, to which office he was appointed on February 13, 1918; as a member of the War Council, which he entered a month later; as Second Assistant Secretary of War, named by the President on April 6, 1918; as representative of the United States on the InterAllied Munitions Council, Paris, from July, 1918, to the Armistice; and as Special Representative of the War Department in Europe from August, 1918, to December, 1918, he contributed with conspicuous success to the effective prosecution of the war.

His first activities in Washington were directed toward a solution of the munitions supply problem, and particularly toward the coordination of purchases and the adjustment of contracts for munitions and supplies to the military programme. When this situation had been effectively met by the centralization and coordination of the purchase, production, and supply of war material in the United States, he went overseas. He represented the United States War Department on the Inter-Allied Munitions Council and sat in conference with the Ministers of Munitions of England, France, and Italy, in the consideration of measures designed to exercise control over the munitions resources of the Allies and to direct their utilization in the general interest of the Allied cause.

In addition to discharging abroad other duties specifically assigned to him by the Secretary of War, he gave to General Pershing, Commander-in-Chief of the A.E.F., in the language of General Pershing's citation, "invaluable assistance in varied and important matters," these matters involving problems of supply, the administration of the financial transactions of the A.E.F., and, after the Armistice, the setting-up of organizations for the cancellation of contracts and the liquidation of the business affairs of the A.E.F. in Europe. Not the least of the services rendered by Mr. Stettinius were the signally successful negotiations with our Allies in the procurement of munitions which were required abroad in consequence of the large number of troops sent abroad in the spring, summer, and fall of 1918.

Subsequently Mr. Stettinius returned to the United States, and, as a result of his study and recommendations, the United States Liquidation Commission, War Department, was formed to assume general charge of the sale of supplies and the liquidation of the affairs of the A.E.F. in Europe. He made a second journey to Europe in the spring of 1919 with members of the Commission, assisting them in organization and serving in an advisory capacity until July, 1919.

For his services to the War Department he received the Distinguished Service Medal. The French Government, in recognition of what his labors had contributed, not only to the effectiveness of the French supply of munitions from the United States, but also to the whole Allied cause, conferred upon him the rank of Commander of the Legion of Honor. The Belgian Government conferred upon him the rank of Commander of the Crown.

Appendix K

Secret A.E.F. orders, October 7, 1918
Secret 1st Army, A.E.F.
Field Orders 7 October, 1918. 12 Hours
No. 46.
(MAPS: Same as Field Order No. 20)

1. No change in the hostile situation.
The Allied Armies continue their attack.

2. The 1st American Army will seize and hold the heights west of Romagne-sous-Montfaucon and the Côtes de Meuse east of Consenvoye on October 8, 1918.

3. (A) The 5th Corps

(1) The 5th Corps, reinforced by the 1st Division and by one brigade of infantry of the 91st Division, will attack at an hour designated by the Corps Commander.

(2) It will capture the heights west of Romagne-sous-Montfaucon while covering its right by capturing and holding the Cunel heights. Special precautions will be taken to cover the left flank of the attack, especially on the front Fléville—Sommerance exclusive.

(3) Zone of action:

Right Boundary — No change.

Left Boundary — Baulny exclusive; Exermont inclusive; Montrefagne inclusive; Fléville exclusive.

(B) The 17th French Corps will attack in accordance with F.O. No. 39.

(C) 4th Corps, 2d Colonial Corps, 33d French Corps — No change in mission.

(D) The 3d Corps

(1) The 3d Corps will protect the flanks of the attack of the 5th Corps and 17th Corps.

(2) It will push reconnaissances to the front and assist the attack of the 5th and 17th Corps with artillery fire. It will be prepared to attack and seize the heights in its immediate front upon orders from the Army Commander. The 33d Division will be held in readiness to carry out the stated plans of the 17th Corps.

(E) The 1st Corps

(1) The 1st Corps will protect the left of the attack of the 5th Corps.

(2) It will push reconnaissances to the front and assist the attack of the 5th Corps with artillery fire. It will be prepared to advance upon orders of the Army Commander.

(3) Zone of Action:

Right Boundary—Baulny inclusive; Exermont exclusive; Montrefagne exclusive; Fléville inclusive.

Left Boundary — No change.

(F) The Army Artillery will support the attack of the 5th and 17th Corps and will concentrate upon the hostile batteries and positions in the heights Bois de Gesnes west of Romagne and on the east bank of the Meuse.

(G) Changes in corps zones of action and the attachment of the 1st Division and one brigade of the 91st Division to the 5th Corps will take effect at 17 hours, October 7.

4. Administrative details — No change.

5. P. C.'s and Axis of Liaison — No change.

By command of General Pershing:

H. A. Drum
Chief of Staff

Appendix L

Correspondence concerning appointment of Charles Dawes as
Commander of the Legion of Honor, November 1918

France, November 24, 1918
Colonel Duchene
Cabinet du Maréchal Pétain
Grand Quartier Général Français

My Dear Colonel:

The Chief of Staff of the Armies of the North and of the Northeast
has submitted to General Pershing a proposition to appoint to the grade
of Commander of the Legion of Honor, General Charles G. Dawes, of
our service, and to the grade of Chevalier of the Legion of Honor, 1st
Lieutenants Thomas Cassady and Alexander Hune Keith.

General Pershing is very pleased to learn of the distinction which it
is proposed to confer upon these officers, and would be glad to see them
decorated provided these propositions still maintain.

Very truly yours,
Carl Boyd
Colonel, A.D.C.

American Candidature for a decoration in the Legion of Honor
Proposition made by the President of the *Comité Interallié des Ravitaillements*

For the grade of: Commander of the Legion of Honor.

In favor of: Dawes, Charles G.

Grade: Brigadier-General.

Corps or Service: Engineer Corps.

Functions: President of the Purchasing Board, Representative of the
American Army on the Comité Interallié des Ravitaillements.

Date of arrival in France: August, 1917.

Date on which relations were established with the French Service
making propositions: April, 1918.

Duration of these relations: Still in course, nine months.

French decorations already received: None.

General appreciation: Has always had at heart to ensure the most intimate liaison and the most complete cooperation between the French and
American Services; always endeavored to smooth out all difficulties and

to assure the most cordial understanding between the two armies, as well as the most effective aid from the American Army to the French Army.

The D.G.C.RA.

President of the Comité Interallié des Ravitaillements

Signed: Ch. Payot

Appendix M

Correspondence Related to the Awarding of the Distinguished Service
Medal to Charles G. Dawes, 1919

General Headquarters American Expeditionary Forces Personal
Division, France, January 9, 1919

From: The Adjutant General, American E.F. To: Brigadier-General
Charles G. Dawes, U.S. Army. Subject: Distinguished Service Medal.

I. Cablegram number 2414-R received from the War Department January
8, 1919, announces the award to you, by the President, of the Distinguished
Service Medal for exceptionally meritorious and distinguished service as
set forth below:

Brigadier-General Charles G. Dawes:

For exceptionally meritorious and distinguished services.

He rendered most conspicuous services in the organization of the
General Purchasing Board, as General Purchasing Agent of the
American Expeditionary Forces, and as the representative of the United
States Army on the Military Board of Allied Supply. His rare abilities,
sound business judgment, and aggressive energy were invaluable in se-
curing needed supplies for the American Armies in Europe.

2. You will be informed later in regard to the time and place of the
presentation of the Medal awarded you.

By command of General Pershing:
J. A. Ulio
Adjutant-General

American Expeditionary Forces Office of the Commander in Chief
France, March 28, 1919

Brigadier-General Charles G. Dawes
General Purchasing Agent
American E.F.
My Dear General:

Now that active operations have ceased, I desire to convey my sincere
appreciation and heartiest congratulations to you and the members of
your splendid organization on the great results accomplished and invaluable assistance rendered to our cause. Due to the tireless, patriotic efforts
of yourself and your highly competent assistants, your organization has
not only succeeded in securing a vast amount of supplies greatly needed in
the course of operations, but has accomplished this object in a scientific,

business-like manner that warrants more laudable expressions than ordinary terms of commendation.

With unswerving zeal, coupled with the gift of picking assistants who possessed the highest degree of specialized ability in multifarious lines of endeavor, you had built up an organization that stood unparalleled; fulfilling every demand made upon it with celerity and thoroughness.

The magnitude of your task was enormous; the innumerable demands made upon your organization would have disheartened any other but unselfish, patriotic, able Americans; yet you and the men of large affairs who responded so readily to the call have achieved success.

Likewise may it be said of the lesser personnel in your organization, who, actuated by a high sense of duty, have performed their work so admirably. In the name of the American Expeditionary Forces, I thank them one and all. These few words of appreciation are indeed but small reward for the magnificent service you rendered the common cause.

Sincerely yours,
John J. Pershing

Appendix N

Farewell Telegram from 17th Engineers to Charles G. Dawes,
March 9, 1919.

Telegram
Headquarters, Seventeenth Engineers (railway)
Base Section No. 1, S.O.S., A.E.F.

March 9, 1919 (1.30 P.M.)
Brig-Gen Charles G. Dawes
General Purchasing Agent, A.E.F.
Paris

It is with deep regret that the officers and men of the Seventeenth Engineers bid farewell to their former Lieutenant-Colonel. Each and every member of the original Seventeenth, as well as the replacements, consider you as their own true friend. Your personal magnetism, combined with your rare executive ability, has won for you the friendship and admiration of all. We are unable to express in words the thanks which we owe to you for the service rendered to the regiment. We wish you continued success in your great undertaking. Good-bye.

Coe

Appendix O

Correspondence concerning the awarding of the *Croix de Guerre* to
Charles G. Dawes, July 1919

Le Maréchal
Commandant En Chef
Les Armeés Alliées
Etat-Major
Le 6 Juillet, 1919
20 Section
Paris, 4 Bis Boulevard
Des Invalides No. 3132.
Le Maréchal De France, *Commandant en Chef les Armeés Alliées*.
To Brigadier-General Charles G. Dawes, *Representative of the American Army on the Military Board of Allied Supply, 104 Ave. des Champs- Élysées.*

I have decided to cite you to the order of the army, in recognition of the eminent services you have rendered during the operations to the Franco-American cooperation and to the general cause of the Allies

Being obliged to absent myself, I regret not to be able to present to you myself the Croix de Guerre before your departure. I have delegated General Payot to present it to you in my name.

By order:
Weygand
Chief of Staff

Commandement En Chef
Des Armeés Alliées Etat-Major General
Direction Genérale
Le 8 Juillet 1919
Des Communications et
Des Ravitaillement
Aux Armées No. 578/C.R.
Le Général Payot, *Directeur Général des Communications et des Ravitaillements aux Armées, Président du Comité Interallié des Ravitaillements.*
To Monsieur Le Brigadier-Général Dawes, *Comité Interallié des Ravitaillements.*

I have the honor to inform you that by order No. 3127, dated July 6, 1919, the Marshal of France, Commander-in-Chief of the Allied Armies, has decided to cite you in the orders of the Army.

I am happy to quote you below the motif of your citation: "In the course of the operations of 1918, has assured a complete union over the supplies between the American and French Armies. By his breadth of spirit and his constant effort to put in common the resources of the two armies, he has permitted to be realized under the best possible conditions the community of efforts which conducted the Americans and French together to Victory."

Ch. Payot

Selected Bibliography

Chase, Joseph Cummings. *Soldiers All: Portraits and Sketches of the Men of the A. E. F.* New York: George H. Doran Company, 1920.

Chernow, Ron. *The House of Morgan: An American Banking Dynasty and the Rise of Modern Finance.* New York: Grove Press, 1990.

Ciment, James and Thaddeus Russell, editors. *The Home Front Encyclopedia: United States, Britain, and Canada in World Wars I and II.* Volume 1. Santa Barbara, CA: ABC-CLIO, 2007.

Cooke, James J. *Pershing and His Generals: Command and Staff in the AEF.* Westport, CT: Praeger Publishers, 1997.

Cowley, Malcolm. *Exile's Return: A Literary Odyssey of the 1920s.* (1934) New York: Penguin Books, 1951.

Crowell, Benedict and Robert Forrest Wilson, *The Road to France, Vol. II. The Transportation of Troops and Military Supplies.* New Haven, CT: Yale University Press, 1922.

Dawes, Charles G. *Essays and Speeches.* Boston: Houghton Mifflin, 1915.

--------. *A Journal of the Great War. Boston:* Houghton Mifflin, 1921.

--------. *A Journal of the McKinley Years.* Chicago: The Lakeside Press, 1950.

--------. *A Journal of Reparations.* New York, Macmillan, 1939.

--------. *Notes as Vice President, 1928-1929.* Boston, Little, Brown, 1935.

Dickon, Chris. *Americans at War in Foreign Forces: A History, 1914-1945.* Jefferson, North Carolina: MacFarland and Co, 2014.

Eisenhower, John S.D. *Yanks: The Epic Story of the American Army in World War I.* New York: Free Press, 2001.

Eksteins, Modris, *Rites of Spring: The Great War and the Birth of the Modern Age.* Boston: Houghton Mifflin, 1989.

Farell, Cullom Holmes. *Incidents in the Life of General John J. Pershing.* Chicago: Rand McNally and Company, 1918.

Farwell, Byron. *Over There: The United States in the Great War, 1917-1918.* New York: W.W. Norton and Company, 1999.

Fredriksen, John C. *American Military Leaders.* Volume 2. Santa Barbara, CA, ABC-CLIO, 1999.

Fussell, Paul. *The Great War and Modern Memory.* London: Oxford University Press, 1975.

Goedeken, Edward A. "The Dawes-Pershing Relationship During World War I," *Nebraska History* 65 (1984): 108-129.

Grotelueschen, Mark Ethan. *The AEF Way of War: The American Army and Combat in World War I.* Cambridge: Cambridge University Press, 2006.

Illinois in the World War: An Illustrated History of the 33rd Division. Chicago: States Publications Society, 1920.

Lacey, Jim. *Pershing, A Biography*. New York: Palgrave Macmillan, 2008.

Leach, Paul R. *That Man Dawes*. Chicago: The Reilly and Lee Co, 1930.

MacMillan, Margaret. *Paris 1919: Six Months That Changed the World*. New York: Random House, 2001.

Marcosson, Isaac Frederick. *S.O.S. America's Miracle in France*. New York: John Lane Company, 1919.

Mead, Gary. *The Doughboys: America and the First World War*. Woodstock, NY: The Overlook Press, 2000.

Mosse, George L. *Fallen Soldiers: Reshaping the Memory of the World Wars*. New York: Oxford University Press, 1990.

Perry, John,. *Pershing: Commander of the Great War*. Nashville: Thomas Nelson, 2011.

Pershing, John J. *Final Report of General John J. Pershing*. Washington, D.C.: Government Printing Office, 1919.

--------. *My Experiences in the World War*. Volume 2. New York: Frederick A. Stokes Company, 1931.

--------. *My Life Before the World War, 1860-1917: A Memoir*. Lexington, KY: University Press of Kentucky, 2013.

Proctor, Tammy M. *Civilians in a World at War, 1914-1918*. New York: New York University Press, 2010.

Seymour, James William Davenport, ed., *History of the American Field Service in France*. Boston: Houghton Mifflin Company, 1920.

Snyder, Alice Ziska and Milton Valentine Snyder, *Paris Days and London Nights*. New York, E. P. Dutton and Co., 1921.

U.S. House, Select Committee on Expenditures in the War Department, Hearings Before Subcommittee No. 3 (Foreign Expenditures), Testimony of Hon. Charles G. Dawes. Washington, D.C.: Government Printing Office, 1921.

U.S. Senate, Hearings Before the Subcommittee on Military Affairs, U.S. Senate, Reorganization of the Army, Statement of Charles G. Dawes, November 4, 1919. Washington, D.C.: Government Printing Office, 1919.

U.S. War Department, *Final Report of the United States Liquidation Commission*. Washington, D.C.: Government Printing Office, 1920.

U.S. War Department. *Organization of the Services of Supply*. Washington, D.C.: Government Printing Office, 1921.

Votaw, John. *The American Expeditionary Forces in World War I*. Oxford, UK: Osprey Publishing, 2005.

Williams, Chad L. *Torchbearers of Democracy: African American Soldiers in the World War I Era*. Chapel Hill: University of North Carolina Press, 2010.

Wilson, Adam P., *African American Army Officers of World War I: A Vanguard of Equality in War and Beyond*. Jefferson, NC: McFarland and Company, Inc., 2015.

Woodward, David. *The American Army and the First World War*. Cambridge University Press, 2014.

Connor, General Fox, 14, 194, 221, 287, 301, 313, 323.

Coolidge, Calvin, 8, 374, 402, 356.

Cravath, Paul Drennan, 184, 188, 189, 209, 370.

Cutcheon, F[ranklin] W[arner] M., 140, 144, 159, 178, 207.

Damrosch, Walter, 200, 211, 212, 285, 293.

Davidson, Jo, 298, 300, 318, 326-327.

Dawes, Beman Gates, Sr., 3, 17, 37, 101, 102, 299, 302, 304, 305, 306, 307, 314, 315, 335, 336, 342, 344, 345, 350, 392, 396.

Dawes, Beman Gates, Jr., 82, 90, 101-102, 126, 129, 137, 155, 178, 185, 275, 278, 280, 344, 345, 346, 347, 350, 379, 392-393, 396.

Dawes, Captain Sandys, 305, 306, 308, 328, 329.

Dawes, Carlos Burr, 342, 390.

Dawes, Caro Blymyer, 3, 4, 5, 20, 23, 25, 37, 39, 46, 65, 97, 102, 137, 208, 335, 336, 340, 341, 342, 343, 350, 376, 396.

Dawes, Charles Cutler, 102, 137, 155, 158, 203, 275, 280, 337, 341, 344-347, 350, 378, 392, 394, 396.

Dawes, Charles Ambrose William, 306, 310, 328, 329.

Dawes, Colonel Bethel, 269, 306.

Dawes, Betty, 306, 307.

Dawes, Betsey Gates (Hoyt), 24, 38, 47, 335, 386, 390.

Dawes, Dana, 4, 20, 25, 39, 40.

Dawes, Dorothy, 336.

Dawes, Ephraim Cutler, 45, 249, 262, 274, 310, 389.

Dawes, Henry May, 3, 4, 5, 14, 24, 37, 39, 104, 324, 335, 337, 339, 340, 341, 342, 348, 349, 350, 352.

Dawes, Janet Newton, 350, 379, 396.

Dawes, Joan Prideaux (Selby), 328.

Dawes, Margaret Booker, 342, 389.

Dawes, Marico, 339, 377.

Dawes, Mary Beman Gates, 4, 18, 19, 20, 24, 45, 47, 65, 118, 126, 270, 278, 299, 304, 336, 340, 341, 342, 344, 345, 348, 353, 369, 370, 389.

Dawes, Mary Frances (Beach), 24, 38, 335.

Dawes, Martha Frances Bosworth, 389.

Dawes, Neil B., 339, 351, 372.

Dawes, Rufus Fearing, 19, 20, 22, 23, 33, 65, 97, 98, 126, 140, 323, 336, 345, 347, 352, 354, 372.

Dawes, General Rufus Robinson, 17-18, 19, 30, 32, 45, 99, 262, 273, 274, 277, 310, 336, 370.

Dawes, Virginia (Cragg), 4, 20, 25, 39-40, 339, 377.

Dawes, William C., 90, 269, 302, 306, 328, 329.

Dawes, William Mills, 82, 102, 126, 135-136, 137, 157-158, 229, 233, 249, 280,

285, 338, 337, 342, 345, 346, 347, 349, 378, 350, 392-393, 396.

Dawes, William Ruggles, 339, 342, 349, 351, 389.

Dawes, William M., of Boston, 46, 249, 310, 347.

Dawes, William, of Sudbury, 308.

De Ceuninck, Armand, 120, 153,

Decoration Day, 328, 352, 371.

Delta Upsilon Fraternity, 38.

Dyar, William Wade, 131, 155, 199.

Ericson, Caroline (Maxey), 322.

Ericson, Carolyn Dawes, 4, 19, 32, 65, 322, 323, 340, 341, 343, 391.

Ericson, Charles, 2, 322.

Ericson, Melvin Burton, 285, 322, 323, 341.

Evanston, Illinois, 2, 3, 5, 35, 36, 37, 40, 47, 102, 104, 167, 297, 310, 322, 323, 326, 327, 331, 336, 339, 341, 342, 343, 344, 350, 361, 373, 386, 389, 392, 401, 403, 404.

Felton, S. M., 2, 35, 36, 37, 65, 97, 202, 414.

Field, Marshall, 45.

Foch, General Ferdinand, 41, 55, 56, 59, 145, 146, 147, 148, 161, 167, 168, 169, 171, 173, 176, 178, 190, 192, 193, 195, 197, 198, 200, 201, 207, 208, 217, 218, 219, 220, 221, 223, 224, 227, 229, 230, 231, 232, 235, 236, 245, 246, 247, 248, 249, 250, 251, 252, 254, 255, 257, 262, 276, 311, 314, 315, 330, 445, 446, 447, 457.

Forbes, Charles R., 366, 407.

Ganne, Maurice, 139, 158, 178, 191, 192, 202, 223, 245, 247, 256, 281, 313, 315.

Gates, Charles Beman, 45-46.

Gibbons, Floyd, 386, 323, 349.

Graham, William J., 355, 356, 361, 362, 400, 402, 405.

Grasty, Charles H., 253, 263.

Greenslet, Ferris Lowell, 400.

Haig, Sir Douglas, 88, 103, 128, 167, 168, 169, 170, 171, 201, 227, 250, 251, 252, 256, 272, 273, 279, 305, 457.

Hammond, Percy, 286, 323, 349, 353.

Harbord, General James Guthrie, 14, 82, 83, 93, 100, 101, 103, 127, 128, 131, 134, 139, 149, 167, 168, 171, 176, 195, 197, 199, 200, 203, 205, 207, 210, 211, 217, 218, 219, 222, 224, 225, 227, 229, 230, 235, 237, 246, 248, 255, 256, 257, 258, 261, 264, 270, 271, 275, 276, 277, 278, 279, 280, 281, 282, 284, 285, 287, 288, 293, 296, 297, 298, 301, 302, 311, 314, 315, 318, 319, 330, 346, 347, 370, 438, 448, 459.

Harding, Warren G., 7, 37, 357, 358, 359, 362, 364, 365, 366, 371, 383, 406.

Harjes, Henry Herman, 38, 96, 106-107, 115, 116, 118, 120, 122, 131, 132,

Moseley, General George Van Horn, 185, 194, 209, 221, 223, 230, 232, 236, 241, 245, 247, 248, 280, 313, 319, 367, 453, 455.

Mulloney, Lieutenant Dalton H., 5, 270, 319, 321.

Murphy, Grayson, 105, 152, 370.

Nye, Gerald P., 405.

Olcott, Charles S., 357, 400-401.

Otis, Emily, 342, 351.

Otis, George Webster, 289, 292, 324, 336, 339, 351, 352, 372, 386, 397.

Otis, Joseph, 324, 336, 351, 387.

Page, Thomas Nelson, 160, 207.

Patten, Jack, 344, 392.

Patten, James A., 392.

Payot, General Jean Marie Charles, 11, 15, 56, 59, 192, 195, 196, 197, 198, 200, 201, 202, 203, 217, 218, 219, 220, 221, 222, 223, 227, 228, 232, 233, 235, 236, 237, 238, 241, 242, 245, 247, 249, 251, 252, 259, 262, 276, 280, 281, 283, 284, 296, 311, 312, 313, 314, 315, 318, 319, 370, 455, 457, 465.

Pershing, Warren, 22, 101, 297, 350, 396.

Pétain, Philippe, 88, 103, 106, 134, 138, 154, 161, 173, 195, 220, 221, 222, 227, 232, 236, 250, 251, 266, 271, 276, 311, 330, 456, 464.

Resco, Micheline, 338, 388.

Rockenbach, Samuel D., 75, 78, 99, 249, 288.

Roop, Colonel J. C., 232, 261, 283, 319.

Rosehill Cemetery, Chicago, 372.

Rosenwald, Julius, 44, 402.

Rothschild, James Edouard, 251, 263, 315.

Sanborn, Colonel Joseph Brown, 297, 326.

Savenay, 324, 351, 397.

Scaife, Roger Livingston, 400, 401.

Schwab, Charles M., 14, 43, 287, 323, 370.

Sewell, Colonel John S., 65, 66, 69, 71, 73, 74, 75, 76, 77, 79, 80, 82, 83, 97, 112, 118, 128, 137, 140, 195, 203, 303.

Sharp, William G., 115, 116, 131, 143, 152, 154, 256.

Shedd, John, 32.

Shedd, William Ambrose, 311, 330.

Sims, Admiral William Sowden, 92, 95, 104.

Smither, Colonel Henry Carpenter, 173, 195, 197, 208, 220, 221, 224, 256, 260, 367, 458.

Soissons, 203, 205, 212, 225.

SS *Leviathan*, 5, 318, 319, 320, 331, 335.

St. Mihiel, 46, 158, 228, 233, 238, 242, 247, 260, 261, 278, 450.

Stanton, Colonel Charles E., 81, 115, 152.

About the Editor

A graduate of San Francisco State University, Jenny Thompson has an MA in American Studies from the George Washington University and a PhD in American Studies from the University of Maryland. She has taught courses in American history and culture at the University of Maryland and at Roosevelt University in Chicago. Her work focuses on 20th and 21st century American history and culture, the cultural history of American wars, and the history of images. Her publications include *War Games: Inside the World of 20th-Century War Reenactors* (Smithsonian Books, 2004) and *My Hut: A Memoir of a YMCA Volunteer in World War I* (editor, 2006). Her essays and reviews have appeared in various anthologies and publications, including the *New York Times*. She currently serves as Director of Education at the Evanston History Center and works as a consultant on a variety of public history projects.